P9-DDB-629

Current Directions in Computer Music Research

System Development Foundation Benchmark Series

1. *Robotics Science*, 1989 Michael Brady, editor

2. *Current Directions in Computer Music Research*, 1989 Max V. Mathews and John R. Pierce, editors

Current Directions in Computer Music Research

edited by
Max V. Mathews and John R. Pierce

System Development Foundation Benchmark Series

The MIT Press
Cambridge, Massachusetts
London, England

This book was set in Times Roman by Asco Trade Typesetting Ltd., Hong Kong, and printed and bound by Halliday Lithograph in the United States of America.

Library of Congress Cataloging-in-Publication Data

Current directions in computer music research/edited by Max V. Mathews and John R. Pierce.

p. cm.—(System Development Foundation benchmark series: 2)
Includes index.
ISBN 0-262-13241-9
1. Computer music—History and criticism. I. Mathews, Max V. II. Pierce, John Robinson, 1910– . III. Series.
ML 1380.C87 1989
789.9′9—dc 19 88-21777
CIP
MN

Contents

Current Directions in Computer Music Research

1 Introduction

John R. Pierce

Information and communication have always been central to civilization. In the past, they have been served by a host of arts, including writing, postal service, printing and publishing, the reproduction of diagrams and pictures through woodblocks, etchings, engravings and lithographs, photography, and motion pictures. These arts, and telegraphy, telephony, the phonograph, and radio and television have served government, commerce, and the arts, as have primitive calculating machines, duplicating processes, and punch cards.

The devising of effective general-purpose computers has created a revolution in those parts of our lives that depend on information and communication. This was not apparent in the early relay computers of a half-century ago, nor in their vacuum-tube successors. It was only about thirty years ago that computers were used successfully to simulate the sort of information processing that had previously been carried out through a variety of different analog arts.

With the coming of large-scale integrated circuit chips and cheap disk memory, the process of simulation is rapidly becoming a process of replacement. Voice, pictures, and diagrams can be stored more accurately and permanently in digital than in analog form. Drawings and diagrams as well as text can be generated in digital form, for use in manufacture, to be stored as information, or to be transmitted to one destination or to many destinations over digital networks.

We are experiencing what has been called a convergence of modes, or a convergence of service modes. The arts of generating, manipulating, storing, and transmitting information are becoming part of one digital art, whether the information is text, pictures fixed or moving, or sounds, or a combination of these. A look inside the equipment cannot tell us what sense modality it serves; we see a lot of chips. It is only in the interface with the users and in problems of special chips to speed specialized operation, and in problems of software and application, that we find a difference.

Problems involving the human interface are among the most challenging problems of our new digital age. Some of these problems are concerned with sound as an organized aspect of human life.

Around 1960, the computer was first used to analyze and synthesize complex sounds. This has made experimental study far faster, easier, and more accurate.

A good deal of the ensuing study has been traditional psychoacoustics, which includes the investigation of loudness, masking, binaural phenomena, and an extensive study of the perceived pitch of a host of sounds, many far from sounds ever heard in nature. Such sounds have been presented in contexts foreign to much human experience. These investigations have cast some light on human hearing, but hearing is a process that is extremely complex. We are far from having an adequate description of human hearing.

Hearing is more than a laboratory phenomenon; it is a sense essential to man's life and to his behavior in his environment. When scientists study animals in a natural environment, they are much concerned with the animal's ability to perceive and interpret the sounds in that environment.

Man does not live in the wild; he lives and functions in a man-made environment. He listens most attentively to highly organized, man-made sounds. These are chiefly the sounds of speech and music.

Historically and persistently, both speech and music have been important to man, and speech the more important. Yet if we are to learn about the capabilities of our hearing, a study of musical sound may be as rewarding, or more rewarding, than a study of the sounds of speech. In an important way, music is more suited to learning about complex sounds and their part in our lives than speech is.

The sense of hearing is central to speech and language. Aspects of memory for written words reflect the associated sounds. Yet a great deal of the study of language is concerned with its linkage with particular information about the external and the internal worlds—with meaning, if you will. Phoneticians make sharp and complex judgments of the sounds of various languages, and those who analyze and synthesize speech study the generation and nature of its sounds deeply. But the range of sounds is limited compared with the perceptual abilities of the ear, and in the study of speech, intelligibility tends to take precedence over the perception of subtle variations in speech sounds.

As in the case of speech, much of what we perceive in music we perceive as part of complicated, overlearned art. There is nothing in the defective pitch of a sung note that makes its acoustical properties wrong; we perceive it as wrong because, through a highly overlearned skill, we find it wrong in its musical context. Yet in music the acoustical qualities of sounds play a far greater part than they do in speech.

Since computers were first used to generate complex musical sounds at Bell Laboratories around 1960, the art has spread to many places in many lands, as we can see from the diversity of those who have contributed to this book. Much important work has been supported through grants to various institutions made by the System Development Foundation. Through work at various places, a number of simple but important things have been learned about sounds and their perception. I list a few of these as an example:

A sharp rise or attack followed by a slower decay gives the impression of a plucked or struck sound, whatever the waveform or spectrum.

The higher harmonics must rise later than the lower harmonics in order to produce a sound like that of a brass instrument.

A common vibrato tends to fuse various frequency components into a common tone, while different vibratos on different frequency components tend to cause them to be heard separately.

We easily sense the difference between one instrument playing and several instruments playing together. When several instruments are playing with acceptable deviations in pitch, their harmonics combine, and in place of each harmonic we have a sine-like component that fluctuates in amplitude and phase. The fluctuations are different for each harmonic. The fluctuations in phase are more important in giving the sense of several instruments than are the fluctuations in amplitude.

A sound can be made to seem distant by decreasing the intensity and adding reverberation. In a room we hear mostly direct sound when someone speaks very close to us, but mostly sound reflected repeatedly from the walls if he speaks from a distance.

Simply increasing sound intensity is a poor way to try to give a sense of loudness. Shouts and instruments played loudly have relatively more energy at high frequencies than at lower frequencies, and this gives an indication of loudness that is independent of intensity at the ear.

These simple examples illustrate a few general things that have been learned through study of sound motivated by musical interests. Much more has been learned, and this book illustrates some of this new knowledge of sounds and hearing, through descriptions of how sounds are generated and through digital recordings ("sound examples" on an accompanying compact disk) illustrating sounds and their musical utility.

While this is a book about musical sound, it is also a book about one aspect of man's civilization, about his environment of man-made sound, and about how he can understand and manipulate that environment.

Work reviewed here, much of it supported by the System Development Foundation, has been motivated by interest in music itself as an important aspect of man's civilization. Such work has led to clever and effective ways of analyzing, processing, and generating complex musical sounds, and of understanding something about their perception.

The understanding itself and the ways of analyzing, processing, and generating sounds have importance beyond their impact on music. As in the challenge of understanding human speech, the complexity of musical sounds has been the spur to the inspired analysis and synthesis that have increased man's general capabilities in the area of sound and hearing.

We owe a great deal to the System Development Foundation for supporting the preparation of this book, as well as for support of parts of the work described in it.

2 Compositional Applications of Linear Predictive Coding

Paul Lansky

An area of digital synthesis that has occupied much of my time and interest is the creative application of linear predictive coding (LPC) [2–5]. This is a well-known data reduction technique originally developed for speech synthesis and analysis. It has the virtue of being simple, robust, computationally efficient, and relatively effective.

Briefly, the process involves the analysis of a digitized signal to yield a time-based series of *n*-pole infinite impulse response (IIR) filters whose poles approximately fall on the formant regions of the analyzed signal. We construct a new filter for roughly each 1/100th of a second of signal. The coefficients for these filters are computed in the analysis process by attempting to construct finite impulse response filters that would have the effect of converting the original signal into a pulselike signal, called the residual. This is often called "minimizing the residual." To resynthesize the signal, the filters are inverted, making them IIR filters. If the residual signal were then passed through these inverted filters, the result would be identical to the original signal. Instead we excite these filters with an artificially created pulselike signal [7] in which we have control over periodicity. As a result we can change the pitch of the signal in resynthesis while retaining its speed and timbre. The name "linear prediction" derives from the fact that this is a linear system that predicts the amplitudes of a signal. Similarly, if we change the rate at which the filter coefficients change, the frame rate, we are able to change the speed of the original signal. We therefore have independent control over pitch and speed, unlike the situation in which a tape is played faster or slower. In order to make the frame-to-frame transition smooth (a process taken care of by image retention in the eye in the case of film, for example) we overlap by 50% segments as they are analyzed (so that each frame consists of half of the signal of its neighbors, and there is interpolation between coefficients if the frame rate is slowed down in the resynthesis). This interpolation is not mathematically accurate but usually works well if overlap was used and the frames are stable.

A critical factor in the analysis process is neither to underspecify nor overspecify the number of poles. In the former case the resultant IIR filter would contain very little useful information and the timbre of the resynthesized signal would bear little resemblance to the original. In the case of overspecification the filter might place its poles on the harmonics of the original signal rather than on the formants, and as a result, a component of any resynthesis would be the pitch of the original signal. If the pitch of the signal is not modified in the resynthesis process, overspecification will yield superior results, but there will be little room for manipulation. We want the poles to capture the formant areas, the natural curve in the sequence of amplitudes of the signal's harmonics. The order of the filter is also dependent on the frequency of the analyzed signal, to a certain extent. We want fewer poles for higher frequencies, since there is less information due to the limitation imposed by the sampling rate. There is a certain amount of magic in computing the number of poles needed, but for speech we have found that a number slightly greater than the sampling rate/1000 seems to work well. For instruments the case is not so clear, and the application of LPC is often not so easy. This is probably because for speech the residual signal created in the analysis process is similar to the pulsetrain created by the vocal folds, and the filter has an effect similar to the resonance created by the mouth, head, and chest. Instruments may be quite different. The driving function for a violin, for example, is probably more like a sawtooth wave, since the movement of the bow against the strings results in a series of small grab/release motions.

Along with each set of filter coefficients we store several data values that yield other pieces of information about the signal. These are the pitch of the original signal for each frame, the rms (root-mean-square) amplitude of the original signal, the rms amplitude of the residual signal, and a number that is a ratio of the two rms values and an approximate indication of the amount of noise in the original signal at that point. The theory behind this latter point is that the residual of a signal with a strong harmonic component will probably have a small rms amplitude, relative to the rms of the original (since the amplitudes of a pulselike signal are near zero most of the time), while the analysis of noise will not have much luck in locating formant peaks and the rms amplitude of the residual will probably be much larger in relation to the original. By comparing the two we get a quick indication of the likelihood that we are looking at unvoiced speech, instrumental noise, etc. In the resynthesis process this "error" number can trigger a switch from a pulselike excitation function for the filter to a noiselike one. This is a crude method but is generally satisfactory. It fails, however, to the extent that most signals are not usually made all of one or the other, and in most musical sounds noise is constantly present in subtle but significant ways. To get around this we often resort to heuristic methods that mix voiced and unvoiced signals continuously in ratios roughly guided by the error number.

The rms of the residual is used as an amplitude multiplier for the excitation function in the resynthesis. In most cases the amplitudes of individual formant regions will change significantly with changes in overall amplitude, and the use of this guide gives much more realistic results. This is critical in speech synthesis, particularly in the transitions from voiced to unvoiced speech, where amplitude levels will be significantly different. In some violin synthesis I have done, the amplitude and frequency modulation of the vibrato was directly reflected in modulation of timbral characteristics, and it was therefore critical to maintain the relations between these factors.

Similarly, I have found that the use of the original pitch as a guide to making alterations in the pitch of the resynthesis is critical. There are probably two reasons for this. First, there seem to be natural fluctuations in the amplitudes of formant regions as functions of pitch. If there is some correlation between the pitch of the synthesis and these fluctuations, the result seems to have a more natural quality, even if the direction of change is different. The second reason is simply that these pitch contours are complicated and have small amounts of random deviation. These deviations seem to lessen the "buzzy" quality of resynthesis with an artificial pulse signal. If the frame rate of the resynthesis is slowed down significantly with respect to the original, the use of artificially created, faster-moving, small random deviations seems to help as well.

Two of the basic methods used in the analysis process are called the covariance method and autocorrelation [3, 4]. The latter creates filters that are always stable, but the former seems to give more accurate results. To take advantage of the superior quality of the covariance method we take the additional step of testing the resultant filters for stability. If they are unstable, we alter the coefficients by solving the polynomial, finding the unstable roots, correcting them, and reconstructing the filter.

With this technique, then, we have independent control over frequency and time in the resynthesis process, and can alter the nature of sounds in interesting and creative ways. By using one further option, the ability to alter the formants themselves, we have the additional means of changing the apparent size of the initial resonating object. This technique was discovered by Kenneth Steiglitz [6] and involves making modifications in the coefficients and the past outputs of the IIR filters. With this technique we can change a violin into a cello, a man into a boy, etc. The shift of the formants is not linear across the spectrum and therefore has to be done carefully.

LPC does not generally give excellent results. All-pole synthesis in particular fails to capture nasals. There is often a "buzzy" quality to the resynthesis. Many aspects of the timbre, such as the constant noise component, are not modeled at all. Pole-zero synthesis would probably do a better job, but the computational complexity is much greater and it is no longer a simple linear system. There have been interesting new developments, such as "multipulse" LPC [1], and there are a significant number of articles published each year on improvements and new approaches. (Keeping up with the latest scientific research is not easy for a composer, particularly one with only one lifetime to devote to music, but I hope soon to experiment with some of these new approaches.) From a composer's point of view, however, the issue is not always to be able to render perfect resynthesis, but rather to have a method that is easy to manipulate, and is robust.

A set of sound examples are given on the accompanying compact disk (CD) and described in the appendix at the back of the book.

Bibliography

[1] Atal, B. S., and J. M. Remde. 1982. "A New Model of LPC Excitation for Producing Natural-Sounding Speech at Low Bit Rates." Proc. 1982 IEEE Conference in Acoustics, Speech and Signal Processing. Paris France, May.

[2] Cann, R. 1979–1980. "An Analysis Synthesis Tutorial." Part 1, *Computer Music Journal* 3(3):6–11; Part 2, *Computer Music Journal* 3(4):9–13; Part 3, *Computer Music Journal* 4(1):36–42.

[3] Makhoul, John. 1975. "Linear Prediction: A Tutorial Review." *Proceedings of the IEEE* 63(4):561–580.

[4] Markel, J. D., and A. H. Gray, Jr. 1976. *Linear Prediction of Speech*. New York: Springer.

[5] Moorer, J. A. 1979. "The Use of Linear Prediction of Speech in Computer Music Applications." *Journal of the Audio Engineering Society* 27(3):134–140.

[6] Steiglitz, K., and P. Lansky. "Synthesis of Timbral Families by Warped Linear Prediction." *Computer Music Journal* 5(3):45–49.

[7] Winham, G., and K. Steiglitz. 1970. "Input Generators for Digital Sound Synthesis." *Journal of the Acoustical Society of America* 47(2, Part 2):665–666.

3 On *Speech Songs*

Charles Dodge

Speech Songs[1] is a group of four short songs for which I used synthetic voices to articulate texts by the American poet Mark Strand. I realized the songs at the Bell Telephone Laboratories in late 1972 and early 1973. These songs constitute one of the first computer music works to be based directly on the computer analysis of recorded sound.

This sort of composition begins with a recording. Then the sound material for the composition is made by manipulating the computer analysis of the recording and synthesizing sounds that result from that process. Finally, the material is made into a composition through a variety of means that usually includes splicing and mixing.

In a sense all computer music synthesis entails synthesis-by-analysis, because the synthesist must base the decisions about the musical sound on something, and that something is most often some notion or concept derived from the acoustical analysis of musical sound. In the type of work discussed in this chapter, however, there is a major difference. Here the synthesis is not based on an entirely abstract notion about musical sound. Rather, all the synthesized sounds take much of their nuance directly from the recording on which they are based. In *Speech Songs*, for example, not only is the speed and register of the speech recording of importance, but even the regional accent of the particular speaker can make a difference.

Thinking back over the almost fifteen years since I composed *Speech Songs*, I have tried to reconstruct some of the musical thinking and technological considerations that went into making the work. I had several motivations for using synthetic voices to realize electronic vocal music. First of all, in the experimental atmosphere of that period, it seemed to be an idea whose time had come. There were a number of composers already experienced in computer music synthesis who showed an interest in making computer vocal music. Godfrey Winham began his work in musical speech synthesis at Princeton at about this time, and Wayne Slawson had already composed and recorded at least one computer vocal work.[2] Ercolino Ferretti had made a very impressive example of singing choral tone at MIT in the mid-1960s, as well. I am sure, too, that we were all aware of the rendition of "A Bicycle Built for Two" made with computer voice synthesis at Bell Labs by John Kelly and Carol Lochbaum in the early 1960s.[3] Computer voice synthesis probably seemed to a number of us to be the next logical development for computer music synthesis to undertake.

I felt a personal, artistic motivation during the period of doing *Speech Songs* from the influence of a group of "text-sound composers" in Stockholm whose work I had heard there the previous year. The works of Lars-Gunnar Bodin, Sten Hanson, and Bengt-Emil Johnson had made an especially strong impression, and I was eager to make a contribution to that growing collection of works.

Text-sound composition makes use of many of the same techniques for manipulating the recorded voice that Pierre Schaeffer and others had developed for "musique concrete."[4] These were mainly means of altering the sound through change of tape speed, mixing, and filtering. I thought that the technique of synthesis-by-analysis would represent a potential improvement over the techniques of "musique concrete" in that with this computer technique one could change the timing of the voice without introducing a radical change in its spectrum. Similarly, using the computer, one could alter the fundamental frequency of the voice while retaining the rhythm of the speech articulation. And, of course, the computer does not involve tape techniques that are awkward and build up noise. It seemed possible that by using the computer one could make a kind of talking music.

Unlike the Swedish text-sound composers, I did not also write poetry, so finding a text was crucial fcr me. I was aided greatly by my acquaintance with Mark Strand. He had spent the summer of 1971 writing a collection of short, ironic, aphoristic and often humorous poems.[5] As he read some of them to me over the telephone that fall, I thought they might lend themselves to computer realization. I was particularly encouraged by the first line of the first poem he read:

When I am with you, I am two places at once.

The computer-synthesized voice seemed an ideal medium for representing the ambivalence indicated in the line. I could do so directly in sound, I thought, by making a voice that, literally, would do two things at once: articulate the poetry and delineate a pitched musical line.

While working on *Speech Songs*, I was most fortunate to have access to a succession of computer speech synthesis systems developed by Bell Laboratories research scientist Joseph Olive. The four songs trace a change in speech synthesis technique. The first three songs were made with a formant tracking system for voice synthesis.[6] The fourth song, "The Days Are Ahead," was realized with Mr. Olive's implementation of the linear predictive coding technique that had been recently invented, also at Bell, by B. S. Atal.[7]

Figure 3.1 shows a block diagram of the synthesis-by-analysis scheme. First, I recorded a reading of the poem to be synthesized. I quickly learned, with Olive's helpful advice, that the reproduction of the original voice recording was better if it was made at a high level, in a quiet, nonreverberant room and spoken somewhat more slowly than normal speech. Sound Example 1 (given on the accompanying compact disk) is the recording of the poem for the fourth song, "The Days Are Ahead," as read by the composer and recorded onto analog tape:

The days are ahead.
1,926,346 to 1,926,345.
Later the nights will catch up.

First, I digitized the recording, and subsequently I processed the digitized speech with two different analysis programs, one to track the fundamental frequency of the voice and the other to derive parameters necessary for resynthesizing the speech. In the formant tracking analysis used for the first three songs, these parameters were the center frequencies of bandpass filters set at the formant frequencies of the speech. In the linear predictive coding analysis used in the fourth song, these parameters were the coefficients for an all-pole filter necessary to remake the waveform of the speech. The particular technique used in both of Olive's programs for tracking the fundamental frequency of the voice was the Cepstrum analysis first described by A. Michael Noll.[8] The analysis systems processed the speech into a succession of "frames" (by analogy to the motion picture), where the parameters for a single frame represented the data necessary for synthesis of .01 second of the speech.

The feature that made Olive's programs uniquely suited to musical use is shown in block (5) of figure 3.1: One could alter the parameters of the speech prior to synthesis. A standard synthesis-by-analysis system would make speech automatically from the parameters derived from analysis, and the result would be a more-or-less-faithful reproduction of the original speech. Using Olive's system, the composer could change the analytic parameters prior to resynthesis and, by so doing, make music out of the recorded speech.

Figure 3.2 provides a closer look at the scheme implemented for the synthesis stage shown in block (6) of figure 3.1. The program first reads the

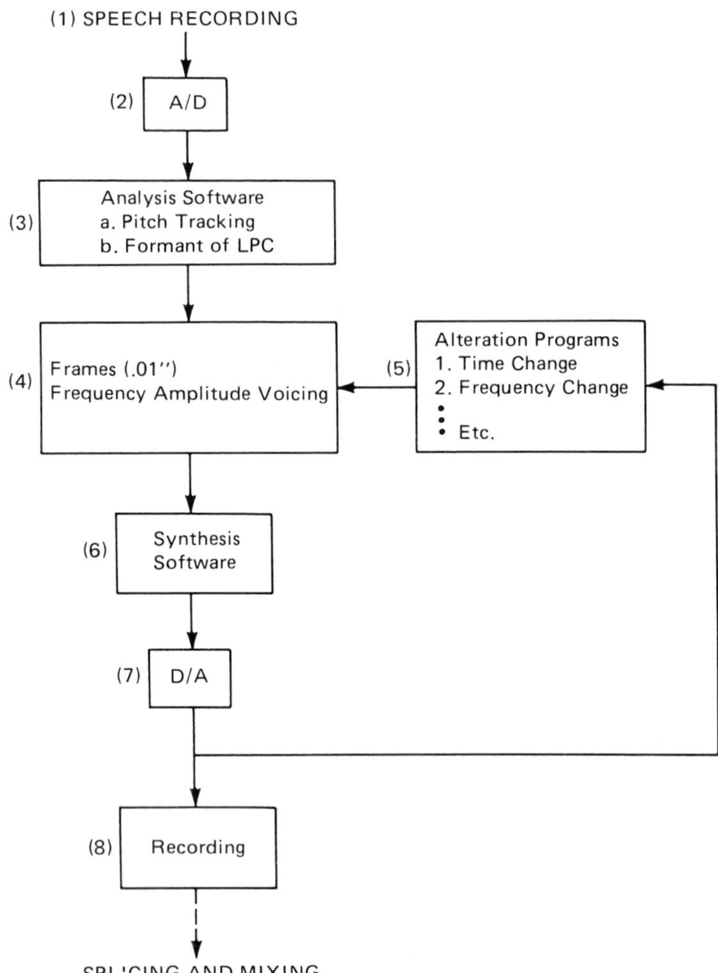

Figure 3.1
Block diagram of the computer program used to produce *Speech Songs*.

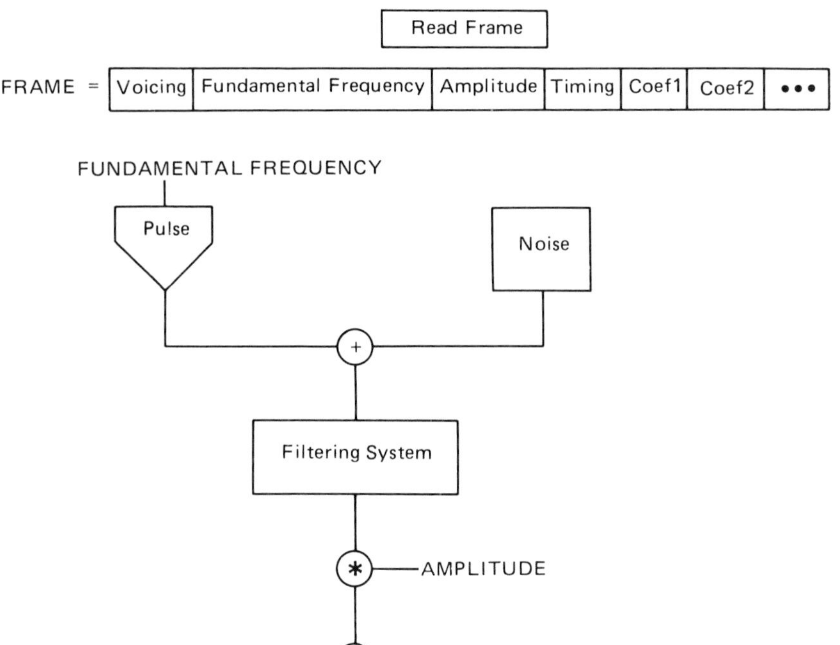

Figure 3.2
More detailed block diagram of the synthesis program used to produce *Speech Songs*.

parameter values of the frame. Then, depending on the value of the "voicing" parameter, it generates a source signal for the synthetic voice from either a periodic pulse or noise. These are used in simulating, respectively, the "voiced" parts of speech (those using the vocal cords) and the "unvoiced" parts of speech (those made by producing turbulence in the vocal tract). Then, for the synthesis of every frame, the appropriate source is fed into the filter system and multiplied by a gain factor. The time variation of speech is accomplished through the change in parameter values from one frame to the next. The hardware formant synthesizer used by Olive has been described by Rabiner et al.[9] Atal and Hanauer discuss the method for synthesizing speech by means of linear predictive coding in their article cited above (see note 7).

The most musically useful feature of this system was the feedback loop connecting block (7) with block (5). One could sit at the computer console and repeatedly synthesize, alter, and audition the results of the synthesis. This is a normal feature of most computer music environments of the late 1980's, but it was a rather unusual arrangement in the early 1970s. In those days one was often able to hear the results of computer synthesis only after a considerable wait. The length of the delay was typically several days and could easily extend to over a week. (Imagine trying to learn to play a musical instrument with such a long delay between performance action and sound!)

As earlier stated, the composer could use the alteration mode of the system to modify independently the perceptually important features of the speech, including its timing, fundamental frequency, amplitude, voicing, and (for formant synthesis) formant frequencies or (for linear predictive coding synthesis) values of the predictor coefficients.[10] The computer system was very nicely outfitted with peripheral devices for input and output. Thus, there were a number of options for implementing particular edits. It had a well-developed graphics capability, too, eliminating some of the tedium of editing sound parameters with numbers. One could, for example, alter a time series of values either by typing new desired values as numbers from the computer console keyboard or by drawing, with a light pen, a new function of time seen on a CRT (cathode-ray tube) display. A cursor could be invoked to display the numerical values of the analysis, at the proper points in time on the graphic display. Thus one had the accuracy of detail available from the numerical values of the parameters and at the same time the "gestalt" enabled by the graphing of the whole segment of speech.

Using the editor was quite straightforward. The particular type of edit was indicated by setting "sense switches" on the computer console. The position of these switches was monitored by the software and thus could be used to control branching in the speech-editing program. Any parameter could be changed either by using the cursor on the CRT or by typing new values on the console typewriter. Setting sense switch number 3, for example, would signal an alteration to the time span of a segment. To accomplish this with the cursor, one first set the cursor to the beginning of the segment by turning a knob on a special function box peripheral. When the cursor was in position, one marked the beginning of the segment by pressing a button on the function box. Then one set the end of the segment by repositioning the cursor with the knob and marking the end point with the push button.

The computer responded by typing the numbers of the beginning and ending frames on the console typewriter. The change in duration was specified by typing the number of frames (centiseconds) into which to map the indicated segment. Alternatively, the entire change could be made at the typewriter by typing three numbers, separated by spaces, indicating beginning frame number, ending frame number, and the number of frames into which to map the segment. A separate program was then invoked (by setting another sense switch) to synthesize the segment—block (6)—and then, finally, to play the result—block (7).

Sound Example 2 is of repeated syntheses of the opening of the poem. It shows the effect of changes to the timing of the voice in successive synthesis runs. Setting a different sense switch enabled an alteration to the fundamental frequency of the speech, for which several means were available. The simplest was to draw a new frequency contour freehand on the CRT. Another possibility was to signal the beginning and end of the segment via the cursor/push button arrangement described above and then type the desired edits to the frequency. It was also possible simply to transpose the entire segment, whether it had been edited or not, by adding or subtracting a constant. Frequency, in any case, was specified as the number of samples per pitch period. Sound Example 3 is of "The Days Are Ahead" synthesized with an edited pitch contour. Here the words, edited from the same analysis of the original recording as that used for Sound Example 2, are set with a melody composed of a new musical pitch for every syllable of the text.

Sound Example 4 demonstrates another type of alteration to the speech—interpolation applied to its fundamental frequency. Here, after specifying the beginning and ending frames of the segment to be altered, a program is invoked to interpolate between the frequencies of the initial and final frames. The sound of this alteration is heard extensively in the middle of the fourth song, where glissandoing voices counting the numbers in the text follow each other up and down. This example displays three different glissandi each with a different timing and interval span. The first glissando sounds twice and the second and third glissandi three times each.

As I implied near the beginning of the chapter, Joseph Olive's computer system for speech synthesis underwent a number of major changes during the period I worked at Bell Labs. For the first three songs, the system was capable of creating only a single line. Furthermore, because the computed samples were held in the main memory of the computer and the computer's memory was quite small, the longest musical fragment possible was about 4 seconds, even at the low sampling rate of 10 kHz used throughout *Speech Songs*. This imposed a stringent limitation on the compositional process. Most of the musical phrases, especially in the first three songs, had to be made out of more than one synthesis run, after which the recorded results were spliced together by hand. The first of the songs probably contains well over 100 splices in its 93-second length.

Around the time I began to work on the fourth song, Mr. Olive enhanced the system to include the possibility of polyphony. The method was quite simple and direct. To make a musical passage with more than a single voice, one first created a separate file on the digital tape for each voice and then invoked a separate program to copy the voices to the disk and add them together. All the files to be mixed had to be the same length, so the shorter ones were padded with silence to make their overall duration equal to that of the longest file. The two arguments to the mixing program for each separate component were sound file number (starting track on the disk) and gain multiplier (to prevent exceeding the dynamic range of the system). Sound Example 5 shows how several syntheses were put together one at a time in order to hear the buildup of the chorus to the desired density.

The final sound example, Sound Example 6, is of the entire song. It consists of a variety of textures from a single synthetic voice to choruses of up to six synthetic voices. (All the vocal sounds are synthetic, even those that sound simply spoken.) The segments for the song were computed separately and recorded onto analog tape. The composition was assembled by splicing together the analog tape. As indicated above, all the mixing was done in digital form on the computer disk.

It is certainly true that the analysis/synthesis techniques used in *Speech Songs* produce an artificial-sounding voice. For certain applications the strong hint of artificiality could be quite detrimental, but in *Speech Songs* it is, for me, a benignly and only mildly artificial sound. I believe the good humor of the poems is well expressed by a synthetic voice. I am sure that much of the humor and many of the surprising juxtapositions benefit from the slightly unnatural, sometimes slurred quality of the synthetic voice. And to be sure the path to "naturalness" in synthesizing sound is a continuum. The sound of the voices in *Speech Songs* would be judged by most to represnt a significant improvement over altering the sound of the recorded voice by varying the playback speed of a tape recorder, although voices made with this latter technique can produce some really fine "chipmunk speech," especially by using accelerated laughter.

Since 1972 I have based many compositions on techniques for the analysis and synthesis of the voice, but *Speech Songs* remains my favorite work. I think this special fondness must be due, in part at least, to the freedom of action I had available as one of the first to compose in a new medium. It was an adventure to be able to chart a new course for computer music and establish a new way of making works of electronic music.

Speech Songs initiated a new genre of composition that many computer music composers now pursue—computer music compositions based on the computer analysis of recordings of a wide variety of material including, among other things, speech, song, and musical instruments. The range of media of works in the genre includes works for tape alone, tape with musical instruments, tape with voice, radio plays, and works of musical theater. A list of composers using the analysis-based synthesis method would include some of the most distinguished names working in the medium.

Notes

1. Dodge, Charles, "Speech Songs." CRI Records, CRI SD348, 1975.

2. Slawson, Wayne, "Wishful Thinking about Winter." Decca Records, DL 710180, 1967.

3. Mathews, Max, John Kelly, and Carol Lochbaum, "A Bicycle Built for Two." Decca Records, DL 79103, 1963.

4. Schaeffer, Pierre, *La Musique Concrete*. Paris, Presses Universitaires de France, 1967.

5. Strand, Mark, *The Sargeantville Notebook*. Elmgrove, RI, Burning Deck Press, 1973.

6. Joseph Olive, "Automatic Formant Tracking in a Newton-Raphson Technique." *Journal of the Acoustical Society of America*, 50(2), 1971, 661–670.

7. Atal, B. S., and S. L. Hanauer, "Speech Analysis and Synthesis by Linear Prediction of the Speech Wave." *Journal of the Acoustical Society of America*, 50, 1971, 637–655.

8. Noll, A. M., "Cepstrum Pitch Determination." *Journal of the Acoustical Society of America*, 47, 1967, 293–309.

9. Rabiner, L. R., L. B. Jackson, R. W. Schaffer, and C. H. Coker, "A Hardware Realization of a Digital Formant Synthesizer." *IEEE Transactions in Communication Technology*, Com-19, 1971, 1016–1020.

10. For a discussion of a more elaborate speech editing system, see Dodge, Charles, "*In Celebration:* The Composition and Its Realization in Synthetic Speech," in *Composers and the Computer*, edited by Curtis Roads, Los Altos, William Kaufman, Inc., 1985, 47–73.

4 Synthesis of the Singing Voice

Gerald Bennett and Xavier Rodet

4.1 Introduction

These examples (refer to the accompanying compact disk) demonstrate digital synthesis of singing voices by the CHANT program developed at the Institut de Recherche et Coordination Acoustique/Musique in Paris. Although CHANT has evolved into a complex program of both synthesis and sound processing since its beginnings in 1978, all of these examples were made using a single technique: the replication of the wave form of each of five formants of an imaginary singer's voice. The examples demonstrate primarily the imitation of natural singing voices, beginning with a madrigal by Carlo Gesualdo (ca. 1506–1613), then illustrating some of the techniques used to give the impression of liveliness of the voice, concluding with an excerpt from the Queen of the Night's coloratura from the aria "Der Hölle Rache kocht in meinem Herzen" from *The Magic Flute*. A final example shows the use of this synthesis technique to obtain nonvocal sounds.

4.2 Synthesis of Formant Wave Functions

CHANT was first written to produce sung vowels. It is based on an acoustical model of the vocal tract and of the singing voice (for the development of an acoustical model for speech, see Fant [2], to which the program CHANT is much indebted). The principles of CHANT have been explained at length elsewhere (Rodet et al. [5]); therefore, we shall give only a brief summary of the theory of the synthesis here.

The sonic wave of the voice is produced by air passing from the lungs into the vocal tract through the larynx to the lips and nostrils. Sound can be produced by three principal sources, the larynx (voiced sounds), the constricted vocal cavity (fricatives), and closing and rapidly opening the vocal cavity (plosives). The vocal tract is a series of connected cavities. These cavities act as resonators, favoring some frequencies, attenuating others. The resonances arising at the favored frequencies are formants.

Consider the spectral representation of the voiced source (figure 4.1) and the spectral representation of five resonances formed by the vocal tract (figure 4.2). Figure 4.3 shows then the spectral representation of the resulting vowellike sound with prominent formants.

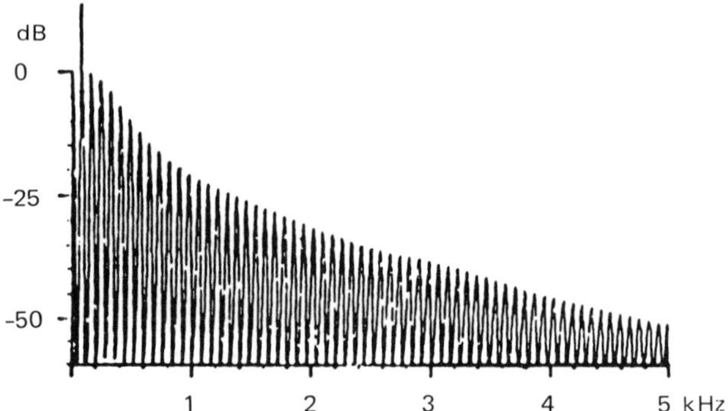

Figure 4.1
Spectrum of a model of the voiced source.

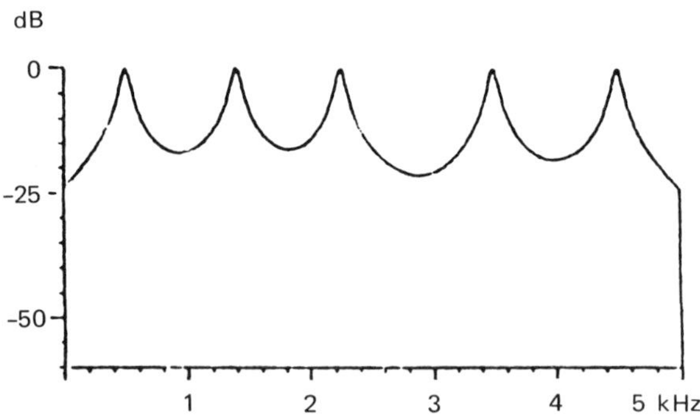

Figure 4.2
Hypothetical transfer function $h(z)$ of five resonances formed by the vocal tract.

The transfer function shown of the filter in figure 4.2 can be represented as five elements in parallel. Thus the response $h(k)$ of the filter can be written

$$h(k) = \sum_{i=1}^{5} s_i(k),$$

where

$$s_i(k) = G_i e^{-\alpha_i k} \sin(\omega_i k + \Phi_i)$$

and

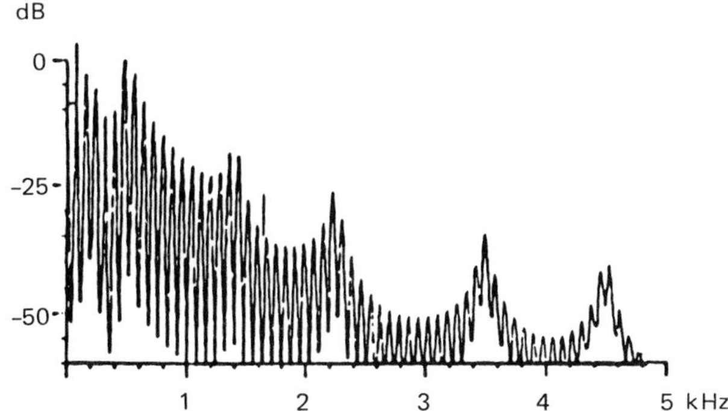

Figure 4.3
Vowellike sound resulting from passing the voiced source shown in figure 4.1 through the resonance system shown in figure 4.2.

$s_i(k)$ is the response of a parallel resonant element,

G_i is the gain of the resonance,

α_i specifies the decay time of the resonance,

ω_i is the frequency of the resonance,

Φ_i is the phase of the resonance, and

k is the sample index.

This corresponds to the sum of products of sinusoids by exponential envelopes. However, natural sounds do not have the instantaneous excitation presupposed here. Therefore, in the synthesis we use a slightly different formant wave form:

$$s(k) = \begin{cases} 0 & \text{for } k < 0 \\ 1/2(1 - \cos[\beta k])e^{-\alpha k}\sin[\omega k + \Phi] & \text{for } 0 \leq k \leq \pi/\beta \\ e^{-\alpha k}\sin(\omega k + \Phi) & \text{for } \pi/\beta < k, \end{cases}$$

which has the form shown in figure 4.4A, where β determines the attack time of the formant.

The shape of the formant is determined principally by its "attack time"—more precisely, the attack time of the corresponding formant wave function. The slower this attack, the steeper the sides ("skirts") of the spectral representation. Figure 4.4B illustrates three attack times and the resulting formant shapes.

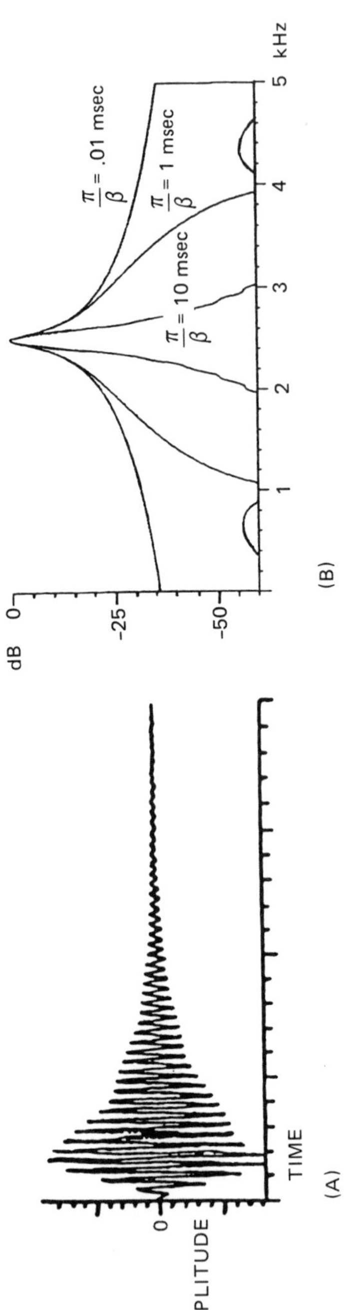

Figure 4.4
A time-domain representation of a formant wave form.

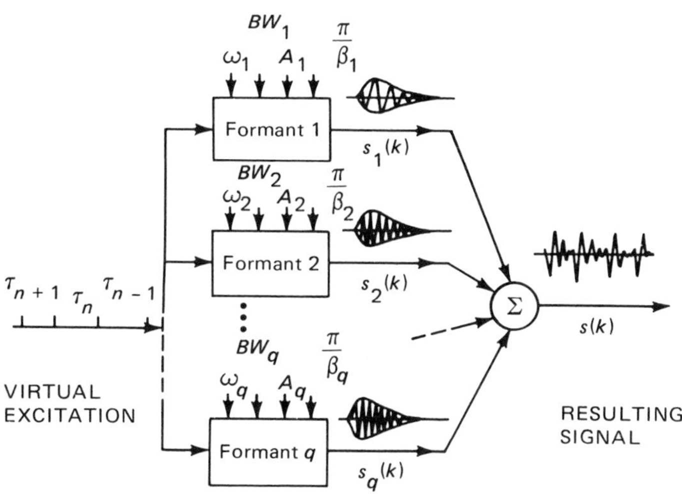

Figure 4.5
For each virtual excitation or period of the fundamental, a waveform is synthesized for each formant. The formants are summed before output.

To make voiced singing sounds, each formant is synthesized separately for each period of the pseudosource (there is in general no easy manipulation of the vocal source in this synthesis model) and then summed with the other formants (figure 4.5). There is no synthesized sound for the fundamental; it arises from the periodicity of the repeated formant waveforms, each of which has its own frequency.

One correction is made to the basic synthesis. The formants synthesized by this technique are symmetrical in form, having equal amounts of energy on both sides of the center frequency. However, the spectrum of a singer's glottal wave form decreases at about 6 dB (decibels) per octave, which means that natural formants tend to have more energy below their central frequencies than above them. To introduce this asymmetry, the final signal is filtered before output by a filter of second order whose center frequency is 100 Hz, whose bandwidth is 450 hz, and whose transfer function is shown in figure 4.6.

This synthesis model has proved to be both very rich in musical possibilities and relatively straightforward to use. The main parameters for each formant (center frequency, bandwidth, amplitude and shape of

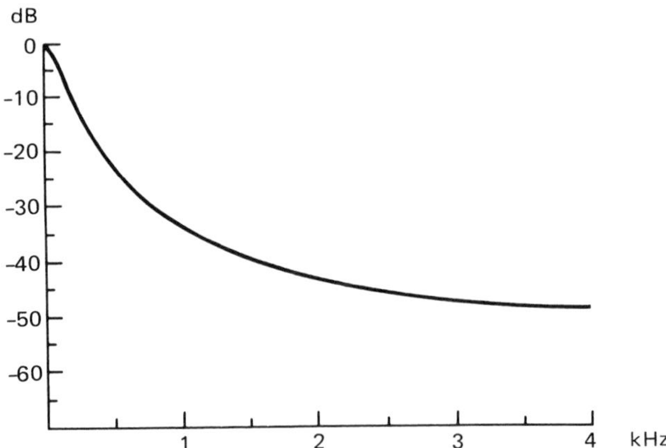

Figure 4.6
The transfer function of the second-order filter used to correct the symmetry of the formants resulting from the calculation of formant waveforms.

the formant) are perceptually relevant, within intuitive reach, and can even be directly measured if one is trying to model real sounds. The only important drawback has seemed to be the producing of unnaturally deep "valleys" between adjacent formants, which changes the overall amplitude of a synthesized sound from what was expected and renders the timbre somewhat nasal. This happens when components of opposite phase are synthesized in neighboring formants, thus cancelling each other out. The fault may be corrected by dephasing the response of one element with regard to the other (see Rodet et al. [5]).

4.3 Rules Modifying the Synthesis on the Basis of Analysis of Singing Voices

Loudness and Spectral Tilt

The timbre of the singing voice changes with loudness, reflecting greater or lesser effort of the vocal folds during phonation. The voice models used for our synthesis represent "loud" singing and hence great effort. We simulate timbral change by calculating a term of correction to be applied to the formants f_2 to f_5 according to the following formula (amplitudes in dB):

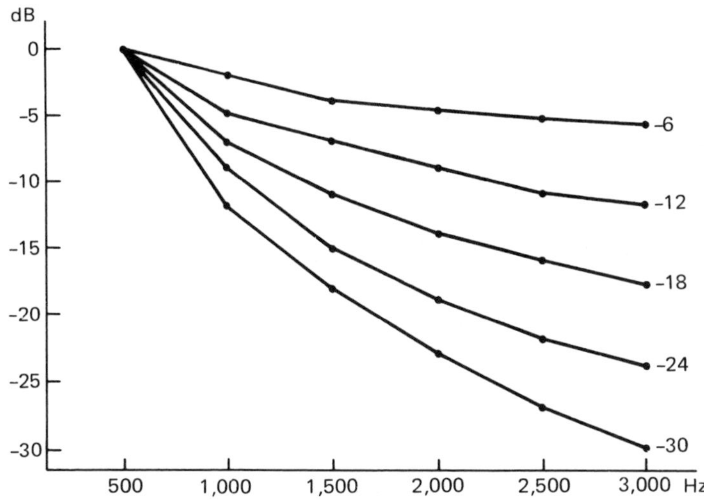

Figure 4.7
The "spectral tilt" applied to all sounds of less than maximum amplitude to correct for vocal effort. Here the first formant, which is not corrected, is at 500 Hz. The perceived spl can be read at the right of the figure. The curves show the corrections to be applied to the nominal formant amplitudes, not the resulting amplitudes.

$$\text{term}_i = k \cdot (\log(\text{freq}_i) - \log(\text{freq}_1)),$$

where $k = \text{spl}/(\log(3{,}000\ \text{Hz}) - \log(\text{freq}_1))$ and spl is the sound pressure level required. (3,000 Hz was chosen as the frequency at which the correction is equal to the spl required.) Figure 4.7 shows the correction for various spls and formant frequencies.

The form of the spectrum of any sound familiar to us, thus especially of vocal sounds, together with the perceived amplitude of the sound, gives an important cue for the distance of the sound's source. So for instance, if the spectrum is rich in high frequencies, one assumes that the effort required to produce the sound is great. If this sound is perceived as soft, one assumes the source is far away; if it is perceived as loud, one assumes that the source is near. In CHANT, the actual amplitude of the synthesized sound is scaled according to a separate parameter after the calculation of the amplitudes of the individual formants so as to have control over this important perceptual cue.

The Formants in Female Singers

Female singers adjust the frequencies of f_1 and f_2 according to the fundamental frequency of the note sung much more than do male singers (Sundberg [6]). It is easy to understand why. The fundamental of the sung note can lie above the nominal frequency of the first formant; without correction, the first formant resonance would not be excited. Even when the fundamental is below the first formant, the partials can be so widely spaced that only a fraction of the available energy falls on the resonances, thus forcing the singer to work much harder to maintain a proper amplitude. Thus for reasons of efficiency, above a certain threshold, most female singers adjust f_1 and f_2 to be close to a partial of the tone sung. This correction accounts for the usually poor vowel quality in high-pitched notes in natural (and synthetic) voices. In CHANT, when the fundamental required is above 260 Hz, we set f_1 to a semitone above the fundamental and f_2 to an octave and two semitones above the fundamental in those vowels whose f_2 lies below about 1,500 Hz ("back vowels": /a/, /o/, /u/).

In those vowels with a high second formant ("front vowels": /e/, /i/), a second phenomenon has been observed (Sundberg [6]). As the fundamental rises, the singer opens her mouth wider. The jaw drops, and with it the tongue, thus lessening the constriction of the vocal tract responsible for the high second formant: the second formant drops in pitch, gradually returning to a "neutral" position around 1,500 Hz. In CHANT, we make a correction of f_2 for vowels having a nominal second-formant frequency above 1,500 Hz according to this formula (all values are in hertz):

$$f_{2\,\mathrm{corr}} = \frac{f_{2\mathrm{nominal}}}{(f_0/260)^{0.2}}.$$

Figure 4.8 shows the shift of the frequencies of the first two formants in the five vowels /a/, /e/, /i/, /o/, /u/ as the fundamental rises. The pattern of shift agrees very well with the shift observed in singers (Sundberg [6]) and shows clearly that for fundamentals above about 800 Hz, the first two formants track the first two partials.

4.4 Consonants

The synthesis of consonants using formant wave functions is much more difficult than the synthesis of vowels. This is because the formants follow

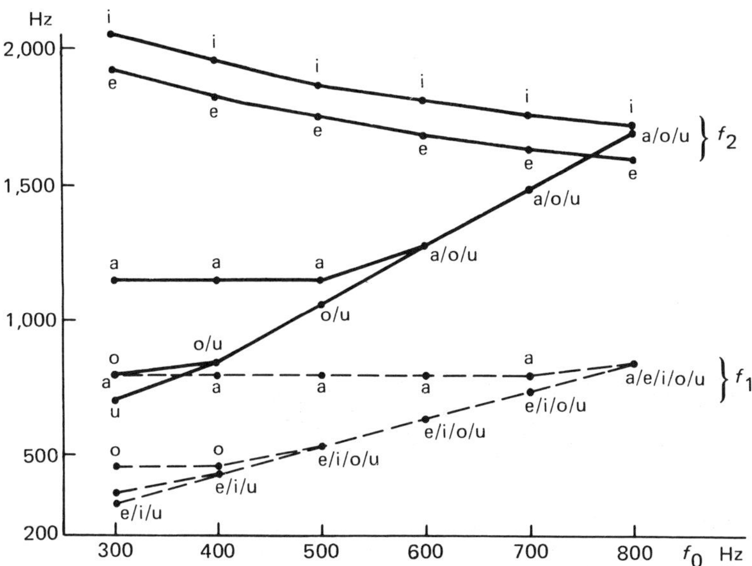

Figure 4.8
The shift in center frequencies of f_1 and f_2 in female voices as performed by CHANT.

very specific trajectories in the passage from consonant to vowel or vowel to consonant: all four important parameters—center frequency, amplitude, bandwidth, and excitation time (the "attack time" of the resonance determining the formant's shape)—are continually changing. In figure 4.9, a sonogram of the sound /ala/ spoken in French, the changing frequencies of the formants (particularly of the lower two), the amplitude (especially for f_2), and the widening of the formant bandwidth can be clearly seen.

In the synthesis, simple tabulated functions form the basis of the formant trajectories; for the /l/ of /ala/ two functions are used: a sine function taken between $-\pi/2$ and $+\pi/2$ for every trajectory except that of the fundamental frequency in the transition consonant-vowel, for which a sine function taken between 0 and $\pi/2$ is used. Clearly, the duration and the exact shape of the transition are of great perceptual and expressive importance and are precisely controllable in CHANT. Figure 4.10A shows more precisely than the sonogram the movement of the center frequencies of f_1 and f_2 in /ala/. Figure 4.10B shows the derived functions for the synthesis.

While the synthesis of vowel sounds in CHANT can be largely automated, leaving one to tend only to matters of musical and expressive

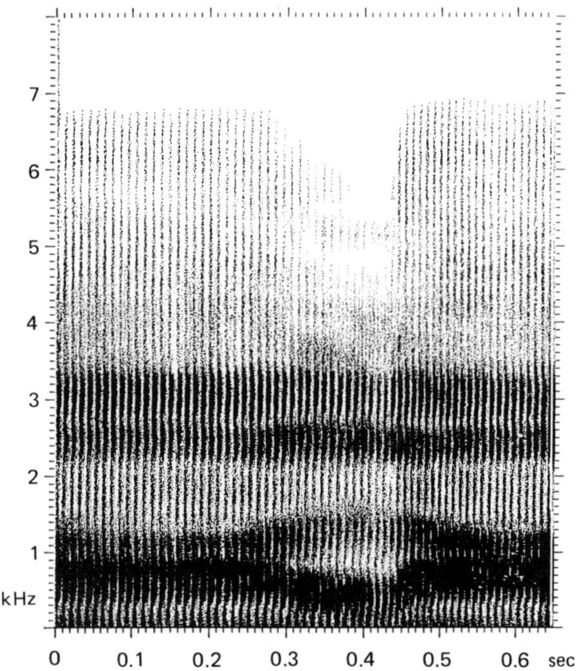

Figure 4.9
Sonogram of the spoken syllable /ala/.

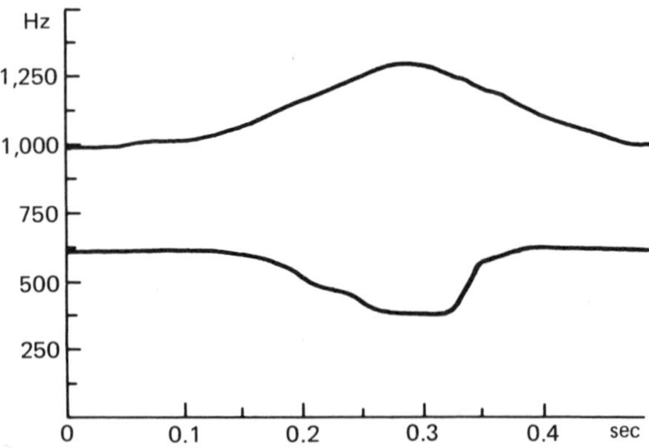

Figure 4.10A
A more accurate measurement of the frequency trajectories of f_1 and f_2 in the spoken syllable /ala/.

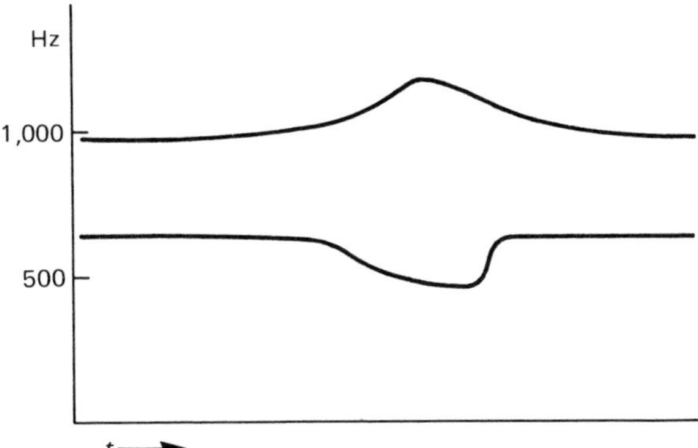

Figure 4.10B
The same frequency trajectories as synthesized by CHANT.

content, the synthesis of consonants must still be done principally by hand. Details of the calculation of the formant trajectories can be found in Rodet and Delatre [4].

Example 14

In this polyphonic example each voice was first synthesized separately. The five voices were then mixed digitally to form the ensemble. Each voice has its own score of pitches and durations as well as its own dynamic evolution. We found that because our voices are synthesized by rule, any two voices were likely to be doing similar things—for example, formant shift as a function of fundamental pitch—at the same time. Also, two voices beginning notes at precisely the same time are in danger of being phase locked (depending of course on the ratios of their various formant frequencies). In the synthesis, we took pains to decouple the voices as much as possible. We made sure that no two voices ever began their notes exactly together; here differences of from 20 to 200 msec were used. Each voice has a different vibrato rate and amplitude, and these parameters are constantly changing (as linear functions) in each voice. Finally, because the higher formants are at similar frequencies in all the voices, we found it important to keep the voices at a moderate dynamic level to avoid too much energy around the "singer's formant" (2,500–2,800 Hz), exactly as the professional soloist does when singing in ensembles.

Here are the actual durations in seconds of the first 10 notes of the soprano voice with the corresponding musical notation (at the beginning of this example the quarter-note has a nominal metronome marking of about 92, or a duration of .65 sec):

seconds: .6 .53 1.15 .57 1.36 1.41 2.74 .73 .8 1.4 · · ·

Two factors are at work here, an inner suppleness of the voice itself (for instance, the exaggerated shortness of the second note) and a gradual slowing of the general tempo leading to the seventh note. This superposition of several independent temporal evolutions is typical for classical music.

Examples 15a–15e

These five vocalises (for bass, tenor, countertenor, alto, and soprano voices, respectively) using the syllables "a-la-la" are examples of consonant synthesis, but they illustrate more especially the five different voice qualities. The voice type (soprano, bass, etc.) is determined almost exclusively by formant frequency. Differentiation within the same vocal type depends on many factors—vibrato, random fundamental variation, attack patterns, etc.—but also on the way these individual characteristics change as a function of pitch and vocal effort (Bennett [1]).

Examples 16a–16d

These examples demonstrate the elements that contribute to the impression of liveliness of the synthesized voice. They all are sung on the g below middle c (196.3 Hz) using the vowel /o/ by our model bass. Each of these examples has a duration of 5 sec.

Example 16a shows the raw synthesis by formant wave function, using the bass voice model for the vowel /o/ shown in the table in the appendix.

Example 16b adds attack and decay. Particularly attack time and also decay time (until masked by room reverberation) are very important means of expression, so rules can hardly be given. Here the attack goes from −30 dB to maximum amplitude in 50 msec; the decay goes from maximum to −30 dB over 150 ms. The transition is logarithmic.

Example 16c adds vibrato. Vibrato is essentially frequency modulation of the fundamental pitch. Here the vibrato frequency moves linearly from 5.2 to 5.5 Hz during the note. The deviation or depth of the vibrato increases from 0 to ±4% (or ±8 Hz at this fundamental frequency) in about 60 msec, roughly parallel to the amplitude attack.

Example 16d adds a random variation to the fundamental frequency. In all singers we observe a small random variation of fundamental frequency. CHANT approximates this "jitter" by adding to the nominal fundamental frequency a term that is the sum of three components whose values are obtained by interpolation between independent, periodic random frequency deviations. In this example component 1 had a period of 8 msec and a deviation of ±0.5%, component 2 a period of 71 msec and a deviation of ±1%, and component 3 a period of 619 msec and a deviation of ±0.3% of the fundamental frequency. The composite "jitter" behaves like a deviation having the spectrum $1/f$.

Examples 17a–17c

Example 17a shows a crescendo-decrescendo without change of timbre. The spectrum is that of a sound 24 dB softer than maximum amplitude (see figure 4.7 for the correction to the spectrum). The amplitude goes logarithmically from −30 to 0 dB and back over 5 sec, where 0 dB is the maximum amplitude representable in 16-bit format. The effect is that of turning up the volume control on an amplifier.

In example 17b the spectrum evolves with the dynamic function, also going from −30 to 0 dB and back. The effect is much more lifelike.

In example 17c the vibrato amplitude (depth) also changes synchronously with the dynamic function, going from a ±2.5% deviation to ±7% at maximum amplitude and falling back to ±6% at the end of the note.

Examples 18a and 18b

Example 18a illustrates a jump of an octave where the change of the fundamental frequency is virtually instantaneous. The effect is, at best, to give the impression of an accent on the second note.

In example 18b the fundamental makes a rapid glissando from the lower pitch to the upper in the form of one-half sinusoid ($-\pi/2$ to $+\pi/2$). The duration of this transition is 200 msec. Shorter durations than about 140 msec do not sound legato for larger intervals, but here again it is difficult to give rules, as the speed of the transition from note to note is an important expressive means.

Example 19

The principal work on this example was done by Yves Potard at IRCAM in 1981. Again, analysis preceded synthesis. A special technique was developed to detect the formants at such high pitches. This technique consisted essentially of monitoring each partial of the recorded example separately and noting sudden increases of amplitude that would indicate passage through a formant.

Several rules were derived for the synthesis.

a. Each note has its own "portamento," a deviation away from the nominal pitch of the note of a few percent. The deviation takes the shape of a sinusoidal arc.

b. The spectral tilt increases during each note, representing increasing vocal effort. In contrast to examples 17b and 17c, the vocal effort here continues to increase for some time after the maximum amplitude for the note has been reached. In staccato notes, the maximum effort is reached just before the end of the note.

c. Vibrato frequency and amplitude increase and then decrease within each note.

d. The amplitude function for each note has a characteristic shape: linear attack and decay, rounded maximum.

e. For notes above a certain limit, the first two formants were placed on or near the first two partials of each note. This gave good homogeneity of timbre.

Example 20

This example is a short excerpt from a work for tape, *Winter (1980)*, by Gerald Bennett, realized at IRCAM in 1980. The music was synthesized entirely with the program CHANT. The example illustrates some of the nonvocal sounds that can be made with CHANT. Over the years, CHANT has proved itself a very rich and supple synthesis tool, capable of producing virtually any sound that can be represented as a sum of resonances.

Appendix

The following table and accompanying figures illustrate the voice models actually used for the synthesis by CHANT. In the table, "Frequency" indicates the center frequency of the formant. "Amplitude" is the amplitude of the formants f_2–f_5 relative to the first formant for a sound perceived to be of loud amplitude. "Band-width" is the size of the formant in the spectral representation of the vowel, measured at 3 dB below the maximum amplitude for that formant.

Frequency and bandwidth are given in hertz, amplitude in decibels relative to f_1.

Table of formant values for vowel sounds in CHANT: soprano

	f_1	f_2	f_3	f_4	f_5
[a]					
Frequency	800	1,150	2,900	3,900	4,950
Amplitude	0	−6	−32	−20	−50
Bandwidth	80	90	120	130	140
[e]					
Frequency	350	2,000	2,800	3,600	4,950
Amplitude	0	−20	−15	−40	−56
Bandwidth	60	100	120	150	200
[i]					
Frequency	270	2,140	2,950	3,900	4,950
Amplitude	0	−12	−26	−26	−44
Bandwidth	60	90	100	120	120
[o]					
Frequency	450	800	2,830	3,800	4,950
Amplitude	0	−11	−22	−22	−50
Bandwidth	70	80	100	130	135
[u]					
Frequency	325	700	2,700	3,800	4,950
Amplitude	0	−16	−35	−40	−60
Bandwidth	50	60	170	180	200

Soprano /a/

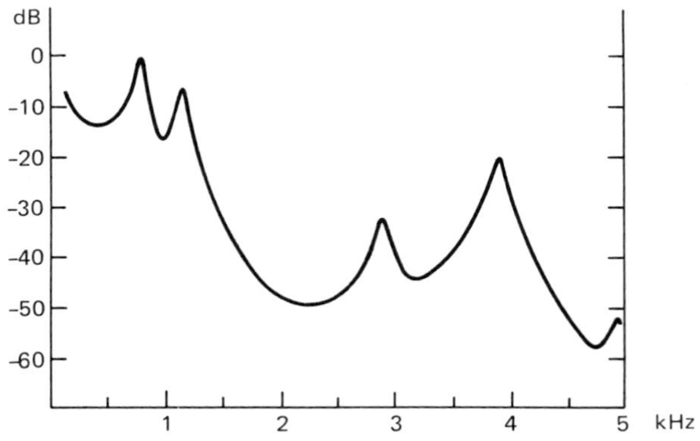

Soprano /e/

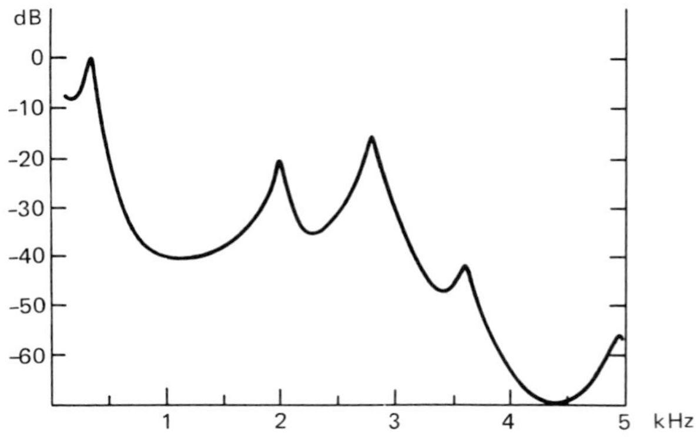

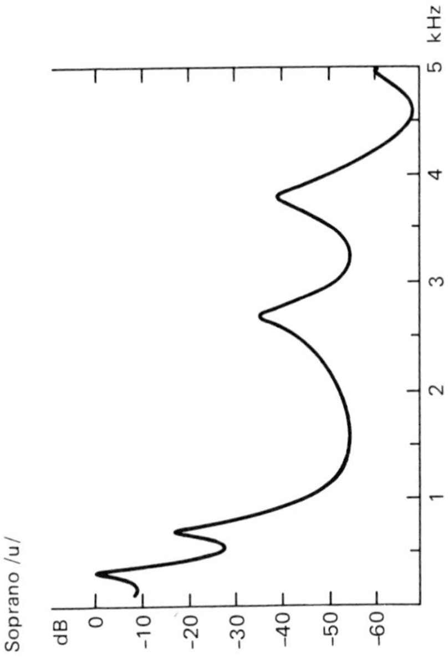
Soprano /u/
dB
0
-10
-20
-30
-40
-50
-60
1
2
3
4
5 kHz

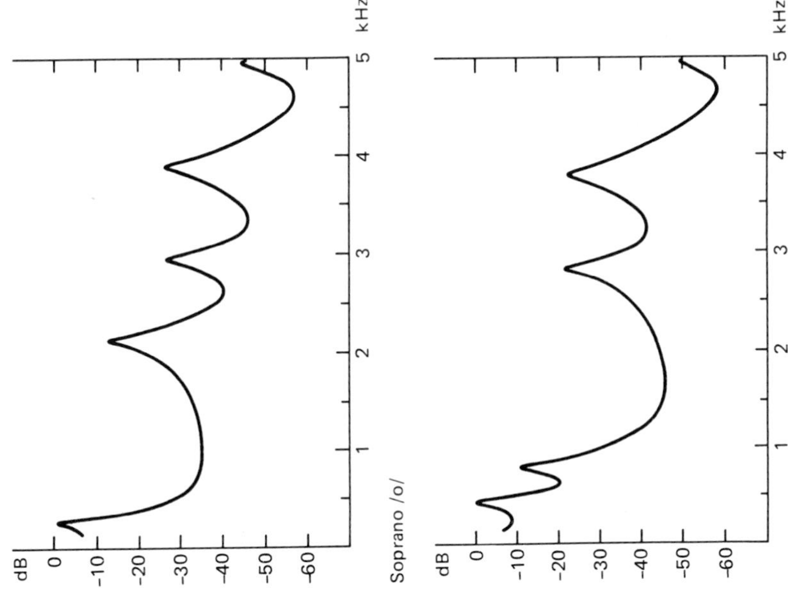
Soprano /i/
dB
0
-10
-20
-30
-40
-50
-60
1
2
3
4
5 kHz
Soprano /o/
dB
0
-10
-20
-30
-40
-50
-60
1
2
3
4
5 kHz

Table of formant values for vowel sounds in CHANT: alto

	f_1	f_2	f_3	f_4	f_5
[a]					
Frequency	800	1,150	2,800	3,500	4,950
Amplitude	0	−4	−20	−36	−60
Bandwidth	80	90	120	130	140
[e]					
Frequency	400	1,600	2,700	3,300	4,950
Amplitude	0	−24	−30	−35	−60
Bandwidth	60	80	120	150	200
[i]					
Frequency	350	1,700	2,700	3,700	4,950
Amplitude	0	−20	−30	−36	−60
Bandwidth	50	100	120	150	200
[o]					
Frequency	450	800	2,830	3,500	4,950
Amplitude	0	−9	−16	−28	−55
Bandwidth	70	80	100	130	135
[u]					
Frequency	325	700	2,530	3,500	4,950
Amplitude	0	−12	−30	−40	−64
Bandwidth	50	60	170	180	200

Alto /a/

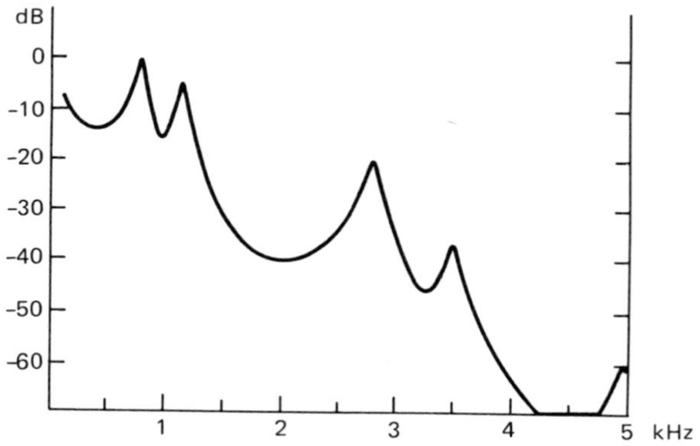

Alto /e/

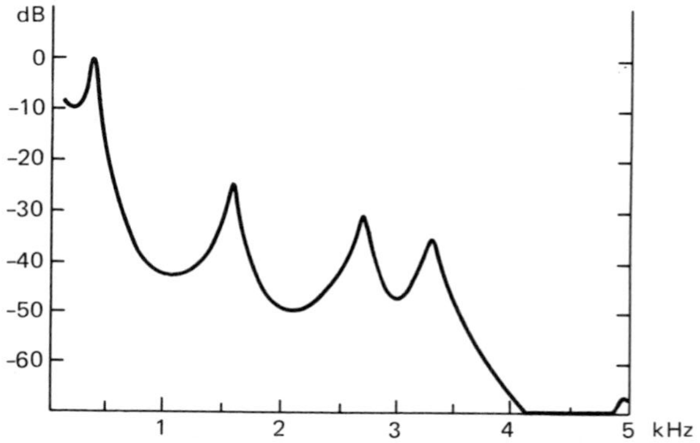

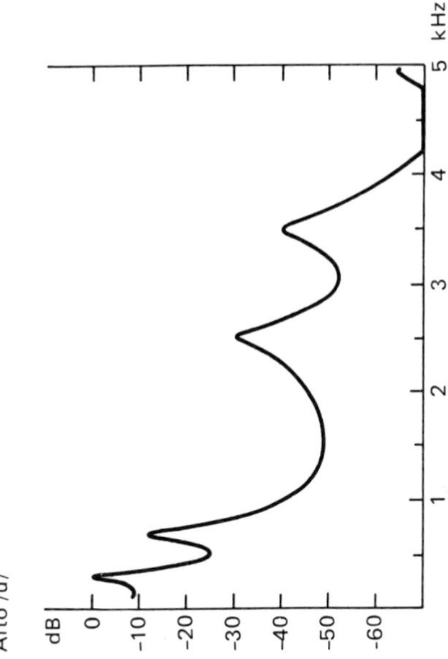
Alto /u/
dB
0
-10
-20
-30
-40
-50
-60
1
2
3
4
5 kHz

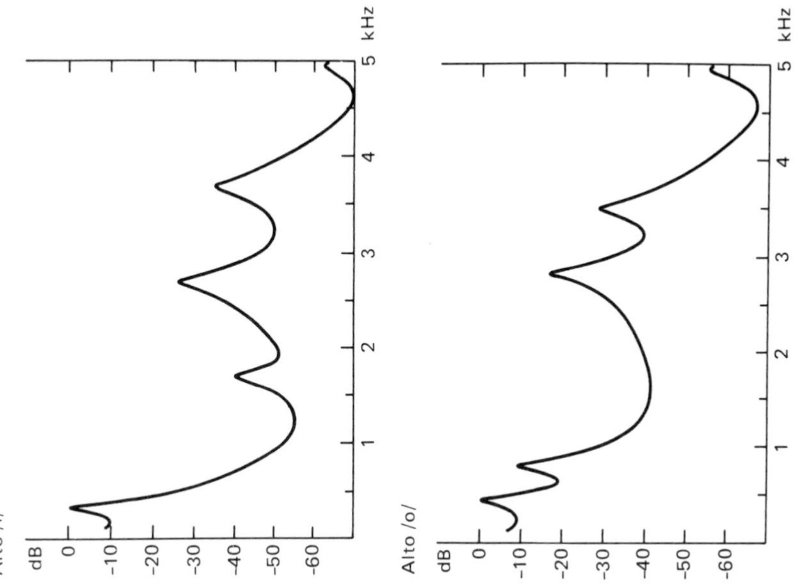
Alto /i/
dB
0
-10
-20
-30
-40
-50
-60
1
2
3
4
5 kHz
Alto /o/
dB
0
-10
-20
-30
-40
-50
-60
1
2
3
4
5 kHz

Table of formant values for vowel sounds in CHANT: countertenor

	f_1	f_2	f_3	f_4	f_5
[a]					
Frequency	660	1,120	2,750	3,000	3,350
Amplitude	0	−6	−23	−24	−38
Bandwidth	80	90	120	130	140
[e]					
Frequency	440	1,800	2,700	3,000	3,300
Amplitude	0	−14	−18	−20	−20
Bandwidth	70	80	100	120	120
[i]					
Frequency	270	1,850	2,900	3,350	3,590
Amplitude	0	−24	−24	−36	−36
Bandwidth	40	90	100	120	120
[o]					
Frequency	430	820	2,700	3,000	3,300
Amplitude	0	−10	−26	−22	−34
Bandwidth	40	80	100	120	120
[u]					
Frequency	370	630	2,750	3,000	3,400
Amplitude	0	−20	−23	−30	−34
Bandwidth	40	60	100	120	120

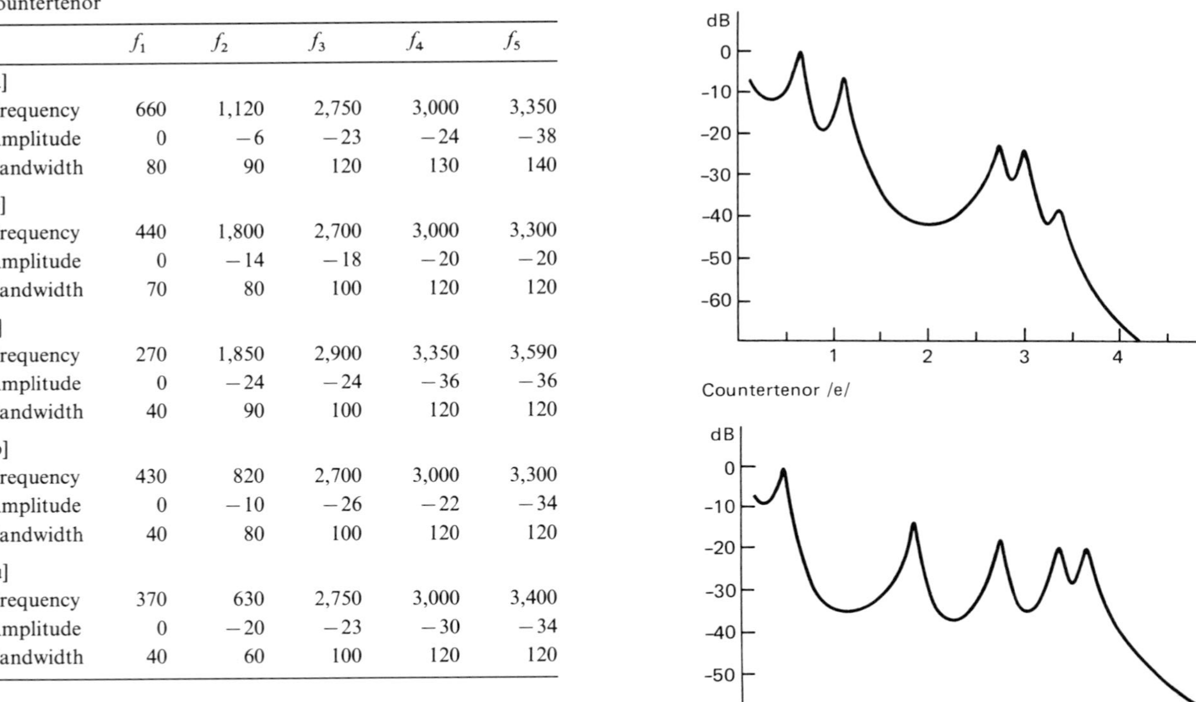

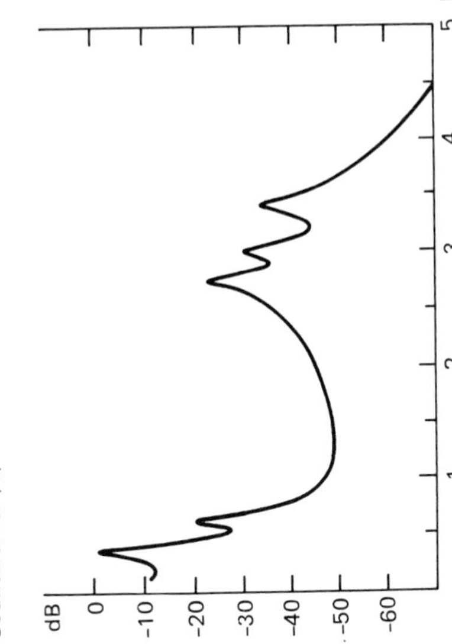
Countertenor /u/
dB
0
-10
-20
-30
-40
-50
-60
1
2
3
4
5 kHz

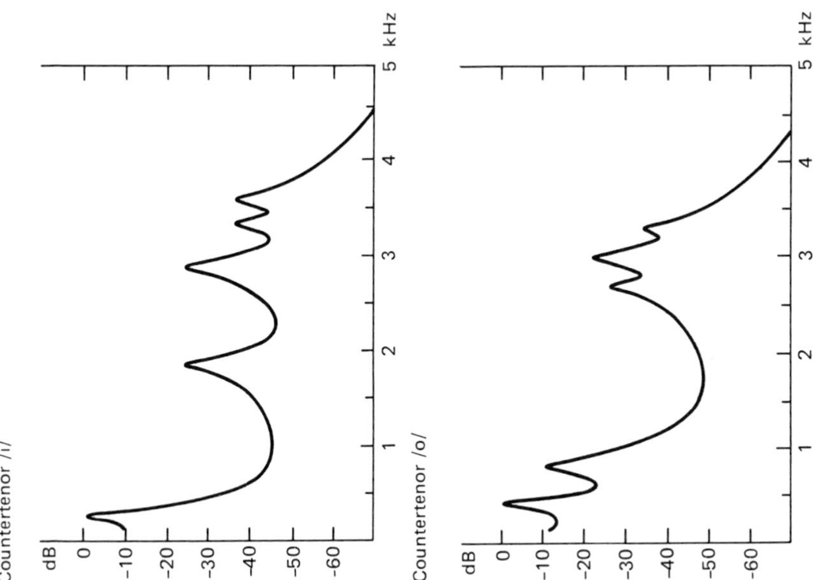
Countertenor /i/
dB
0
-10
-20
-30
-40
-50
-60
1
2
3
4
5 kHz
Countertenor /o/
dB
0
-10
-20
-30
-40
-50
-60
1
2
3
4
5 kHz

Table of formant values for vowel sounds in CHANT: tenor

	f_1	f_2	f_3	f_4	f_5
[a]					
Frequency	650	1,080	2,650	2,900	3,250
Amplitude	0	−6	−7	−8	−22
Bandwidth	80	90	120	130	140
[e]					
Frequency	400	1,700	2,600	3,200	3,580
Amplitude	0	−14	−12	−14	−20
Bandwidth	70	80	100	120	120
[i]					
Frequency	290	1,870	2,800	3,250	3,540
Amplitude	0	−15	−18	−20	−30
Bandwidth	40	90	100	120	120
[o]					
Frequency	400	800	2,600	2,800	3,000
Amplitude	0	−10	−12	−12	−26
Bandwidth	40	80	100	120	120
[u]					
Frequency	350	600	2,700	2,900	3,300
Amplitude	0	−20	−17	−14	−26
Bandwidth	40	60	100	120	120

Tenor /a/

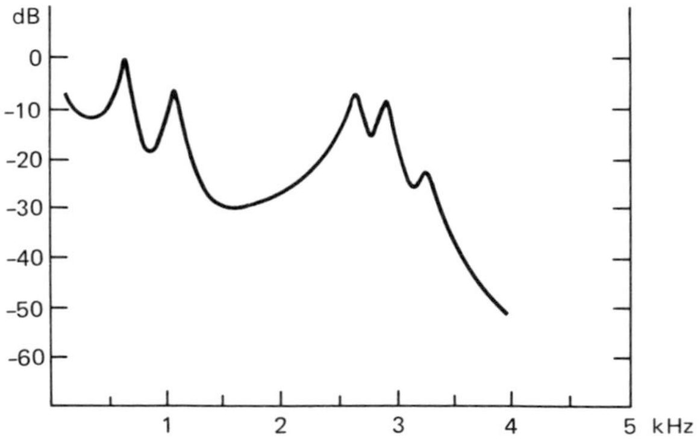

Tenor /e/

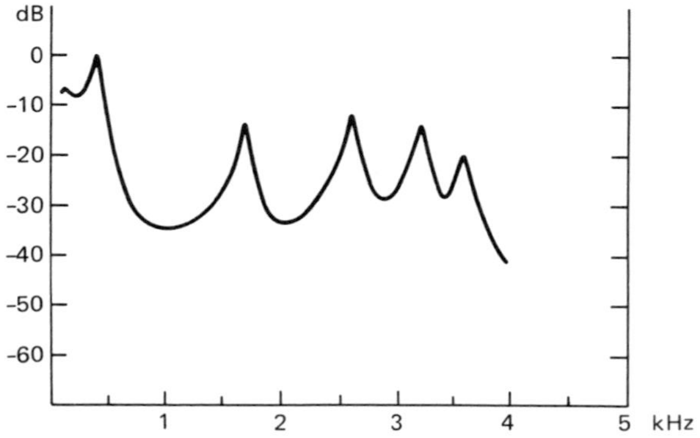

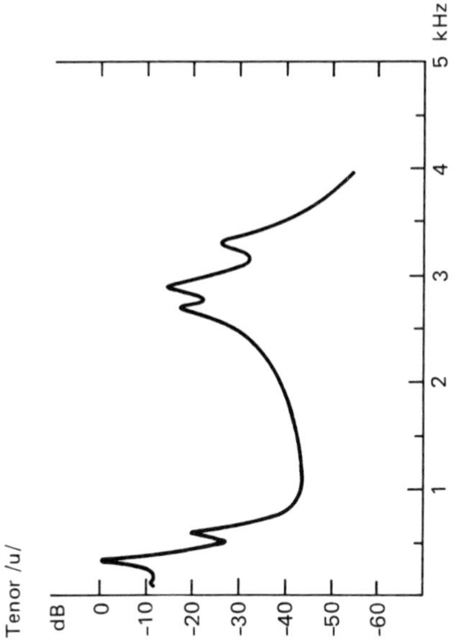
Tenor /u/
dB
0
-10
-20
-30
-40
-50
-60
1
2
3
4
5 kHz

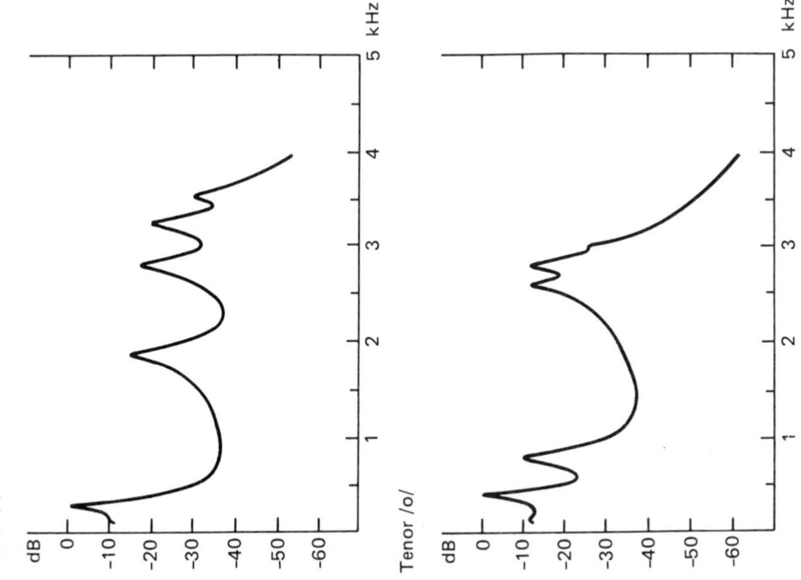
Tenor /i/
dB
0
-10
-20
-30
-40
-50
-60
1
2
3
4
5 kHz
Tenor /o/
dB
0
-10
-20
-30
-40
-50
-60
1
2
3
4
5 kHz

Table of formant values for vowel sounds in CHANT: bass

	f_1	f_2	f_3	f_4	f_5
[a]					
Frequency	600	1,040	2,250	2,450	2,750
Amplitude	0	−7	−9	−9	−20
Bandwidth	60	70	110	120	130
[e]					
Frequency	400	1,620	2,400	2,800	3,100
Amplitude	0	−12	−9	−12	−18
Bandwidth	40	80	100	120	120
[i]					
Frequency	250	1,750	2,600	3,050	3,340
Amplitude	0	−30	−16	−22	−28
Bandwidth	60	90	100	120	120
[o]					
Frequency	400	750	2,400	2,600	2,900
Amplitude	0	−11	−21	−20	−40
Bandwidth	40	80	100	120	120
[u]					
Frequency	350	600	2,400	2,675	2,950
Amplitude	0	−20	−32	−28	−36
Bandwidth	40	80	100	120	120

Bass /a/

Bass /e/

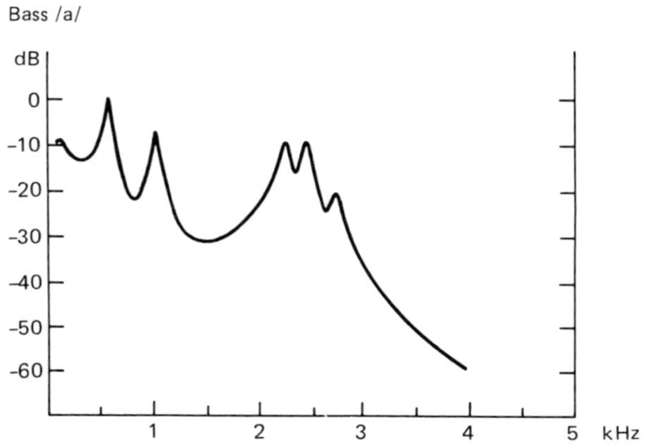

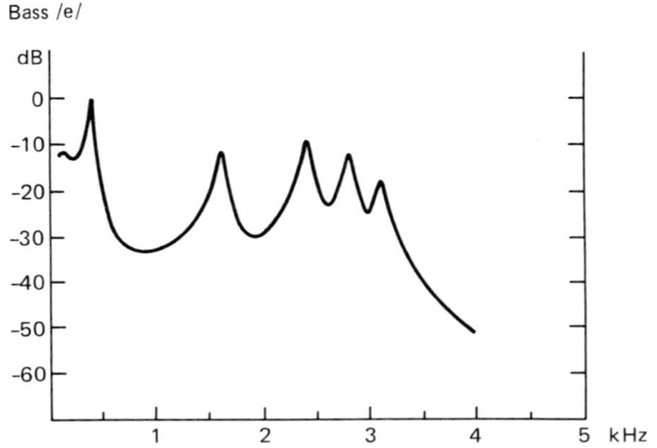

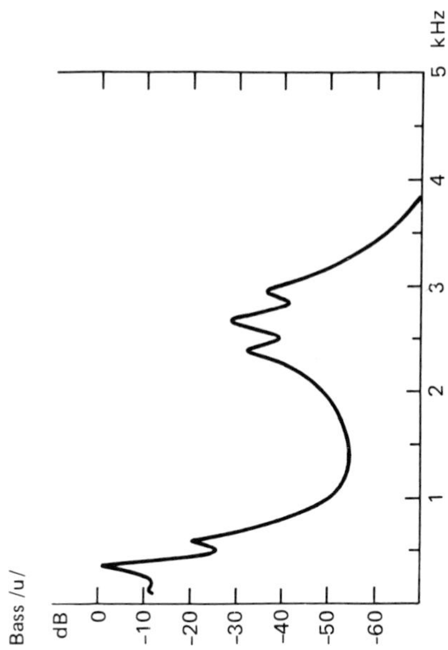
Bass /u/
dB
0
-10
-20
-30
-40
-50
-60
1
2
3
4
5 kHz

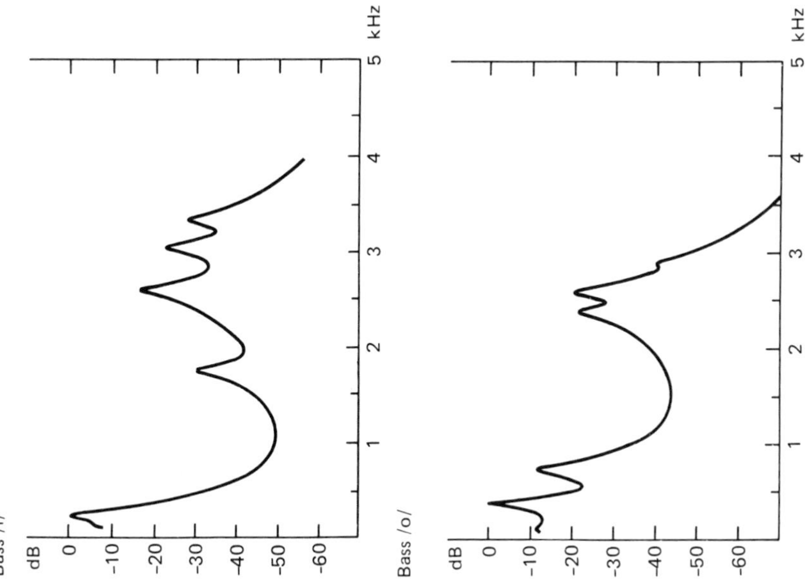
Bass /i/
dB
0
-10
-20
-30
-40
-50
-60
1
2
3
4
5 kHz
Bass /o/
dB
0
-10
-20
-30
-40
-50
-60
1
2
3
4
5 kHz

Acknowledgment

The authors would like to acknowledge their deep indebtedness to Johan Sundberg for insight into many of the questions of singing synthesis treated in this chapter. To begin with, he provided much of the formant data (center frequencies, amplitudes, and bandwidths) used in the actual synthesis. The original studies to determine an algorithm for spectral tilt were done with Sundberg at IRCAM in early 1979; the formula for the correction of second-formant frequency in front vowels is his, as is the technique of frequency transition illustrated in example 18b.

References

[1] Bennett, G. 1981. "Singing Synthesis in Electronic Music." In *Research Aspects on Singing*, ed. J. Sundberg. Publication 33. Stockholm: Royal Swedish Academy of Music, pp. 34–50.

[2] Fant, G. 1970. *The Acoustic Theory of Speech Production*. The Hague: Mouton.

[3] Rodet, X., and G. Bennett. 1980. "Synthèse de la voix chantée par ordinateur." In *Conférences des Journées d'Etudes 1980*. Paris: Festival International du Son, pp. 73–91.

[4] Rodet, X., and J.-L. Delatre. 1979. "Time-Domain Speech Synthesis-by-Rules Using a Flexible and Fast Signal Management System." In *Proceedings of the ICASSP 1979*. Washington, DC: IEEE.

[5] Rodet, X., Yves Potard, and Jean-Baptiste Barrière. 1984. "The CHANT Project: From the Synthesis of the Singing Voice to Synthesis in General." *Computer Music Journal* 8(3): 15–31.

[6] Sundberg, J. 1975. "Formant Technique in a Professional Female Singer." *Acustica* 32: 89–96.

[7] Sundberg, J. 1978. "Synthesis of Singing." *Swedish Journal of Musicology* 60(1): 107–112.

[8] Sundberg, J. 1987. *The Science of the Singing Voice*. Dekalb, IL: Northern Illinois University Press.

5 Synthesis of Singing by Rule

Johan Sundberg

5.1 Singing

Much has been written about the synthesis of musical performance on instruments. Musical performance should obey the same rules regardless of whether music is played on an instrument or the human voice is used as the instrument. Yet the voice has special features that instruments lack, and vice versa. I recount here some of the experiences I have had in synthesizing singing. I shall give examples that appeared to me to be revealing when I heard them.

5.2 Equipment

The instrumentation used is basically the same as that shown in figure 5.1. Sound is produced by the MUSSE synthesizer. This is a formant synthesizer controlled by an Eclipse minicomputer (Larson [3]). The basic MUSSE consists of a source oscillator generating a sawtooth signal with variable dc offset connected to five cascaded formant circuits with variable frequencies and, for the three lowest formants, also variable bandwidths. The manually controlled bandwidths of the two highest formants are set at 150 Hz. A higher-pole correction is provided by a resonance circuit at 4,500 Hz with a wide bandwidth. For fricatives, there are two computer-controlled noise generators, one at the glottal end of the formant chain and one at the lip end. As the noise generated at the glottis has to travel through the formant chain, the former generator is programmed to produce a higher amplitude signal than the latter.

5.3 Vowels and Consonants

The basic strategy for consonant synthesis is to use target (locus) values for formant frequencies and bandwidths and for the source parameters. These locus values and the vowel formant frequencies are given in table 5.1. In this table, all those cases have been marked in which the loci are modified by contest-dependent rules, modeling coarticulation. The transitions are smoothed by means of programmable filters. The characteristics of this smoothing are illustrated in figure 5.2.

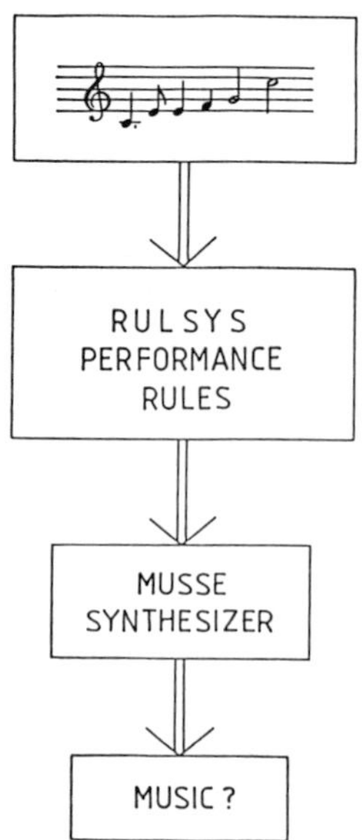

Figure 5.1
System to synthesize singing.

As the formant circuits are cascaded, the amplitudes of the formants are automatically tuned according to the acoustic theory of voice production, and reflecting a source spectrum envelope slope of −12 dB/octave. Consonant duration varies between 70 and 150 msec, depending on the context as illustrated in figure 5.2. These figures also show the associated patterns for the source amplitude and the formant frequencies and bandwidths.

5.4 Timing of Pitch Change

Now let us consider some very basic questions concerning the exact location of the boundary between notes. If there is a pitch change, where is it supposed to take place? We may hypothesize that the new note should start on the new pitch rather than with a pitch transition. However, one may equally well assume that a note keeps its pitch toward the end, so that the

Table 5.1
Formant frequency values in Hz for the vowels, given in IPA symbols, and locus values for consonants

Vowels								
	F1	F2	F3	F4	F5	B1	B2	B3
a:	550	1,000	2,550	2,900	3,300	40	70	100
a	600	1,000	2,450	2,900	3,100	40	70	100
y:	330	1,650	2,170	2,670	3,400	40	70	100
å:	400	750	2,400	2,600	2,900	40	70	100
å:	450	850	2,500	2,950	3,250	40	70	100
i:	300	1,800	2,500	3,000	3,300	40	70	100
i	350	1,750	2,500	3,000	3,300	40	70	100
e:	400	1,620	2,400	3,000	3,380	40	70	100
e	500	1,500	2,400	3,000	3,300	40	70	100
o:	350	680	2,350	2,750	3,000	40	70	100
Consonants								
	F1	F2	F3	F4	F5	B1	B2	B3
d	200[a]	1,500[a]	2,500[a]	2,950[a]	3,200[a]	40	80	120
f	400	1,150	2,020	2,610	3,200	70	100	250
g	280[a]	2,200?[a]	2,200[a]	3,450	4,030[a]	60	80	120
h	Same as following vowel					100	200	250
j	280[a]	1,650[a]	2,500[a]	3,000[a]	4,500[a]	50	120	120
k	400	1,700	1,800	3,020	3,300	80	40	110
l	300	1,200[a]	2,300[a]	2,900[a]	3,100[a]	25	40	30
m	250	1,200	2,200	2,750	3,500	25	250	250
n	200	1,450	2,070	2,500	2,700	20	200	100
p	200	960	1,960	2,470	3,100	50	80	120
r	400	1,350	2,000	2,400	3,000	50	80	120
s	200[a]	1,600[a]	2,600	3,600	4,300	40	80	120
t	200	2,300	3,000	3,800	4,500	80	100	200
v	400	1,100[a]	2,300	3,100	3,500	130	120	175

a. Context-dependent values; for details see figure 5.2.

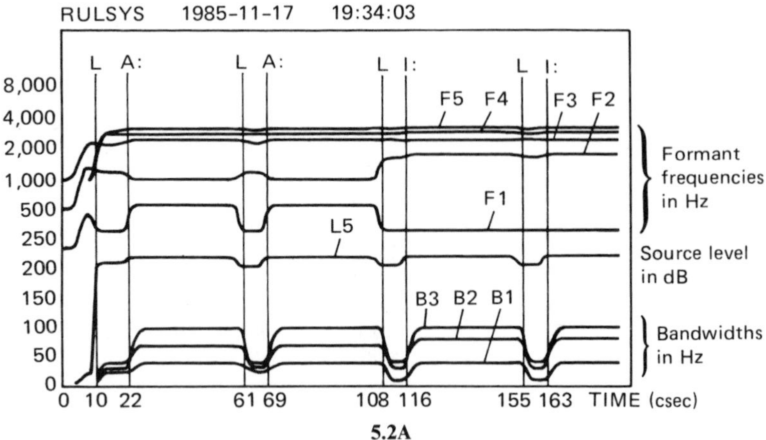
RULSYS 1985-11-17 19:34:03
L A:
L A:
L I:
L I:
F5 F4 F3 F2
F1
L5
B3 B2 B1
8,000
4,000
2,000
1,000
500
250
200
150
100
50
0
0 10 22 61 69 108 116 155 163 TIME (csec)
Formant frequencies in Hz
Source level in dB
Bandwidths in Hz

5.2A

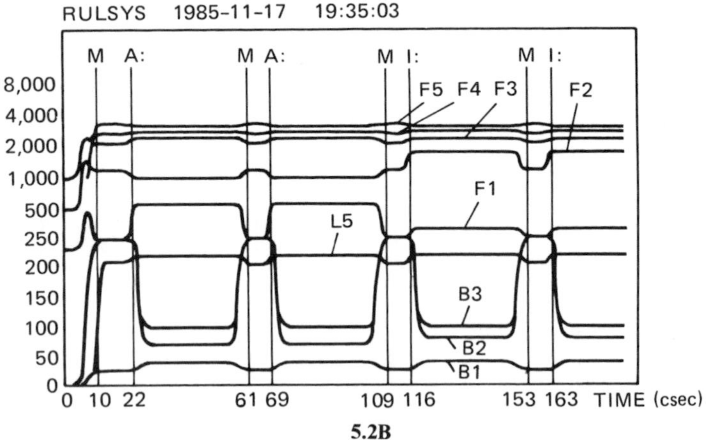
RULSYS 1985-11-17 19:35:03
M A:
M A:
M I:
M I:
F5 F4 F3
F2
F1
L5
B3
B2
B1
8,000
4,000
2,000
1,000
500
250
200
150
100
50
0
0 10 22 61 69 109 116 153 163 TIME (csec)

5.2B

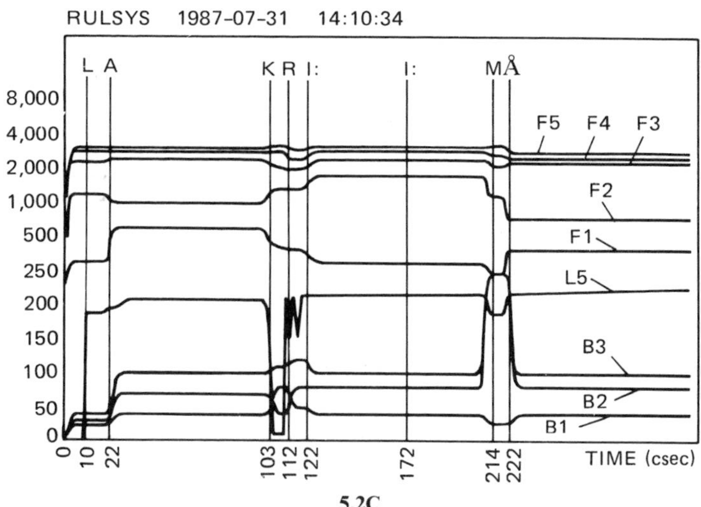

5.2C

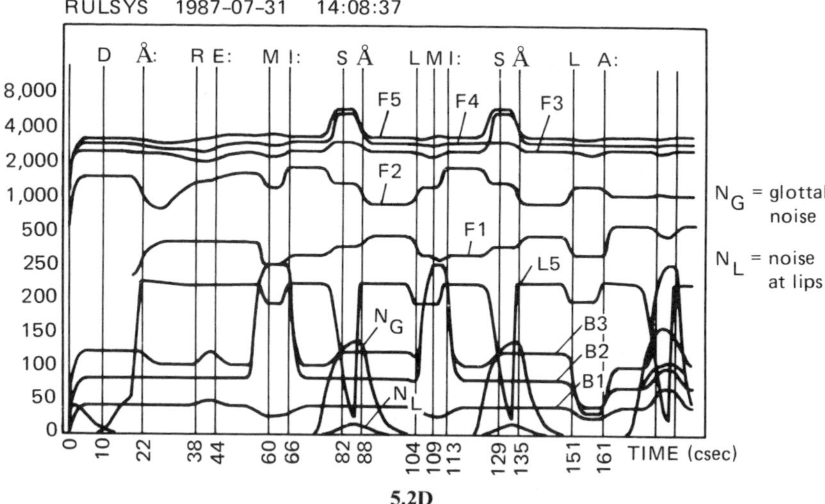

5.2D

Figure 5.2
Examples of the parameter values used in the synthesis. The text is shown at the top.

pitch change is left to the onset of the next note. Both alternatives are given in sound example 21 (given on the accompanying compact disk). There seems to be no doubt that the second alternative is the correct one. Thus, the singer executes the pitch change at the end of the old note, and not during the beginning of the new note.

5.5 Long and Short Vowels and Consonants

More questions present themselves when we synthesize singing that includes consonants as well as vowels. As we see in sound example 22, it is appropriate to use a long vowel (as /a:/) on stressed, and a short vowel (as /a/) on unstressed notes.

What about consonants? As in speech, a consonant should be lengthened if it appears after a short vowel, and shortened when it appears after a long vowel.

5.6 Location of Syllable Boundaries

There are other aspects of the timing of consonants. We know that there are syllables and notes, but how, exactly, are these coordinated? In particular, if we use both long and short consonants and vowels, where do we start to take the duration of these consonants? Up to now we have taken the time needed for the consonants from the vowel following them. There is another solution: to let the vowel preceding the consonant offer the duration needed. This proves to be correct, as we see in sound example 23.

5.7 Effects of Chords

Through synthesis of instrumental sounds, I have shown that crescendos and diminuendos are essential to musical playing, and of course this is true also in singing. This is illustrated in sound example 24.

A crescendo is never a matter of amplitude only. In the human voice, as well as in most musical instruments, an increase in sound level is associated with a shift in the overall tilt of the spectrum. Figure 5.3 shows a typical example for a singer and a nonsinger. Typical spectral implications of a change in loudness of phonation observed in a singer and a nonsinger are shown. The curves show the level in various spectral bands, the center

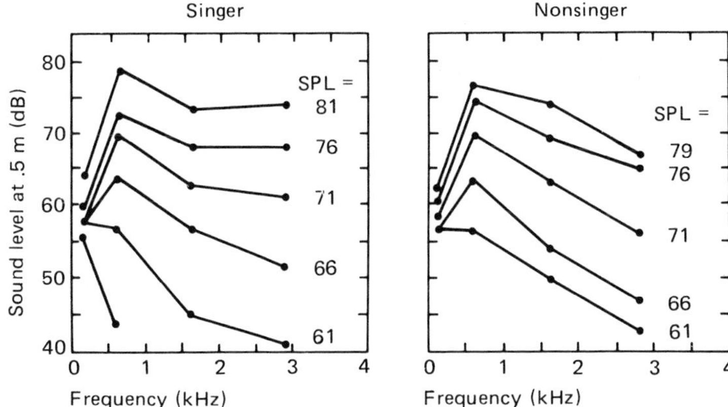

Figure 5.3
Energy in various frequency bands at different loudnesses for singer and nonsinger.

frequency of which is the horizontal axis. The curves are labeled according to the overall sound level (SPL) of the vocalizations. As loudness is increased, the higher spectrum partials gain more in amplitude than the lower spectrum partials. We have included this feature by inserting a so-called physiologic volume control circuit in the synthesizer. This effect, also, is included in sound example 24.

In addition to this, I have added one more characteristic that varies directly with the sound level, and that is the vibrato amplitude. The vibrato, we recall, is a modulation of the fundamental frequency. The vibrato is characterized by two parameters: the frequency, that is, the number of undulations per second, and the amplitude, that is, the magnitude of departures from the mean frequency. While the frequency of the vibrato, or its rate, generally remains rather constant for a particular singer, the magnitude, or extent of variation of the frequency, increases with level.

5.8 Coloratura

Coloratura is a term used for a rapid succession of short notes that are sung without interspersed consonants. Sound example 25 demonstrates some aspects of coloratura.

Figure 5.4 shows the fundamental frequency variations for a professional singer's rendition of the coloratura exercise shown at the top. The singer's

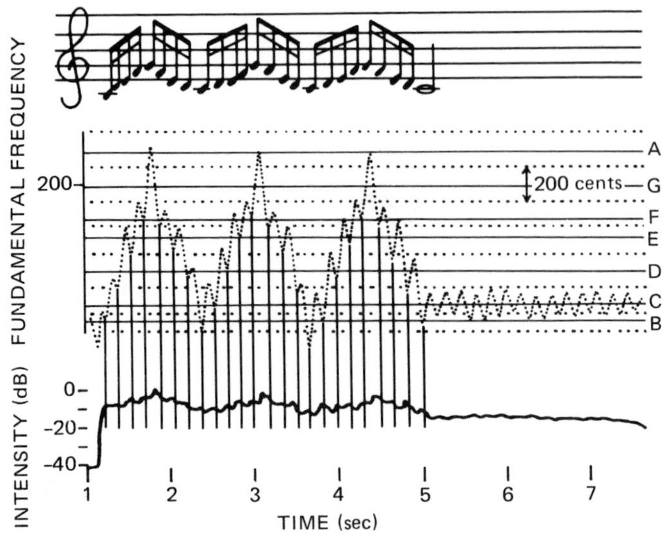

Figure 5.4
Fundamental frequency pattern for a baritone singer performing the passage shown above. Solid vertical lines show the frequencies of the notes, and dotted lines the boundaries midway between them.

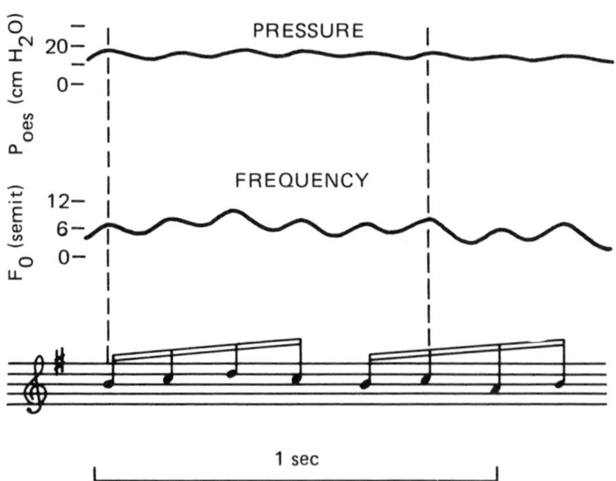

Figure 5.5
Oesophageal pressure (P_{oes}) and fundamental frequency (F_0) for male singer performing a fast coloratura passage. Note: cm H_2O = centimeters of water (a measure of pressure used by physiologists); semit = semitones of musical pitch.

fundamental frequency curve is placed on a grid of which the solid lines represent the target frequencies according to the equally tempered scale, given the frequency of the last note. The dotted lines are drawn midway between the targets, so that they represent the boundaries between notes. In examining the pitch trace of the voice in relation to the grid, we see that the singer apparently attempts to let the fundamental frequency make one sweep up and one sweep down around the center frequency for each of the tones. However, this does not mean that he always succeeds in doing so.

Together with Curt von Euler and Rolf Leanderson, I have had the opportunity of studying the performance of such rapid passages. Figure 5.5 shows a typical registration from an experienced male singer. The top curve shows the pressure swings in the esophagus, the variations of which reflect the variations in the subglottal pressure. We can see that esophageal pressure varies at a rate of about 6 variations per second. We conclude that during coloratura singing the subglottal pressure is rising and falling at a rate of about 6 times a second.

The same figure also shows the synchronization between these pressure undulations in the esophagus and the fundamental frequency. We can see that the synchronization is almost perfect; the pressure and the voice pitch frequency reach their peaks at nearly the same moments. From this we conclude that coloratura is performed by means of pressure undulations that are synchronized in phase with fundamental frequency undulations.

Sound example 25 illustrates the use of these effects.

5.9 Formants as Flags

The voice frequency and amplitude can be used to mark certain tones. The formant frequencies can probably also be used for that purpose. This is the conclusion that I draw from sound example 26.

5.10 Let Formants Sing

Synthesis allows us to improve our understanding of reality. It also offers the opportunity to innovate, because machines may be skilled in doing things that humans find difficult.

From the theory of vowel production we know that vocal tract resonances, or formants, enhance those partials of the spectrum that are closest to the center frequencies of these formants, or formant frequencies. Such enhancing is actually an increase in the intensities of these partials. Under certain conditions, the intensity of a particular partial may be so strong that the partial may be perceived as a single tone with the pitch of the partial.

It is easy to play around with the formants in order to play melodies. As long as we keep the fundamental frequency constant, we have available only the series of natural harmonics, as in a trumpet without valves.

We can make things a bit more complicated if we can change the fundamental frequency one-fifth up and one-fifth down. We thus gain access to all the tones of the complete diatonic scale. Hence, we can play all melodies that use the tones of the diatonic scale only.

This is hard but not impossible for human beings. Some singers do practice this special kind of singing. The so-called Harmonic Choir, working in New York and Paris, is one example.

In sound example 27, harmonics of heightened intensity are used to play tunes.

5.11 Discussion

We have seen how the performance of short excerpts can be improved from a musical point of view in various ways. Earlier, I presented rules for instrumental performance. Here I have extended most of these rules to the synthesis of singing. I have added several rules that seem specific to singing, rules that have effects that seem phonetic rather than musical.

Analysis-by-synthesis is an excellent strategy for developing a description of the important features of very complicated systems. However, in a sense it can only provide relative evidence, and can never prove that the description tried is the best possible. For instance, we would not like to pretend that our recipes for synthesizing singing is the best possible. What we want to pretend is that, at least with the quality you have heard in the examples, singing can be synthesized by means of a rule system of ordered, context dependent rules that operates on the music and the phonetic text.

References

[1] Rapp, K. (1971), "A Study of Syllable Timing," Speech Transmission Laboratory Quarterly Progress and Status Report 1/1971, 14–19.

[2] Carlson, R., and Granström, B. (1975), "A Phonetically Oriented Programming Language for Rule Description of Speech," in *Speech Communication*, G. Fant, ed., Almqvist and Wicksell, Stockholm, Vol. 2, 245–253.

[3] Larsson, B. (1977), "Music and Singing Synthesis Equipment (MUSSE)," Speech Transmission Laboratory Quarterly Progress and Status Report 1977/1, KTH, Stockholm, 38–40.

[4] Frydén, L., Sundberg, J., and Askenfelt, A. (1982), "From Music to Sound. A Rule System for Musical Performance of Melodies," Proc. of the International Computer Music Conference, Venice, T. Blum and J. Strawn, eds., 426–436.

[5] Zera, J., Gauffin, J., and Sundberg, J. (1984), "Synthesis of Selected VCV-Syllables in Singing," Proc. of the International Computer Music Conference, IRCAM Paris, W. Buxton, ed., 83–86.

[6] Sundberg, J., and Frydén, L. (1985), "Teaching a Computer to Play Melodies Musically," in *Analytica, Festschrift for Ingmar Bengtson*, publications issued by the Royal Swedish Academy of Music Nr. 47, 67–76.

[7] Thompson, W. F., Friberg, A., Frydén, L., and Sundberg, J. (1986), "Evaluating Rules for the Synthetic Performance of Melodies," Speech Transmission Laboratory Quarterly Progress and Status Report 2–3/1986, 27–44.

[8] Sundberg, J., and Frydén, L. (1987), "Melodic Charge and Music Performance," in *Harmony and Tonality*, publication Nr. 54 issued by the Royal Swedish Academy of Music, Stockholm, 53–58.

[9] Sundberg, J., "Computer Synthesis of Music Performance," in *Generative Processes in Music*, J. A. Sloboda, ed., Oxford: Clarendon Press, 52–69.

6 Frequency Modulation Synthesis of the Singing Voice

John M. Chowning

6.1 Introduction

The work represented here demonstrates above all that acceptable synthesis of a sung tone demands careful attention to rather simple characteristic details of the real target tone that are largely independent of the synthesis technique. While the particular spectral content of a wave may be achieved by a variety of synthesis techniques, "naturalness" depends upon the temporal characteristics of very basic descriptors, such as pitch and loudness, and spectral changes during the attack-decay portions of the tone. Although frequency modulation (FM) synthesis has been used to simulate some orchestral instrument tones (Schottstaedt [6], Morrill [4]), the singing voice seems to remain in the province of synthesis models borrowed from speech research (Sundberg [7], Moorer [3]). The purpose of this chapter is to show a strategy for the use of FM in the synthesis of the soprano singing voice.

Inasmuch as the basic concepts underlying FM synthesis are by now well-known (Chowning [1]) and synthesis programs have a large degree of commonality (MUSIC V, MUSIC10, CMUSIC, etc.), detailed descriptions will not be presented here.

6.2 Frequency Modulation Tone Synthesis

The fundamental FM algorithm is based upon the output of a modulating oscillator that adds to the frequency term of a carrier oscillator, thereby producing a complex waveform. This is expressed in the equation

$$e = A \cdot \sin[6.28 \cdot fc \cdot t + I \cdot \sin(6.28 \cdot fm \cdot t)], \tag{1}$$

where

e = the instantaneous amplitude of the modulated carrier,

A = the peak amplitude of the carrier,

fc = the carrier frequency,

fm = the modulating frequency, and

I = the index of modulation.

The ratio of the carrier and modulating frequencies, fc/fm, determines the relative interval of the component frequencies in the modulated carrier signal, while the modulation index and Bessel functions determine the amplitudes of the components and the overall bandwidth of the signal. The modulation index, I, is the ratio of the depth of modulation or peak deviation to the modulating frequency. Of particular interest in the application of FM to voice synthesis presented below are ratios of frequencies where

$fc = N \cdot fm$ and N is a positive integer.

The spectra resulting from this class of ratios are such that the frequency components form the harmonic series, where fm is the fundamental, f0.

There are a number of useful extensions of this basic algorithm—(1) summing the outputs of two or more copies of the basic algorithm in parallel, (2) one carrier oscillator and two or more modulating oscillators in parallel, (3) one carrier oscillator and two or more modulating oscillators in series, and (4) two or more carrier oscillators and one modulating oscillator—to name some of the basic types of extensions. It is the last of these that is particularly appropriate to voice synthesis or indeed any tones that have prominent resonances.

6.3 General Characteristics of Soprano Tones

Spectral representations of the attack, quasi-steady-state, and decay portions of recorded soprano tones show that for most vowel timbres and through the greater part of the range

1. There is a weighting of the spectral energy around the low order harmonics with the fundamental as the strongest harmonic above 400 Hz, thus supporting the theory that in the female voice the lowest formant tracks the pitch period (Sundberg [7]).

2. There are one or more secondary peaks in the spectrum depending on the vowel and fundamental pitch.

3. The formants are not necessarily at constant frequencies independent of the fundamental pitch, but rather follow formant trajectories that may either ascend or descend, depending on the vowel, as a function of the fundamental frequency (Sundberg [7]).

4. Only the lowest formant is significant at the amplitude thresholds of the attack and decay portions of a tone, while the upper formants become significant as the overall amplitude of the signal approaches the quasi steady-state.

5. The upper formants decrease in energy more rapidly than does the lowest formant when a tone is sung at decreasing loudness.

6. A crescendo, then, must depend upon an increase in the overall amplitude where the contribution of the upper formants is proportionally greater at maximum amplitude.

7. There is a small but discernible variation of the pitch period even in the singing condition without vibrato.

6.4 FM Model for the Soprano Voice

For the FM model of sung soprano tones three formants are considered. One oscillator can be used to modulate the three carrier oscillators with a separate index scaling for each, or three parallel simple FM pairs can be used. The frequency of the modulating oscillator(s) is always set to the frequency of the pitch of the tone, f0, while the frequencies of the carrier oscillators are set to those harmonic frequencies closest to the appropriate formant frequencies. In this model various parameters, or terms, of the FM equation are computed from the basic musical descriptors of overall amplitude and fundamental pitch and from a set of tables that form the data base for the terms at selected pitches through the soprano range. In this sense, then, it is an adaptive algorithm since all of the computation is based upon the following two performance variables:

A = overall amplitude of the signal, where $0 < A \leq 1.0$,

f0 = fundamental pitch frequency, where F3(185.0 Hz) $\leq$ f0 $\leq$ F6(1,480 Hz).

The modulation signal is defined to be

$$M = \sin(6.28 \cdot fm \cdot t), \qquad (2)$$

where

M = the modulating signal to be scaled by the indices and

fm = the modulating frequency = f0.

The signal resulting from the sum of the three modulated carriers is

$$e = A^{.5} \cdot A1(t) \cdot \sin(6.28 \cdot fc1 \cdot t + I1 \cdot M)$$
$$+ A^{1.5} \cdot A2(t) \cdot \sin(6.28 \cdot fc2 \cdot t + I2 \cdot M)$$
$$+ A^{2} \cdot A3(t) \cdot \sin(6.28 \cdot fc3 \cdot t + I3 \cdot M), \quad (3)$$

where

e = the instantaneous amplitude of the sum of the three modulated carrier signals,
$fc1$ = the first carrier frequency = round($fmt1$/f0),
$fc2$ = the second carrier frequency = round($fmt2$/f0),
$fc3$ = the third carrier frequency = round($fmt3$/f0),
$A1(t)$ = the relative amplitude of the first carrier,
$A2(t)$ = the relative amplitude of the second carrier,
$A3(t)$ = the relative amplitude of the third carrier,
$I1$ = the modulation index of the first formant,
$I2$ = the modulation index of the second formant,
$I3$ = the modulation index of the third formant, and
round ( ) is a function that rounds its argument to the nearest integer.

The data base used for the computation of the carrier frequencies, amplitudes, and indices of modulation is in the form of tables, where there is a table for each vowel. Within the table the data are arranged in three groups, one for each formant, including the formant frequency, its amplitude, and index at 1/2 octave intervals as shown in table 6.1. The table specifies the break-point frequencies for the pitches

F#3 C4 F#4 C5 F#5 C6 F#6

and the data for the intervening pitches are computed by interpolation. Thus, for the frequency of the second carrier, $fc2 = N \cdot fm$, the integer N is computed by dividing the interpolated value of the formant frequency at the value f0 by f0 and rounding to the nearest integer.

Note that the relative contribution of the three carriers varies with the overall loudness of the tone. With decreasing values of A, the amplitudes of

Table 6.1
Format data for vowel ah

*fmt*1	*A*1	*I*1		
, , , ,	, , , ,	, , , ,		
175	.400	0.1	at	F#3
262	.400	0.1	at	C4
392	.800	0.1	at	F#4
523	.800	0.1	at	C5
784	.800	0.0	at	F#5
1,046	.800	0.0	at	C6
1,568	.800	0.0	at	F#6
*fmt*2	*A*2	*I*2		
, , , ,	, , , ,	, , , ,		
350	.800	0.5	at	F#3
524	.800	0.1	at	C4
784	.400	0.1	at	F#4
950	.200	0.1	at	C5
1,568	.100	0.0	at	F#5
2,092	.100	0.0	at	C6
3,136	.000	0.0	at	F#6
*fmt*3	*A*3	*I*3		
, , , ,	, , , ,	, , , ,		
2,800	.150	1.6	at	F#3
2,700	.150	1.6	at	C4
2,500	.150	1.6	at	F#4
2,450	.150	1.6	at	C5
2,400	.150	1.6	at	F#5
2,350	.100	1.5	at	C6
4,500	.100	1.0	at	F#6

the individual carriers decrease according to the exponents .5, 1.5, and 2, respectively [equation (3)]. The high frequency energy falls off more rapidly with decreasing effort than does the low frequency energy. This is a very important property of this model since without this scaling, tones at decreasing loudness sound to be increasing in distance from the listener rather than decreasing in effort, i.e., sung more softly.

For the same reason, the rapid increase and decrease of energy in the vocal tract during the attack and decay portion of the tone may, for some vowels, also follow these conditions; the amplitude envelopes for the three formants have different attack and decay slopes.

Further, a crescendo and decrescendo would similarly manifest a change in the proportion of contribution of formant energy according to overall loudness. Therefore, the attack and decay portions of the amplitude envelopes for each formant are divided into two parts, a1, a2, d1, and d2. In the normal case the first and second attacks (a1 and a2) and the first and second decays (d1 and d2) will have a small constant duration. However, in the case of a crescendo through the course of a note the attack will have the following value,

$$a2 = D - (a1 + d1 + d2), \tag{4}$$

where

$D =$ the duration of the note and

$a1 = d1 = d2 = 0.08$ are typical attack and decay values.

Here, for any value of D substantially greater than 0.32 sec, the attack segment a2 will provide for the increasing contribution of the 2nd and 3rd formants as the crescendo evolves. For a decrescendo equation (4) would be solved for d1. A variety of articulations can thus be realized in the distribution of $D - (a1 + d2)$ between a1, the steady state, and d2.

Finally, a small amount of periodic and random vibrato is applied in equal amounts to the frequency terms in equation (3), according to the relation

$$\text{vibrato percent deviation} = 0.2 \cdot \log(f0)$$

at a frequency that ranges from 5 Hz to 6.5 Hz according to the fundamental frequency range of F#3 to F#6. Without vibrato the synthesized tones are unnatural sounding. The small fluctuation in pitch is therefore a key attribute of the singing voice. In addition, a slight portamento or pitch glide is included during the attack portion of the tone.

6.5 Conclusions

The research presented here serves to show that a nonlinear synthesis technique can be used to synthesize sung vocal tones and serves to confirm previous research results in regard to formant trajectories for the soprano voice. It suggests, as well, two areas for future research: (1) the physical correlates to performance dynamics (loudness) and (2) a more precise understanding of the effect of microfrequency fluctuation on perceptual fusion.

Acknowledgments

The author wishes to express his gratitude to Jean-Claude Risset and IRCAM, Paris, for the support of this work, to Johan Sundberg for his encouragement and sharing of his extensive knowledge of the singing voice, and to Gerald Bennett and Xavier Rodet for their helpful comments; a special indebtedness is owed to Michael McNabb, who first revealed the significance of random pitch fluctuation in vocal tone synthesis.

References

[1] J. M. Chowning (1973). "The Synthesis of Complex Audio Spectra by Means of Frequency Moduation," *J. Audio Eng. Soc.* 21, pp. 526–534, reprinted in *Computer Music Journal*, 1:2, pp. 46–54 (1977).

[2] M. Le Brun (1977). "A Derivation of the Spectrum of FM with a Complex Modulating Wave," *Computer Music Journal*, 1:4, pp. 51–52.

[3] J. A. Moorer (1979). "The Use of Linear Prediction of Speech in Computer Music Applications," *J. Audio Eng. Soc.* 27:3, pp. 134–140.

[4] D. Morrill (1977). "Trumpet Algorithms for Computer Composition," *Computer Music Journal*, 1:1, pp. 46–52.

[5] M. V. Mathews (1970). *The Technology of Computer Music*, MIT Press.

[6] W. G. Schottstaedt (1977). "The Simulation of Natural Instrument Tones Using Frequency Modulation with a Complex Modulating Wave," *Computer Music Journal*, 1:4, pp. 46–50.

[7] J. Sundberg (1978). "Synthesis of Singing," *Swedish J. of Musicology*, 60:1, pp. 107–112.

7 Spatial Reverberation: Discussion and Demonstration

Gary S. Kendall, William L. Martens, and Shawn L. Decker

7.1 Introduction

When a sound event is transduced into electrical energy by a microphone and reproduced over loudspeakers or headphones, the experience of the sound event is altered dramatically from what would result if the listener were located at the position of the microphone. One of the primary reasons for the change in the experience is that information regarding the spatial location of the sound event and of the sound reflected from the environment has been lost. Multichannel recording and reproduction can retain some spatial information, but conventional techniques do not attempt to recreate the spatial sound field of a natural environment and, therefore, create a listening experience that is spatially impoverished. This is despite the fact that many recordings include reverberation from a natural environment in order to provide the listener with a general impression of an acoustic environment. There is a need for improved techniques to spatialize recorded sound, but the need is even more urgent for synthesized sounds that have no spatial attributes save those provided by signal processing.

The goal of the work described here is to provide composers with a comprehensive control of auditory space percepts in music. Our effort in this regard has had two primary components. The first is the formulation of idealized spectral cues for use in directionalizing sound. We know, for example, that spectral cues induce spatial percepts even when other types of cues are absent. The second is the simulation of environmental reverberation that retains the spatiality of reflected sound. By combining spectral cues for directional hearing with such reverberation, we are attempting to recreate the experience of listening in natural environments entirely from computer simulation. We use the term "spatial reverberation" for this synthesis of directional cues and simulated reflected sound. It is our hope that techniques like ours will stimulate composers to produce a kind of music that not only takes place in space but is spatially conceived.

7.2 Directional Hearing Cues

7.2.1 Interaural Differences

The two cues that classical psychoacoustics holds as primarily responsible for identifying the direction or incidence angle of a sound source are interaural intensity difference (IID) and interaural time delay (ITD). The physical basis for these cues is as follows: As a sound source moves on the horizontal plane toward the side—away from directly ahead or directly behind the listener—IID grows from 0 dB up to roughly 20 dB depending on frequency, and the ITD grows from 0 to about 650 microsec (Feddersen et al. [8]). Because the head blocks only those frequencies with wavelengths shorter than the diameter of the head (about 1 kHz and above), the acoustic "head shadow" responsible for the IID is frequency dependent. For pure tones, IID is a salient cue only at frequencies higher than 1 kHz. Because the periods of high frequencies are shorter than the maximum ITD, ITD is a salient cue for pure tones only below about 1.5 kHz. The potential confusion between waveform periods and ITDs is abolished if the high-frequency stimuli have time-varying amplitude (e.g., Nuetzel and Hafter [12]) or time-varying frequency (e.g., Blauert [4]).

In actuality, IID and ITD provide the auditory system only with information on whether a sound source is to the left or right of a listener. This is especially clear in headphone listening when cues to externalize the sound source are eliminated (Sakamoto et al. [14]). Sound images with IID and ITD cues are perceived on a left/right axis inside the head. This is referred to as "lateralization" and has been the subject of considerable research in the last century. The fact that listeners have some basis for identifying the direction of sound sources above, below, in front, and in back did not become a general research topic in psychoacoustics until the late 1960s. In order to visualize a point on this left/right lateralization axis projected into three-dimensional space, we must imagine a plane containing the point placed perpendicularly to the axis. For a given distance from the listener represented by a sphere, the plane cutting through the sphere makes a circle as shown in figure 7.1. This circle is a representation of the possible locations in three-dimensional space at which the lateralized sound might have originated.

7.2.2 Spectral Cues

Within the last 20 years, we have come to recognize that an additional cue for directional hearing is provided by the reflection of sound off the convolutions of the pinna (outer ear), the shoulders, and the upper torso. These short latency reflections impose directional information on the spectrum of the source signal. The most important of these reflections are those contributed by the pinnae. Because the pinnae have an asymmetric

Figure 7.1
The left/right lateralization dimension and the up/down/front/back circles upon which sounds can be located at a given distance from the listener.

arrangement of ridges, the composite sound reflections create a unique spectral profile for every sound direction. The auditory system uses these spectral profiles to remove the spatial ambiguity that results from IID and ITD cues alone. It is the spectral cues produced by the pinna, shoulders, and upper torso that enable the auditory system to determine the position of the sound source on the circle represented in figure 7.1: above, behind, below, or in front of the listener.

Numerous researchers have studied the relationship between the direction of a sound source and the acoustic transformation produced by the pinna. It is a reasonable approximation to imagine that a discrete reflection from a ridge of the pinna will produce a notch in the spectrum of the source signal and that a collection of reflections will produce a complex spectral shape with many notches of varying depth. Even though some empirical measurements of the pinna made in the ear canal conform to this approximation, most measurements indicate that reflections are not discrete and that there is no simple correspondence between single reflections and spectral notches. Understanding of the relationship between time-domain and frequency-domain representations of the pinna responses was historically slow to evolve. Batteau (1967) [2] was the first researcher to develop a model of the relationship between the physical characteristics of the pinna and the acoustic information used for directional hearing. He attempted to identify individual reflections responsible for judgments of azimuth and for elevation. Shaw and Teranishi (1968) [17] measured the acoustic effects of the pinna in the frequency domain and demonstrated that the relationship between pinna filtering and the directional location of a sound source is very complex, but they did not attempt to explain how the auditory system used this information. Blauert (1969) [3] hypothesized that pinna cues were evaluated by the auditory system in terms of spectral "preference bands" that constituted a signature of certain source directions. It was not until 1974 that Wright, Hebrank, and Wilson synthesized Batteau's and Blauert's views into a concept that bridged the time-domain/frequency-domain distinction and demonstrated the essential similarity of both views.

Despite the fact that pinna transfer functions are highly complex and difficult to adapt to a simple model, they have easily identified spectral features. A quick examination reveals that they contain spectral notches and peaks whose frequencies are dependent on the incidence angle of the source signal. Almost every researcher has noted that individual pinna transfer functions vary tremendously from each individual ear to the next. Careful examination reveals that in spite of the variety of details, there are numerous common trends. For example, on the lateral plane (the plane defined by the left/right dimension and the above/below dimension), the frequencies of the two most prominent spectral notches generally increase with increasing elevation. The exact shapes of the head-related transfer functions can differ as shown here for subject MDL (figure 7.2A) and subject GSK (figure 7.2B), but both show the same trend in the migration of these spectral notches. This might suggest that the directional information supplied by the pinna can be characterized largely in terms of these spectral notches, although there are several other observable global trends involving spectral peaks and overall spectral contour. In fact, one can separate to some extent the individual spectral features contributed by the head and the pinna. Binaural recordings and studies such as that by Butler and Belendiuk [6] demonstrate that it is quite possible for one person to utilize the spatial hearing cues recorded with another person's ears, but the issue of how the auditory system evaluates the complex spectral profile at the two ears has not been adequately investigated and may require many more years of research.

7.2.3 Simulating Cues for Directional Hearing

For the purposes of simulating cues for directional hearing in computer music or any kind of audio reproduction, one must determine a set of "idealized transfer functions" that will provide the best possible image of the sound direction for the general population. It has already been estab-

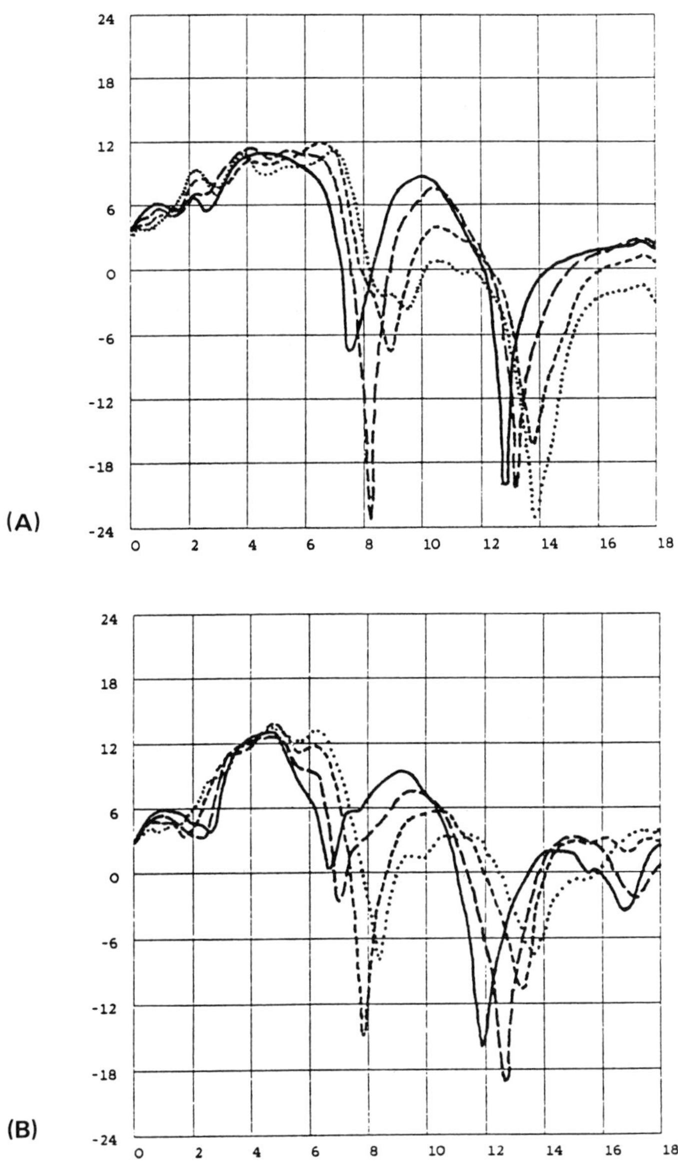

Figure 7.2
Head-related transfer functions for two subjects (MDL in 7.2A and GSK in 7.2B) illustrating trends in spectral features for increasing source elevation in the lateral plane. The sound was located 2 meters to the left of the subject and was moved from ear level (0°) to an elevation 30° above ear level (solid line, 0°; long dashes, 10°, short dashes, 20°; dotted line 30°). Abscissa is frequency in kHz, ordinate is gain in dB.

lished that measured pinna responses display tremendous variability at the detail level, but that in spite of this variability individuals are able to localize sounds recorded through the pinnae of others. Idealized transfer functions cannot be determined by averaging techniques because directional judgments may well be based on spectral features that averaging would smooth away. Notches may appear to be at different frequencies for different individuals, but all individuals have notches. Then too, it may be possible to create spectral cues that produce superior directional images to those associated with "natural" cues. In this regard, research by Butler and Belendiuk [6] is supportive. They demonstrated that "some pinnae ... provide more accurate cues for MSP [median sagittal plane] localization than do others." Butler and Belendiuk did not attempt to identify experimentally the exact features that improve directional hearing, but their data did enable them to speculate that "the migration of the notch in the frequency response curves appears more orderly" in the superior pinna.

Our own approach to this problem has been to synthesize directional cues on the basis of considerable visual study of pinna measurements. We have recorded head-related transfer functions for sound sources located 10° apart in azimuth and 20° apart in elevation. We have analyzed our empirical data in order to identify those spectral features that seem to be the most common to all subjects and most likely to present the auditory system with usable information. Large-scale trends are taken into account in creating a table of spectral features and their relation to perceived direction. It is hoped that, by combining the best and most regular features of many different pinnae, a set of spectral manipulations can be devised that not only match the saliency of natural cues but actually support superior directional perception for many people.

Once we have arrived at a decision on the important spectral features for a given spatial direction, a list of these features is passed on to a filter design program. This program is able to construct a pole-zero filter that matches the prescribed characteristics. Figure 7.3A shows transfer functions measured inside the ear canal for two subjects. Figure 7.3B shows the transfer function of a digital filter designed to match ideal spectral features derived from such empirical measurements. The problem of designing these filters is somewhat complicated by the fact that one may need to produce continuous changes in direction between the analyzed points. This means that there must be steady migration of poles and zeros as intended direction is changed, or else the resulting signal discontinuities would produce notice-

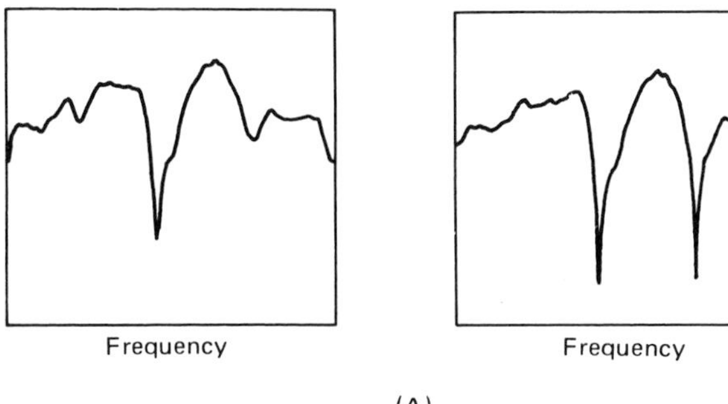

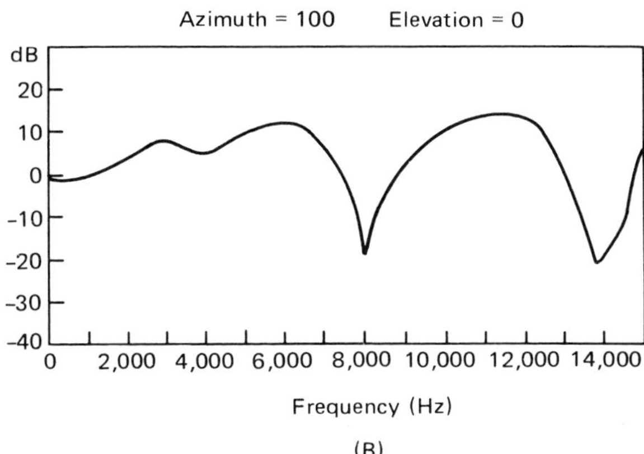

Figure 7.3
Comparison of measured head-related transfer functions for two subjects (upper panels: maximum is 18 kHz) and our simulation (lower panel: maximum is 15 kHz).

able noise. In effect, the filters must be designed for the entire ensemble of directions taken together.

7.3 Simulating Reflected Sound

7.3.1 The Spatial Reverberation Concept

Our particular experience with pinna cues led us to the conclusion that in order to simulate the spatial cues of real environments, one must capture the total spatiotemporal pattern of reflected sound. For this reason, we have sought a reverberator design that models an actual room and that

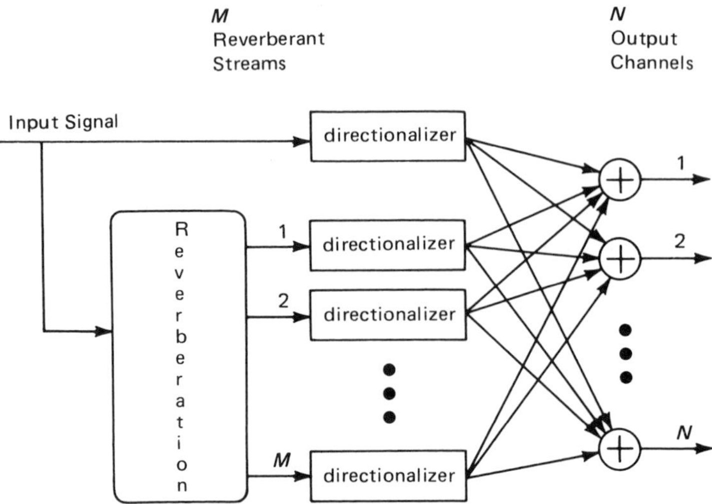

Figure 7.4
Basic signal-processing network for spatial reverberation.

accurately replicates the spatial and temporal distribution of reflected sound. The design must differentiate between large and small rooms and allow us to place the reverberated sound source anywhere in three-dimensional space, not just at the speaker positions. A basic signal-processing network for spatial reverberation requires two subsystems (figure 7.4). One is a reverberation subsystem that takes an input signal and produces multiple outputs, each of which is a unique "reverberation stream." The temporal pattern of each stream must match the reflections in a small spatial region of the model room. The other is a "directionalizer" subsystem that superimposes directional hearing cues such as pinna filtering. Each reverberation stream is individually directionalized to position the simulated reflections in the correct region of the model room. The sum of all reverberation streams taken together captures the entire spatiotemporal pattern of reflected sound in the model room.

We believe that this spatiotemporal pattern creates the context in which judgments of direction and distance are made. A mental model of the acoustic environment develops rapidly from this context during normal experience in a novel environment. If one is denied normal exposure to an environment, such mental models are not formed and localization accuracy is significantly degraded (Musicant and Butler [11]). We also believe that the spatiotemporal pattern formed by the reflected sound can serve to clarify the position of the sound source in the environment, especially once the sound source begins to move. The reflected sound is particularly important to directional judgments when other directional cues, such as the cues for distinguishing between front and back positions, are weak. Thus, our primary goal is that the spatial reverberator produce the kind of spatially distributed reverberation that will help listeners localize sounds and impart a very strong impression of the reverberant environment.

7.3.2 Implementing the Image Model with Recirculating Delays

The technique of recirculating delays has served as the basis for reverberation simulation in computer music and digital audio production ever since the publication of Manfred Schroeder's pioneering work in 1962 [15]. The Schroeder reverberator prescribes small units of recirculating delays combined in a predominantly serial network. The complete reverberation network suggested by Schroeder consists of four comb filters in parallel followed by two all-pass filters in series. Although the comb filters produce a series of spectral notches in the reverberated signal, the four filters in parallel produce a density of notches akin to that measured in real rooms.

In 1970, Schroeder expanded his reverberation network to include an initial delay buffer that replicates the kind of the early reflection pattern typical of concert halls [16]. This model, including both the frequency-dependent recirculating delays and the simulation of early reflections, was refined by Moorer [10], who produced the best-sounding reverberation network of this type. A significant advance in the goals of such networks was achieved by Chowning [7], who combined the basic serial network of recirculating delays with time-variant controls to simulate moving sound sources.

These and other contemporary approaches to reverberation attempt to replicate the global reverberation typical of large reverberant rooms like concert halls without attempting to capture any of the exact characteristics that distinguish one room from another. Since these methods do not actually model a room, matching the reverberation to the characteristics of a particular room is largely a matter of guesswork. Even Chowning's system for simulating moving sound sources does not change the pattern of reflected sound in a way that captures the changes typical of real rooms.

For simple rooms the "image model" of reverberation (Allen and Berkeley [1]) provides a method for predicting both the spatial and the temporal pattern of reflected sound from the room dimensions and the positions of the sound source and the listener within that room. For this model, each ray of reflected sound is viewed as originating from a "virtual sound source" outside of the actual physical room. Each virtual sound source is contained within a "virtual room" that replicates the physical room or is a mirror image of it. We use three-dimensional coordinates (x, y, z) to specify individual virtual sound sources or virtual rooms (figure 7.5). The pattern of reflected sound in the physical room can be viewed as the composite sound reaching the listener from all virtual sources. A vector connecting the position of the listener in the physical room and these virtual sources will predict the direction from which the reflected sound emanates and the distance that the sound must travel before reaching the listener. Even though real walls usually have irregularities that cause reflections to be spatially diffused, the image model provides a good approximation of the direction and timing of the most important reflections.

Until now, the image model was computationally too expensive for use in audio and music production since it could only be implemented by convolution with an entire simulated room impulse response. It has also been generally believed that the image model could not be captured with recirculating delays. The reverberation network described in the following section is able to capture image model reverberation with recirculating delays.

Delays for the Source and First-Order and Second-Order Reflections. This basic signal-processing network can be realized in a number of ways. Figure 7.6 illustrates the version of the system implemented by the *space18* program currently in use at Northwestern Computer Music. The input signal to *space18* is passed into three different nonrecirculating delay buffers. Digital signal interpolation must be performed on all buffers when the delay times change (Smith [19]). The first buffer captures delays for the source itself. Its input is scaled and filtered to capture intensity and spectral changes due to distance; its output is passed directly to a directionalizer. The source signal enters the inner reverberation network through two delay buffers with multiple taps. Each buffer is preceded by a filter that captures the spectral changes due to air and wall absorption. The first buffer produces the delays for the six first-order reflections predicted by the image

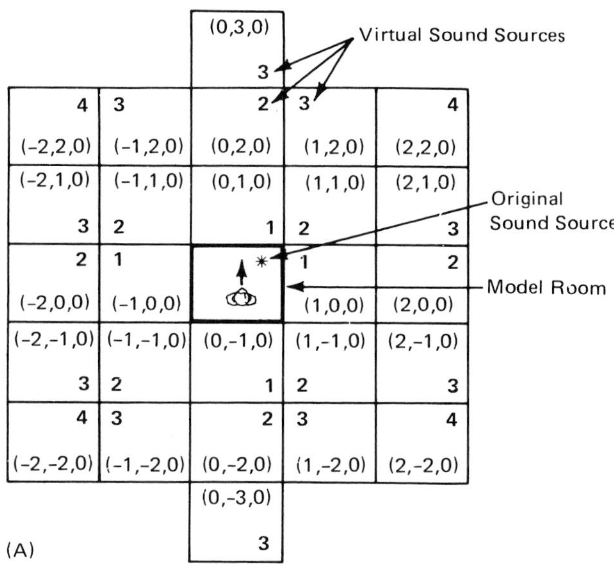

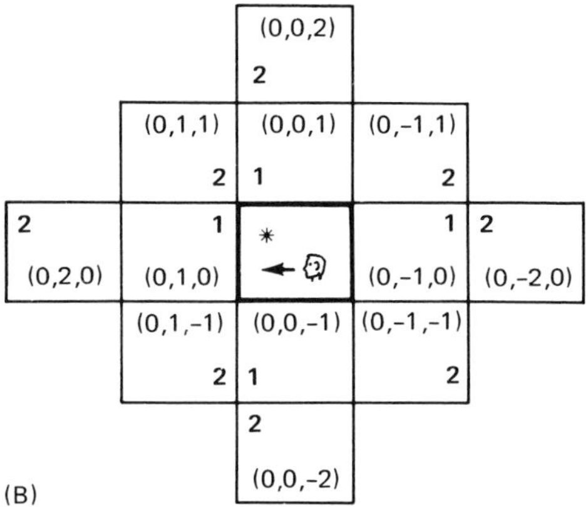

Figure 7.5
Two-dimensional cross section of virtual rooms: (A) horizontal plane and (B) Median plane.

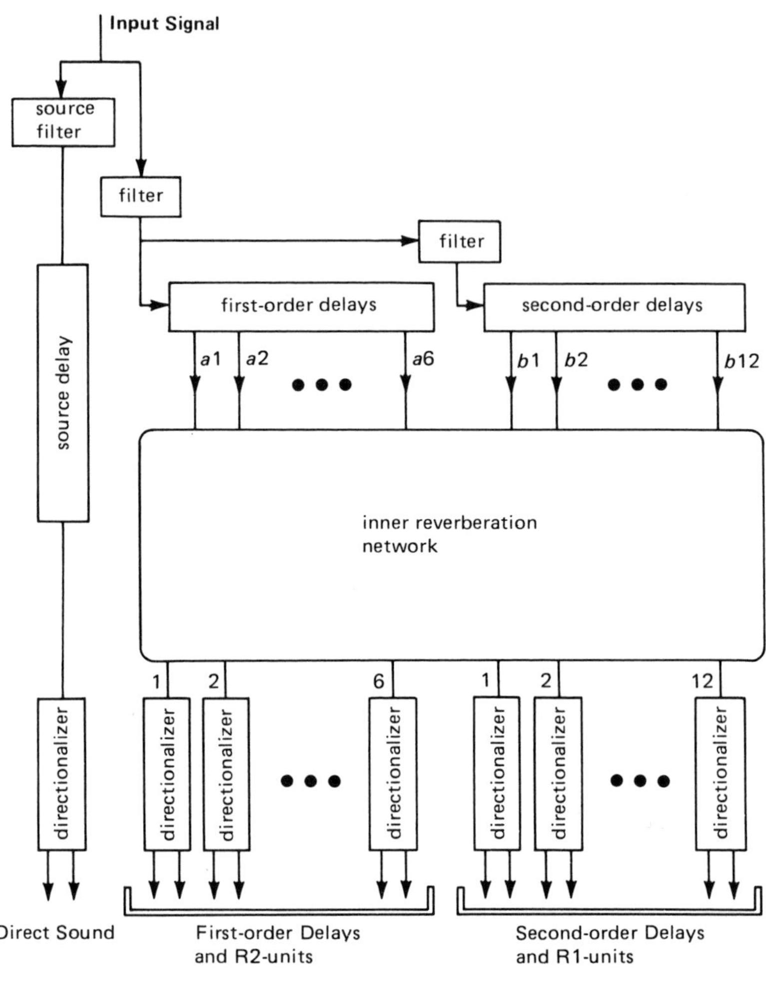

Figure 7.6
Signal-processing network for spatial reverberation as implemented in *space18* program.

model that emanate from virtual rooms behind the six walls of the model room. These first-order virtual sources are contained in the following virtual rooms:

$(1,0,0)$ $(0,1,0)$ $(-1,0,0)$ $(0,-1,0)$

$(0,0,1)$ $(0,0,-1)$

The gain of each reflection is produced by multiplication with the scaling coefficients, $a1$ through $a6$. The signal from each of these delay taps is passed to the inner reverberation network.

The image model predicts a total of eighteen second-order reflections. Six of these second-order reflections originate in virtual rooms directly behind the first-order virtual rooms and will be produced within the inner reverberation network. The remaining twelve second-order delays originate in second-order virtual rooms that extend from the junction of two walls in the model room. Twelve taps from the second delay buffer replicate the time delays for these reflections, and the gain of each reflection is produced by multiplication with the scaling coefficients, $b1$ through $b6$. The signals are passed directly into the inner reverberation network, where they are used to generate reverberation streams that begin with these second-order reflections. These second-order virtual sources are contained in the following virtual rooms:

$(1,0,1)$ $(0,1,1)$ $(-1,0,1)$ $(0,-1,1)$

$(1,1,0)$ $(-1,1,0)$ $(-1,-1,0)$ $(1,-1,0)$

$(1,0,-1)$ $(0,1,-1)$ $(-1,0,-1)$ $(0,-1,-1)$

The exact delay and direction of each reflection is computed from the position of the listener in the model room and the position of the virtual sound source.

Figure 7.7 shows a two-dimensional slice of image rooms for the horizontal plane. Virtual sound sources in the darkly shaded virtual rooms are captured by the initial nonrecirculating delays.

Reverberation Units. There are two types of recirculating delay units within the reverberation subsystem, which will be referred to as the R1-unit and the R2-unit. Both units include a path for the input signal from the delay buffers to be added directly into the output; this path passes the first- and second-order reflections from the nonrecirculating delays into the

10	9	8	7	6	5	6	7	8	9	10
9	8	7	6	5	4	5	6	7	8	9
8	7	6	5	4	3	4	5	6	7	8
7	6	5	4	3	2	3	4	5	6	7
6	5	4	3	2	1	2	3	4	5	6
5	4	3	2	1	0	1	2	3	4	5
6	5	4	3	2	1	2	3	4	5	6
7	6	5	4	3	2	3	4	5	6	7
8	7	6	5	4	3	4	5	6	7	8
9	8	7	6	5	4	5	6	7	8	9
10	9	8	7	6	5	6	7	8	9	10

Image Model Reflections Accounted for by

Figure 7.7
Two-dimensional cross section of virtual images rooms. The shading indicates those virtual rooms accounted for by initial delay buffers, R1- and R2-units, and crossfeeding.

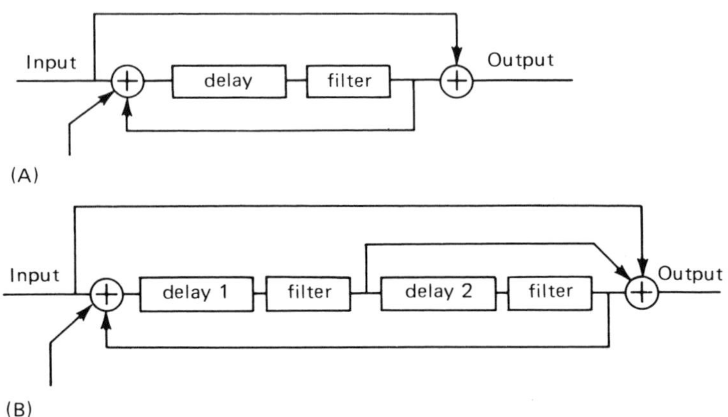

Figure 7.8
Reverberation units: (A) R1-unit and (B) R2-unit.

reverberation streams. There is also an input for signals generated in the crossfeeding process (described below) to be passed into the recirculation. The remainder of the R1-unit is a recursive comb filter similar to that discussed by Schroeder [15]. Schroeder's original version contained a delay buffer and a feedback loop. The amount of feedback was governed by a feedback coefficient in the loop. Moorer [10] implemented a digital realization of Schroeder's suggestion for a RC-section in the feedback loop by incorporating a one-pole, low-pass filter. The response of the filter in the R1- and R2-units is scaled by the attenuation factor for the feedback. Other aspects of the filter are discussed below. The design presented in figure 7.8 places a feedback filter at the end of the delay buffer, but in other respects mimics the Schroeder design. As shown in figure 7.8B, the R2-unit contains a pair of delay buffers with a feedback filters. The actual feedback occurs after the second delay buffer and its feedback filter. The output of the unit is the sum of the outputs of each delay-buffer pair after filtering. This unit produces a pattern of alternating long and short delays that is essential to capturing image model reverberation.

A signal-processing network for spatial reverberation requires a different structure from the Schroeder reverberator, because it must produce parallel streams of reverberation. Schroeder, Moorer, and others use combinations of reverberation units in parallel and series with the final output mixed down to a single reverberation stream. Even in cases where the processing path separates at the end and distinguishes the reverberation streams sent to the individual reproduction channels, the basic combination of reverberation units is in series. The general solution to the problem of producing multiple streams is to place reverberation units in parallel, where each unit produces a unique reverberant stream.

Each of the delay taps from the buffer for first-order reflections is fed into the input of a R2-unit. Each R2-unit is associated with a reverberant stream emanating from a second-order virtual room directly behind the first-order room. For example, a second-order room $(2, 0, 0)$ is directly behind a first-order room $(1, 0, 0)$. The delay lengths in the R2-units are taken from the time of arrival difference of first- and second-order reflections and of second- and third-order reflections, respectively. For the unit associated with room $(2, 0, 0)$, the delay times are given by

$$\text{delay\_1} = T(2, 0, 0) - T(1, 0, 0),$$

$$\text{delay\_2} = T(3, 0, 0) - T(2, 0, 0),$$

where $T(x, y, z)$ is the predicted time of arrival for a virtual sound source from the virtual room (x, y, z). As shown in figure 7.7, the pattern of reflections emanating from image rooms behind the first-order rooms has a characteristic pattern of alternating short and long delays, especially when the sound source is near a wall. The R2-unit recreates this pattern and thus captures the reverberation for the series of image rooms extending from every wall in the model room.

Each of the delay taps from the buffer for second-order reflections is fed into the input of an R1-unit that is associated with a reverberation stream emanating from a fourth-order virtual room directly behind a second-order room at the junction of two walls. For example, the fourth-order room $(2, 2, 0)$ is directly behind second-order room $(1, 1, 0)$. As shown in figure 7.7, the pattern of reflections emanating from the wall junctions also demonstrates this pattern of short and long delays. However, the long/short pattern is only exaggerated when the sound source is in the corner, and the reflection stream from the wall junction becomes high order twice as fast as the wall reflection stream. Therefore, for the sake of efficiency we chose to implement these delays with the R1-unit, even though it cannot produce a long/short delay pattern. (If greater accuracy is desired, an alternative realization of the inner reverberation network can be created using R2-units in place of the R1-units.) The time delays for the R1-units are taken from the time of arrival difference of second- and fourth-order reflections. For the unit associated with virtual room $(1, 1, 0)$, the delay times are given by

$$\text{delay} = T(2, 2, 0) - T(1, 1, 0).$$

The lightly shaded virtual rooms in figure 7.7 are accounted for by the R1- and R2-units. Together, the eighteen reverberation units produce reverberation streams for eighteen directions in three-dimensional space. Six streams emanate from walls, and twelve streams emanate from the junction of walls. Figure 7.9 shows all the delays calculated for a room 6.2 meters by 12.3 meters by 8 meters.

Crossfeeding of Reverberation Units in Parallel Combination. The elements of the inner reverberation network explained so far replicate all reflections originating in the eighteen lines of virtual rooms extending behind each wall and behind each junction of two walls. Even though this accounts for a large number of reflections, it omits those reflections pre-

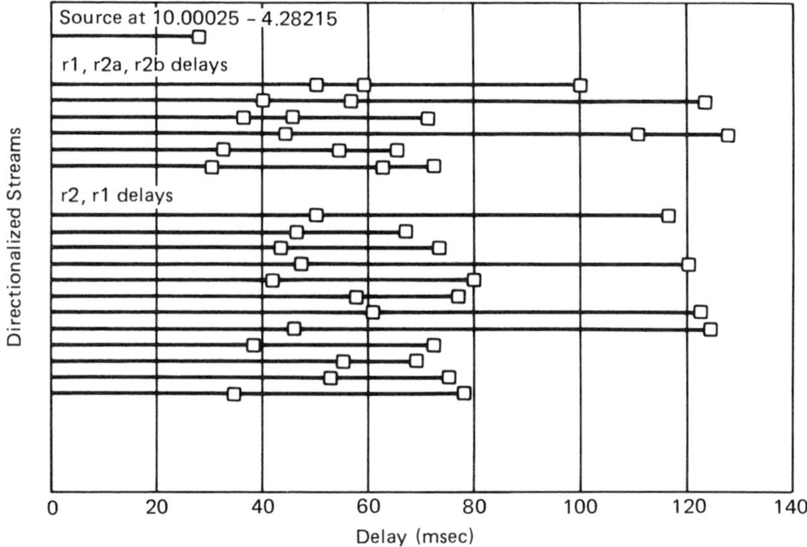

Figure 7.9
Delays calculated for a room 6.2 meters by 12.3 meters by 8 meters. Represented are the source delay, first-order reflection and R2-unit delays, and second-order reflection and R1-unit delays.

dicted by the image model that originate in virtual rooms that lie between those eighteen directions. Close to the source room, there are very few missing rooms. As reflections emanate from farther away in higher-order image rooms, the number of missing rooms greatly outnumbers the rest. Without the "in-between" rooms, the density of reflections does not increase with time.

In order to capture the missing reflections, the output of the R1-units must be fed into the R2-units for spatially adjacent streams. The crossfed signal is added into the initial summation node for each unit. Figure 7.10 represents the crossfeeding process for a single quadrant of a two-dimensional plane. Figure 7.10A shows all of the image rooms up to the fifth order for this region; the source room is to the left. The sequence of reflections emanating from the image room behind the wall, (1, 0, 0), is captured by the R2-unit. The sequence of reflections emanating from rooms behind the two wall junctions, (1, 1, 0), and (1, −1, 0), are produced by R1-units. When the output of each R1-unit is fed immediately into the R2-unit, each reflection is delayed by the R2 delays. The R2 delays are

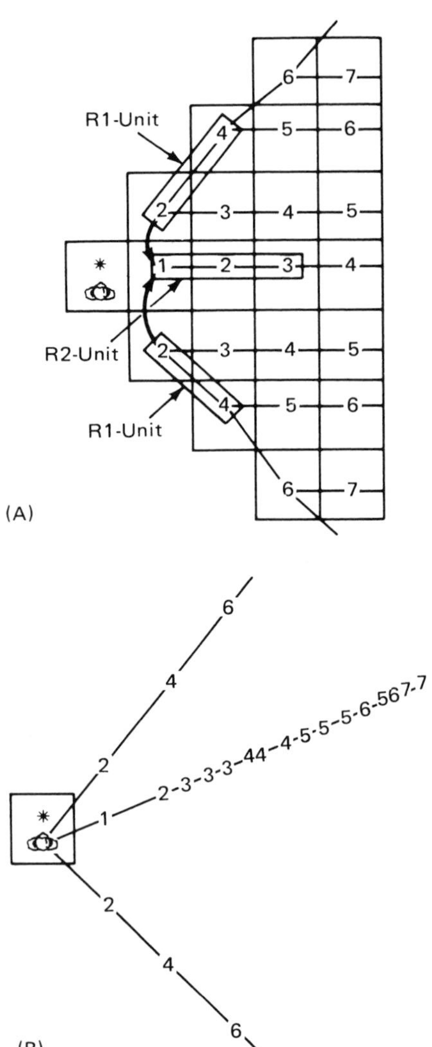

Figure 7.10
Two-dimensional crossfeeding: (A) interaction of R2- and R1-units and (B) the resulting reverberation streams.

approximately equal to the delays between the R1 reflections and those from the next adjoining image rooms to the right. For example,

$T(2,1,0) \simeq T(1,1,0) + \text{R2\_delay } 1,$

where R2_delay 1 $= T(2,0,0) - T(1,0,0)$. As the R2-unit recirculates its input, it creates the sequence of reflections whose delay is approximately equal to those emanating from the next set of image rooms between the R1 and R2 rooms. For example,

$T(3,1,0) \simeq T(1,0,0) + \text{R2\_delay } 1 + \text{R2\_delay } 2,$

where R2_delay 2 $= T(3,0,0) - T(2,0,0)$. As the process continues, the number of reflections is exactly that predicted by the image model. The delay times are entirely accurate for first- and second-order reflections; reflections beyond the second are approximately correct. The output of each R2- and R1-unit can be directionalized toward the leading first- or second-order reflection; the reverberation streams produced are those shown in figure 7.10B.

The crossfeeding illustrated in figure 7.10 is easily extended to all three dimensions. The R2-units are each crossfed from two spatially adjacent R1-units in the horizontal two-dimensional plane and are crossfed themselves into the R1-units that are spatially adjacent in the vertical two-dimensional plane. For example, the R2 stream emanating from the virtual room $(1,0,0)$ is spatially adjacent to R1-units associated with the second-order virtual rooms: $(1,0,1)$ and $(1,0,-1)$. Reflections are created for all of the "missing" virtual image rooms from all three dimensions (with the exception of eight third-order rooms). A more intuitive understanding of how the system operates can be gained from figure 7.11, which shows a three-dimensional representation of the network. The *space18* program provides accurate spatial placement for the source and the initial reflection in each reverberation stream, i.e., a total of nineteen sound directions.

7.4 Software for Controlling Spatial Reverberation

To simulate a model listening environment, the user must specify a spatial configuration consisting of 11 parameters: room size (3 dimensions), sound source location (3 coordinates), listener location (3 coordinates), and listener orientation (the direction the listener is facing, specified by azimuth and elevation angles). All of these parameters may be dynamic; the source

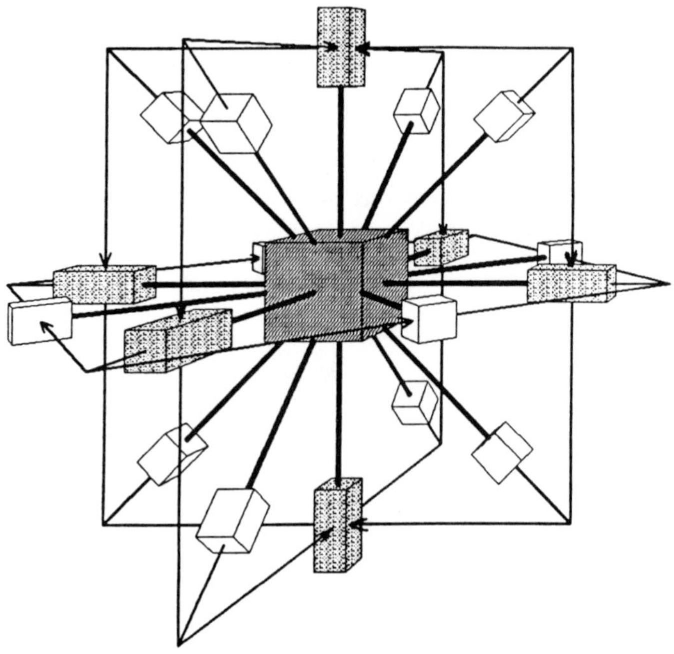

Figure 7.11
Three-dimensional configuration of reverberation units. Crossfeeding signal paths are indicated for the closest R2-unit.

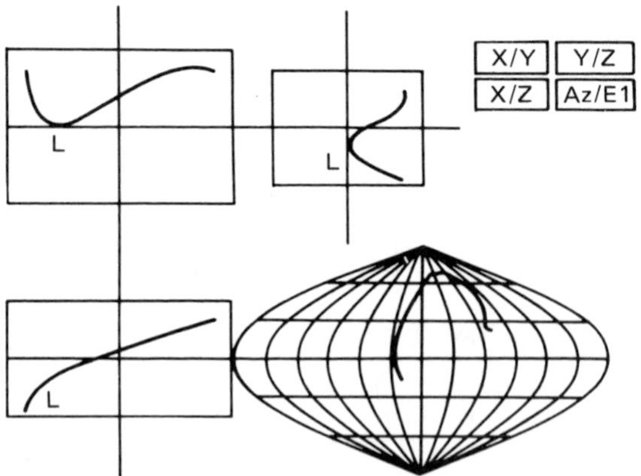

Figure 7.12
Graphic depiction of source path produced by the *trace* program.

and listener may follow an arbitrary path, and room dimensions may also change arbitrarily (the walls of the room follow a "path" as well). The first of the control programs, *framer*, samples the paths for each parameter at regular time intervals determined by a *frame rate*. Its output is a series of *frames* that contain a single value for each of the 11 parameters at a point in time. All subsequent programs, including the reverberator, operate on a frame-by-frame basis.

The user defines paths for all parameters by a list of target values to be reached at particular times, called "anchors," and intermediate values that control curvature, called "attractors." Bezier curves (Rogers and Adams [13]) are used to interpolate a smooth path. The user develops the spatial paths by graphical interaction with the program *trace*. A sample screen is shown in figure 7.12. Once the path has been specified, the program *framer* generates a series of snapshots of the interpolated path at the frame rate.

The first step in modeling a spatial configuration is to determine the spatiotemporal distribution of reflections predicted by the physical model. *Image18*, the second control program in the pipeline, solves the image model (see below) for the spatial configuration and calculates delays and directions for a number of reflections. As described below, the signal-processing network of the reverberator approximately captures high-order reflections with recirculating delays, and so only a small number of reflections must be modeled exactly. The output of *image18* is a series of frames, each of which specifies delays and directions of reflections at a point in time.

7.5 Conclusion

The spatial reverberator is the first reverberation system that recreates the full spatiotemporal sound field of a natural environment. This reverberator is also the first using recirculating delays to create reverberation based on the image model. It is our intention that the physical modeling of acoustic space will provide a point of departure for a more perceptually oriented study of spatial hearing and its relationship to computer music and audio reproduction. A physical model is only useful to the extent that it aids the user in realizing creative intentions. A great deal still needs to be learned about the relationship of spatial sound perception to music perception in general. It is our hope that spatial reverberation will be a tool in this study.

Acknowledgments

This work has been supported by a grant from the System Development Foundation. Special thanks must be given to Charles Smith, without whose commitment to new ideas this project would not have been possible. We also give our thanks to Carl York, whose continuing interest and support has meant a great deal to us.

References

[1] Allen, J. B., and Berkeley, D. A. (1979). Image method for efficiently simulating small room acoustics. *JASA*, 65(4), 943–950.

[2] Batteau, D. W. (1967). The role of the pinna in human localization. *Proceedings of the Royal Society of London*, 168(series B), 158–180.

[3] Blauert, J. (1969). Sound localization in the median plane. *Acustica*, 22, 957–962.

[4] Blauert, J. (1981). Lateralization of jittered tones. *Journal of the Acoustical Society of America*, 70, 694–698.

[5] Blauert, J. (1982). *Spatial Hearing*, trans. John S. Allen. MIT Press (Cambridge, MA). Originally entitled *Raumliches Hören*, S. Hirzel Verlag (Stuttgart), 1974.

[6] Butler, R. A., and Belendiuk, K. (1977). Spectral cues utilized in the localization of sound in the median sagittal plane. *Journal of the Acoustical Society of America*, 61, 1264–1269.

[7] Chowning, J. M. (1971). The simulation of moving sound sources. *Journal of the Audio Engineering Society*, 19, 2–6.

[8] Feddersen, W. E., Sandel, T. T., Teas, D. C., and Jeffress, L. A. (1957). Localization of high-frequency tones. *Journal of the Acoustical Society of America*, 29, 988–991.

[9] Moore, F. Richard (1983). A general model for spatial processing of sounds. *Computer Music Journal*, 7(3), 6–15.

[10] Moorer, James A. (1979). About this reverberation business. *Computer Music Journal*, 3(2), 13–28.

[11] Musicant, A. D., and Butler, R. A. (1980). Monaural localization: an analysis of practice effects. *Perception and Psychophysics*, 28, 236–240.

[12] Nuetzel, J. M., and Hafter, E. R. (1976). Lateralization of complex waveforms: effects of fine structure, amplitude, and duration. *Journal of the Acoustical Society of America*, 60, 1339–1346.

[13] Rogers, D. F., and Adams, J. A. (1976). *Mathematical Elements for Computer Graphics*, 139–144.

[14] Sakamoto, N., Gotoh, T., and Kimura, Y. (1976). On "out-of-head localization" in headphone listening. *Journal of the Audio Engineering Society*, 24, 710–715.

[15] Schroeder, M. R. (1962). Natural-sounding artificial reverberation. *Journal of the Audio Engineering Society*, 10, 219–223.

[16] Schroeder, M. R. (1970). Digital simultion of sound transmission in reverberant spaces. *JASA*, 47(2), 424–431.

[17] Shaw, E. A. G., and Teranishi, R. (1968). Sound pressure generated in an external-ear replica and real human ears by a nearby point-source. *Journal of the Acoustical Society of America*, 44, 240–249.

[18] Sheeline, C. W. (1982). An investigation of the effects of direct and reverberant signal interaction on auditory distance perception. PhD dissertation, Department of Hearing and Speech Sciences, Stanford.

[19] Smith, J. O. (1984). An all-pass approach to digital phasing and flanging. *Proc. ICMC*, 1984, 103–109.

[20] Wright, D., Hebrank, J. H., and Wilson, B. (1974). Pinna reflections as cues for localization. *Journal of the Acoustical Society of America*, 56, 957–962.

8 Spatialization of Sounds over Loudspeakers

F. Richard Moore

8.1 Introduction

Auditory events are related to sound events much as pitches are related to frequencies: the former terms refer to subjective percepts while the latter refer to physical phenomena. An auditory event need not coincide with a physical sound source. For example, auditory events can occur at positions where nothing is visible to a listener, including positions behind, above, or below, as well as "beyond the walls" of a listening space (Blauert [2]).

The term "spatialization" in computer music refers to the use of digital signal-processing techniques to affect the subjective "locatedness" of auditory events, despite the fact that the sounds responsible for these percepts emanate from loudspeakers sitting at fixed locations inside a listening space. Spatialization is related to methods used in sound recording to achieve "stereo imaging" effects with extensions into specific techniques for controlling the apparent distance, direction, trajectory, size, and shape of auditory events.

The question of how human beings localize auditory events is the subject of an extensive body of psychophysical research. If a physical sound source is located, say, 3 meters in front of and slightly to the left of a listener, the sound emitted by it will reach the listener's left ear slightly before it reaches the right. That the interaural time difference (ITD) of wave front arrival provides a localization cue to a listener has been known for some time (Rayleigh [10], von Békésy [1]). It might occur to one to simulate such a cue by positioning a listener between two loudspeakers and slightly delaying the sound in the right channel. While this procedure actually works, if the listener's head is not precisely between the speakers or is turned slightly this cue becomes distorted, yielding an unintended auditory event.

During loudspeaker playback, a listener's left ear will receive some sound from the right speaker and vice versa. While it is possible to cancel such "crosstalk" for a given listening position for the most part, localization cues generated in this way are again distorted at other positions. In addition, the well-known "precedence" effect (Haas [3]) tends to make all the sound seem to come from whichever loudspeaker is closest to the listener.

If computer sound spatialization is to be a practical tool for musicians, it is necessary to address its applicability to typical musical situations. In a concert hall, or even in a living room, it is generally impractical to control the relative positions of listeners and loudspeakers. A possible solution is to design music specifically for audition over headphones, but this is hardly practical for concert hall presentation, especially when live performance on traditional instruments is combined with computer-processed sound. The work described here provides an approach to sound spatialization that can produce vivid impressions of auditory event location and motion with a minimum of dependence on the relative positions of the listeners and the loudspeakers.

8.2 The Conceptual Model

Beyond some mimimum distance, a well-designed loudspeaker approximates a point (or line) source of sound. If loudspeakers are placed along the walls (or in the corners) of a listening space, facing inward, they approximate apertures, or "holes" in the walls, through which an acoustic field existing on "the other side of the walls" can be thought of as reradiating. Such sound sources would create a complex sound field according to their radiation patterns and locations (or trajectories) in conjunction with the acoustic properties of the "illusory space" (Chowning [4]) in which they are embedded. Rather than attempting to place the listener directly into this imaginary sound field, which is the intent of most localization simulation techniques, the present spatialization model replaces the *listener* with the *listening space*. The essence of this procedural model, then, is a room within a room. The inner room is the listening space (with holes in its walls) occupied by one or more listeners. The acoustic characteristics of the interior of the listening space and the positions of listeners within it are taken to be undefined. The outer room is an imaginary one with any acoustic properties the computer musician wishes to impute to it, in which auditory events are free to move (Moore [7]).

Before delving into some of the details of this model, a thought experiment is useful. Imagine that you are sitting in a living room with a pair of loudspeakers located in front of you. Now imagine that the living room is somehow (miraculously!) transported into the center of a large cathedral sanctuary in which a concert is taking place, and that the loudspeakers are replaced by holes in the walls. Ahead may be heard an organ, an orchestra, and a choir, but behind there is also an antiphonal choir and another section of the organ. The processing techniques described here cause the loud-

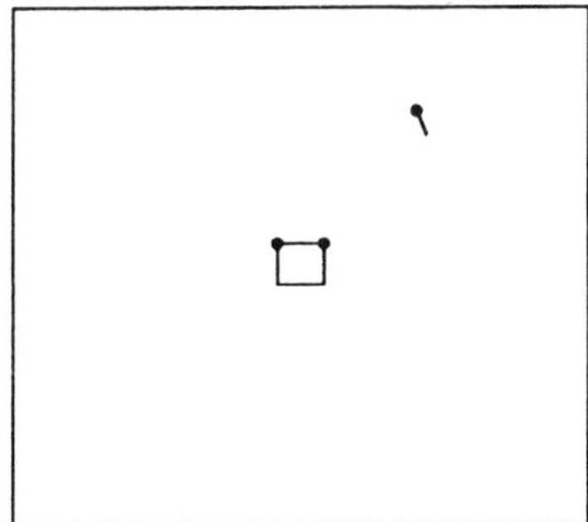

Figure 8.1
A listening room with two loudspeakers located within an imaginary acoustic space, with an imaginary sound source radiating southeast.

speakers to approximate the sound as it would be heard through the holes. If more loudspeakers are available, they could be used to simulate more "holes" elsewhere in the walls of the listening room. Note that additional "apertures" into the surrounding sound field would not affect the sound coming from the front apertures, although they certainly would affect the sound inside the listening space. In fact, any number of loudspeakers could be used, with each loudspeaker "sampling" the acoustic field imagined to exist just beyond the walls of the listening room.

Imagine now that a soloist from the choir sings while walking slowly around the outer perimeter of your listening room. The spatial impression you would gain of the moving soloist would approximate one gained by listening from inside such a "perforated" room. In particular, the impression of auditory event locations in such a circumstance may not be critically dependent on your relative position or that of the loudspeakers—precisely what is desired when spatialized sound materials are to be presented in a concert setting.

8.3 The Spatialization Procedure

The principle components of this spatialization procedure are shown in figure 8.1. Loudspeaker placement is arbitrary as long as it is along or near any wall of the listening space (two speakers are marked by dots in the front corners of the inner room in figure 8.1). The relative dimensions and shapes of the inner room and outer acoustic spaces may also be chosen arbitrarily.

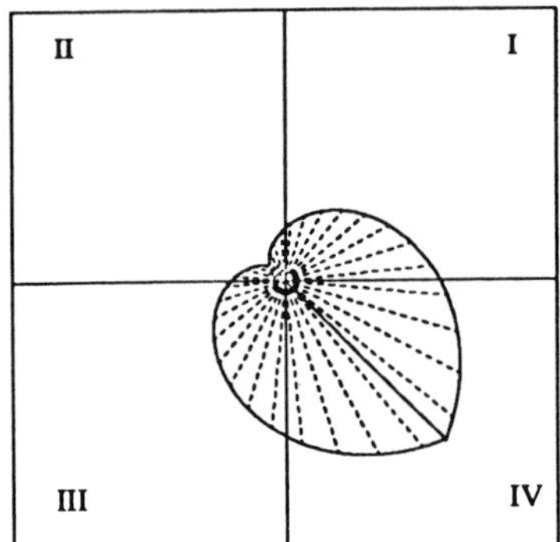

Figure 8.2
A source radiation vector pointing southeast with back radiation equal to 0.1 times the main radiation amplitude.

A single imaginary sound source is depicted in figure 8.1, located in the front right quadrant of the outer room and radiating differentially toward the southeast.

8.4 Radiation Vectors

To model the directional characteristics of physical sound sources we may use a source radiation vector such as the one shown in figure 8.2. This source "points" southeast, with the length of the arms of the radiation vector showing relative sound amplitudes radiated in various directions.

A radiation vector such as the one in figure 8.2 is completely described by its position in space, the direction in which it points, and the relative amount of forward versus back radiation. Its supercardiod shape results from a square-law interpolation between the forward and back radiation values. In figure 8.2, for example, the back radiation is taken to be one tenth the amplitude of the forward radiation (i.e., the back-to-front radiation ratio is -20 dB).

The supercardiod shape is determined in two dimensions by the formula

$$r(\phi) = \left(1 + \frac{(back - 1)|\theta - \phi|}{\pi}\right)^2,$$

where θ is the angle (in radians) in which the radiation vector points, and *back* specifies the relative amount of radiation in the direction opposite to θ. Setting *back* to zero results in a strongly directional sound source (figure

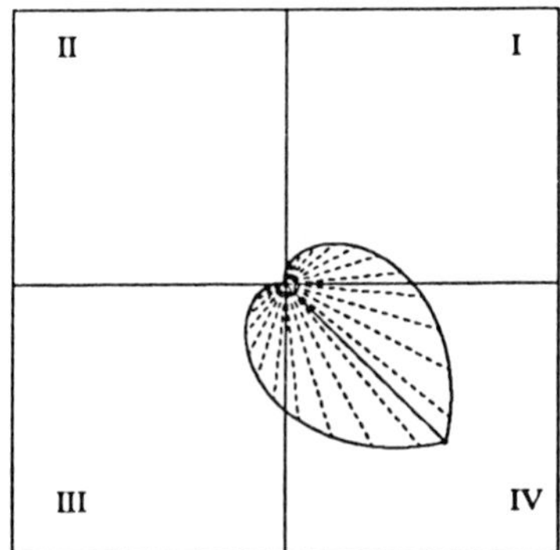

Figure 8.3
A strongly directional radiation vector.

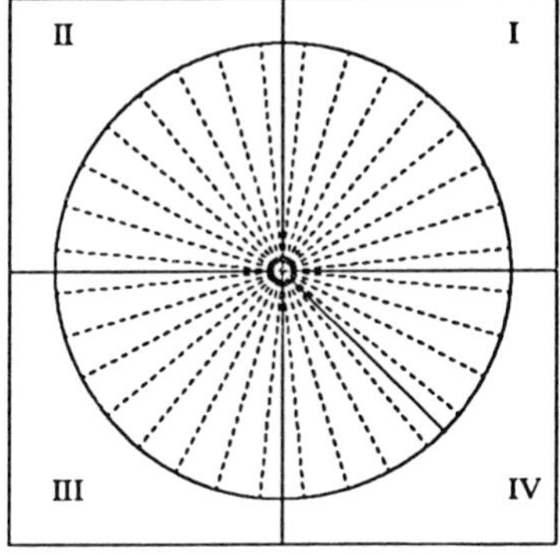

Figure 8.4
An omnidirectional radiation vector.

8.3), while setting *back* to one results in an omnidirectional source (figure 8.4).

Radiating sound *surfaces* (as opposed to points) may be approximated to any desired degree of precision with multiple radiation vectors, as shown in figure 8.5.

8.5 Sound Paths

A radiation vector specifies an imaginary point source of sound in the imaginary acoustic space surrounding the listening room. For each such

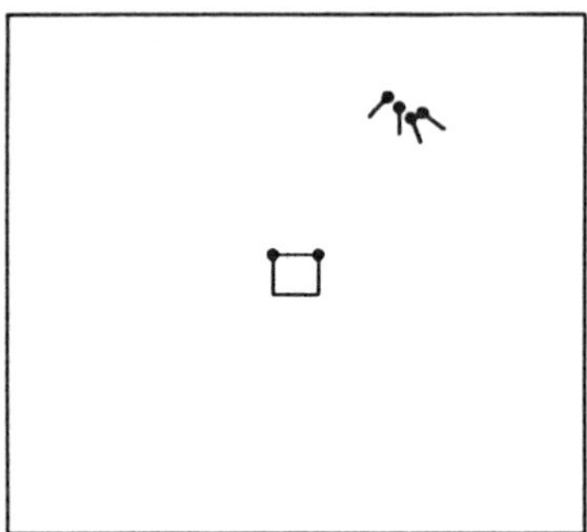

Figure 8.5
Multiple radiation vectors approximate a radiating surface.

point source, direct and reflected paths of sound may be calculated to each loudspeaker positioned along the walls of the listening space. Sound attenuation and delay along these paths determine how a source is represented in each loudspeaker.

For a source in a fixed position we may consider its loudspeaker representation as consisting of multiple copies of the original source sound, one copy for each sound path. Each copy—or echo—of the source sound has a path-dependent amplitude (which may be frequency-dependent) and a path-dependent delay time. The attenuation associated with each path may be modeled either as a simple path length-dependent gain (less than unity), or as a frequency-dependent gain that takes into account frequency-dependent absorption characteristics of air and reflecting surfaces. The delay time is determined by the length of the complete path.

Psychoacoustic experiments indicate that the first 100 msec or so of these echoes—the so-called "early echo pattern"—provide powerful directional and distance cues to the listener. After 100 msec or so, the echo density becomes so great in real acoustic spaces that its details no longer provide directional information, although the relative amount of direct-to-reverberated signals still provides an impression of the distance between the listener and the sound source.

From the geometry of the rooms and source and speaker positions, we may calculate the early echo pattern based on both direct (figure 8.6) and reflected (figure 8.7) sound paths between the source and the loudspeakers. The first-order reflections shown in figure 8.7 are the "principal" reflections from each surface of the illusory outer room (the ones with the

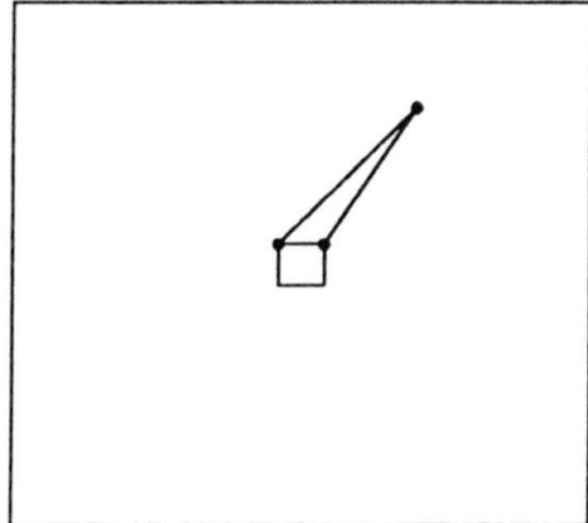

Figure 8.6
Direct sound paths from one source to two loudspeakers.

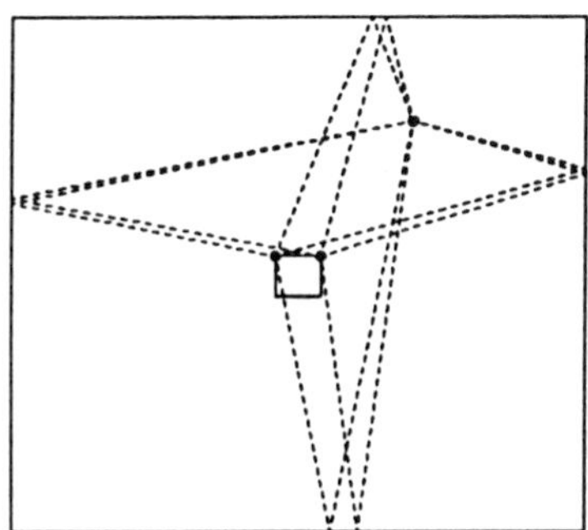

Figure 8.7
Reflected sound paths from one source to two loudspeakers. Some of these paths will be "cut" by the absorbing outer surface of the listening space walls.

shortest possible path lengths and hence having the greatest amplitude). Higher-order reflections may be used as well. Reflection paths that pass through the interior of the listening space are effectively "cut" (removed) by the model in order to account for the shadowing effect of the listening room embedded within the imaginary acoustic space.

Additional loudspeakers may be placed at specified positions along the listening room walls. The direct and reflected sound paths (see figure 8.8) are used to calculate the characteristics of finite impulse response (FIR) filters (one for each speaker) that model the early echo response of the room for a given configuration. Dense reverberation is modeled by feeding some percentage of the outputs of the FIR filters into an infinite-impulse re-

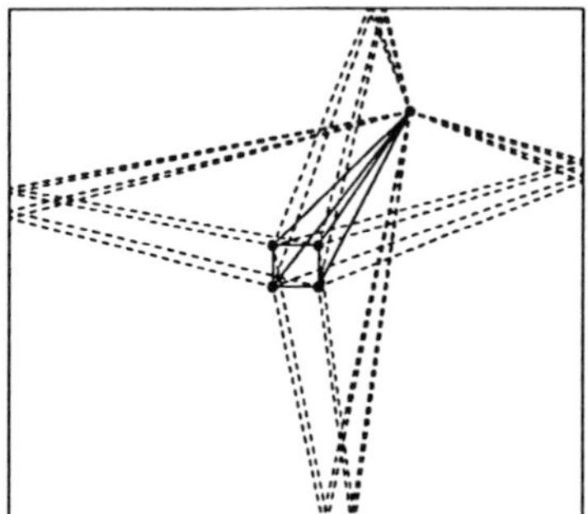

Figure 8.8
Direct and first-order reflected paths for one source and four loudspeakers (paths crossing through the inner room are suppressed).

sponse (IIR) filter network. In general it is desirable to use IIR filters with lowpass filters in their feedback loops (Moorer [9]). These lowpass filters may then be adjusted to account for frequency-dependent absorption of reflections. The output of the IIR "global" reverberator network is mixed back into the loudspeaker channels through all-pass filters used to decorrelate (Schroeder [11]) the dense reverberation signal coming from each loudspeaker. An overall signal flow graph for this spatialization procedure is shown in figure 8.9.

8.6 Moving Sound Sources

The direct and reflected paths are recomputed whenever the imaginary sound source location or orientation changes. In general it is *not* sufficient to round or truncate path delays to the nearest sample period because even the tiny waveform discontinuities that result are audible—especially in the presence of reverberation. Simple linear interpolation, though, works well enough in practice as a means to obtain a dynamically changing delay. The following C function illustrates one method of implementing a dynamic linear interpolation delay with a circular buffer.

```
/*
 * do_delay looks up a sample delayed by tau samples (note that tau is of
 * type float and need not be an integer) using interpolation on a circular
 * buffer buf of length len with present sample at buf[now] and previous
 * sample at buf [ (now + 1)% len ]
```

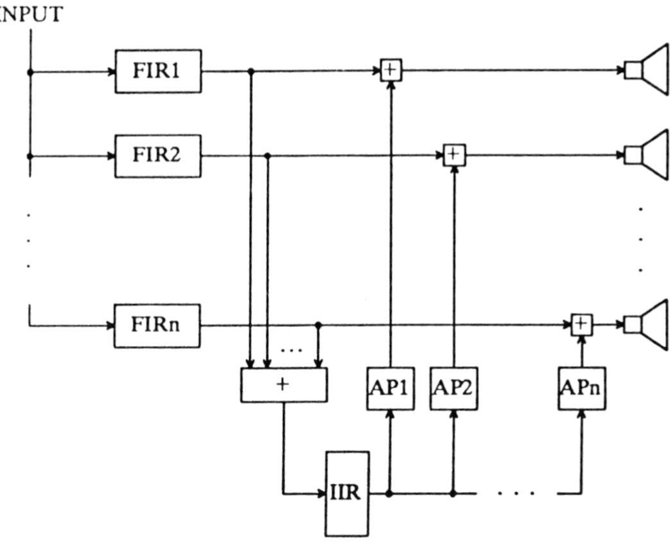

Figure 8.9
Signal flow graph for n-channel spatialization system. FIR filters model early echoes for each loudspeaker channel, an IIR filter network models dense reverberation, and APs (all-pass filters) decorrelate channel signals.

```
 */
float
do_delay( buf, len, now, tau )
 float buf[ ] ; float tau ; long len, now ;
{
 register long t1, t2 ;
   t1 = now + tau ;
   while ( t1 >= len )
      t1 -= len ;
   t2 = t1 + 1 ;
   while ( t2 >= len )
      t2 -= len ;
   return( buf[t1] + (tau - ( (int)tau ))*(buf[t2] - buf[t1]) ) ;
```

In the above programming example, buf[now] is assumed to hold the current sample, buf[now + 1] the previous sample, and so on. The circular buffer is implemented by decrementing now at each sample, adding len to it if it is less than zero, then installing the current sample in the buffer at buf[now].

A satisfying feature of using the above procedure for implementing dynamically changing delays is that a sound source moving, say, toward the listener will undergo a frequency change precisely equivalent to a Doppler shift due to the continual shortening of the delay. The FIR sections shown in figure 8.9 may therefore be implemented by calculating the delay times and gains associated with each sound path and applying the above procedure directly, with the added benefit that Doppler shift is a free side effect.

Another issue related to moving sound sources involves the sound paths that are cut by the listening space when the source moves "around a corner" from a speaker. It is necessary to reduce the amplitude of the associated path signal gradually to avoid a click. Again, a simple linear interpolation with a characteristic time of about 50 msec seems sufficient to mask this effect.

The delay time in samples τ_i associated with the ith sound path is given by the relation

$$\tau_i = \frac{R \times \text{Length}_i}{c},$$

where R is the sampling rate in Hz, Length_i is the total length of the path, c is the speed of sound, and τ corresponds to the variable tau in the previous programming example.

In addition to the delay, the attenuation along each path must be modeled as well. The total attenuation for each path is the product of attenuation factors, as follows:

$$\alpha_i = \rho_i K_i B_i D_i,$$

where α is total attenuation, ρ is the amplitude scalar determined by the radiation vector associated with the sound source (i.e., ρ depends on the value of the radiation vector for the angle at which the path leaves the sound source), K is the "cut factor" (ramped to 0 if cut and 1 if not), B accounts for absorption at reflection points, and D is attenuation due to distance (the length of the path). These attenuation factors would in reality be frequency-dependent, but the vividness of the spatialization effect is sometimes reduced if they are implemented as such. This is presumably because each of these sources of attenuation tends to suppress high frequencies (which provide more powerful localization cues) more than low frequencies. A propos of the distinction between the auditory events as opposed to a "sound source," it is interesting to note that the most effective spatialization procedure is not necessarily the most accurate model of the physics of room reverberation. A further example of such perception-specific behavior is given in the next section.

Once the delay times and attenuations for each path are calculated, multiple calls to the do_delay function described previously may be used to implement the FIR filters shown in figure 8.9.

8.7 Distance Laws

It is well-known that the intensity of a sound source falls off with the inverse square of its distance, i.e.,

$$I \propto \frac{1}{D^2},$$

or, equivalently,

$$A \propto \frac{1}{D},$$

where I is intensity, A is amplitude, and D is distance. The two formulas given are equivalent due to the fact that sound intensity is proportional to the square of amplitude. In order words, when we compare the loudnesses of two identical sound sources in an anechoic environment, one of which is twice as far from the listener as the other, the physical intensity (or amplitude) of the two sounds differs by a factor of about 6 dB. Yet, when people are asked to estimate doublings or halvings of *loudness*, two remarkable things result: the first is that people tend to be remarkably consistent in such judgments, and the second is that their "half loudness" judgment is quite inconsistent with the inverse square law stated above for distance. If we wish to spatialize two sounds so that one sounds twice as *distant* as the other, we therefore have a choice: *to* model nature (make one sound 6 dB louder than the other) or to explore the subjective association of half *loudness* with a doubling of distance.

Psychoacoustic research (Stevens [13]) indicates that subjective loudness is approximately proportional to the cube root of intensity, i.e.,

$$L \propto I^{1/3},$$

where L is subjective loudness in *sones*. If the *subjective impression of distance* follows loudness rather than intensity (as I find that it does especially for unfamiliar sounds), we can adjust for this in our spatialization procedure by using an inverse cube law to associate intensities (or amplitudes) with distances along sound paths as follows:

$$I \propto \frac{1}{D^3},$$

or, equivalently,

$$A \propto \frac{1}{D^{1.5}}$$

Using this procedure, a doubling or halving of distance would be associated with an intensity or amplitude change of about 9 dB. This in turn would impart a subjective loudness that becomes half as great when a sound source moves twice as far away. Such a direct relationship between subjective loudness and distance—while contrary to natural behavior—may be musically desirable when the geometry of the trajectory along which an imaginary sound source moves is to be made clear to the listener.

8.8 Conclusion

The procedure described briefly here illustrates but one possible approach to the problem of sound spatialization over loudspeakers. It principle advantage lies in its ability to produce vivid spatialization with a mimimum of dependence on the precise locations of listener and loudspeaker. Like all spatialization models, however, it is not entirely immune to the playback circumstances, particularly the acoustics inside the listening room. Just as sound engineers currently compensate for an uneven room frequency response, sound spatialization may require compensation for uneven room spatiotemporal response. Even the most robust of spatialization techniques can be made to fail when the listening room confounds the intended signals sufficiently. Directions for future research, therefore, include understanding how to compensate adaptively—via real-time feedback and signal processing—for the enormously variable effect of listening room acoustics.

Appendix

In order to give a flavor of how the cmusic program's space unit generator may be used to spatialize any sound, the following cmusic score file is included here. It is the precise file used to generate sound example 4b (given on the accompanying compact disk).

```
{
  preliminary setup—include standard cmusic macros
}
#include <carl/cmusic.h>
set list ;                  { output a listing file }
set srate       = 48K ;     { sampling rate = 48K (49152) Hz (each
                              channel) }
set func        = 8K ;      { set wavetable default length to 8192 }
{
  the following macro sets up for stereo spatialization within a
  square illusory space 17 meters on a side with a listening space 3 meters
  on a side at its center
}
STEREO(3, 17);
Set revscale    = 0.5 ;     { attenuation for global reverb input }
set direct      = 1.5 ;     { select inverse cube law for direct
                              sound }
set reflect     = 1.5 ;     { select inverse cube law for reflected
                              sound }

{
  soundfile containing source sound for spatialization
}
var 0 s1 "/sndc/frm/twang" ;
{
  instrument definition for elliptical paths centered at arbitrary point on
  midline
}
ins 0 s ;
  shape       b4 f3 d ;             { rotation speed control }
  iosc        b2 p7 b4 f1 d;        { x-axis control }
  iosc        b3 p8 b4 f2 d ;       { y-axis control }
```

```
   adn            b3 b3 p9 ;                  { center control }
   sndfile        b1 p5 p6 s1 1 0 -1 d d ;    { read in soundfile }
   SPACE(b1,1)    b2 b3 0 1 1 ;               { spatialize it }
end ;
{
   generate wavetables
}
GEN5(f1) 1, 1, 90 ; { cosine path for x }
GEN5(f2) 1, 1, 180 ;                          { inverse sine path for x }
{
   the following function controls the rate of rotation along path
}
GEN1(f3) 0, 0 .125, 0 .5, 3 Hz 1 -.125, 0 1, 0 ;
{
   move sound along specified path—parameters:
   p1 = note command
   p2 = starting time (0)
   p3 = instrument name
   p4 = duration (8 seconds)
   p5 = amplitude scalar (1)
   p6 = soundfile increment (1)
   p7 = x path amplitude (4 meters)
   p8 = y path amplitude (3 meters)
   p9 = midline position (+5 meters)
}
note 0 s 8 1 1 4 3 5 ;
section ;
{
   pad with 2 seconds of silence to let reverberation die away
}
terminate 2 ;
```

References

[1] von Békésy, G. 1936. Zur Theorie des Hörens: Über das Richtungshören bei einer Zeitdifferenz oder Lautstärkeungleichheit der beidseitigen Schalleinwirkungen. *Phys. Z.* **31**: 824–838, 857–868.

[2] Blauert, J. 1983. *Spatial Hearing*. Cambridge, MA: MIT Press.

[3] Hass, H. 1951. Über den Einfluss eines Einfachechos auf die Hörsamkeit von Sprache. *Acustica* **1**:49–58.

[4] Chowning, J. 1971. The simulation of moving sound sources. *J. Audio Eng. Soc.* **19**:2–6.

[5] Haustein, B. G. 1969. Hypothesen über die Einohrige Entfernungswahrnehmung des menschlichen Gehörs. *Hochfrequenztech. u. Elektroakustik* **78**:46–57.

[6] Moore, F. R. 1982. The computer audio research laboratory at UCSD. *Computer Music J.* **7(1)**:18–29.

[7] Moore, F. R. 1983. A general model for spatial processing of sounds. *Computer Music J.* **7(3)**:6–15.

[8] Moore, F. R. 1985. The cmusic sound synthesis program. in *The CARL Startup Kit*, published by the UCSD Center for Music Experiment, La Jolla, CA.

[9] Moorer, J. A. 1979. About this reverberation business. *Computer Music J.* **3(2)**:13–28.

[10] Lord Rayleigh 1907. On our perception of sound direction. *Phil Mag.* **13(6th series)**: 214–232.

[11] Schroeder, M. R. 1979. Binaural dissimilarity and optimum ceilings for concert halls: more lateral diffusion. *J. Acoust. Soc. Amer.* **65**:958.

[12] Stevens, S. S. 1970. Neural events and the psychophysical law. *Science* **170**:1043.

[13] Stevens, S. S. 1955. Measurement of loudness. *J. Acoust. Soc. Amer.* **27**:815.

9 Fourier-Transform-Based Timbral Manipulations

Mark Dolson

9.1 Introduction

An area of digital signal processing that has received considerable attention of late within the speech and communication communities is the design of analysis-synthesis filter banks for subband coding. As might be expected, the results of this research are applicable not only to speech but to music as well. Realizing the full musical potential of these new algorithms, however, requires an evolving process in which both engineer and musician participate equally. In this chapter, I describe some of the fruits of this collaboration between myself and composers at UCSD's Computer Audio Research Lab (CARL).

9.2 Short-Time Fourier Analysis-Synthesis

An important subset of analysis-synthesis algorithms are those that can be implemented via short-time Fourier analysis-synthesis. Analysis-synthesis techniques attempt to fit signals to some underlying model that has been identified as a potentially more useful way of representing the signal without compromising fidelity. At CARL, the analysis-synthesis technique that we have explored most extensively is the so-called phase vocoder.

The phase vocoder basically attempts to decompose an audio signal into a representation in which temporal and spectral features can be manipulated independently. In particular, the phase vocoder represents the signal as a sum of sinusoids, each with a different time-varying amplitude and time-varying frequency. A crucial feature of this representation is that none of the information in the original audio signal is destroyed. As a result, it is always possible to reconstruct the original signal exactly. In practice, this ability of the phase vocoder to function as an analysis-synthesis "identity system" is both what distinguishes it from its predecessor, the "channel vocoder," and what makes it fundamentally attractive for music.

A mathematical description of the phase vocoder is given in the appendix to this chapter. However, the fact that any signal can be reconstructed exactly by a phase vocoder is not so startling as it may seem. Imagine a bank of overlapping bandpass filters, each having the same band shape and linear phase. Imagine that at every frequency the sum of the voltage gains

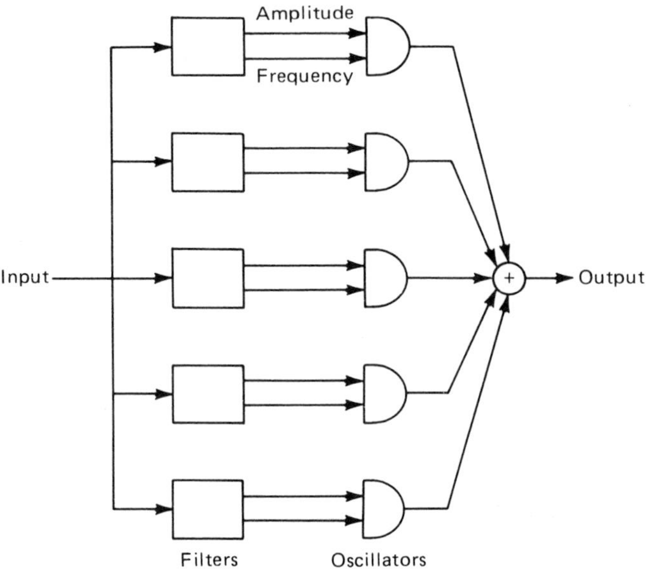

Figure 9.1
The filter-bank interpretation.

of all filters is constant. If we add the outputs of all of the filters, we shall get the original signal, for the amplitude and phase of any sinusoidal input component will have been reconstructed perfectly. Yet, if the filters are narrow, the output of each filter will be approximately sinusoidal, no matter what the input.

The most interesting musical applications of the phase vocoder arise when modifications are introduced between the analysis and synthesis operations. In principle, these modifications may be completely arbitrary, but the goal of our work at CARL has been to identify systematic modifications with predictable and desirable effects on the resulting sound. The underlying idea is that the phase vocoder's capacity for perfect reconstruction in the absence of modifications should also enable it to perform certain classes of modifications with comparably high fidelity.

The phase vocoder analysis-synthesis algorithm can be understood from either of two complementary perspectives. On the one hand, as shown in figure 9.1, the phase vocoder analysis can be seen as a bank of bandpass filters in which the output of each filter is represented as a time-varying

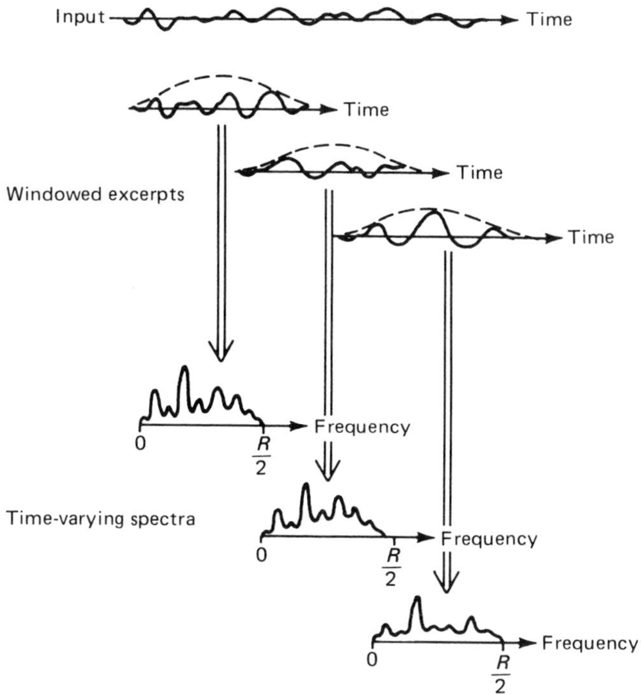

Figure 9.2
The Fourier-transform interpretation.

amplitude and a time-varying frequency. This interpretation is particularly attractive when the filters are aligned in frequency so that each filter extracts exactly one harmonic from the signal. The synthesis can then be understood in terms of a bank of oscillators in which the time-varying amplitude and frequency of each oscillator is controlled by the corresponding filter outputs.

But the phase vocoder is not necessarily restricted to dealing with periodic signals. This is more easily understood in terms of the second, complementary perspective. In this view, as shown in figure 9.2, the phase vocoder analysis consists of a succession of overlapping, finite-duration, discrete Fourier transforms in which the real and imaginary terms are converted to magnitudes and phases. Thus, the phase vocoder essentially steps along in time, taking "snapshots" of the evolving spectrum. The synthesis consists of taking the inverse discrete Fourier transform of each spectral snapshot, overlapping the resulting finite-duration signals, and adding them all back together.

I have elsewhere presented a lengthy explication of these two contrasting viewpoints (Dolson [2]). Musicians generally find the filter-bank perspective easier to relate to, but it is the Fourier-transform perspective that is ultimately the more powerful (see, for example, Moorer [4] or Crochiere and Rabiner [1]). From the point of view of the novice user, however, neither of these understandings is essential. Rather, the crucial point is simply that the phase vocoder makes available to the musician some very powerful "handles" for the modification of recorded sounds, handles that exceed in flexibility, in fidelity, and in ease of use nearly all others available at present.

9.3 Implementation

Probably the best way to appreciate the musical potential of short-time Fourier analysis-synthesis techniques such as the phase vocoder is via actual sound examples. The examples that follow were all generated on the CARL system at UCSD, a VAX 11/780 running Berkeley UNIX, with 16-bit A/D and D/A converters operating (in this instance) at a rather low sample rate of 16, 384 samples per second. The phase vocoder was implemented as a program written in C with standard FFT subroutines performing the bulk of the computation. Sounds were digitized and stored on computer disk, processed by the phase vocoder algorithm, and then played back from disk through the D/A converters at a later time. Typically, a 1-second sound required nearly 2 minutes of VAX CPU time to be processed by the phase vocoder.

Two aspects of this implementation merit further discussion. First, because of the UNIX orientation toward pipes and device-independent graphics, the control mechanisms provided with the phase vocoder program were almost entirely in the form of parameter settings via command-line arguments. Second, as the above paragraph makes clear, the turn-around time for a single run was frequently substantial. Thus, many of the applications tended to be of the form, "What one, monolithic change can I make to the following sound via the phase vocoder?" With currently available hardware and graphic interfaces, neither of these constraints need apply, and a whole new world of interactive musical applications should soon be open for exploration. Thus, the examples that follow should be taken only as an initial indication of some of these new possibilities.

9.4 Time Scaling

Perhaps the most striking sonic modification engendered by the phase vocoder is that of "time scaling" (i.e., changing the duration of a sound without altering its pitch). From the point of view of the user, this is accomplished by varying the value of a single parameter. Inside the program, the time scaling is implemented by essentially recomputing the time scale of the time-varying amplitude and frequency control signals for each oscillator. This causes the composite signal to evolve more slowly or rapidly (whichever was chosen) without changing the actual frequencies present in the sound. A different way of saying the same thing is that the spectral "snapshots" (i.e., the Fourier transforms) are spaced closer or farther apart upon synthesis than they were upon analysis. In either case, the essential feature of time scaling, from a mathematical perspective, is that it attempts to speed up or slow down the evolution of the time-varying spectrum.

It is important to realize, though, that time scaling itself is not a mathematically well-defined operation. There is no rigorous definition as to what would constitute a perfectly time-scaled signal; hence, there is no mathematical means to evaluate the success of the phase vocoder in this regard. To be sure, related mathematical measures could be devised; for now, though, we have been content to conduct our evaluations primarily via listening tests. Sound Examples 1–4 (given on the accompanying compact disk) illustrate time scaling.

9.5 Pitch Transposition

If we can modify duration without altering pitch, then we can equally well change the pitch without affecting the duration. For example, to transpose up an octave, we can simply time expand by a factor of two, and then play back at twice the sample rate. The most obvious musical application for this technique is in the adjustment of precise tunings. But, as with time expansion, the most interesting applications are those that transform familiar sonic material into something familiar yet different. Sound Examples 5–8 illustrate pitch transposition.

9.6 Time-Varying Filtering

A third class of intriguing musical effects that can be obtained with the aid of the phase vocoder are those that may be characterized as "time-varying filtering" effects. Actually, these effects can be obtained with any short-time Fourier analysis-synthesis technique, but the phase vocoder provides a useful unified framework for conceiving and implementing them.

As with all phase-vocoder-related effects, time-varying filtering can be understood in either of two ways. On the one hand, it can be seen as a separate time-varying gain applied to each harmonic of a sound. On the other hand, it can be seen as a frequency-dependent, time-varying weighting of successive spectral snapshots, where each snapshot is basically a short-time Fourier transform of the input sound. This latter view is particularly suggestive, because it presents the possibility of using the spectrum of one sound to shape dynamically the spectrum of another. This is explored further in the final sound example.

9.7 Conclusion

Our experience with the phase vocoder and related short-time Fourier analysis-synthesis techniques has convinced us that they will play an important role in future computer music systems. This prediction is predicated upon the introduction of more powerful number-crunching boxes and graphic interfaces, but such advances seem certain to occur. Indeed, the "sound design" software packages now being marketed for personal computers in conjunction with digital "sampling synthesizers" can be viewed as a first step in this direction. These packages are particularly good candidates for phase-vocoder-based augmentations.

Last, it should be noted that virtually no audio signal-processing technique is immune to "surprises" in working with naturally produced sounds. In the case of the phase vocoder, these surprises are most apparent when working with sounds that resist the attempted decomposition into separate temporal and spectral components. For example, sounds with very closely spaced harmonics or sounds with substantial noise components can give rise to unanticipated audible results in the course of attempted modifications. Whether these unexpected results are seen as good or bad is largely a matter of taste because, for example, there is no "real" sound to which a time-expanded sound can be compared. In any event, it seems clear that short-time Fourier analysis-synthesis techniques will be popular and musically productive for some time to come.

Appendix: Mathematical Analysis of Phase Vocoder

Mathematically, the short-time Fourier transform $X(n,k)$ of the signal $x(n)$ is a function of both time n and frequency k. It can be written as

$$X(n,k) = \sum_{m=-\infty}^{\infty} x(m)h(n-m)e^{-j(2\pi/N)km}, \tag{1}$$

where $h(n)$ is a window or filter impulse response as described below.

The short-time Fourier transform is the analysis portion of the analysis-synthesis procedure. A general resynthesis equation is then given by

$$x(n) = \sum_{m=-\infty}^{\infty} f(n-m)\frac{1}{N}\sum_{k=0}^{N-1} X(m,k)e^{j(2\pi/N)km}, \tag{2}$$

where $f(n)$ is another window or filter impulse response. In the absence of modifications—and with certain constraints on $h(n)$ and $f(n)$—this equation reconstructs the input perfectly.

The analysis equation (1) can be viewed from either of two complementary perspectives. On the one hand, it can be written as

$$X(n,k) = \sum_{m=-\infty}^{\infty} \left(x(m)e^{-j(2\pi/N)km}\right)h(n-m). \tag{3}$$

This describes a heterodyne filter bank. The kth filter channel is obtained by multiplying the input $x(m)$ by a complex sinusoid at frequency k/N times the sample rate. This shifts input frequency components in the vicinity of k/N times the sample rate down near 0 Hz (and also up near twice k/N times the sample rate). The resulting signal is then convolved with the lowpass filter $h(m)$. This removes the high-frequency components and leaves only those input frequency components originally in the vicinity of k/N times the sample rate (albeit shifted down to low frequency). Thus the output $X(n,k)$, for any particular value of k, is a frequency-shifted, bandpass-filtered version of the input.

On the other hand, equation (1) can be regrouped as

$$X(n,k) = \sum_{m=-\infty}^{\infty} (x(m)h(n-m))e^{-j(2\pi/N)km}. \tag{4}$$

This is the expression for the discrete Fourier transform of an input signal $x(m)$ that is multiplied by a finite-duration, time-shifted window $h(n - m)$. Thus the output $X(n,k)$, for any particular value of n, is the Fourier transform of the windowed input at time n. Instead of representing the output of a bank of parallel heterodyne filters, $X(n,k)$ now represents a succession of partially overlapping Fourier transforms.

References

[1] Crochiere, R. E., and Rabiner, L. R. (1983). *Multirate Digital Signal Processing*. Englewood Cliffs, NJ: Prentice-Hall.

[2] Dolson, M. (1987). "The Phase Vocoder: A Tutorial." *Computer Music Journal*, Winter, 1987.

[3] Dolson, M., and Boulanger, R. (1985). "New Directions in the Musical Use of Resonators." Unpublished manuscript.

[4] Moorer, J. A. (1978). "The Use of the Phase Vocoder in Computer Music Applications." *Journal of the Audio Engineering Society*, 24(9), 717–727.

[5] Vetterli, M. (1987). "A Theory of Multirate Filter Banks." *I.E.E.E. Transactions on Acoustics, Speech, and Signal Processing*, ASSP-35(3), 356–372.

10 VLSI Models for Sound Synthesis

John Wawrzynek

10.1 Introduction

Very large-scale integrated circuit (VLSI) technology is here and is changing the way scientists work. It is a powerful medium that is flexible enough to support a wide variety of ways of computing. With the help of VLSI we have an opportunity to rethink old problems and tackle new ones. Ideas that were once only reasoned about and simulated can now be built and experimented with.

The generation of realistic musical sounds is an interesting and important problem for several reasons. It has not been studied with respect to VLSI, although VLSI holds the possibility for large benefits. Sound synthesis is representative of many other computational tasks—therefore, any insight and understanding gained is likely to be applicable in other areas. Besides being computationally expensive, musical sound synthesis faces directly the issues of machine-man interface.

Sound synthesis is not an easy problem, partly because human hearing and perception are not well understood. But listening tests can be performed, making the problem more tractable. It is clear when one is progressing in the right direction. This is an attribute sound synthesis shares with computer graphics—results are clearly visible. Also, in the same way that computer graphics can help us understand human vision, computer sound synthesis can help us understand human hearing.

Sounds that come from physical sources can be naturally represented by differential equations in time. Since there is a straightforward correspondence between differential equations in time and finite difference equations, we can model musical instruments as simultaneous finite difference equations. Musical sounds can be produced by solving the difference equations that model instruments in real time.

In the past the enormous computation bandwidth of sound generation has been avoided by using musical shortcuts such as waveform table lookup and interpolation. While this approach and those built upon it can produce pleasing musical sounds, the attacks, dynamics, continuity, and other properties of real instruments simply cannot be captured. In addition, traditional methods suffer from the shortcoming that the player of the instrument is given parameters that do not necessarily have any direct physical interpretation and are simply artifacts of the model. An even larger problem with the shortcut methods of the past is that they have produced models that require updates of internal parameters at a rate that is many times that which occurs in real musical instruments. The control, or update, of parameters has become an unmanageable problem.

In this chapter I present a solution to the problem of the generation of realistic musical sounds. The solution is based on using physical modeling and a VLSI implementation.

Section 10.2 summarizes past attempts at sound synthesis and presents an alternative approach based on physical models. Section 10.3 presents our computational idiom, that is, a method of computing musical sounds, and describes the implementation of musical instrument models. Section 10.4 presents a computer architecture based on VLSI and our computational idiom.

10.2 Modeling Musical Instruments

This section presents an approach to the synthesis of musical sounds. I present computational models for two representative musical instruments. The form that the models take is strongly dependent on the implementation strategy, or computational metaphor, that we have adopted.

10.2.1 Methods of Sound Synthesis

Many techniques for electronic sound synthesis have been developed over the years. In cases where the methods have worked in realtime, they have produced low-quality sounds. Other techniques have produced higher-quality results but have failed to work in realtime. For a complete summary of existing sound-synthesis techniques and equipment see [3] and [13].

Most real-time synthesis techniques are attempts to imitate the sound of the instrument rather than the instrument itself. Therefore, the user is not provided with a meaningful parameterization of the physical instrument. It is a complicated and sometimes impossible task to go from a physically caused phenomenon to a set of synthesis parameters.

The parameterization, or control, problem is just one of a variety of problems that exist due to the fact that nowhere in the sound-synthesis technique is there a model of the physical instrument. Most nonphysical sound models do not contain a representation of the state of the instrument, and as a result each note cannot depend on the history (last sequence of notes) in any way. Not only is interaction between successive notes disallowed, but also the previous one is usually terminated when a new note is begun. A dramatic example of the need to represent the state of the instrument is apparent in a repetitively struck church bell. The sound resulting from each strike is a function of the nature of the strike *and* of the state of the bell at the instant that it is struck. Some strikes sound harder and others softer, depending on the surface of the bell at the exact instant the hammer contacts the surface. In addition, because the bell has many long-lived modes, the effects of many strikes all exist simultaneously within the system. Similar effects occur in all physical instruments.

Another aspect of sound generation that has not been captured by the methods of the past are effects due to coupling between resonant members of the same instrument. Consider the piano as an example. The timbre of a struck string (or set of strings) depends not only on the state of the string and how it is struck, but also on the state of the bridge, the soundboard, and certain other strings (the ones without a damper). All the strings couple through the bridge and soundboard, affecting the sound of a struck string and producing synpathetic vibrations. The way strings couple with one another depends on which keys are pressed (and thus which dampers are released) at the time a new key is pressed.

The human hearing system has evolved to be extremely sensitive, particularly with respect to transient behavior. The nonphysical sound-modeling techniques, except for sampling, start notes off in a very simple and pure way, contrary to the way sounds from physical instruments are started. The sounds from most musical instruments in reality begin with an almost chaotic behavior before the instrument develops coherence and produces a pure tone.

In spite of these drawbacks these techniques have enjoyed popularity for three reasons:

1. Under controlled conditions, for certain sounds, people can be fooled into hearing natural sounds.
2. The electronic instruments have developed on their own merit as new instruments with new sounds.
3. Nothing better has been available.

An obvious step is to develop a method of generating sounds by mathematical modeling of the motions of the physical musical instrument. Generating sound by solving the equations of motion of an instrument captures a natural parameterization of the instrument and includes many of the musically important physical characteristics of the sound. A large literature exists concerned with mathematical modeling of musical instruments, or at least pieces of musical instruments. Most of these projects have not had the benefit of humans being able to listen to the results, and progress has been slow. Human hearing is complex and itself is poorly understood, so it is difficult to refine models without the benefit of listening tests. Weinreich is a notable exception [17]. He has been primarily interested in understanding the physics of musical instruments and has used listening to synthetic sound as a way to check his theories and models. Hiller and Ruiz solved the wave equation for a string using finite differences on a conventional computer as a way to generate sound [4]. Their research resulted in interesting experiments with a natural parameterization of a string, including density, elasticity, stiffness, and rigidity of string end supports.

10.2.2 Physical Modeling

In this section, we step back and explore the possible techniques for emulating the physical behavior of musical instruments. The conventional way of representing acoustical systems, and perhaps the most general way, is as a set of coupled partial differential equations (PDEs) in time and the three spatial dimensions. If such an approach is practical, in many ways it is the ideal way to produce sound. All the problems mentioned with traditional sound-synthesis techniques are avoided naturally. In fact, few people would argue that, implementation issues aside, a PDE representation for musical instruments is the best representation; the problems arise because of the impracticality of numerical solutions to such systems. The power of the PDE technique lies in the fact that the interesting and complex behavior of most musical instruments arises from the interaction of their pieces. (A notable exception to this theory is the Chinese gong, the timbre of which evolves as the result of a nonlinearity in the metal due to hammering during construction.) The behavior of each constituent piece is close to that of an ideal theoretical case. The rich interaction among elements is also what has eluded researchers in arriving at simple closed-form solutions for such systems over a wide range of parameters.

The two popular techniques for numerically solving a system of PDEs are the methods of finite elements and finite differences. Both methods discretize the systems in the spatial and temporal dimensions. Variables are used to represent the state of each element or each discrete piece of the system. Local laws based on conservation of energy govern the interactions among the elements of the system. The system can be solved by sequentially updating the state of each piece of the system represented in the memory of a conventional computer, or by simultaneously updating them on a parallel computer. These methods work well for most physical systems because the behavior of the system is described very accurately by local effects. The question is: How powerful a computer do we need to model interesting instrument behavior in this fashion?

A simple analysis shows that the requirements of this method cannot be met by any computer in existence today nor probably for some time to come. A way to reduce the computational complexity of the task without giving up the physical essence of the representation is to attempt to reduce the dimensionality of the problem. Stretched strings, for example, can be approximated as one-dimensional structures, as can the air columns of woodwind and brass instruments. Accurate simulations of plates and membranes require a two-dimensional representation. Interfaces between the various elements of the system still exist, but each element takes on a lower-dimension form. Not enough work has been done in these areas, however, for us to know what is lost sonically in such approximations.

One-dimensional approximation takes one of two forms: The most obvious form is simply a one-dimensional finite-element or finite-difference approach. The finite-difference method was used by Hiller and Ruiz [4] to simulate the motion and sound of a string. A much more efficient simulation for some computers uses the concept of wave impedance. Media are approximated by coupled sections of constant impedance. A forward and backward wave moves through each section unchanged but delayed in time. There is a strong correspondence between these systems and scattering theory, and the well-known ladder and lattice filter structures used in signal processing. The interface between each constant impedance section forms a scattering interface where there is a wave transmission and reflection. The form of the computation at each interface can be formulated from conservation of energy. Nondispersive media or mildly dispersive media may be implemented quite efficiently, using delay lines with computation joining them. The delay lines simulate the propagation of the wave through a section of constant impedance, and the computation joining each section computes the scattering. These systems have been explored by J. Smith in an approach to modeling he calls *waveguide digital filters* [14]. Corrections having to do with representing a nonideal medium with an ideal one—

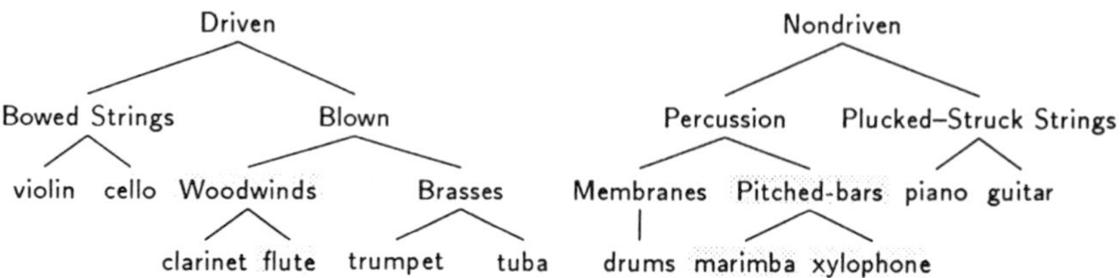

Figure 10.1
Partial taxonomy of modern orchestral instruments.

namely, memory—sometimes can be lumped into the ends of the lines where the computations take place.

The next logical step in lowering the dimensionality of the elements is to approximate coarsely the spatial dimension by forming a *lumped* system for each element, similar to conventional linear filters or lumped electrical circuits. The instrument model that results is a system of coupled ordinary differential equations (ODEs) in time. This is the approach we have taken in this work. The ODEs are approximated by finite-difference equations and are solved concurrently.

Figure 10.1 shows a taxonomy of modern orchestral instruments; it is not complete and for clarity does not necessarily use the proper technical names for each category. The primary division separates *driven* instruments, those with a forcing function, from *nondriven* ones, those which are excited and then allowed to sound freely. The two instrument classes differ significantly in their sound production mechanisms. We have investigated one case from each of the two classes of instruments and have developed models used to compute sound. From the driven class we have chosen the flute, recorder, and organ pipe instruments, all of which share a common sound production mechanism. From the nondriven class we have chosen the bar-percussion instruments, which with minor modifications can be extended to emulate plucked strings and struck bells and chimes.

10.2.3 Computational Model for Organ Pipes and Flutes

Organ pipes, recorders, and flutes all share a common sound-production mechanism. This mechanism is fairly well understood and has been presented in the literature ([1], [2]). As is true of our response to most other musical instruments, nonlinear effects play an important role in our perception of the generated sound. These nonlinearities make musical instru-

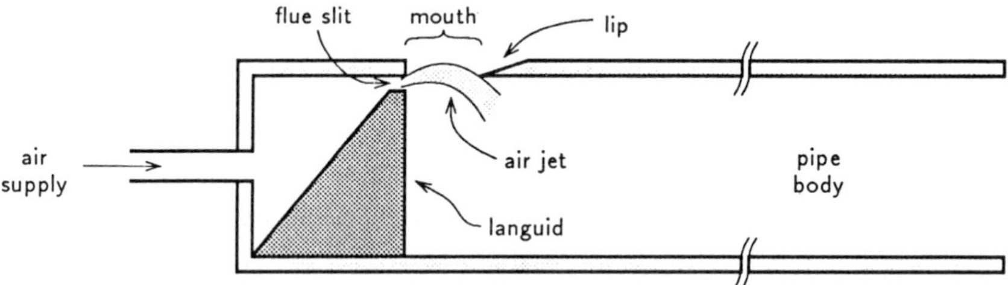

Figure 10.2
Organ pipe.

ments particularly difficult systems to study analytically, for a formulation of a closed-form model of such a system requires the solution of coupled nonlinear equations. This difficulty has led to the development of time-domain models [7]. The time-domain models provide the basis for efficient numerical solutions and thus a method for simulation.

One fortunate feature of flutes and other woodwind instruments is that there are two separable systems. The nonlinear effects are essentially concentrated at the blowing mechanism and thus can be split off from the remainder of the system, leaving a linear system. This lumping of pieces of the system into distinct parts is essential to efficient simulation.

A typical organ pipe is shown in figure 10.2. Air is forced through the *flue*, across the mouth of the pipe where it hits the *lip*. In the flute, the player's mouth and lips play the role of the flue slit. The air forced through the flue interacts with the air within the pipe body so as to generate a sustained oscillation. From basic linear-system theory, the system must contain a negative resistance (or positive feedback) if it is to sustain an oscillation.

In organ pipes, the essence of the oscillation mechanism is the same as it is in clarinets. The air supply is forced out the flue slit across the mouth of the pipe, where it forms a sheet of air. The sheet is a turbulent jet that reacts to the acoustical vibrations of the air within the pipe and is analogous to the reed in the clarinet. If the jet were simply allowed to move in and out with the air in the pipe, the oscillation would be canceled out. As the pressure within the pipe increased, it would force the jet out of the pipe, decreasing the pressure in the pipe. The situation is similar for a low pressure in the pipe. The air jet does not moves as a flat sheet, however; the jet interacts with the acoustical vibration in the pipe, which in turn induces transverse waves on the jet traveling from the flue slit across the mouth. The distance from the flue slit to the lip on the pipe is carefully designed to correspond to one-half the wavelength of the transverse wave on the jet. The delay along the jet results in the jet's alternately blowing in and out of the mouth of the pipe one-half cycle out of phase with the acoustic displacement out of the pipe mouth due to the vibration of the air column. Alternatively, we can describe the jet as behaving as a mass termination, responding one-quarter cycle out of phase with the force acting on it (pressure) and thus one-half cycle out of phase with the displacement. This one-half-cycle delay is the source of the negative resistance.

It is interesting to look in detail at the jet flow in and out of the pipe. Even if the jet deflection at the lip is nearly sinusoidal, the jet flow saturates once it is completely blowing into the pipe and similarly when it is blowing completely out of the pipe. This saturation results in an approximate hyperbolic-tangent function relating jet flow into the pipe to jet deflection. The distortion of the jet deflection by the tanh function injects odd-numbered harmonics into the pipe along with the fundamental frequency of the deflection. Of course, odd harmonics are generated for all the components of the waveform on the jet; however, it has been found by Fletcher and Douglas [1] that, in practice, the fundamental is the primary component surviving the trip along the jet. The pipe body has resonant modes approximately corresponding to the harmonics of the fundamental frequency of the oscillation, and it adds gain at the frequencies of the harmonics, producing a more pleasing musical tone. Even-numbered harmonics are generated by offsetting the lip of the pipe slightly from the center of the flue so that the lip cuts the jet away from its center place. This offsetting causes the waveform of the flow into the pipe to be non-symmetric, and thus to contain even harmonics. Offsetting of the lip is used by pipe-organ builders to adjust the tonal quality of pipes, and also by flute players who direct the air jet relative to the pipe lip to achieve a desired timbre. Timbre is also adjusted by instrument builders by varying the pipe geometry. Narrow-diameter pipes have more efficient higher resonances and thus produce a brighter tone relative to wide pipes, which emphasize the lower frequencies, resulting in a duller tone. Closed-ended pipes are also sometimes used when only odd harmonics are desired.

Basic Model. In this section, I present a model for the sound-generation mechanism in the flute, suitable for simulation. From the line of modeling developed in [7] for the clarinet, we have developed model equations for the

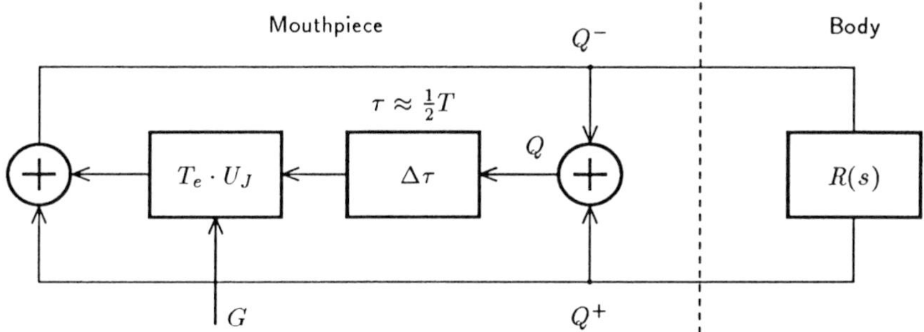

Figure 10.3
Computational model for flute.

organ pipe and transformed them into a description suitable for direct execution within our computational metaphor [15]. The result is summarized in figure 10.3.

The right side of the diagram represents the function of the body of the flute. To a very close approximation, the body is a linear system—and we represent it as its s-transform. Of course, $R(s)$ may be very complex, depending on the reflectivity properties of the flute body. The geometry of the pipe, placement and size of the tone holes, and shape of the bell (if present) all contribute to $R(s)$. The radiation function of the body model is not involved in the interaction between the body and the mouthpiece and, for simplicity, is not shown.

The left side of the diagram represents the mouthpiece portion of the flute. The function U_J represents the flow into the mouth of the pipe due to the jet and its interaction with the vibrations within the pipe. The flow function takes on the nonlinear form shown in figure 10.4.

This curve has the form of a standard saturation curve, with the extremes representing the flow of the jet being totally in or totally out of the pipe. Implicit in U_J is a delay τ introduced by the time for the disturbance of the jet to propagate from the flue slit to the pipe lip. At resonance, τ is approximately one-half the fundamental period of oscillation.

We assume that the function U_J is scaled by a factor G such that it takes the form $G \cdot \tanh(k \cdot P)$, where G roughly corresponds to the maximum flow of the jet or the blowing strength, and k corresponds to the width of the jet. A low-flow jet saturates at a lower level and thus has a smaller G.

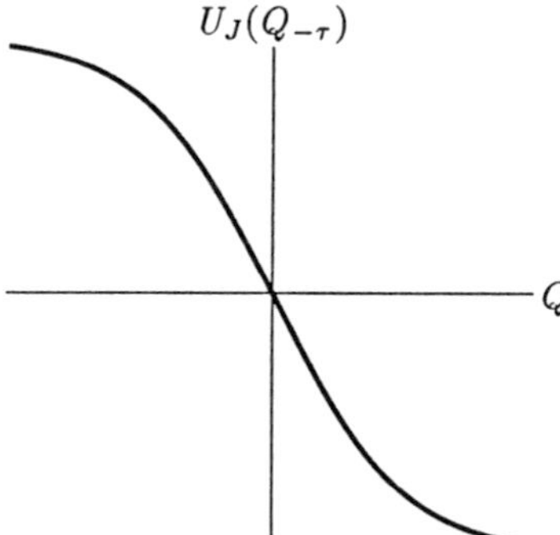

Figure 10.4
Functional form of flow into the pipe.

The following describes an interpretation of the model: When $G = 0$, the output of the functional block $T_e \cdot U_J$ is equal to zero for any input Q, and the output from the mouthpiece Q^- equals the input Q^+; in other words, the jet has no effect, and the incoming displacement wave is simply reflected off the mouth of the pipe and returned. Because R is a passive function, the gain around the loop is less than unity and any disturbance simply dies out exponentially. When $G > 0$, the displacement wave emerges from the mouthpiece with amplification of frequencies near the fundamental. The saturation of the U_J curve limits the amplitude of the oscillation and also distorts the waveform, resulting in sustained oscillation and the generation of harmonics.

Noise. The model presented captures the essence of the sound-production mechanism, including nonlinear effects and the production of harmonics, but fails to generate the noise that is present in real flute tones. It is commonly understood that the presence of noise is important to our perception of flute tones. The noise is the consequence of turbulence in the air jet. In our abstraction of the air jet, all such turbulent behavior is lost. The exact behavior of the jet is complicated, sometimes behaving more as a laminar flow than as a turbulent flow. A detailed simulation of the air jet may be one way to achieve the desired result; however, in practice, a detailed simulation is impractical because of computational expense. A much simpler method captures much of the subjective effect of the turbulence. We observe that (1) the amount of noise injected into the pipe is proportional to the flow into the pipe, and (2) the amplitude of the signal

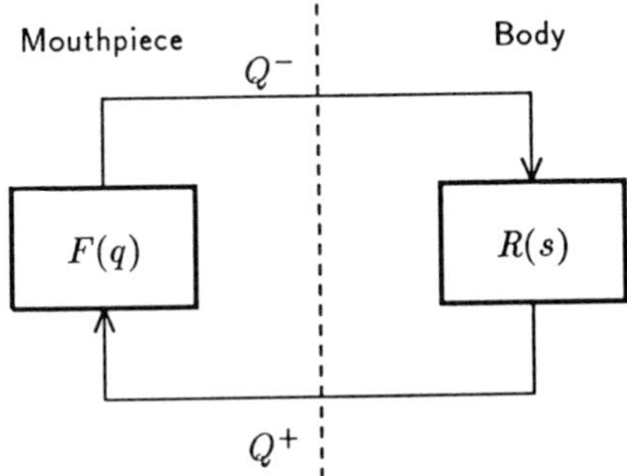

Figure 10.5
Simplified model for flute. The mouthpiece section is modeled with a single function.

generally grows in proportion to the amount of the flow into the pipe. Therefore, an amount of noise proportional to the amplitude of the signal is added to the signal as it leaves the mouthpiece section of the model.

Modifications. The computational model presented thus far and represented in figure 10.3 may be simplified to arrive at a system shown in figure 10.5. The composite function of the mouthpiece, $F(q)$, may be found and replaces the mouthpiece computation in figure 10.3. Such a system is more efficient to compute in some computational metaphors, for instance, where function evaluation is done using table lookup. In addition, because the computation is in a more familiar form, it may lend itself more readily to analysis.

10.2.4 Computational Model for Bar-Percussion Instruments

As we saw in the previous section, blown pipes and flutes have a sound characterized by the way energy is supplied to the system. Now we examine a class of instruments the sound of which is characterized by the way energy is dissipated. This class of instruments includes all nondriven instruments, such as plucked and struck strings, drums, and bar-percussive instruments. Here I restrict the class to those instruments including a *stiff* resonant bar or plate, or those with an *elastic* member with low-amplitude oscillations. The most common instruments in this restricted class include marimbas, vibraphone, glockenspiels, bells, and chimes. Examples of a stringed instruments with low-amplitude oscillations are the Japanese koto and the Chinese guseng. Systems with elastic vibrating members, such as plucked

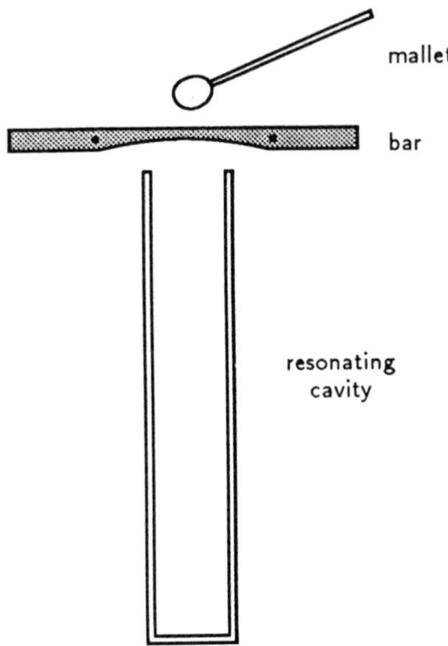

Figure 10.6
Marimba.

strings, where the vibration amplitude is large, include a nonlinear effect that cannot be ignored.

For simplicity, I shall refer only to bar-percussion instruments; however, all results apply equally well to any instrument meeting the constraints outlined. All bar-percussion instruments are composed of one or more vibrating bars, a striking implement, such as a mallet, and in some cases a resonating cavity or tube to modify the sound of the bars. I shall assume that, in a system of multiple bars, the bars are acoustically independent of one another. This assumption is certainly true in the case of marimbas and other such bar instruments but is not true in the case of string instruments. The strings all share a common bridge that couples energy among the strings. (see figure 10.6)

The timbre of the sound from a struck instrument is dependent on two sets of phenomena: (1) the physical dimensions and compositions of the constituent pieces and (2) the manner of striking. Included in the first set is the means of support of the bar and the relative placement of the resonant cavity, if present. The manner of striking includes the force and place of the strike and can be characterized as a time-varying two-dimensional force profile on the surface of the bar. It is probably not accurate to represent the manner of striking simply as initial conditions for the bar. It is well known to students of marimba playing that the act of pulling the mallet away from the bar after a strike is important in the generation of correct timbre.

The Bar. Ideal vibrating bars and strings have been studied for centuries. Theoretical explanations for the motion of a stiff bar and an elastic string following the initial transients have long been given in the literature ([11] and [12]). Most authors treat bars with uniform thickness.

The major distinction between bars and ideal strings is that the general function $f_1(x + ct) + f_2(x - ct)$ is *not* a solution for bars, and the motion cannot be represented by a sum of identical right-going and left-going waves. The velocity of propagation of a wave along a bar is a function of frequency, whereas that in an ideal string is not. This property makes bars a *dispersive* medium—a pulse sent down a bar loses its shape, because the various frequency components travel at different speeds. The consequence to instrument builders is that, even though the spatial periods of the normal modes of vibration of a bar are related closely to a series of integers, the modes do not oscillate with frequencies that lie close to a harmonic series, as they do in the case of stringed instruments.

Instrument builders have developed ways to modify the geometry of bars to force at least one normal mode to oscillate at a musical interval relative to the fundamental [10]. Similar techniques are used by builders of violins to adjust the resonant qualities of the plates in a violin body. Builders of marimbas and other bar-percussion instruments remove material from the underside of the bar at the antinode of a normal mode, resulting in a slightly less stiff bar for that mode and a lowering in frequency. These modifications also mean that most of the solutions for the motions of bars have little practical significance.

Although strange geometries complicate the solution of the wave equation for bars by imposing complicated boundary conditions and violating assumptions about constants in the equation of motion, the form of the solution is not different from that for the ideal bar. The modes are independent and have constant frequency with amplitude and time. Because of these invariants, we can model the bar as a set of independent resonances, each with a damping factor Q and center frequency θ_c. The resonances correspond to the spatial modes of the bar. Note that the resonances cannot be modeled accurately as sine waves, in spite of what the solution of

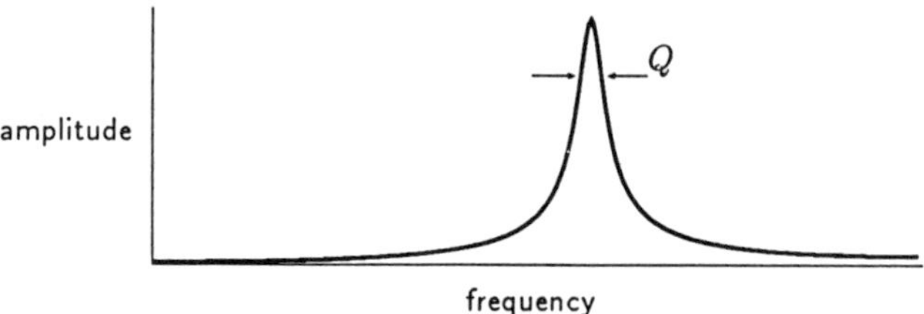

Figure 10.7
Frequency response of bar resonance.

the wave equation may suggest. Like those of most mechanical oscillators in nature, each resonance of the bar has a response to a forcing function, as shown in figure 10.7.

Highly resonant modes have a narrow resonance peak. The use of simple sine oscillators loses this *bandpass* characteristic, which becomes important when considering the presence of forcing functions and the excitation of an already moving mode.

The Mallet and Strike. The bar is not modified in any way by the player of the instrument; therefore, the striking of the bar is the player's sole control over the timbre of the note. The composition and size of the mallet and force of the strike constitute the major controls used by the player. Also important to the production of a musical tone is the placement of the strike and the period of impact. How all these parameters affect the tone of the note played is fairly well understood.

One interesting and musically important aspect of the strike, however, is not well understood and is not treated in the literature. Even in the case of a "clean" blow to the bar, the observed waveform appears "noisy" for the first few cycles, as is evident in figure 10.8. The noise dies out within the first few cycles. The amount of observed noise is more pronounced for forceful strikes, as well as for harder mallets. Part of the "noise" is probably due to the excitation of many low-Q, high-frequency modes. The nearly discontinuous stress profile generated on the bar propagates from the point of impact and interacts with the many degrees of freedom of the bar, generating random movements of the substance composing the bar. These random movements generate heat and are quickly damped, leaving the standing wave motion of the normal modes. Although the details of the noise-generation mechanism are not modeled by the

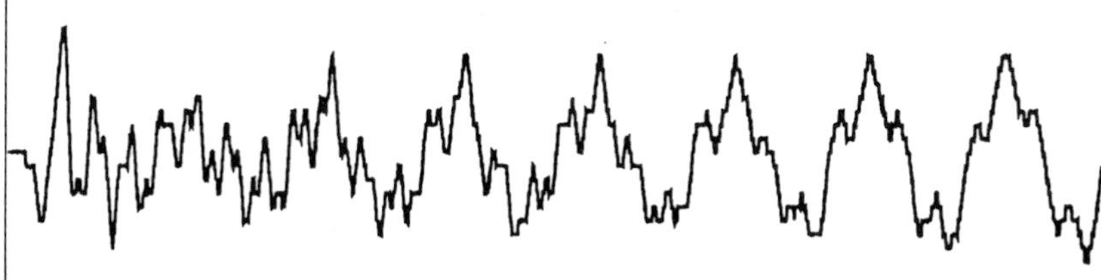

Figure 10.8
Waveform of a marimba strike. The waveform shows amplitude versus time. The bar struck was in the middle range of the instrument. It was struck with moderate force, in its center, with a hard rubber mallet.

equation of motion for the bar, the noise is critically important to our perception of the struck sound and is included in our model. The noisy beginning of the bar's motion may be viewed as an excitation function (forcing function) for the resonances of the bar. To model the qualitative effect of the noise, we need to generate an excitation function containing noise that has an amplitude proportional to the force of the strike and to the hardness of the mallet. It also is important that the noise die out after several cycles.

The key to the qualitative affects of mallet size and hardness lies in the stress generated in the bar for each case. Our hypothesis about the important affects of mallet size and hardness can be viewed as a *footprint*. As we move from a smaller to a larger mallet, the stress footprint on the bar is enlarged, providing relatively less energy to higher spatial modes. The larger the mallet, the more total energy is transferred to the bar, because a larger mallet has more mass and thus generates more force. The hardness of the mallet also effects the size of the stress footprint on the bar, because of the compressibility of the mallet. Perhaps more important, the hardness of the mallet effects the *steepness* of the stress profile into the bar. Harder mallets generate a steep stress profile and provide more energy to higher modes—and generate more noise.

Translation from stress in the spatial domain to the temporal-frequency domain is not straightforward. I use a model that captures the essential qualitative behavior with sufficient parameters to generate musically important control.

The Model. The struck-instrument model is composed of two sections, as shown in figure 10.9. The right circuit models the normal modes of the bar

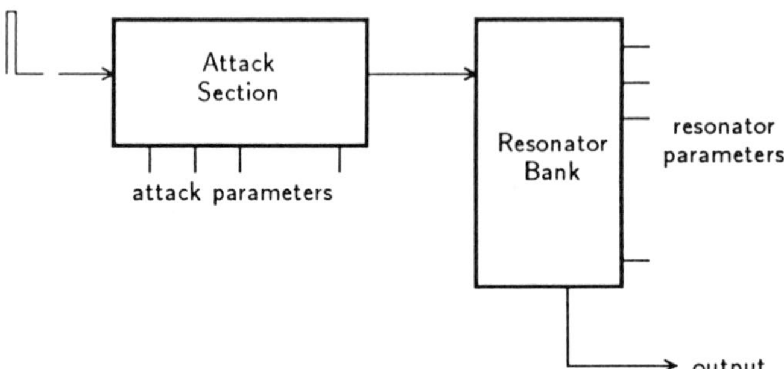

Figure 10.9
Struck instrument model.

with discrete resonances. The circuit used for each mode is called a *resonator*. A weighted sum of resonator outputs is formed by summing a weighted value from the output of each resonator circuit. All the resonators are excited by a common signal from the attack section. The attack section generates a noisy signal to excite the resonators. Parameters of the attack section are changed to model different types of mallets and different force strengths. Details of the struck-instrument model with several parameters useful for specific musical instruments are presented in the next section.

10.3 Computing Sound

This section presents the implementation of musical-sound synthesis. I present the implementation strategy, or computational metaphor, that we have adopted, and present in detail the implementation of the two musical instruments developed in section 10.2.

10.3.1 Implementation Strategy

Our approach to generating musical sounds involves solving difference equations in real time. Musical instruments are modeled as systems of coupled difference equations. A natural architecture for solving systems of finite-difference equations is one with an interconnection matrix between processors that can be reconfigured (or programmed), as illustrated in figure 10.10. A realization of a new instrument involves reconfiguring of the connection matrix between the processing elements, as well as configuring connections to the outside world both for control and for updates of parameters.

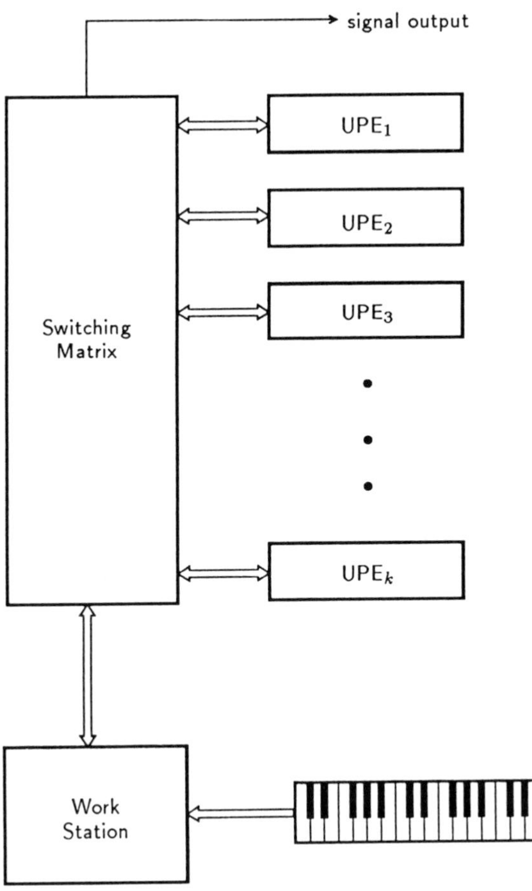

Figure 10.10
Sound-synthesis architecture. Processing elements are connected to each other and to the outside world through a reconfigurable interconnection matrix.

Processing elements are placed together to form an array and then are joined by a reconfigurable interconnection matrix. A general-purpose computer supplies updates of parameters to the processing elements and provides an interface to the player of the instrument. The external computer also supplies the configuration programs for the interconnection matrix. Synthesized signal outputs go to a digital-to-analog converter.

To implement a reconfigurable connection matrix, a bit-serial representation of samples facilitates the use of single-wire connections between computational units, drastically reducing the complexity of implementation. In fact, a bit-serial implementation makes the entire approach possible. Bit-serial implementations also have the advantage in that computational elements are small and inexpensive.

For our computation we have chosen a basic unit we call a Universal Processing Element (UPE) [15] that computes the function

$$A + (B \times M) + D \times (1 - M), \tag{1}$$

It is similar to the bit-serial multipliers proposed by Lyon [6]. In its simplest mode of computation, where $D = 0$, the function of a UPE is a multiplication and an addition. This simple element forms a digital integrator that is the basic building block for solving linear difference equations. If D is not set to zero, the output of the UPE is A plus the linear interpolation between B and D, where M is the constant of interpolation.

All the inputs and outputs to the UPE are bit serial. UPEs can be connected to each other with a single wire.

10.3.2 Musical-Instrument Models

This section describes two simple musical instrument models based on UPEs. Both models have been implemented, and we have used them to generate musical sounds. Although these models have been used to produce extremely high-quality timbres of certain instruments, they are certainly not capable of covering the entire range of timbres of the instruments. The development of a new timbre can be thought of as building an instrument, learning to play it, and then practicing a particular performance on it. This activity requires a great deal of careful study and may involve extensions or modifications to the model.

Struck Instrument. Struck or plucked instruments are those that are played by displacing the resonant element of the instrument from its resting

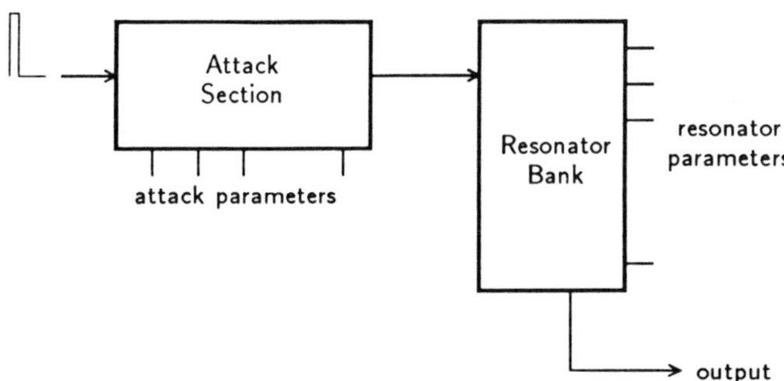

Figure 10.11
Struck instrument implemented with UPEs.

state and then allowing it to oscillate freely. Tone quality in such instruments is a function of how the system is excited, and of how it dissipates energy. Examples of plucked and struck instruments include plucked and struck strings, struck bells, and marimbas.

Figure 10.11 illustrates a struck-instrument model implemented with UPEs. The model can be decomposed into two pieces: the *attack section* and the *resonator bank*. The attack section models the impact of the striking or plucking device on the actual instrument. An impulse is fed to a second-order section that is tuned with a Q value close to critical damping. A detailed version of the attack section is shown in figure 10.12. In this figure, the output of the *attack resonator* is fed to the input of the *noise-modulation section*. The noise-modulation section generates the function

$$y = NM \cdot x \cdot RNG + SG \cdot x,$$

where RNG is the output of a random-number generator. This computation adds to the signal input x an amount of noise proportional to the level of x. The balance of signal to noise is controlled by the ratio $SG : NM$, and the overall gain is controlled by $SG + NM$.

The output of the noise-modulation section is used to drive a parallel connection of second-order sections used as resonators. The resonators are tuned to the major resonances of the instrument being modeled. The parameters of the attack section—attack resonator frequency and Q value, signal-to-noise ratio, and attack level—are all adjusted to produce a variety of musical timbres.

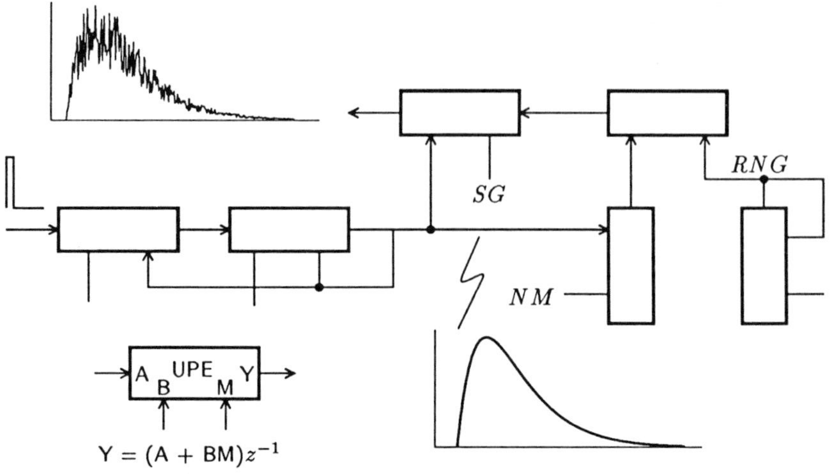

Figure 10.12
Attack section.

Second-order sections are combined to form a resonator bank, as shown in figure 10.13. The output of each resonator is connected to a single UPE that scales the output of the resonator and adds the signal to the signal from the other resonators.

In a typical application, a pianolike keyboard is used to control the instrument. The pressing of a key triggers the following actions: (1) the key position determines the coefficients loaded into the resonator bank; (2) the key velocity controls the level of the coefficient *NM* in the attack section (higher key velocities correspond to more noise being introduced into the system and hence a higher attack level); and (3) the key press generates an impulse that is sent to the attack resonator.

Table 10.1 shows the parameters developed to synthesize the sound of a struck aluminum bar suspended on two loops of string at a distance of one-quarter of its length in from each end. The bar is similar to the ones used in vibraphones, without the arch cut in its underside. The bar was struck with moderate force, on its center, with a hard rubber mallet. The gain of the attack resonator is the coefficient *SG*. EQ_R and EQ_G refer to the two coefficients of a resonator normalization circuit. The frequency, Q, and gain of each resonator were found empirically, using spectrum analysis of the physical bar. The bar has length of 211 mm, width of 37.5 mm, and

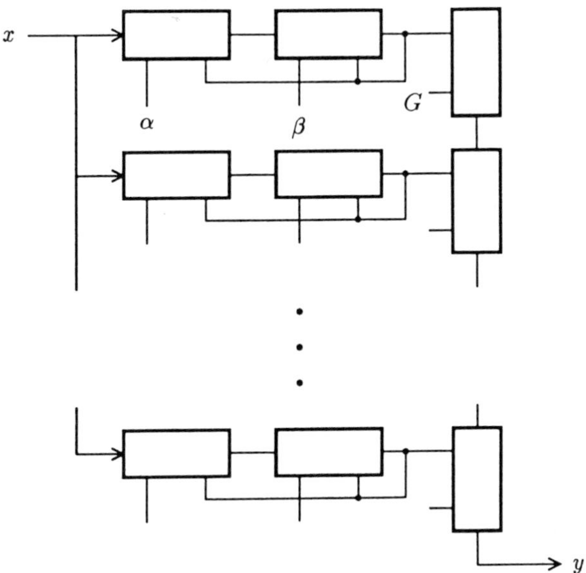

Figure 10.13
Resonator bank implementation.

Table 10.1
Aluminum bar synthesis parameters[a]

Resonator	Frequency	Q	Gain
1	1,077	2,000	1.0
2	2,160	500	0.7
3	2,940	500	0.7
4	3,220	500	0.6
5	3,520	500	0.4
6	3,940	2,000	0.4
7	5,400	500	0.3
8	5,680	2,000	1.0
9	6,900	2,000	1.0
10	7,840	500	1.0
Attack	2,000	0.5	0.004

a. $EQ_R = 0.0$, $EQ_G = 1.0$, noise gain = 0.0004, and impulse value = 1.0.

Table 10.2
Marimba synthesis parameters[a]

Resonator	Frequency	Q	Gain
1	261.63	240	1.0
2	1,041.29	200	1.0
3	2,668.63	150	1.0
Attack	261.63	0.5	0.05

a. $EQ_R = -1.0$, $EQ_G = 1.0$, noise gain = 0.025, and impulse value = 1.0.

thickness of 9.5 mm. It was found to have many normal modes. Only the 10 most prominent modes were included in the simulation. Under normal listening conditions, the synthesized sound was indistinguishable from that of the physical bar.

Table 10.2 shows parameters developed by Lounette Dyer for a struck marimba. The effect of the resonating cavity under the bar is incorporated into the parameters for the resonators that model the normal modes. As with those for the aluminum bar, the parameters for the resonators were found empirically, using spectrum analysis of recorded marimba sounds. Again, the strikes were of moderate force, on the center of the bar, with a hard rubber mallet. Although the parameters are shown for one particular bar (middle C), with one particular mallet type, and one particular strike, we have generalized them to simulate all the bars of the marimba, as well as other mallets, and other strike forces. We performed generalization by devising functions that scale the parameters according to user input (for example, key position and velocity) and additional input (such as mallet hardness). The scaling covers the full range of a normal marimba and also allows for experimentation with fanciful marimbas, for example, those that extend well beyond the normal range of a physical marimba and those with mallets that change size automatically to match better the size of the bars.

Figure 10.14 shows the first few cycles of the waveform generated by the parameters in table 10.2. It compares favorably with the waveform of a recorded marimba strike (figure 10.8), and with nonexpert listeners in an informal listening environment it sounds virtually indistinguishable from a recorded marimba strike.

Solving the wave equation for an ideal string clamped at its ends yields normal modes, the frequencies of which are integer multiples of the fundamental. The parameters for the resonators for a plucked-string sound in table 10.3 are based on this idea. The parameters for the attack section were

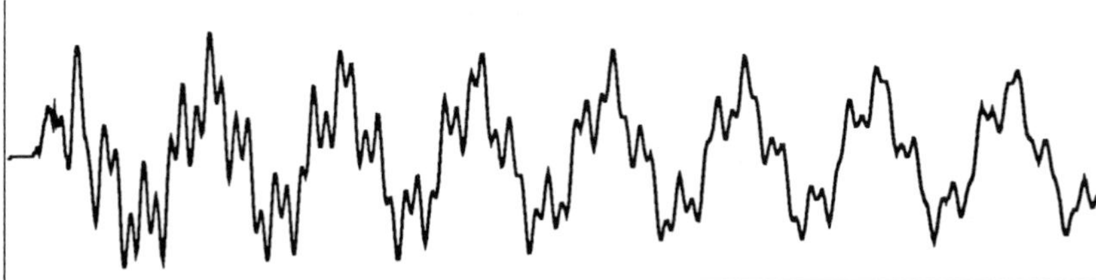

Figure 10.14
Synthesized marimba strike. The waveform shows amplitude versus time. The synthesis parameters are from table 10.2

Table 10.3
Plucked string synthesis parameters[a]

Resonator	Frequency	Q	Gain
1	440	300	0.70
2	880	300	0.80
3	1,320	300	0.60
4	1,760	300	0.70
5	2,200	300	0.70
6	2,640	300	0.80
7	3,080	320	0.95
8	3,520	300	0.76
9	3,960	190	0.87
10	4,400	300	0.76
Attack	2,000	0.5	0.004

a. $EQ_R = 0.0$, $EQ_G = 1.0$, noise gain = 0.02, and impulse value = 1.0.

found by trial and error. The resulting sound is that of a plucked, tightly strung string.

Dynamic Model. Figure 10.15 shows a simple model for blown instruments, implemented using UPEs. In section 10.2 I presented a computational model for organ pipes, flutes, and recorders based on their physical behavior. The basic observation used to develop the model was that a blown musical instrument can be viewed as a nonlinear forcing function at the mouthpiece, exciting the modes of a linear tube. In this section, I present an implementation of the model using UPEs.

We found that the computational model is composed of three pieces: (1) a linear element representing the flute body or pipe, (2) a nonlinear element

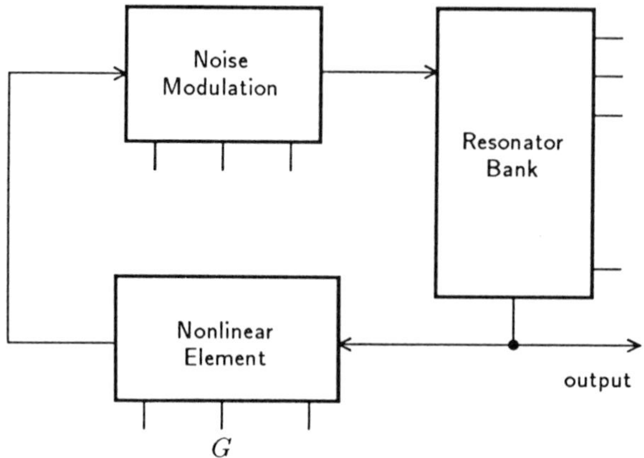

Figure 10.15
Dynamic model used for blown instruments.

representing the interaction of the air jet with the pipe, and (3) a noise-modulation section. The linear and nonlinear elements are shown explicitly in figure 10.5; the noise-modulation section is implicit in the mouthpiece. We can translate the model into a form directly solvable on a system of UPEs by interpreting the model in Figure 10.5. The mouthpiece section serves two functions: (1) it terminates the body at the blowing end by reflecting incoming waves back into the body, and (2) it supplies energy to complement the acoustical vibrations within the body. Considering only the first function of the mouthpiece, the system is a pipe open at both ends. Such a system has normal modes of vibration, the frequencies of which are proportional to the length of the pipe and the relative amplitude and damping of which are dependent on the material composing the pipe and the width of the pipe. As we did in developing the struck-instrument model, we model the normal modes of the tube explicitly, using digital resonators.

The function at the mouthpiece, not including reflection of the incoming wave, is a hyperbolic-tangent function relating the outgoing wave to the incoming wave. For a limited range of input values, a cubic polynomial is a good approximation to a tanh, as seen in figure 10.16.

The noise-modulation scheme is the same as in the struck-instrument model: Noise is added to the signal in an amount proportional to the amplitude of the signal.

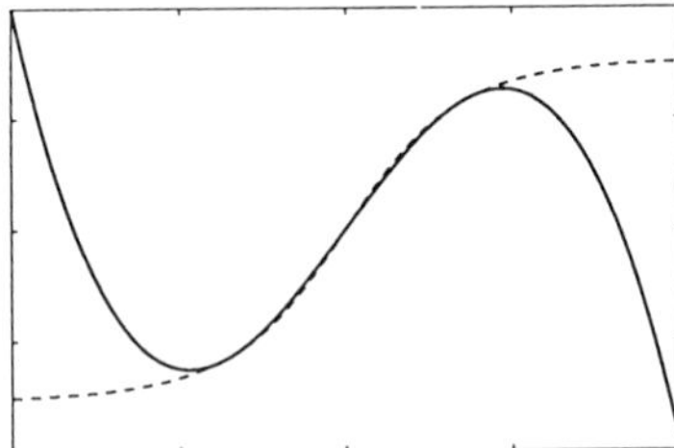

Figure 10.16
Comparison of tanh and cubic plynomial.

In summary, the UPE dynamic model is composed of three pieces: (1) the nonlinear element that computes a third-order polynomial; (2) the noise-modulation section, which adds an amount of noise proportional to the size of the signal at its input; and (3) the resonator bank, which has second-order resonators tuned to frequencies corresponding to the resonances of the pipe.

These elements are connected in a cascade arrangement, forming a closed loop. When the closed loop gain is sufficiently high, and the system is disturbed, the system oscillates with modes governed by the tuning of the resonator bank. Typically, the gain of the loop is controlled by the gain of the nonlinear element G. For small values of G, the feedback is too small and the system does not oscillate. If G is just large enough, the system oscillates with a pure tone as it operates in the nearly linear range of the nonlinear element. If the nonlinear gain G is set to an even higher value, the signal is increased in amplitude and is forced into the nonlinear region. The nonlinearity shifts some energy into higher frequencies, generating a harsher louder tone.

In a typical application, the loop gain is set by controlling the nonlinear gain G according to the velocity of a keypress on a pianolike keyboard. A slowly pressed key corresponds to a small value for G and thus generates a soft pure tone. A quickly pressed key corresponds to a larger value for G and hence to a louder, harsher tone. When the key is released, G is returned to some small value—one that is just under the point where the loop gain is large enough to sustain oscillation. Because G is not returned to zero, the signal dies out exponentially with time, with a time constant that is controlled by the value of G used.

A small amount of noise in injected constantly into the loop, using the noise-modulation section, so that the system will oscillate without an impulse being sent to excite it.

This model has been used successfully for generating flutelike tones. It works surprisingly well, considering that the tanh function is only approximated with a cubic polynomial. The essence of the physical sound seems to be captured by the combination of a nonlinearity in a feedback loop with a linear element.

In physical organ pipes, the nonlinear function is nonsymmetric—it is offset and does not pass through the origin. The same effect can be achieved in our polynomial function, and we have had great success generating sounds of various timbres.

In physical organ pipes, it has been observed that only the fundamental frequency and a small number of harmonics survive the interaction of the jet with the air column [1]. This observation implies that, for high-frequency harmonics, the pipe acts as a passive radiator, suggesting a modification to our model: Not all the resonator outputs are summed and fed back to the nonlinear element, but instead a subset is summed independently and behaves passively. Experiments with this idea have yielded encouraging results. The system was much more stable and controllable, producing a wider range of timbres than could be achieved before the modification.

Composite Model. Because both models contain several parts in common, they can be combined into one structure, with the addition of an extra coefficient to control the feedback, as shown in figure 10.17. A detailed view of the composite model is shown in the form of a computation graph for our computing engine in figure 10.18. Each rectangle in the graph represents the operation of add-multiply-delay and, optionally, mod 2^{32}.

10.4 A VLSI Architecture

In this section I present a computer architecture designed specifically for the finite-difference computations used in generating musical sounds. Our computational task is the real-time evaluation of the fixed computation graphs of the variety presented in the previous section. In these graphs, each computation node is one or more members of the set of operations: plus, times, mod 2^{32}, and delay. Input to each node is either the output of another node or an externally supplied coefficient. Samples and coefficients

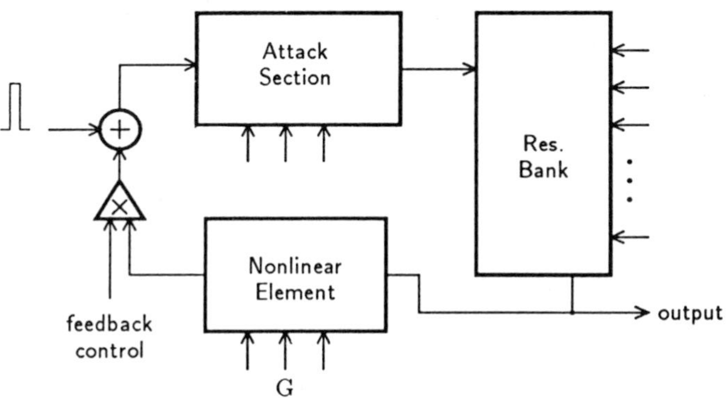

Figure 10.17
Composite instrument model.

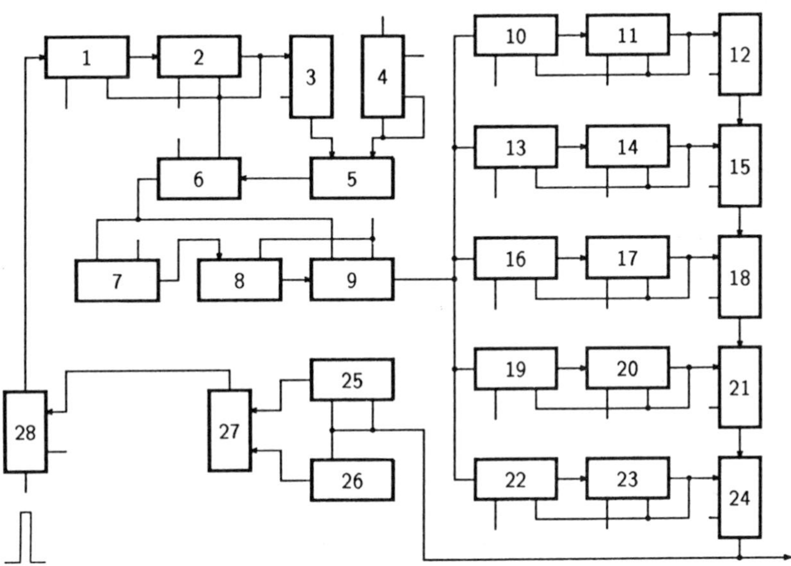

Figure 10.18
Computation graph for composite model.

flow to computation nodes across the arcs of the graph. Each processor in our computer is mapped to one and only one node, and each communication channel in our machine is mapped to one and only one arc. This concept of a one-to-one mapping is a deviation from the traditional approach, in which a single processor is time multiplexed to perform the function of each node sequentially, and memory is used to form "interconnect."

10.4.1 Architectural Overview

Our machine is structured as a number of intercommunicating chips, each responsible for computing a piece of a computation graph. We assume that our task may be organized such that somewhat independent subgraphs may be split off and solved fairly independently in a small number of clustered chips (possibly just one), alleviating the need for very high bandwidth between chips and between clusters of chips. Musical sound synthesis has this locality property.

Figure 10.19 shows a typical system configuration (many others are possible). The chips are organized in a ring structure with each chip communicating to its nearest neighbors. They are controlled by a global master, or *host*, that provides initialization information and coefficient updates during the computation. The host also provides an interface either to an external controlling device, such as a pianolike keyboard, or to a disk file containing musical-score information.

Each chip comprises three major pieces, as illustrated in figure 10.20. An array of identical processing elements responsible for arithmetic and delay operations forms the first piece. The second piece is a buffer for holding coefficients supplied by the host; these coefficients, with the outputs of other processing elements, serve as operands for the processing elements. The third piece is an reconfigurable interconnection matrix that serves all the chip's communication needs; it connects processing elements to one another, to the output of the coefficient update buffer, and to input and output connectors of the chip. The exact patterns of communication are determined by setting switches in the matrix prior to the computation. Throughout a computation, these switches remain constant, and thus the topology of the computation graph is fixed; topology can be changed, however, between computations.

10.4.2 The Processors

Bit serial processing offers two attractive features for our application. First, the processing elements are physically small, so large numbers of

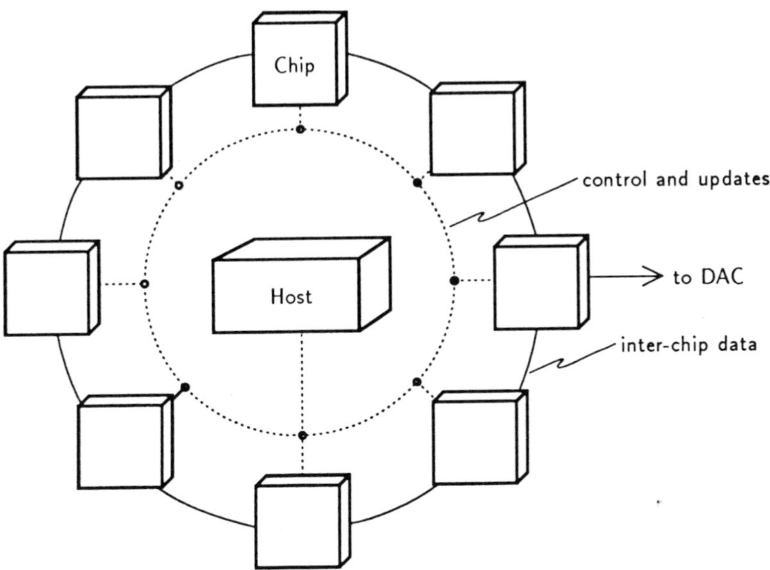

Figure 10.19
Typical system configuration.

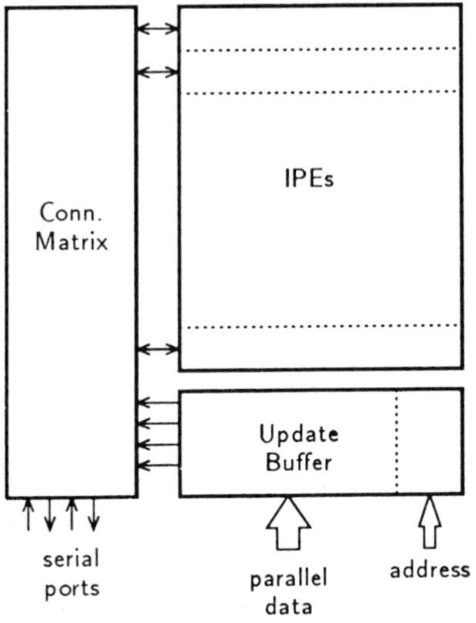

Figure 10.20
Chip organization.

them can be integrated on a single chip. Bit serial processing also facilitates bit serial communication, simplifying communication channels; single wires can be used to interconnect processing elements. One potential drawback is the *latency* incurred with each operation—the time from the operand's arrival until the total answer's arrival at the output. In our application, however, we *want* a delay at each processing step, so the latency is an advantage.

Various bit serial multiplication schemes have been implemented and presented in the literature [5]. We wanted to provide maximum processing power per unit chip area that was possible with current technology. Therefore, we chose the simplest multiplication scheme that met the constraints placed by standard digital audio rates. The CMOS implementation of our processor is a serial-parallel multiplier structure capable of one multiply-add-delay step per word time; we call it an *inner product element* (IPE). The multiplier structure is simple and therefore requires little space to implement in silicon [9]. Inputs arrive one bit at a time, least significant bit (LSB) first, and the output is generated one bit at a time. All inputs and outputs have the same number representation; therefore, there are no restrictions for interconnection of processors or the connection of coefficients.

10.4.3 The Connection Matrix

The connection matrix provides points-to-point communication between processors, from the update buffer and bidirectionally with the outside world. The matrix is *programmable*; the interconnection patterns within the matrix are not fixed but are changeable through external control, made possible by a storage cell located at each cross point in the matrix and circuitry to set the state of the storage cells. In addition to programmability, the connection matrix also takes advantage of the inherent locality in sound synthesis computations and is discretionary in the allowable interconnection patterns, saving in the chip area and providing for growth of the processing power of VLSI implementations.

Figure 10.21 shows the basic structure of the connection matrix and its interface to the other components. Note that the horizontal wires, or *tracks*, are used to bring in signals from off-chip and to send signals off-chip, as well as to provide communication between processing elements. One possible configuration is to dedicate one track-per-processing element output, which guarantees that any IPE can communicate with any other IPE. Such a configuration, however, grows as the square of the number of

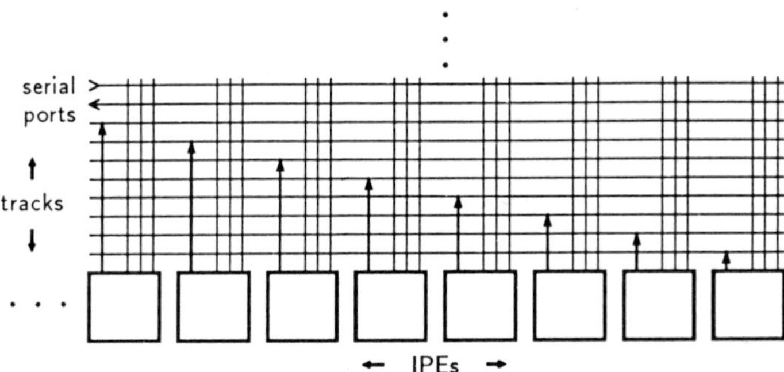

Figure 10.21
Basic structure of connection matrix.

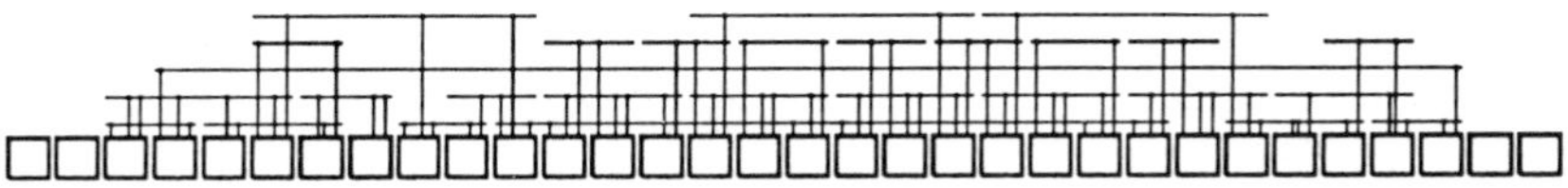

Figure 10.22
Mapping of computation graph to processor array.

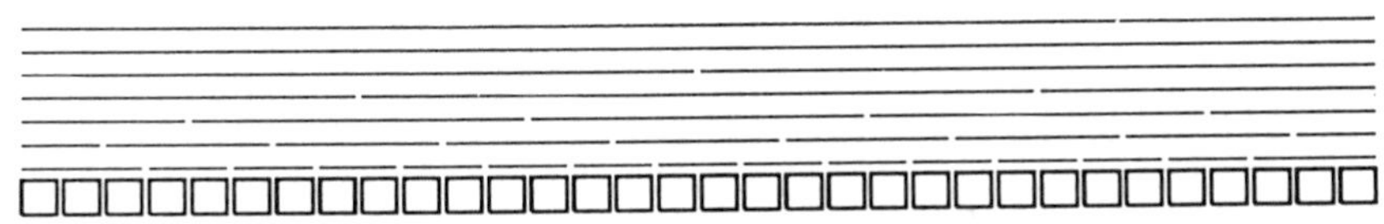

Figure 10.23
Discretionary interconnect matrix.

processing elements; in musical sound synthesis applications, it is a waste of chip area. In figure 10.22, we have mapped the computation graph in figure 10.18 onto the processor array by assigning nodes of the graph to IPEs and routing the interconnections, assuming that tracks could be broken arbitrarily. The assignment of processors to nodes in the graph was ordered from left to right across the array for consecutively numbered nodes. Clearly, all tracks have many breaks and there are a large number of small links and a relatively small number of larger links, and so on. In the modification shown in figure 10.23, tracks no longer span the entire array of IPEs, but rather are split at one or more points along their lengths. There is one track of links for length 2, one for length 4, and so on, doubling the length of the

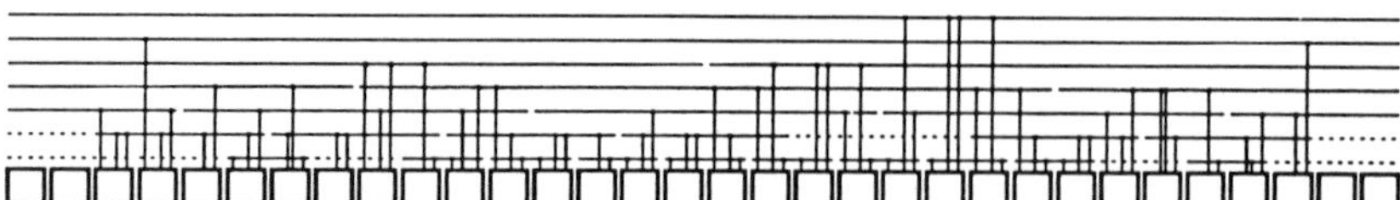

Figure 10.24
Mapping of computation graph to modified matrix.

links for each track until the entire length of the array is spanned in one link. The breaks in the tracks are arranged to avoid any two breaks lining up vertically, and consequently to maximize the potential communication between pairs of processors. This matrix grows as $N \log N$—rather than N^2, as does the earlier version—thus saving area. The computation graph of figure 10.18 has been mapped into the new structure, in figure 10.24. The ordering of the nodes in the graph has been perturbed to make a better match. All but one network is routed in the modified matrix; one additional track is used to handle that network.

It is not known what the optimal configuration for the connection matrix is, and what are the best algorithms for assignment of computational nodes to processors in the array. Although the assignment problem is NP-complete, heuristic algorithms that find the inherent localities in our applications perform very well and are aided through the addition of a few extra tracks in the matrix and a few extra processing elements in the array.

10.4.4 The Update Buffer

The update buffer is simply a register bank to hold coefficients (that is, inputs to the processing elements supplied from the host computer). Input to the update buffer is a parallel connection to a standard computer memory bus. The outputs of the update buffer are bit serial lines that run through the connection matrix to the processing elements. For maximum flexibility in the assignment of processing elements, no a priori correspondence is made between update buffer registers and processing elements; this assignment is made by programming the connection matrix.

One important feature of the update buffer is that it is double buffered. Coefficients can be sent from the host computer to the update buffer without affecting the ongoing computation. Only after all the coefficients of a new set of updates have arrived in the buffer is a signal sent to update them simultaneously. If some coefficients were allowed to change before others did, instability could result.

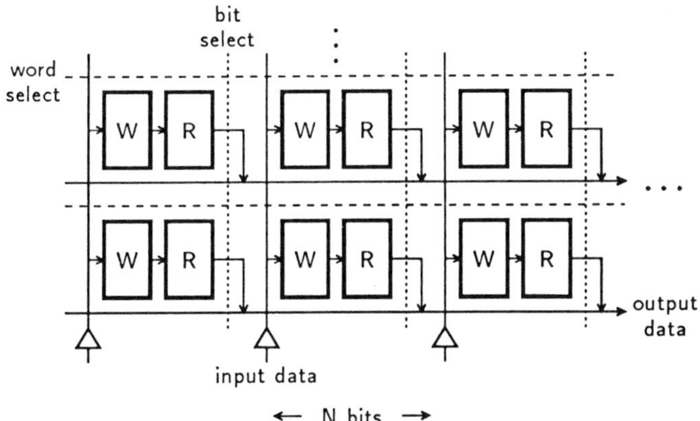

Figure 10.25
Dual RAM structure of update buffer.

Empirically, we have found that our applications average about one coefficient per processing element. This fact constrains the nominal number of registers in the update buffer to be the same as the number of processing elements, with a few spares to cover exceptional cases.

The structure of the update buffer comprises two random access memory (RAM) structures laid one on top of the other (figure 10.25). The first RAM is writable from the parallel input bus with a decoder that selects one coefficient (row). The second RAM is readable one bit (column) at a time, all coefficients being read simultaneously. A select signal cycles through the columns of the second RAM one bit at a time, sending the bits of the registers to the output, LSB first. Under control from the host computer, a transfer signal copies the contents of the first RAM to the second one.

10.4.5 CMOS Layout Summary

The cells of the three major blocks of the chip implementing our computing engine were laid out to interconnect by abutment rather than by wires. In some cases, cells were stretched to match up with neighboring cells. Consequently, the size of each block is slightly larger than is absolutely necessary to perform the function of that block, but the block composition contains no wiring channels and thus is extremely area-efficient. In general, the layout makes efficient use of silicon area.

Figure 10.26 shows the floor plan for a typical version of the chip. Most of the area is taken up by the processing elements and the connection

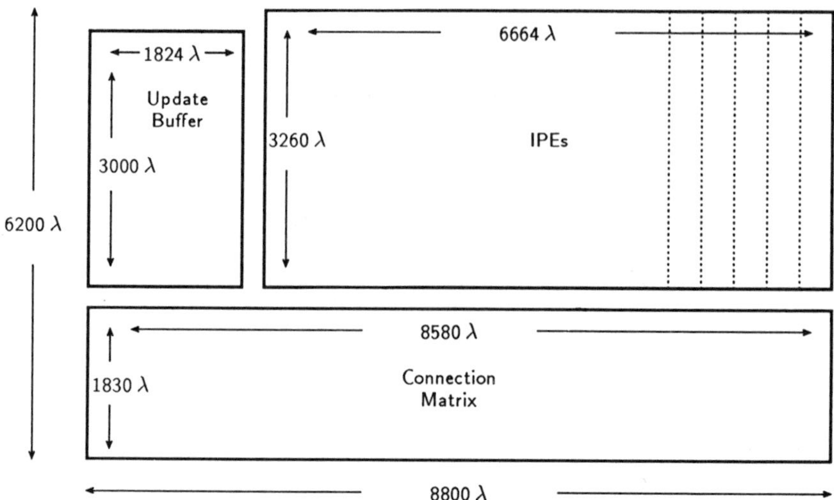

Figure 10.26
Layout dimensions of chip. Dimensions are not shown for pads.

matrix. The sizes, in lambda [8], shown in the figure are for a 32-IPE array of 32 bits each, with 32 words of update buffer capacity, and a 44-channel connection matrix. The largest version of the chip fabricated to date was an experimental version with this configuration, but with a connection matrix of 64 channels.

10.5 Conclusion

This chapter presents (1) a new approach to the production of musical sounds, (2) the application of this approach to several musical instrument models, and (3) the design of a custom computing engine to support the approach.

Our solution to the problem of sound synthesis is one that employs the flexibility provided by VLSI to build an architecture that is tailored to the computation involved in modeling the dynamics of musical instruments. The key to the efficiency of our machine differentiates it from other concurrent architectures; no processing cycles are used for communication; the processors are dedicated to arithmetic operations, and the connection strategy is preprogrammed to provide the communication for a specific task.

This chapter described two simple musical instrument models. Although the instrument models have been used to produce extremely high-quality timbres of certain instruments, they are certainly not capable of covering the entire range of timbres of the instruments. They are simplistic models of the physics of the musical instruments that they emulate, and are meant as examples and a basis for future study. The activity of modeling requires a great deal of careful study and will involve extensions and modifications to the models.

Results in modeling may lead to architectural changes. A possible change in the architecture may be to incorporate into its design the use of large amounts of temporary memory configured as delay lines of the type required for *scattering models*. Commercially available memory could be used in this application. Scattering models are efficient for emulating wave propagation in uniform mediums such as uniform air columns and for simulating physically large systems such as reverberant performance halls. The approach we have presented is more general but may be relatively expensive in some simple cases. A hybrid system could include the best of each approach.

Acknowledgments

I would like to acknowledge the many contributions by Carver Mead and Lounette Dyer to the music project at Caltech. Carver was my thesis advisor and the source of many of the ideas presented here. Lounette developed the software interface to our prototype system and did much of the work on developing parameters for the musical instrument models. She also generated many of the recorded sound examples. John Pierce and Max Mathews jointly stirred up interest in computer music at Caltech, and for that I am very grateful. Many thanks to Charles Smith, Carl York, and the System Development Foundation for funding this research and computer music research at other institutions.

References

[1] Fletcher, N. H., and Douglas, L. M. (1980). "Harmonic Generation in Organ Pipes, Recorders and Flutes." *Journal Acoustic Society* 68(3).

[2] Fletcher, N. H., and Thwaites S. (1983). "The Physics of Organ Pipes." *Scientific American* 248(1):84–93.

[3] Gordon, J. W. (1985). "System Architectures for Computer Music." *Computing Surveys*. 17(2): 191–233.

[4] Hiller, L., and Ruiz, P. (1971). "Synthesizing Musical Sounds by Solving the Wave Equation for Vibrating Objects: Parts I and II. *Journal Audio Engineering Society* 19(6): 462–470 and 19(7): 542–550.

[5] Lyon, R. F. (1976). "Two's Complement Pipeline Multipliers." *IEEE Transactions on Communications*, April, 418–425.

[6] Lyon, R. F. (1981). "A Bit-Serial VLSI Architecture Methodology for Signal Processing." *VLSI 81 Very Large Scale Integration* (Conf. Proc., Edinburgh, Scotland, John P. Gray, editor), Academic Press: New York.

[7] McIntyre, M. E., Schumacher, R. T., and Woodhouse J. (1983). "On the Oscillations of Musical Instruments." *Journal Acoustic Society America* 74(5).

[8] Mead, C. A., and Conway, L. A. (1980). *Introduction to VLSI Systems*, Chapter 9. Addison Wesley: Reading, MA.

[9] Mead, C. A., and Wawrzynek J. C. (1985). "A New Discipline for CMOS Design: An Architecture for Sound Synthesis." *1985 Chapel Hill Conference on Very Large Scale Integration*, edited by Henry Fuchs, Computer Science Press.

[10] Moore, J. L. (1970). "Acoustics of Bar Percussion Instruments." Ph.D. Dissertation, Music Department, Ohio State University.

[11] Morse, P. M. (1936). *Vibration and Sound*. McGraw-Hill: New York.

[12] Rayleigh, J. W. S. (1945). *The Theory of Sound*. Dover Publications: New York.

[13] Roads, C., and Strawn J. (1985). *Foundations of Computer Music*. MIT Press: Cambridge, MA.

[14] Smith, J. O. (1985). *Waveguide Digital Filters*. Internal Report, Center for Computer Research in Music and Acoustics (CCRMA), Dept. of Music, Stanford University, Stanford, CA.

[15] Wawrzynek, J. C. (1987). "VLSI Concurrent Computation for Music Synthesis." Doctoral Thesis, Department of Computer Science, Report No. 5247 : TR : 87 California Institute of Technology Pasadena, California, April.

[16] Wawrzynek, J. C., and Mead C. A. (1985). "A VLSI Architecture for Sound Synthesis." In *VLSI Signal Processing*, Denyer & Renshaw, Addison Wesley: Reading, MA, pp. 277–297.

[17] Weinreich, G. (1979). "The Coupled Motions of Piano Strings." *Scientific American* 240(1): 118–127.

11 Paradoxical Sounds

Jean-Claude Risset

11.1 General Description

Three examples of paradoxical sounds are presented. The first consists of Roger Shepard's [10] sequence of tones of ever ascending pitch. The second consists of an endlessly speeding-up beat made by Ken Knowlton at Bell Labs. The final example, lasting 40 sec, presents a sound with several paradoxical features. The pitch glides down the scale, yet it becomes gradually shriller, and it ends much higher than where it started. The sound is scanned by a pulse that constantly slows down, yet that is much faster at the end than at the beginning. Finally this sound, played in stereo, should also give the illusion of rotating in space.

These are only instances of the effects that can be obtained by exploiting both the precision of computer synthesis and the specificities of auditory perception. I have used this sound in the third movement of my piece "Moments Newtoniens" [5].

11.2 Technical Description

I first synthesized a sound going down the scale but ending higher in pitch at Bell Laboratories (1969); this was a generalization of the endless chromatic scale generated at Bell by Roger Shepard [10]. The rhythmical effect, which extends the endlessly speeding-up beat generated in Bell Labs by Ken Knowlton around 1974, was synthesized in 1975 in Marseille-Luminy ([6], [4]). The illusion of movement exploits the work of John Chowning [1], using the ratio of direct to reverberant sound as a cue for the distance of the source.

The sound was generated with the MUSIC V program [3]. The MUSIC V score is presented in the appendix; comments will explain the differences between the version of the program used to generate the sound and the original version as described in Max Mathews's book [3]—in particular, the original version did not include any reverberation unit generator).

I shall now present a detailed description of the construction of the sound example, so that it can be replicated if desired. The description examines in succession the recipe for the pitch effect, the rhythm effect, and the spatial effect. This description does not require knowledge of the

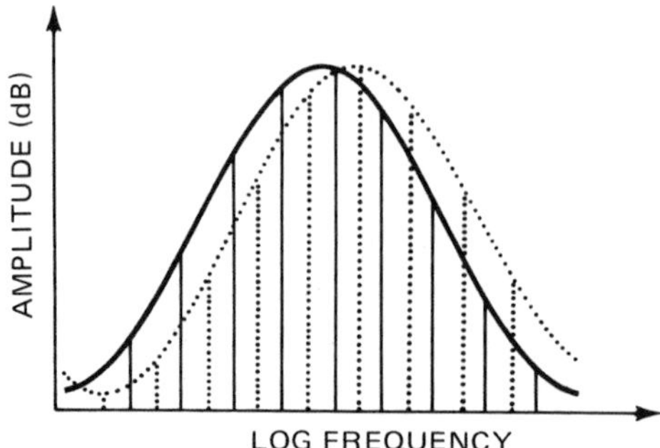

Figure 11.1
Spectrum of sound used to generate a pitch paradox.

MUSIC V program and its input language; yet it includes sections intended to clarify the MUSIC V implementation: these sections do require some knowledge of MUSIC V. It should be very easy to replicate the sound with any version of MUSIC V or with similar synthesis programs (like CMUSIC or MUSIC 11) provided they include the necessary units, such as reverberators. It is hoped that the general description is clear and complete enough to provide a detailed knowledge of the structure of the sound and to permit a replication with different tools, such as digital synthesizers. (The pitch and rhythm effects can be approximated by singers or instrumentalists.)

11.2.1 Pitch Effect

The pitch effect is obtained by adding together 10 sinusoidal components in octave relation, that is, with frequencies f, 2f, 4f, . . . , 256f. At the beginning of the sound, f = 31.25 Hz, so that the component frequencies (in Hz) are 31.25, 62.5, 125, 250, . . . , 8,000 Hz. The fundamental frequency goes down 2 octaves, following an exponentially decaying curve going down one octave every 20 sec. Thus all components glide down the pitch scale, maintaining their octave intervals. At the same time, the amplitude of each component is controlled separately, in order to move the peak of the spectrum toward the high frequencies. The way this is done is illustrated in figure 11.1, displaying the amplitude of the components as a function of their frequency. The frequency scale is logarithmic, so that components one octave apart are represented as equally spaced. The spectral envelope is a bell-shaped curve, with extreme values about 80 dB below the peak; the formula used to generate 512 samples of this curve is

$$F(x) = \exp\{\log(.008)[1 - \cos(6.28(x - 255.5)/511)]\}.$$

The solid lines show the components at the beginning of the sound; the dotted lines show them 10 sec later: all components have then gone down in frequency by half an octave, while the spectral envelope has moved upward by about 1 octave. (As represented in the figure, the spectral envelope, as it moves "upward," does not actually extend above 8,000 Hz: the portion that would be above 8,000 Hz, if the transformation were a mere translation, is actually brought back near the origin.) Thus all 10 components glide down 2 octaves, staying at octave intervals, while the peak of the distribution goes up by about 4 octaves.

Notes on the MUSIC V Implementation of the Pitch Effect. The sound structure described above is realized in instrument #2 much like example #514 of my sound catalog [5]. The amplitudes of the 10 components are controlled by function F5 in the first oscillator of instrument #2, and their frequencies are controlled by function F6 in the second oscillator. Each frequency component corresponds to a note played on this instrument. For these notes, the increment (specified in P7) for the amplitude-controlling oscillator is the same for all components, and it corresponds to a period of 66 sec. However, the amplitudes of the components are different because the initial "sums," specified in P8 (that is, the initial abscissa of the table lookup of function F5) are, respectively, $0, 511/10, 2 \cdot 511/10, \ldots, 9 \cdot 511/12$ —the function length is 511 samples: thus the amplitudes are as in figure 11.1, and F5 corresponds to the bell-shaped spectral envelope. Similarly, the increment for the frequency-controlling oscillator (specified in P10) is the same for all components, corresponding to a period of 200 sec, and the initial sums are also $0, 511/10, 2 \cdot 511/10, \ldots, 9 \cdot 511/10$. Since the frequency-controlling function F6 corresponds to an exponential descent of 10 octaves, the components go down one octave in 20 sec, while staying at octave intervals. The contributions of the components are added into box B6, which has to be zeroed, since only B1 and B2 are zeroed automatically; this is done by instrument #1, which also zeroes B7 and B8 (see below).

11.2.2 Rhythm Effect

The gliding sound described above is essentially constant in amplitude: the rhythm effect is realized by modulating the amplitude of the sound by recurring percussive envelopes, which adds a rhythmical beat. The rhythm paradox is realized much like the pitch paradox; several beats are superimposed (5 in this example), which are also in "rhythmical octave" relation —that is, their respective repetition rates are r, $2r$, $4r$, $8r$, and $16r$. At the beginning of the sound, $r = 1.25$ Hz, so that the number of beats per second are respectively 1.25, 2.5, 5, 10, and 20 for each of the 5 simultaneous beats. Initially the slowest beats are dominant in amplitude. During the example, r diminishes regularly—it is divided by 8 in 40 sec; meanwhile, the peak of the amplitude distribution is a broad bell-shaped curve, to ensure a gradual passage from one dominant beat to one with a repetition rate twice as fast. The peak shifts to a component beating twice as fast in less time than it takes for r to be divided by 2: in this example, it takes 13 sec for the fundamental rate to slow down by a factor of 2, whereas it takes only about 6.5 sec for the amplitude distribution to move from one component to the one which is twice as fast. Thus, while the beats are all slowing down, faster beats become dominant; during the 40 sec of sound, r is slowed down by a factor of 4, yet at the end the dominant beat is about 4 times faster than at the beginning.

Notes on MUSIC V Implementation of the Rhythm Effect. The rhythm effect is implemented in instrument #3, which modulates in amplitude the outputs of instrument #2 (which have been added into I/O box B6) by a beat that changes in speed and amplitude. The beat corresponds to a recurring amplitude envelope specified by function F4; its maximum amplitude is controlled by function F2—a smooth bell-like curve—and its rate is controlled by function F3, which is a decaying exponential going from 1 to 1/32. Each rhythm component corresponds to a note played on instrument #3. Here again, the increments, specified in P8, for the oscillator controlling the amplitude, are the same for all components: they correspond to a period of 36 sec; but the components have different initial "sum" values, specified in P10 as 0, 51/5, $2 \cdot 511/5, \ldots, 4 \cdot 511/5$. Similarly the increments, specified in P9, for the oscillator controlling the repetition rate are the same for all components, corresponding to a period of 66 sec, also with initial "sum" values, specified in P1, of 0, 511/5, $2 \cdot 511/5, \ldots,$ $4 \cdot 511/5$. Function F9 is a general envelope that just ensures a smooth beginning and end of the 40-sec sound. The beats are added into I/O block B7 (which is initially zeroed by instrument 1). The remainder of instrument #3 is used to implement the spatial effect (see below).

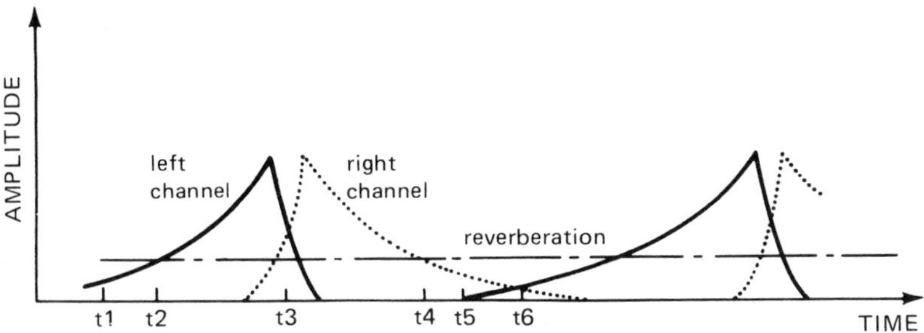

Figure 11.2
Amplitude and reverberation functions used to control apparent spatial location of sound.

11.2.3 Spatial Effect

The combined pitch and rhythm effects yield a mono sound. A portion of this sound (15% of the amplitude) is sent to a simulated reverberator; the sound itself is fed in equal proportion to a left and to a right channel in order to manufacture a stereo sound. Both channels are then modulated in amplitude by two different functions of time, as shown in figure 11.2. Function F10, drawn with a continuous line, controls the amplitude of the direct sound in the left channel, and F11, drawn with a dotted line, controls the amplitude of the direct sound in the right channel. The line shown in figure 11.2 parallel to the time axis represents the level of the reverberated sound, which is approximately constant (it is added in equal proportions to the left and to the right channel). At time t1 (figure 11.2), the sound comes from the left channel only; its level is below the level of the reverberated sound, so the sound seems to come from a source situated far away on the left side [1]. Then the direct sound increases: at time t2, it exceeds the reverberated sound level, and it gives the impression of originating from a source which is closer and closer. Around time t3, the level of the sound from the left channel abruptly decreases, and conversely the level of the sound from the right channel abruptly increases: this gives the impression that the source of sound rapidly moves from left to right, at a speed that depends upon the slopes of the left and right channel envelopes. Later, at time t4, the level of the direct sound in the right channel diminishes below that of the reverberated sound. At time t5, some direct sound begins to originate from the left channel again, and it starts to exceed the level of the direct sound from the right channel at time t6: thus the sound source seems to move from right to left, but far away, because the level of the direct sound in both channels is far below that of the reverberated sound. Thus the illusory movement resembles the trajectory described in figure 11.3. This illusory rotation accelerates from 1 cycle in 5 sec at the beginning to 2 cycles per second at the end.

The reverberators use a "colorless" scheme, as described by Schroeder and Logan [9]. Several reverberators are used with different delays (see [8] and [1]). The delays used here correspond to 1389, 887, 619, 443, and 281 samples; since the sampling rate used in the example is 16,000 samples per second, the values of these delays are 0.0868, 0.0554, 0.0386, 0.0277, and 0.0175 sec. The corresponding amplitudes are .75, .72, .691, .657, and .662. However, the parameters of the reverberation are not critical. The reverberation is applied to the sound prior to its modulation by the envelopes represented in figure 11.2.

Notes on the MUSIC V Implementation of the Spatial Control. In instrument #3, B7 is multiplied by V2, set to .15: the result is stored in B8, for subsequent reverberation by instrument #50. Function F8 controls the acceleration of the spatial cycle from .2 to 2 cycles per second (the maximum value of 2 Hz is set in P12). The varying rate of the spatial cycle is stored in B9. F10 controls the amplitude of the left channel and F11 that of the right channel.

The reverberation is implemented in instrument #50. It comprises 5 reverberators, each of which has delays as specified above (for instance, in the first reverberator, variables V100 to V1379 are reserved to store the 1,389 samples necessary for the first delay). The instrument is turned on during the entire duration of the example.

With the design of instrument #3 used here, all rhythmic components could be spatially controlled at different rates—but the same spatial trajectory is used for all in this example.

Appendix: MUSIC V Score

```
COMMENT UP DOWN SLOWER FASTER LUMINY WITH
ACCELERATING ROTATION;
COMMENT SAMPLING RATE 16000 HZ OR MORE, STEREO;
SIA 0 4 16000; SIA 0 8 1;
COM**************************************;
```

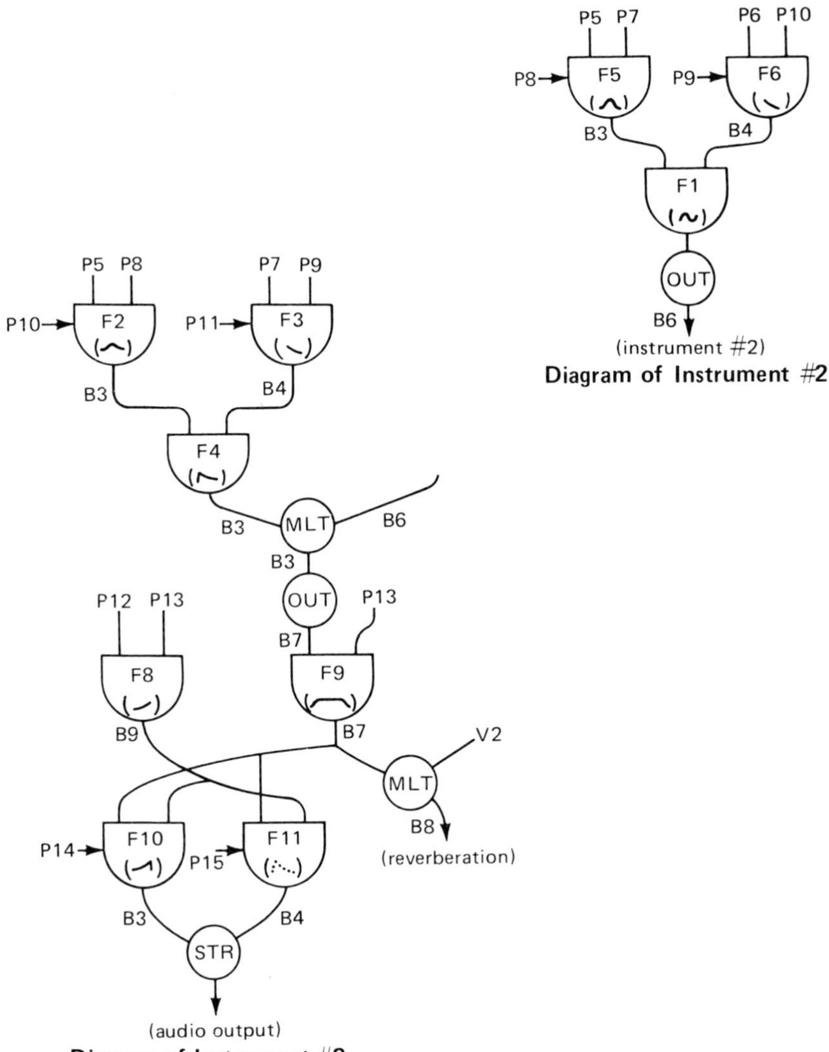

Figure 11.3
Diagram of computer instruments used to produce examples.

```
COM INSTRUMENT DEFINITIONS;
COM A DIAGRAM OF INSTRUMENTS 2 AND 3 IS GIVEN IN
FIG.4;

COM INSTRUMENT 1 TO ZERO I-0 BOXES B6, B7, B8;
INS 0 2; AD2 P5 P6 B6; AD2 P5 P6 B6; AD2 P5 P6 B6; END;

COM INSTRUMENT 2 FOR PITCH EFFECT;
INS 0 2; IOS P5 P7 B3 F5 P8; IOS P6 P10 B4 F6 P9;
IOS B3 B4 B5 F1 P25; OUT B5 B6; END;

COM INSTRUMENT 3 FOR RHYTHM AND SPATIAL EFFECT;
COM RHYTHM;
INS 0 3; IOS P5 P8 B3 F2 P10; IOS P7 P9 B4 F3 P11;
IOS B3 B4 B3 F4 P25;
COM COMBINATION WITH INSTRUMENT 2 AND ENVELOPE;
MLT B3 B6 B3; OUT B3 B7; IOS B7 P13 B7 F9 P24;
COM FEED REVERBERATORS;
MLT B7 V2 B8;
COM ACCELERATING ROTATION IN STEREO;
IOS P12 P13 B9 F8 P16;
IOS B7 B9 B3 F10 P14; IOS B7 B9 B4 F11 P15;
STR B3 B4 B1; END;

COM INSTRUMENT 50 FOR REVERBERATION;
INS 0 50;
RV1 B7 V100   V11379 V90 B7 P10;
RV1 B7 V1380 V2267   V91 B7 P11;
RV1 B7 V2268 V2887   V92 B7 P12;
RV1 B7 V2888 V3331   V93 B7 P13;
RV1 B7 V3332 V3613   V94 B7 P14;
STR B7 B7 B1; END;
COM************************;

COM PROPORTION OF REVERBERATION;
SV3 0 2 .15;
COM WEIGHTS OF REVERBERATORS;
SV3 00 90 .75 .72 .691 .657 .662;
COM****************************;

COM FUNCTION DEFINITIONS;
COM SINE WAVE;
```

```
GEN 0 2 1 1 1;
COM DISTRIBUTION OF REPETITION RATES: BELL-SHAPED
FUNCTION;
GEN 0 10 2 1;
COM EXPONENTIAL DECAY 1 TO 2** (-5);
GEN 0 7 3  -5;

COM PERCUSSIVE ENVELOPE;
COM GEN9 IS SIMILAR TO GEN1 EXCEPT THE
INTERPOLATION BETWEEN POINTS IS EXPONENTIAL
INSTEAD OF LINEAR;
GEN 0 9 44 .001 0 1 10 .001 511;
COM BELL-SHAPED SPECTRAL ENVELOPE;
GEN 0 7 5 0;
COM EXPONENTIAL DECAY 1 TO 2** (-10);
GEN 0 7 6  -10;
COM CONTROL OF BEAT ACCELERATION;
GEN 0 9 8 .1 1 .2 70 1 512;
COM GENERAL ENVELOPE;
GEN 0 9 9 .0001 1 1 10 1 495 .1 506 .0001 511
COM**********************************;

COM CONVERSION FOR P FIELDS; GENERAL CONVERT OF
CATALOG;
SV2 0 3 1;
COM FOR INSTRUMENT 2 P6 IN HZ P7 P10 IN S;
SV2 0 20 3 6  -7  -10;
COM FOR INSTRUMENT 3 P6 P7 P12 IN HZ P8 P9 P13 IN S;
SV2 0 30 6 6 7 12  -8  -9  -13;
COM ENVELOPES FOR SPATIAL EFFECT AS IN FIG 3;
GEN 0 1 10 .15 0 .3 200 1 300  0 310 0 400 .15 511;
GEN 0 1 11  0   0  0 290 1 300 .3 400 0 511;
COM NOTES;

COM THE ZEROING INSTRUMENT MUST BE PLAYED FIRST;
NOT 1 1 42 0;

NOT 1 2 40 200 8000 66     0       0   200;
NOT 1 2 40 200 8000 66   51.1    51.1 200;
NOT 1 2 40 200 8000 66 102.2 102.2 200;
NOT 1 2 40 200 8000 66 153.3 153.3 200;
```

```
NOT 1 2 40 200 8000 66 204.4 204.4 200;
NOT 1 2 40 200 8000 66 255.5 255.5 200;
NOT 1 2 40 200 8000 66 306.6 306.6 200;
NOT 1 2 40 200 8000 66 357.7 357.7 200;
NOT 1 2 40 200 8000 66 408.8 408.8 200;
NOT 1 2 40 200 8000 66 459.9 459.9 200;
NOT 1 3 40 1 0 20 36 66    0      0   2 40 300 310;
NOT 1 3 40 1 0 20 36 66 102.2 102.2 2 40 300 310;
NOT 1 3 40 1 0 20 36 66 204.4 204.4 2 40 300 310;
NOT 1 3 40 1 0 20 36 66 306.6 306.6 2 40 300 310;
NOT 1 3 40 1 0 20 36 66 408.8 408.8 2 40 300 310;

COM THE REVERBERATION INSTRUMENT MUST BE
PLAYED LAST;
NOT 1 50 42;

COM*********TERMINATION*****************;
TER 43;
COM***********END OF MUSIC V SCORE*******;
```

References

[1] J. M. Chowning (1971). The simulation of moving sound sources. *Journal of the Audio Engineering Society* 19, 2–6. (Reprinted in *Computer Music Journal* 1(3) (1977), 48–52.)

[2] C. Dodge and T. A. Jerse (1985). *Computer Music: Synthesis, Composition and Performance*. Schirmer books, New York.

[3] M. V. Mathews (1969). *The Technology of Computer Music*. MIT Press, Cambridge, Mass.

[4] J. R. Pierce (1983). *The Science of Musical Sound* (*with Sound Examples*). Freeman, New York.

[5] J. C. Risset (1969). An introductory catalog of computer synthesized sounds (with sound examples). Bell Laboratories, Murray Hill, N.J.

[6] J. C. Risset (1977). Paradoxes de hauteur (with sound examples). IRCAM Report no. 10, Paris.

[7] J. C. Risset (1979). Mutations: a 33 rpm L.P. record including "Trois moments newtoniens." Collection INA-GRM (distributed by Harmonia Mundi). Cf. also compact disc INA C 1003.

[8] M. R. Schroeder (1962). Natural sounding artificial reverberation. *Journal of the Audio Engineering Society* 10, 219–233.

[9] M. R. Schroeder and B. F. Logan (1961). Colorless artificial reverberation. *Journal of the Audio Engineering Society* 9, 192.

[10] R. N. Shepard (1964). Circularity in judgments of relative pitch. *Journal of the Acoustical Society of America* 36, 2346–2353.

12 Additive Synthesis of Inharmonic Tones

Jean-Claude Risset

12.1 Introduction

The following examples present inharmonic tones produced by additive synthesis. The first example demonstrates the additive synthesis process for a single tone. The second example presents the use of inharmonic tones in a musical context.

12.2 Instances of Additive Synthesis of Inharmonic Tones

The sound example consists of four successive inharmonic tones; each tone lasts 10 sec. Successive tones are separated by a silence of 1 sec.

All four tones use sine wave components (partials) with frequency ratios as follows: .56, .92, 1.19, 1.71, 2, 2.74, 3, 3.76, and 4.07. (This is close to, yet different from, the frequency ratios that are supposed to be appropriate for bell tones, i.e., .5, 1, 1.2, 1.5, and 2.) The respective amplitudes of the components can be read in the score. This example, similar to example #430 of my 1969 sound catalog [1], has been synthesized at CCRMA, Stanford, with the SAMBOX synthesizer. The score for the example is presented here; it uses the PLA input language [2], but the comments should make it easy to read any parameter from the score (except the envelope, described below).

In the first tone, all the frequency components decay synchronously. This gives a very unnatural sound.

In the second tone, the higher the frequency of a component, the faster its decay. Since each component is generated as a separate "note," this is done very simply by shortening the duration of the components above the lowest one (see figure 12.1). This gives a much more natural decay. In most natural sounds, the higher frequency components tend to decay more rapidly than the lower frequency ones, which can be formulated as a principle—the higher, the shorter. Because with additive synthesis one has complete control of the decay rates of all components individually, one can add interest to the computer timbres by occasionally violating the principle.

In the third tone, the durations of the components are as in the second, but some of the partials are split into two components of slightly different frequencies. For example the two lowest partials are split into components 1 Hz apart. This causes a beat, or periodic amplitude modulation, recurring

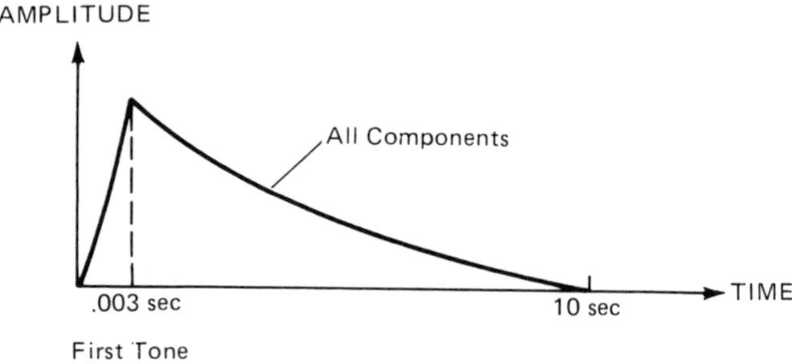

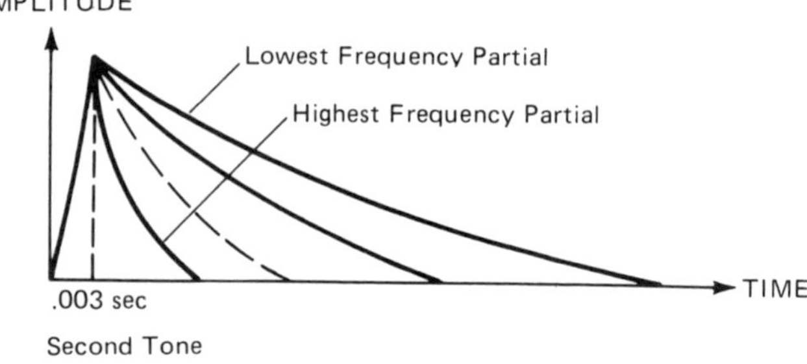

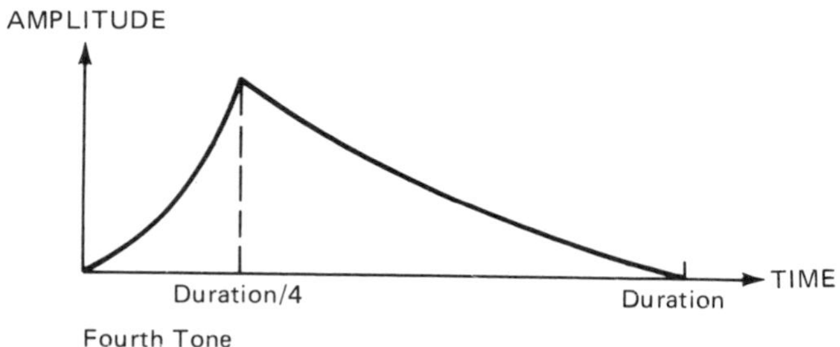

Figure 12.1
Sketch of the envelopes of components used for additive synthesis of inharmonic tones.

Table 12.1
Score for examples of additive synthesis of inharmonic tones

```
Require PARAMS. HDR[PLA, MUS]:          /* Must begin all Pla input files; */
Header: "FUNC EXAMP. FUN";              /* Tells sambox where to get functions */
Voice Add;                              /* Use the ADD instrument */
    BEGIN                               /* Signals start of information for ADD */
  I_only:
    Begin
      Mynotenum ← 42;
    End;
EXPONENTIAL_MODE ← TRUE;                /* Attacks and decays are exponential */
  Dur ← [10, 10, 10, 10, 10,            /* Durations of the frequency compon- */
         10, 10, 10, 10,                /* ents; for the first tone */
         10, 7.5, 5, 4.5, 4, 3,         /* for the second tone: the lower */
         1.5, 1, .7,                    /* the frequency, the longer the */
                                        /* duration */
         10, 9, 7.5, 6.5, 5,            /* for the third tone */
         4.5, 4, 3, 2.5, 1.5
         1, .7,
         10, 9, 7.5, 6.5, 5,            /* for the fourth tone */
         4.5, 4, 3, 2.5, 1.5,
         1, .7];
         AmpAt ← .003;                  /* For notes 1 to 3, attack time 3 ms,
                                           exponential decay */
         If Mynotenum < 12 then         /* For note 4, attack lasts a quarter */
         AmpAt ← Dur * .25;             /* of the note duration */
         Ampdc ← (Dur − .1 − AmpAt);
  beg ← beg + [2, 0, 0, 0,              /* Start of first tone */
           0, 0, 0, 0, 0,
           11, 0, 0, 0,                 /* Start of second tone */
           0, 0, 0, 0, 0                /* 11 seconds later */
           11, 0, 0, 0, 0               /* Start of third tone */
           0, 0, 0, 0, 0, 0             /* 11 seconds later */
           11, 0, 0, 0, 0, 0,           /* Start of fourth tone */
           0, 0, 0, 0, 0, 0];           /* 11 seconds later */
  Pitcho ← [224.5, 368.5,               /* Frequencies in Hz for the */
           476, 684, 800,               /* components of the first tone */
           1096, 1200,
           1504, 1628,
           224.5, 368.5,                /* Frequencies for second tone */
           476, 684, 800,               /* (same as first) */
           1096, 1200,
           1504, 1628,
           224, 225, 368,               /* Frequencies for third tone */
           369, 476, 680,               /* (extra beating components) */
           800, 1096, 1099.7,
           1200, 1504, 1628,
```

Table 12.1 (continued)

```
              224, 225, 368, 369,          /* Frequencies for fourth tone */
              476, 680, 800, 1096,         /* (same as third) */
              1099.7, 1200, 1504,
              1628];
Amp ← [.1, .1, .1, .05, .05, .04,          /* Relative component amplitudes */
          .04, .03, .04,                    /* for first tone */
          .1, .1, .1, .05, .05, .04,        /* id. for second tone */
          .04, .03, .04,
          .05, .05, .05, .05, .1,           /* id. for third tone */
          .05, .05, .04, .04, .04,
          .03, .04,
          .05, .05, .054, .046, .1,         /* id. for fourth */
          .05, .05, .04, .04, .04,
          .03, .04] * 2;
  AmpFun ← "TRAP";                          /* Name of amplitude envelope:
                                               exponential; attacks and decays */
Syntho ← "SINE";                            /* sine wave components */
  End;
```

here every second. There is also a faster beat produced by two higher components—the beat rate corresponds to the difference between the frequencies of two close components. Such beats are important to impart life and warmth to the sound.

In the fourth tone, the frequencies and the durations are as in the third tone, but this time the envelope (i.e., the amplitude as a function of time) is changed to a nonpercussive envelope. The buildup of each component now takes a quarter of the duration instead of 3 msec as in tones 1 to 3. Hence the various components reach their peak amplitude at different times; thus, just as white light can be separated into its colored components by a prism, the tone components can be heard building up in succession out of a fluid texture, instead of fusing into a single percussive tone.

12.3 Inharmonic Tones and Transformations in a Musical Context

This example is in two parts. The first part consists of inharmonic tones synthesized according to the process exemplified by the third tone of the simple example above: it evokes music played on gongs and bells.

The second part consists of exactly the same components—the same frequencies and same durations—as the first part, except that the envelope has been changed to a nonpercussive envelope, as in tone 4 in the example above. Hence the bell-like tones are changed into fluid textures—while they retain the same underlying harmonic pattern. The passage from the first part to the second part thus involves an intimate transformation that keeps the harmonic content invariant but changes the curve that determines the time behavior of the components. In the first part the listener tends to perceive individual objects—"bells"—whereas in the second part, the fusion of partials into individual objects is hindered by the asynchronous envelopes, which helps one hear out the partials in succession. This kind of transformation was used extensively in my piece "Inharmonique" [3]. See table 12.1.

References

[1] J. C. Risset (1969). An introductory catalog of computer-synthesized sounds. Bell Laboratories, Murray Hill, N.J.

[2] W. Schottstaedt (1983). PLA: a composer's idea of a language. *Computer Music Journal* 7(1), 11–20 (1983).

[3] D. Lorrain (1980). Analyse de la bande d'Inharmonique. Rapport IRCAM no. 26, Paris. "Inharmonique" is included in the compact disc INA C 1003, distributed by Harmonia Mundi.

13 The Bohlen-Pierce Scale

Max V. Mathews and John R. Pierce

13.1 Introduction

The diatonic scale has provided a basis for most Western music since the seventeenth century. Harmonies based on major and minor scales, chord progressions, keys, cadences, and modulations have provided a rich and perceptible musical language that has been easily transmitted to other cultures.

Some other musical material appears not to be so easily perceptible or transmittable. The whole-tone scale has had a narrower acceptance than the diatonic scale, and so have other scales. The tone rows of 12-tone or serial music and their inversions and retrogrades may be another example.

With the advent of digital computers, there is much greater freedom in selecting musical systems and scales. One can be free of the constraints of traditional musical instruments and can manipulate the overtone structure of the sounds used. Is it possible that one might devise an easily learnable and attractive scale, different from the diatonic scale and yet exhibiting some of its acoustic and structural properties?

The major triad provides the harmonic basis for the diatonic scale. The frequencies of the just scale can be derived from the 4 : 5 : 6 frequency ratios of the notes of the major triad.

Here we discuss a scale called the BP or Bohlen-Pierce scale. This scale is based on chords different from the major and minor triads of the diatonic scale, yet the chords and the scale have much of the order and acoustical effect of the diatonic scale.

13.2 Intonation Sensitivity

How can we evaluate a new chord and assess its perceptibility as the harmonic basis of a scale? Roberts and Mathews [3] proposed *intonation sensitivity* as a useful measure. Intonation sensitivity is determined by how the preference for a chord varies with the tuning, or mistuning, of the center note. The study showed that the major triad, with frequency ratios 4 : 5 : 6, has a clear pattern of intonation sensitivity, and that two nontraditional chords, with frequency ratios 3 : 5 : 7 and 5 : 7 : 9, have a very similar intonation sensitivity.

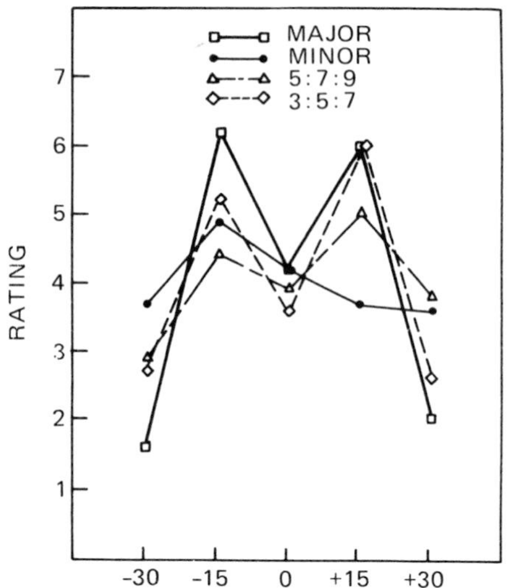

Figure 13.1
Ratings of triads as a function of the tuning of the middle note.

As shown in figure 13.1, Roberts and Mathews found that some subjects prefer the third mistuned by around 15 cents in the major triad (as in equal temperament). These same subjects prefer the middle tone of th 3 : 5 : 7 and the 5 : 7 : 9 chords mistuned by the same amount. Further, those who prefer just intonation in the major triad also prefer just intonation in the new chords.

We can note from figure 13.1 that 3 : 5 : 7 and 5 : 7 : 9 chords are more like diatonic major triads in the way that preference varies with tuning than diatonic minor triads are.

It is clear from the experiments of Roberts and Mathews that the 3 : 5 : 7 and 5 : 7 : 9 chords of the BP scale are chords in their intonation sensitivity. This might be argued from the fact that, as in the diatonic major triad, the frequencies are in the ratio of small ascending whole numbers. It is good, however, to have experimental evidence.

13.3 Scales with 3 : 5 : 7 and 5 : 7 : 9 Chords

Four scales using 3 : 5 : 7 and 5 : 7 : 9 chords were proposed by Mathews, Roberts, and Pierce [2]. The scale then described as the Pierce 3579b scale

Table 13.1[a]

Step	Frequency ratio	Just ratio	Error cents	Closest diatonic ratio	Difference cents
0	1	1	0	1	0
1	1.08818				
2	1.18414			6/5	−22.5
3	1.28856	9/7	+3.7	5/4	+51.9
4	1.40219	7/5	+2.6		
5	1.52583			3/2	+29.0
6	1.66038	5/3	−6.4	5/3	−6.4
7	1.80681	9/5	+6.4		
8	1.96613			2	−28.4
9	2.13591				
10	2.32818	7/3	−3.7		
11	2.53348			5/2	+22.5
12	2.75689				
13	3	3	0	3	0

a. The right two columns list some exact diatonic ratios and accidental approximations to them. 6/5 is a minor third, 5/4 a major third, 3/2 a fifth, 5/3 (an octave less minor third) a sixth, 2 the octave, 5/2 an octave plus a major third, and 3 an octave plus a fifth.

appears to us to be musically the most interesting. We now refer to this as the Bohlen-Pierce, or BP, scale. We found that Bohlen [1] had proposed this scale earlier on the basis of combination tones.

The tones used in the BP scale are selected from a chromatic BP scale in such a way as to approximate the frequency ratios 3 : 5 : 7 : 9. The tones of this chromatic scale are separated by the 13th root of 3. Table 13.1 shows that all frequency ratios are approximated to 6.4 cents or better.

We shall note from table 13.1 that the BP chromatic scale also approximates a number of diatonic intervals, some quite poorly. This may have a distracting effect in listening to BP scales and music, especially for musicians.

Figure 13.2 is a representation of the structure of the BP tempered scale. A circle, representing a 3-to-1 frequency ratio, is divided into 13 equal steps that are the semitones of the BP chromatic scale. These are designated 0, 1, . . . , 12. The 9 tones of the BP scale, designated I, II, . . . , IX, are selected from among the 13 steps. The tenth tone of the scale. I′, is analogous to the octave in the diatonic scale. We call it the tritave (for three) to distinguish it from the traditional octave with its 2-to-1 frequency ratio.

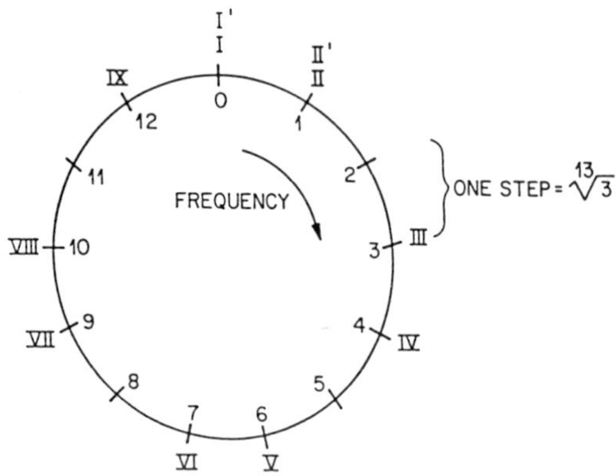

MAJOR CHORDS	MINOR CHORDS
I V VIII	I IV VIII
III VII I'	III VI I'
IV VIII II'	V VIII III'
V IX III'	VII I' V'
VI I' IV'	VIII II' VI'
VIII III' VI'	IX III VII'

Figure 13.2
Representation of the structure of the Bohlen-Pierce scale.

The 2-to-1 octave corresponds to the ratio of the frequency of the first overtone (the second harmonic) to that of the fundamental. The BP scale is intended for use with tones with odd harmonics only. In this case the ratio of the frequency of first overtone (the *third* harmonic) to the fundamental is 3 to 1, the tritave.

We shall note also that for tones with both even and odd harmonics, the octave is musically empty in the sense that if we add a tone an octave above a sounding tone, we add no new frequency components; the harmonics of the added tone are all present in the tone already sounding.

This is not so if the tones have odd harmonics only, for by adding a tone an octave up we add even harmonics of the tone already sounding. But if we add a tone whose fundamental frequency is 3 times (a tritave above) the sounding tone, the tone added will add no new frequency components.

Hence, for tones with odd harmonics only, the tritave plays the role that the octave does for tones with both even and ood harmonics.

13.4 Triads

The 3 : 5 : 7 chord, or major triad of the BP scale, is approximated by a lower interval of 6 semitones and an upper interval of 4 semitones. In the minor triad of the scale the intervals are reversed, to give 4 semitones in the lower interval and 6 in the upper. The 5 : 7 : 9 chord appears as the first inversion of the 3 : 5 : 7 chord.

The positions of the major and minor triads which fall inside a given key are indicated in figure 13.2. There are 6 major traids and 6 minor traids. There is neither a major nor a minor triad on tone II of the scale. All scale tones are in both a major triad and minor triad. Hence, any scale tone can be harmonized by using either a major or a minor chord, in the root position or suitably inverted.

13.5 Modulation

The tonic can be positioned at any one of the 13 semitones that fall in a tritave, thus allowing 13 possible keys. Different keys share various numbers of notes. In particular, each key can modulate to two adjacent keys by changing a single note.

Following the notation of figure 13.2, moving the II note up by one semitone will cause the new tonic to rise to the III note of the original scale (note 3 of the chromatic scale). We shall call this third position the dominant and the corresponding modulation a movement into the dominant key. Moving the IX tone down by one semitone will cause the tonic to fall to the VIII note of the original scale (semitone 10 of the chromatic scale). We shall call this VIII position the subdominant and call the corresponding modulation a change into the subdominant key. A major chord begins on both the dominant and the subdominant.

13.6 Just Scale

By choosing an overlapping set of four major chords we can produce a just version of the BP scale, as shown in figure 13.3. The four chords chosen were V, III, VI, and IV. Each chord contains one note of each of its neighbors. Although it is possible to generate the BP scale using chords

JUST SCALE

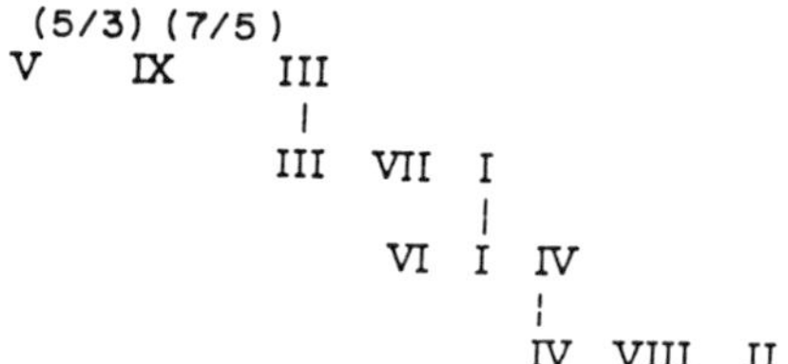

Figure 13.3
Diagram to show how a just Bohlen-Pierce scale may be constructed from four overlapping 3 : 5 :7 chords.

other than those given above, the resulting scales do not differ much from that shown here.

13.7 Consonance Judgments

We felt it appropriate to investigate the consonance of various triads of the BP scale. In addition to the triads that lie in one key, one can play chromatic triads which are arbitrary combinations of the 13 tones of the chromatic scale. Exactly 78 triads can be formed that span no more than one tritave.

Twelve musicians and twelve untrained listeners made judgments of consonance of these chords. Subjects judged consonance using a 7-point scale, where 7 was designated as very consonant and 1 as very dissonant.

The stimuli used had odd-numbered harmonics 1, 3, 5, 7, and 9. The amplitudes were, respectively, 1, $-.35$, $-.19$, .125, and $-.089$. The negative (180° phase) components were chosen to reduce the peak factor.

The principal results of the study are

a. A wide range of perceived consonance is observed between the most consonant and the most dissonant chords. Thus, consonance is a salient property of chords.

b. The strongest factor explaining the dissonance of a chord is the presence of an interval of a semitone.

c. Major and minor chords are relatively consonant compared to average chords.

Table 13.2
Mean consonance ratings for the 8 most consonant and the 8 most dissonant chords for the two groups of listeners and for the major and minor triads

Most consonant				Most dissonant			
Musicians		Untrained		Musicians		Untrained	
Chord	Mean	Chord	Mean	Chord	Mean	Chord	Mean
0, 11, 13	5.31	0, 7, 10	4.97	0, 1, 2	1.61	0, 1, 2	2.47
0, 2, 5	5.25	0, 2, 11	4.94	0, 11, 12	1.67	0, 1, 3	2.64
0, 5, 11	5.22	0, 7, 13	4.89	0, 12, 13	1.89	0, 12, 13	2.75
0, 6, 8	5.17	0, 6, 13	4.83	0, 9, 10	1.89	0, 2, 3	2.81
0, 2, 8	5.14	0, 8, 11	4.81	0, 10, 11	1.94	0, 9, 10	3.06
0, 3, 5	5.03	0, 4, 7	4.78	0, 8, 9	2.00	0, 4, 5	3.06
0, 3, 13	5.11	0, 7, 9	4.78	0, 1, 9	2.06	0, 8, 9	3.11
0, 7, 11	5.08	0, 6, 10	4.75	0, 1, 13	2.22	0,.11, 12	3.11
0, 6, 10	4.39	0, 6, 10	4.75	(major triad)			
0, 4, 10	4.08	0, 4, 10	4.67	(minor triad)			

d. A "critical dissonance model" fits much of the data. (The critical dissonance model will not be discussed here.)

Table 13.2 gives the mean consonance ratings for the 8 most consonant and the 8 most dissonant chords for each group of listeners, and also the ratings for the major and the minor triads.

The major triad does not appear among the chords judged most consonant by trained musicians.

We should note that among the 8 chords rated most consonant by musicians, in the first 5 both intervals are approximately diatonic intervals (see table 13.1). It seems possible that in listening to BP chords and the BP scale, musicians are much influenced by their training with and listening to the diatonic scale—and by their lack of training with or listening to the BP scale.

13.8 Similarity of Chords; Inversions

An experiment was carried out in which musicians and nonmusicians rated the similarity of major and minor triads, both diatonic triads and BP triads. The triads used had various roots; the root position and the first and second inversions were included.

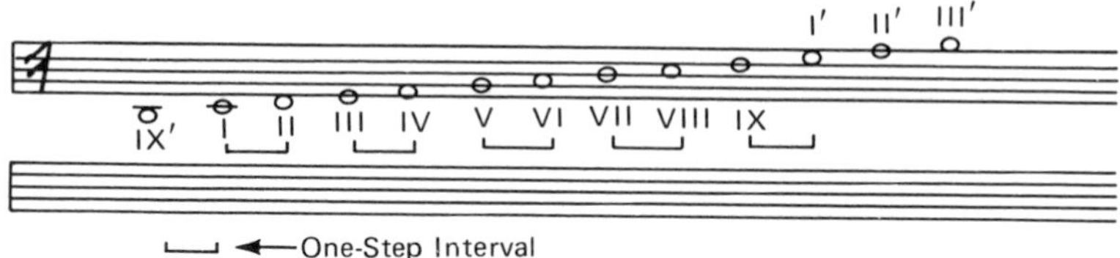

Figure 13.4
Notation for the Bohlen-Pierce scale.

For both musicians and nonmusicians the similarity of BP chords reflected chiefly the pitch height. Chords were rated as very similar if their lowest tones were the same.

The ratings of the nonmusicians for diatonic triads was similar; chords were judged as similar if they had similar pitch heights, and as very similar if they had common lowest tones.

The ratings of musicians were different. Chords in the root position and in the first and second inversions were rated as very similar.

The results of these similarity judgments seem clear. When listeners have not been taught what to listen for, they abstract information mainly about pitch height. As a result of training with a particular scale system (the diatonic scale) they are able to recognize and take into account other information. It seems reasonable that training with the BP scale would make it possible for listeners to recognize and respond to its structure, just as trained musicians recognize and respond to the structure of the diatonic scale and diatonic chords.

13.9 Compositions in the BP Scale

While there is no "standard" notation for the BP scale, the notation shown in figure 13.4 has been used in the compositions of Alyson Reeves.

Various people have composed short pieces using the BP scale. These include Alyson Reeves and Jon Appleton, some of whose pieces are included in the accompanying compact disk. The musical interest of these compositions must be judged by the listener.

It appears to us that it is possible to produce clear and memorable melodies in the BP scale. Counterpoint sounds all right. Chordal passages sound like harmony, but without any great tension or sense of resolution.

13.10 Summary and Conclusions

We have explored a 9-tone scale that is used with tones having odd partials only. The 3 : 5 : 7 triad on which this scale is based has an intonation sensitivity more like that of the 4 : 5 : 6 major triad of the diatonic scale than does the diatonic minor triad.

The scale has 9 tones. In the equal-tempered version, these are 9 of 13 chromatic tones. The structure of the scale resembles that of the diatonic scale in allowing analogs of major and minor triads on various tones of the scale, and in shifting key repeatedly by flatting or sharping tones one at a time.

In ratings of consonance and of chord similarity, trained musicians give somewhat different judgments than do nonmusicians. This suggests that ear training with the BP scale might lead listeners to make better distinctions and evaluations based on the structure of the scale and its chords.

A small number of short pieces have been composed using the scale.

References

[1] H. Bohlen, "13 Tonstufen in der Duodezeme," *Acoustica* 39, 76–86 (1978).

[2] M. V. Mathews, L. A. Roberts, and J. R. Pierce, "Four new scales based on nonsuccessive-integer-ratio chords," *J. Acoust. Soc. Amer.* 75, S10(A) (1984).

[3] L. A. Roberts and M. V. Mathews, "Intonation sensitivity for traditional and non-traditional chords," *J. Acoust. Soc. Amer.* 75, 952–959 (1984).

14 Residues and Summation Tones—What Do *We* Hear?

John R. Pierce

This chapter is about residue pitch and combination tones. The approach will be to discuss various matters briefly, to present sound examples on the compact disk, and to ask the reader to listen and to reach his own conclusions.

Rather than searching the literature myself, I have read with some care an excellent summary on residue phenomena published by E. de Boer in 1976 [1]. I recommend this summary highly.

Residue pitch has sometimes been called *periodicity pitch* or *virtual pitch*. It was first demonstrated unequivocally by Schouten around 1940. Schouten produced a train of pulses at a rate of 200 per second. By adjusting the amplitude and phase of a synchronous 200-Hz sine wave he was able to cancel out the fundamental component of the pulse train. You could hear the 200-Hz component come and go, but the pitch of the stimulus was unchanged. Later I heard this myself in his laboratory.

When we are presented with a sum of sine waves whose frequencies are exact or approximate integer multiples of a missing fundamental frequency, we sometimes hear the pitch of the sound as the pitch of the missing fundamental. That is how we hear the correct pitch of a man with a bass voice talking over a telephone that does not pass the fundamental frequency of his speech. That is how we hear the correct musical pitch of the very low notes of a piano. The lowest key, A0, has a fundamental frequency of 27.5 Hz. Certainly, that does not get through most audio systems, and its importance in listening to the piano directly is probably small or nonexistent.

The pitch of orchestra chimes is that of a missing "fundamental" of partials whose frequencies closely approximate the second, third, fourth, and seventh harmonics of the pitch frequency, which is not present in the sound.

Residue pitch has been studied largely in nonmusical contexts. In a laboratory, carefully trained subjects make pitch matches of an adjustable-frequency sinusoid to a tone composed of a number of sinusoidal components. The components of the tone matched are often but not always harmonically related frequencies.

Existence regions for hearing a residue pitch have been published. Figure 14.1 is based on the work of Ritsma, published in 1962. I shall not discuss it in detail. It is for tones made up of three sinusoids. Up-and-down is frequency spacing of the sinusoidal components, right-and-left is the center

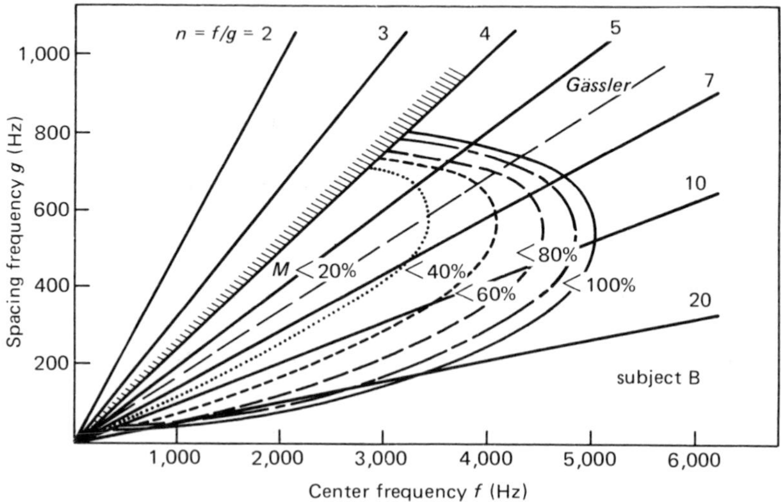

Figure 14.1
Existence region for three-component residue signals. *M* is the modulation depth. The line marked "Gässler" indicates the critical bandwidth. After Ritsma (1962).

frequency of the components, and the curves bound regions in which residue pitch was found for various ratios of the amplitudes of the component sinusoids. According to such curves, almost all of the sounds I present should have residue pitches.

Figure 14.2 shows residue pitch measurements obtained for two equally spaced sinusoidal components as the frequency of the lowest component was raised. At some frequencies the components were successive harmonics of 200 Hz, and at these frequencies the pitch matches gave a frequency of 200 Hz. As the frequency was raised, the residue pitch so measured went up a little, around 15% of the frequency change, until the next harmonic ratio was reached. Then the pitch could have two or more values, including the 200 Hz of the frequency separation.

Figure 14.3 shows similar data for three sinusoidal components spaced 200 Hz apart.

Such results seem to imply that if one used a tone made up of sinusoidal components separated by a constant frequency and played a scale with the lower component, one would not hear a scale. Rather, the pitch heard should skip to the missing fundamental frequency whenever the components are harmonically related.

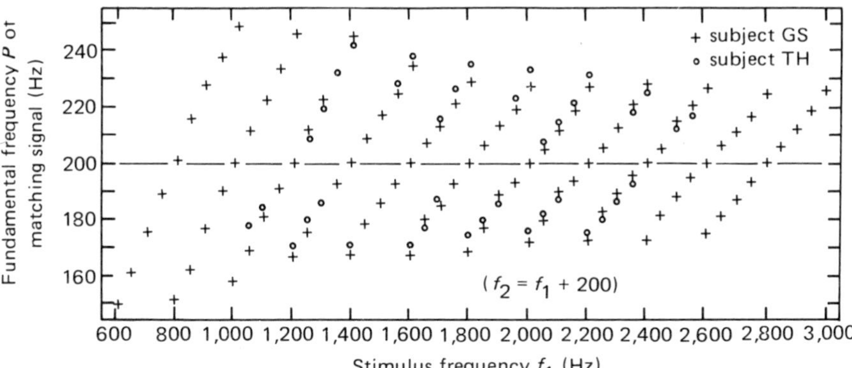

Figure 14.2
Results of pitch measurements for two-component signals: frequency difference of components, 200 Hz; abscissa, frequency of the lower component; ordinate, measured pitch value. After Smoorenburg (1970).

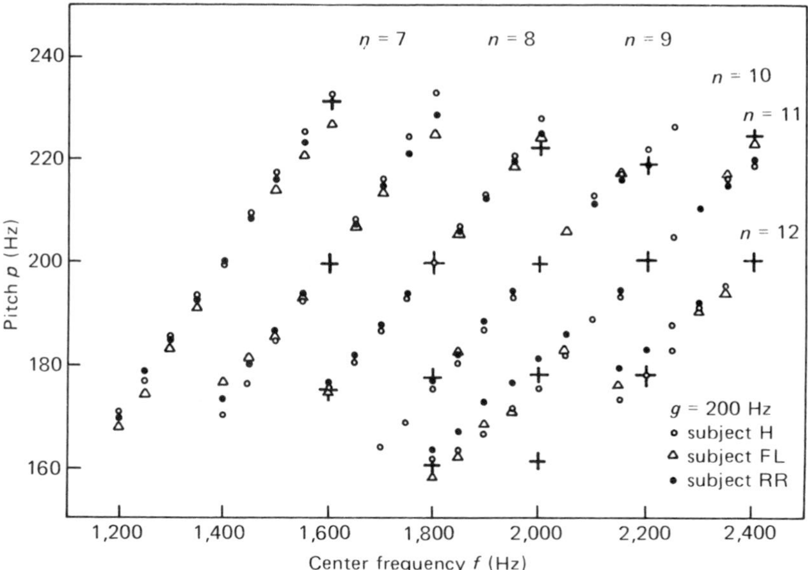

Figure 14.3
Pitch measurements for three-component signals: difference of component frequencies, 200 Hz. After Schouten (1962).

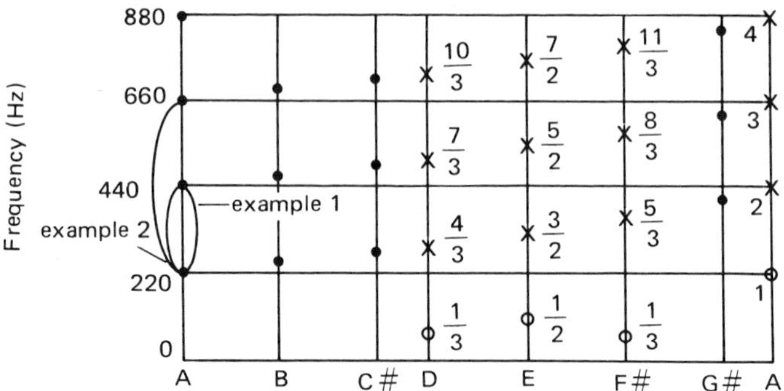

Figure 14.4
Two- and three-component scales.

14.1 Examples 75 and 76

I synthesized two such major scales. The first scale consists of two equal-amplitude sinusoidal components spaced 220 Hz apart. The second scale consists of three equal-amplitude sinusoidal components spaced 220 Hz apart.

These scales are in just intonation. The lowest-frequency component starts at 220 Hz, the A below middle C, and goes up one octave to 440 Hz, the A above middle C. Just after each scale, I play in succession the first and last notes of the scale.

I have shown the frequencies and something about their ratios in figure 14.4. At the start of the scales, 220 Hz, the frequencies for the two-component tones are fundamental and first harmonic, and for the three-component scale the frequencies are fundamental, second harmonic, and third harmonic. The pitch at the start must be 220 Hz.

At the end of the scale, for the two-tone scale the frequencies are the second and third harmonics of 220 Hz—with no fundamental. Do we hear a residue pitch of 220 Hz? At the end of the octave of the three-component scale, the frequencies present are the second, third, and fourth harmonics of 220 Hz, with no fundamental. Do we hear a residue pitch of 220 Hz?

Along the way there seem to be opportunities for other residue pitches. For the three-component scale, at the subdominant of the scale we have the fourth, seventh, and tenth harmonics of 220/3 Hz. At the dominant of the scale we have the third, fifth, and seventh harmonics of 220/2 Hz. At the

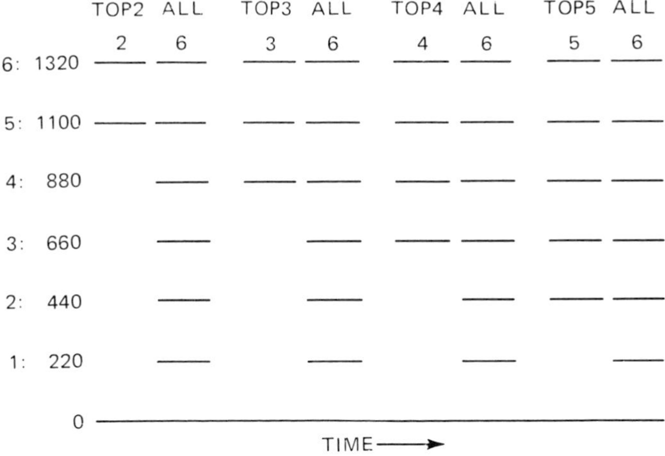

Figure 14.5
Tones that compare the top few partials with all partials.

sixth of the scale we have the fifth, eighth, and eleventh harmonics of 220/3 Hz.

I do not hear any of these residue pitches.

What I hear is scales of rather odd timbre going up an octave. When, after each scale, the final tone follows the initial tone I hear a rise in pitch, not the same pitch, as residue experiments might lead one to believe.

My conclusion is that people hear different pitches in classic residue experiments and in a musical context.

14.2 Example 77

The next sound example is illustrated in figure 14.5. This makes use of a tone with partials of equal amplitude, ranging in frequency from 220 Hz (the fundamental) to 1,320 Hz (the sixth harmonic). This tone is labeled ALL in figure 14.5. The other tones used are TOP2, which has only the top 2 harmonics of ALL, TOP3, which has the top 3 harmonics of ALL, TOP4, which has the top 4 harmonics of ALL, and TOP5, which has the top 5 harmonics of ALL. These four TOP timbres have the same fundamental as ALL, but the fundamental is missing. They might give rise to the same residue pitch.

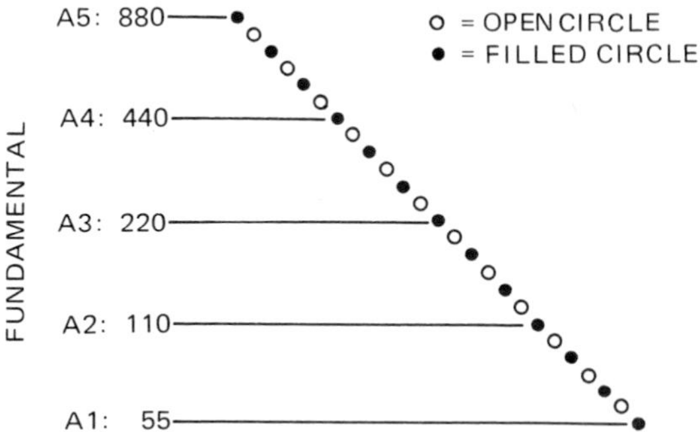

Figure 14.6
Descending whole-tone scale: •, all 6 harmonics; o, top 2, 3, 4, 5 harmonics.

In the recording one hears TOP2 followed by ALL, and other pairs in succession, ending with TOP5 followed by ALL.

The question is, do the successive pairs seem to have the same pitch?

My comment is that TOP2 sounds higher in pitch than ALL, and so does TOP3. TOP5 seems to have the same pitch as ALL. I can convince myself that TOP4 may have the same pitch as ALL, but this is not a certain conviction. Others may hear other pitches.

It seems clear to me that in the case of TOP2 and TOP3 one does not hear a residue pitch equal to that of ALL. Yet in all cases the tones are in a region in which residue pitch has been found in psychacoustic experiments.

14.3 Example 78

The perception of residue pitch is sensitive to the frequency of the fundamental. Let us explore this by listening to the descending whole-tone scale shown in figure 14.6. This descends from a fundamental of 880 Hz, the second A above middle C, to a fundamental of 55 Hz, 4 octaves below the initial tone.

In the first scale played, the successive tones alternate between ALL and TOP2. In successive scales TOP2 is replaced by TOP3, TOP4, and TOP5, in that order.

Do we hear in all cases a pitch that goes evenly down by successive whole tones, a scale in which the fundamental, or missing fundamental, or a residue with a pitch equal to that of the missing fundamental, progresses downward in equal steps?

Listeners' judgments of these scales vary somewhat. Except perhaps for TOP2, all hear a descending scale as the frequency approaches the lower end of the scale, 55 Hz. This shows that residue pitch is most prominent for missing low-frequency fundamentals. Some listeners appear to hear a descending scale near the top end for all but TOP2, but the scale is rather jumpy because of timbre changes. I hear initial jumps up in pitch at the top for all TOP timbres—or at least for all but TOP5.

It seems clear that, for the musical context of a scale, in a number of instances we do not hear the residue pitch of the missing fundamental, even in the regions in which residue pitches are reported in the literature. Generally, residue pitches are heard more clearly or easily at low frequencies and when there are many harmonic components. This is in qualitative agreement with the literature.

14.4 Example 79

I now come to another matter, difference tones, or Tartini tones, tones whose pitches are the difference in the frequencies of two sinusoids. These are a subset of combination tones.

Some have attributed hearing a residue pitch with two-tone stimuli to hearing a difference tone, though this would hardly account for the pitches of pairs of tones that are not harmonically related, like those displayed in figures 14.2 and 14.3.

This example and the following examples explore difference tones by trying to use them to play tunes. In example 79 the two sinusoidal components whose difference frequency plays the melody lie above and below 2,000 Hz. The notes of the melody lie in the range from the A below middle C to the A above middle C. The frequencies of these notes are represented by the frequency difference between the two sinusoids.

I give below the first few frequencies for the pitch entry of the PLA score for the upper tone, followed by the pitch entries of the PLA score for the lower tone:

pitch∅ ← 2000 + .5*[C, C, E, etc.],

pitch∅ ← 2000 − .5*[C, C, E, etc.].

Here C is middle C, 277.18 Hz.

Because of an unfortunate experience with nonlinearities in a sound system, I have recorded the two sinusoidal tones on separate stereo tracks, so that nonlinearities in amplifiers or speakers cannot produce a difference-frequency tone in the sound field. This was suggested to me by Max V. Mathews.

In example 79 the level used first is moderate. I did not hear the tune the first time it was played. The presence of the two frequency components within a critical bandwidth produces a rather rough timbre.

If the tune is known, one may "hear it" in the mind, prompted by the rhythmic pattern.

The same material is then played at a level 20 dB higher. In this case, I hear the tune as a difference frequency pitch that seems to be "in my ear" rather than coming from the speakers.

In listening, it is best to turn one's head from left to right and back in seeking to hear this difference tone and in estimating its source. As the head is turned, the tone may appear or disappear, and may shift from ear to ear because of the spatial variability of the sound field from the two speakers.

14.5 Example 80

This example is presented as a contrast to the difference-tone phenomena of example 79. In example 80 the sinusoidal components are in the same 2,000-Hz region as in example 79. But the components are now played by a waveform that consists entirely of the tenth and eleventh harmonics of a frequency playing the tune. The frequency differences are comparable to the frequency differences of example 79, but in this new case what one hears at low levels is the tune played at pitches around 2,000 Hz.

The tune is then played at a level 20 dB higher. In this case, one may, in moving his head, hear the fundamental of the two harmonics as a low difference frequency playing the tune. The first part of PLA score entry for the pitch of the tune is

pitch∅ ← (200/264)*[C, C, E, etc.].

To me, this example emphasizes the importance of place along the cochlea in musical pitch. In the low-level presentation, one hears a high pitch because the tones excite the basilar membrane near a 2,000-Hz place. At a higher level one can also hear a low pitch, presumably because a low-frequency place is excited through nonlinearities in the ear.

14.6 Example 81

In this example, a different tune is used, played as the difference frequency of two sinusoidal tones in a range around 2,000 Hz. In this case, however, the upper tone goes up and down a scale. The PLA score pitch entries for the two tones are

pitch∅ ← 7*[B/2, C, D, etc.],

pitch∅ ← 7*[B/2, C, D, etc.] − [F, F, E, etc.].

The first square bracket in each pitch represents the scale. The second square bracket in the second pitch entry represents the melody. The frequency of the lower component is less than that of the higher by the pitch frequency of the melody.

The scale motion can be heard in both the low-level and the high-level presentations. It tends to distract one from hearing difference tones.

In the second presentation, at a level 20 dB higher, with care one can hear the tune "in the ear," especially if one moves one's head to a favorable position.

14.7 Final Comments

Musically, residue pitch is an important phenomenon. It accounts for our ability to hear the "correct" pitches of low piano tones over ordinary sound systems. It accounts for the pitches assigned to orchestra chimes. And much more.

However, the literature on residue pitch is much concerned with marginal cases, in which residue pitch is heard with some difficulty in pitch-matching experiments. In an actual presentation of sounds that *might* have a residue pitch, one may hear quite a different pitch, as the examples that I have given demonstrate.

At low levels, difference tones do not give a distinct enough sense of pitch to "play a tune." Indeed, at low levels and with truly linear sound equipment, it is difficult, if not impossible, to hear a musical pitch other than that of the component sinusoids, though, prompted by the rhythmic pattern, one can summon up the pitches from memory.

Pairs of sinusoids do have a rough timbre if they lie within a critical bandwidth.

At higher levels one can hear difference tones as clear musical pitches, but the source seems, as it should, to lie in the ear rather than outside, from the speaker.

Acknowledgment

All tones were generated at the Center for Computer Research in Music and Acoustics (CCRMA) using the Samson Box and the PLA program. I received important help from various CCRMA people. The idea of recording difference tones on two cassette tracks in order to avoid the effects of nonlinearities in amplifiers and speakers was given to me by Max V. Mathews.

Reference

[1] E. de Boer, *On the "Residue" and Auditory Pitch Perception*, Chapter 13 in Volume V of *Handbook of Sensory Physiology*, edited by W. Keidel and W. D. Neff, Springer, 1975.

15 Simulating Performance on a Bowed Instrument

Chris Chafe

15.1 Introduction

The sound examples in the accompanying compact disc demonstrate music synthesized from a physical model and controlled by simulated physical performance gestures. This chapter presents some issues in designing a control system for such a synthesizer. The system that has been developed runs considerably slower than real time and is intended as an environment for answering some questions about live control of an eventual real-time system. The control methods in a playable real-time instrument are similar to those used here, in which the computer interprets the musical score.

The attempt to simulate performance on bowed instruments actually stems from an interest in developing new instruments, rather than pure simulation. A good simulation serves as a useful "benchmark" that provides a starting point for exploration of novel instruments and musical materials for composition.

The control method is specific to synthesis from a physical model of a bowed string. Five time-varying control signals are generated for the model: string length, string damping and bow speed, pressure, and position. Other instrument types could be tested using a similar approach. Articulation rules would be adapted to the particular parameter sets of their synthesis models.

Time-varying envelopes for the parameters are created by concatenation of short envelope segments corresponding to performance gestures. Gestures themselves are not represented in actual physical terms, so there is no notion of the extent or rate of motion of the fingers or bow. Instead, the system represents gestures in terms of their effect on the bowed string parameters.

Musical scores are coded as lists of gestures. The method is a variant of tablature notation, in which a score is described from the point of view of hands manipulating the instrument, rather than pitches on a stave. For example, events described in this fashion include *martelé attack on string III* in the right hand or *hammered pitch at the fifth on string I* in the left hand.

When creating a performance, the system adds details that cause gestures to conform to the changing state of the musical phrase. The intended result is consistency within complex gestures that perform multiple notes as well as some amount of expressiveness.

15.2 Synthesis Method: Physical Modeling

At the outset, it should be mentioned that though computer music synthesis using physical models is promising, it is still largely a theoretical field. Commonly restricted to running in software, sound generation is many times slower than real time. Real-time systems require either new types of synthesizer hardware (which are likely to be built from standard digital signal-processing VLSI) or general-purpose supercomputers.

The bowed string algorithm used in this chapter runs in software. Since the purpose here is to discuss control of the cello model, background concerning the algorithm itself should be found by referring to the following sources: [3, 5, 6, 9, 11].

A physical model of an acoustic source can represent a vibrating system of arbitrary complexity. A complete cellolike synthesizer is constructed by coupling together a number of bowed string models that simulate each string's internal reverberation and the bow's frictional driving mechanism, and that are further coupled to the bridge, the sound box, and the air. Weinreich [10] has termed the bowed string algorithm a method for "synthesis from first principles." It is a simplified, but nonetheless accurate, description of a dynamic physical system. The algorithms representing the four cello strings are iterated in time from some initial state, e.g., an open string at rest. As the bow excites string motion, waves begin to circulate that are emitted as sound at the model's output. Events in the musical score, through the intermediary control system, cause changes to parameters controlling the bow and string components.

A cellist develops skill at manipulation of five basic parameters. *String length*, controlled by fingers on the player's left hand, determines the round-trip time of the recirculating waves and the resulting pitch of the sound. The right hand controls *bow speed, pressure,* and *contact position*, affecting loudness and tone quality. A fifth control, *string damping*, controls the amount of wave recirculation and varies with movement of the fingers and bow touching the string.

In synthesis experiments with a physical model of the cello, a number of advantages have become clear:

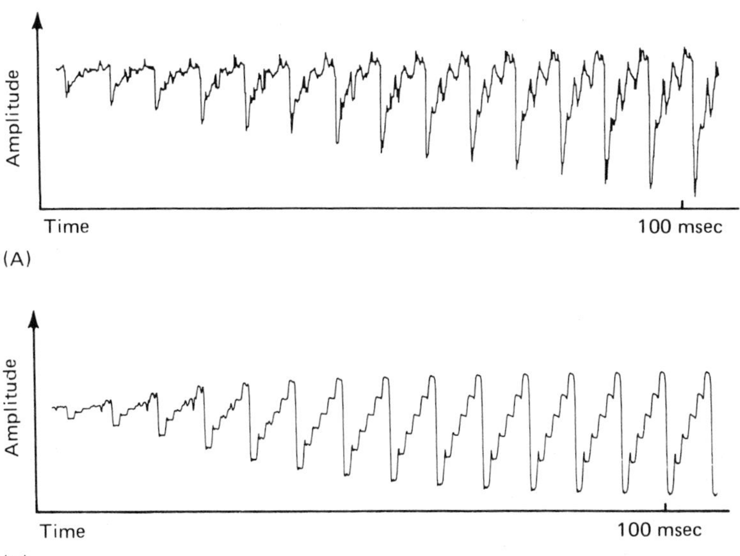

Figure 15.1
(A) sampled waveform and (B) synthesized waveform. The plots compare sampled and synthesized bowed cello waveforms. The upper plot was recorded off an isolated string in the *Celletto*, a bodyless electric cello with sensors implanted in the bridge directly beneath each string. Both traces exhibit sawtoothlike *Helmholtz motion* at the fundamental period modulated by crumples at several times the fundamental frequency.

• **Regimes of oscillation are correct in the time domain.** Self-sustained oscillators such as bowed strings are *dynamical systems*. The system's *attractor* (equilibrium state) under normal bowing conditions is a waveform exhibiting *Helmholtz motion*, named after the acoustician who first described the periodic mechanism of string capture and release by the bow. Figure 15.1 compares real and synthesized bowed waveforms.

• **As in the real instrument, transient behavior of the system is state-dependent.** Response to a particular articulation depends on what the system was doing in the recent past. Sound example number 63 (given in the accompanying compact disc) demonstrates multiple strikes on a physical model of a bell. The repeated strikes sound different because of their interaction with the vibrating system.

• **The model has the same external controls as the physical system.** These are the parameters a cellist develops skill at manipulating.

• **There is an "intuitive feel" to the system's response.** A cellist can recognize and imitate a synthetic articulation and recommend improvements in the control values. The complete range of cello articulations can be synthesized.

The most important restriction concerning control of the model is that the model's state should persist through successive articulations and events, allowing the system to produce real-sounding transients. Traditional speech or music synthesis techniques, e.g., linear predictive coding, formant synthesis, additive synthesis, frequency modulation, or sampling methods, do not easily produce real-sounding transients. In physical models, finely detailed transients are achieved when new events interact with the reverberation of previous events. A particular articulation, played twice, may sound different as it interferes with a system that is already in motion. The state of the system at any given point in time is a result of complex interactions between external control parameters and recent system "memory." Due to this accurate transient behavior, dynamical system models are useful in a wide range of real-world simulations [4].

This accuracy creates, in music synthesis, recognizable instruments. A wide range of acoustic cues contribute to the dynamic signature of an instrument in play, especially features that are covarying. It does not matter particularly *what* is being performed. For instance, the model can produce tones or passages that are recognizably the sort produced on the instrument by unskilled players. Refining the performance of the control system is reminiscent of early exercises on the instrument. When something is amiss, the best approach has been to compensate the controls as if listening to the actual instrument. Tone quality, for example, might be improved by specifying something like ". . . use more bow pressure at that point."

15.3 Scores: Segmenting Performance

Music is performed on the cello synthesizer by a control system that replaces the cellist. Its rules are gesture based, and imitate the effect of the player's actions on the strings. The system also attempts to reproduce some of the interpretive functions of the player, such as musical phrasing. Time-varying envelopes for the synthesis parameters are calculated by rules that correspond to basic gesture segments. Usually, a few of these are concatenated to form the complete envelope of a musical note.

The system operates from musical scores coded in common notation and enhanced with explicit markings for bowing and fingering (to choose which string a particular note is played on). These markings are often added by players to their parts, indicating fingering and bowing choices for performance of a particular passage. Each succeeding pitch is associated with either a fingering change, bow change, or both. The old forms of tablature style scores for lute are reminiscent of this approach, in that they notated the placement of the hands on the strings. Figure 15.2 illustrates an example coded as input for the system.

The gestures that the hands can perform vary in complexity. The simplest items are those that initiate a bow stroke or finger a new pitch. More intricate operations are possible, which result in coordinated activity across multiple strings, such as rolled, or "broken," chords. The system breaks each gesture into smooth sequences of short envelope segments—for example, those resulting in string release, bow acceleration, pitch sustain, or vibrato. The larger gestures described by the musical notation, such as a note sequence, trill, or slur, are formed by compounds of these "atomic" segments.

For each gesture in the score, sequences of segments are cued up in a time-ordered list by the control system. In most cases this sequence contains one or more transition segments paired with a sustain. For example, a change of bow is comprised of a quick deacceleration, a reattack, and a sustain segment.

The extendable duration of sustain segments distinguishes them from transitions whose durations are fixed. Sustainable segments prolong the string state, possibly modulating it with vibrato or tremolo. The intervening transitions determine trajectories for the hands as they move between sustainable motions. For example, left-hand transitionals include sliding, hammering, and homing in on a new pitch.

Each segment contributes to the envelopes of a few synthesis parameters. The number of parameters that will be inflected together depends on the particular segment. In a reversal of bow direction, the reattack segment affects four parameters: bow speed, pressure, pitch, and damping.

Several kinds of phrasing marks are likely to be encountered in a score and are referred to as *phrase controls*. These include dynamic level, vibrato rate, tone quality, and tempo, among others. Separate slow changing envelopes which are internal to the system are generated from marks in the score. Their levels represent the *phrase state* at any given instant.

```
(Time 0.)
  (Strings
    ((4 (G /2))
     (3 (D *1))
     (2 (A *1))
     (1 (E *2))))
  (Dynamic PP)
  (Tempo 0.9 <)
  (Stroke 4)
  (Place_and_Vibrato 4 FS *1)
(After 0.5)
  (Place_and_Vibrato 4 E *1)
  (Dynamic PP <)
(After 0.5)
  (Accent_and_Vibrato 4 D *1)
(After 1.0)
  (Martele 4)
  (Dynamic P)
(After 1.0)
  (Lift 4)
  (Place_and_Vibrato 3 FS *1)
  (Stroke 3)
  (Tempo 1.0 <)
(After 0.5)
  (Place_and_Vibrato 3 A *1)
(After 0.5)
  (Place_and_Vibrato 3 E *1)
  (Dynamic P >)
(After 2.)
  (Martele 3)
  (Place_and_Vibrato 3 FS *1)
  (Dynamic PP <)
  (Tempo 1.1 <)
(After 0.5)
  (Place 3 A *1)
(After 0.5)
  (Accent_and_Vibrato 2 B *1)
  (Stroke 2)
  (Open 3)
  (Light_Stroke 3)
  (Dynamic P)
(After 1.5)
  (Place 3 E *1)
  (Lift 2)
  (Dynamic PP)
(After 0.3)
  (Lift 3)
(After 0.2)
  (Place_and_Vibrato 4 E *1)
  (Martele 4)
  (Dynamic P >)
  (Tempo 1.2)
(After 0.75)
  (Place 4 D *1)
(After 0.25)
  (Accent_and_Vibrato 4 FS *1)
  (Dynamic PP >)
  (Vibrato_Excursion 0.02 >)
(After 1.)
  (Place_and_Vibrato 4 E *1)
(After 1.)
  (Lift 4)
  (Dynamic N)
  (Vibrato_Excursion 0.005)
(After 0.01)
(End)
```

Figure 15.2
Player system input notation. A violin passage has been transcribed as input for the violin player system. The specific choices for fingering and bowing represent one of several possible interpretations for performing the score. Each event in the time-ordered list is specified by an articulation name, the string number, and an (optional) new pitch to be sounded. Phrasing marks such as accents and dynamic changes are included.

Phrase controls are updated by an ever-present background process. These values are relatively stable since they change over the course of seconds or tens of seconds. Though a given control level usually persists longer than a single note, exceptions can occur, for instance, as in a *messa di voce* (a prolonged tone with a swell in dynamic level).

The control system can insert unscored segments when interpreting a score. Some may belong to a particular playing style while others arise from a need to simulate a natural level of "sloppiness." Citing some inaccuracies common in string playing: pitches are rarely placed directly on target by the left hand and spurious sounds often accompany position shifts or string crossings. Computer-perfect synthesis without a dose of nature's noises has a lifeless quality.

15.4 Simultaneity: Multiple Articulators

Novice players are familiar with the burden of the many controls that they must track: the bow, intonation, tempo, loudness, and timbre. In effect, these items can be seen as components of a "polyphonic" texture, containing several independent parts, or "voices," for which the hands are the articulators.

From the instrument's point of view, the two articulators that act on it are sometimes coordinated and sometimes completely independent. Both hands simultaneously contribute to the value of a synthesis parameter. This is clearly the case for the damping coefficient in the string, as well as for string length and the bow parameters.

Two independent processes represent the hands in the control system. These processes will be assigned different kinds of gestures that invoke string excitation, and pitch or damping change. Regarding string excitation, in addition to the right hand bowing the string, the left hand can hammer down a new pitch and either can pluck. Given the possibility for left-hand sounds, the current system allows the left-hand process to add excitation by inflecting the bow parameters (which is departing from the physical analogy). A hammered pitch is simulated by a sharp jerk in the bow envelopes.

Updates to the synthesis parameters occur every 10 msec. Prior to each update, the hand processes evaluate their contribution to the control envelopes and their respective contributions are summed for each of the synthesis parameters.

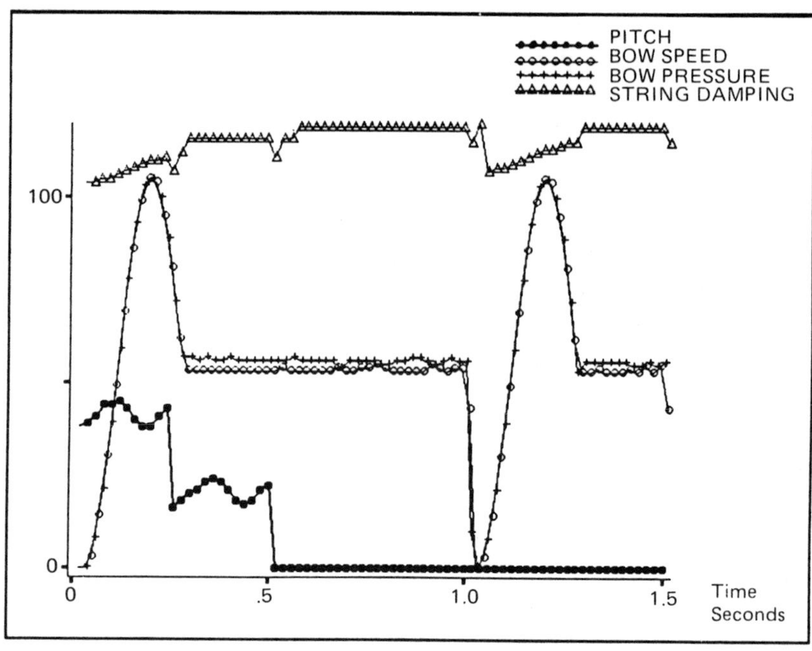

Figure 15.3
Envelopes generated by the player system. The plot provides a detailed view of envelopes for the synthesis of the first four notes of the previous score. To give an approximate idea of scale: the vibrato excursion shown in the graph is almost a semitone. Bow speed and pressure are shown in log units, from minimum to maximum effort divided into a scale of 127 values (as with MIDI control data). String damping is at a minimum at the very top of the scale, where it corresponds to a free ringing string. The graph begins with a three-note slur played in the left hand, followed by a repeated pitch in the bow. As the left-hand finger moves to a new pitch, damping increases slightly until the new note is fully sounded.

Segments in the two hands may be changed synchronously or asynchronously depending on the type of musical material. In typical performance, this texture may switch rapidly from a one-to-one correspondence to many-to-one or entirely independent relationships between the hands. For example, in figure 15.3, several segments have been generated by the system. Due to the initial three-note slur there are more segments for the left hand than for the right.

An additional parallel-executing process evaluates the state of the phrase controls. The hand processes evaluate their segments within this context. The desired effect of this mechanism is that a given gesture or articulation will translate into different envelope shapes depending on the dynamic level or tone quality.

Control processes, synthesis processes, gestures, and segments are objects in the system's computer program. Each has an associated set of execution rules. At initialization time, the instrument configuration is declared giving the number of strings and their tunings. The system then copies the required number of each object prototype. For the sound examples, from 1 to 4 strings were played by 2 hands (of course, being a computer, additional hands can be made available for more difficult scores).

All processes execute each tick in an order that follows a hierarchical pattern [7]. The instrument is the *father* process, and hand, phrase, and string synthesis processes are *offspring*. The father contains a scheduler that cues the time-ordered segments into its offspring processes. The evaluation order (at each update) is as follows: instrument, phrase controls, and then string-by-string—left-hand control and right-hand control. The updated value is sent to the string synthesizer process, which then outputs 10 msec of sound.

15.5 Rule-Based Envelope Generation

Envelopes are calculated by the segments' rules rather than fetched from lookup of envelope tables. There are two principal reasons for taking this approach:

- Multiple synthesis parameters can be inflected in a coordinated way.
- The rules automatically adjust envelopes according to the changing phrase state.

Recorded measurements of violin bowing gestures support the notion that multiple envelopes are often inflected by one articulation [1, 2]. Performance of a bow stroke with a certain desired loudness and tone quality requires balancing of the three bowing parameters. Bow speed, pressure, and contact position are interdependent in a way that is best understood graphically [8]. Plotting these quantities in separate dimensions, there is a locus of "normal tone" in which these quantities are balanced for different dynamic levels. Outside of this region the bowed effects of sul tasto, sul ponticello, flautando, and even undertone (octave splitting) are found. The desired balance of the bowing parameters is determined by rules contained in the bowing segments, as demonstrated in the 84th sound example. It demonstrates variation of dynamic level and contact position while repeating the same articulation.

The rule-based method for envelope generation facilitates coordinating shape and timing of the different articulations. For example, all five synthesis parameters are perturbed together by a *flying spiccato* bow stroke. Bow speed, pressure, and contact position as well as pitch and damping are affected by the abrupt attack as the bow drops on the string.

The following is an illustration of the detail that can be embedded in segment rules: as mentioned before, the left hand excites a small amount of string motion in hammering down on a new pitch when striking the fingerboard hard enough. In the *hammered pitch* segment, a short interval of heavier damping occurs during which the finger stops the string just before it is fully seated on the fingerboard. This brief muting is followed by new excitation from the hammered strike. Similarly, *pulling off* to a new pitch is executed by a segment that includes a left-hand pizzicato.

The use of a "global" phrase state also provides a means for regulating details of envelopes affecting individual strings. Multiple-string gestures such as bowed triple-stop chords can be regulated by rules that look up phrase attributes. In this example, rolled chords are played across three strings. Since the bow is limited to touching two strings at a time, chords are played as a succession of diads. Bowing envelopes that are calculated for the individual strings track the current dynamic level and tone quality and behave in a mutually consistent fashion. Figure 15.4 depicts the energy through time on each of the 4 strings as a country fiddle tune is played in sound example 83.

Certain articulations create strong multiparameter accents. A *sforzando* attack would generally affect vibrato as well as the bow. Such accents are engineered as brief boosts to phrase controls, triggered by the accent segment. Transient bumps imposed on envelopes for timbre, dynamic, and vibrato are short lived and decay exponentially.

15.5.1 Bow Articulations

Segments available in the rule base of the system include representatives from a small "taxonomy" of bowed articulations. Five features have been taken into account in classifying them:

- **Reversal of bow direction.** This distinguishes *detaché* from *legato* bow strokes.

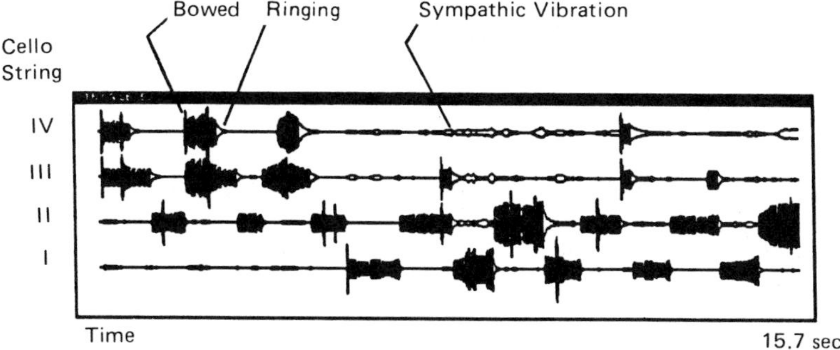

Figure 15.4
Synthesized string motion. Output level has been recorded for each string in isolation in the synthesis of sound example number 83, *Wrassled with a Wildcat*. Shading shows bowed portions, and open areas show either ringing or sympathetic vibration caused by bowing on other strings. The dynamic level of each double stop is coordinated by the global phrase controls.

- **Initial displacement.** Significant bow pressure before the bow starts to move causes a hard attack. The initial string snap that results is sometimes called a *quasi-pizzicato*. Examples are *martelé*, *marcato*, and *staccato*.
- **Pulsed accent.** Soft attacks have no discernible displacement, but can have some degree of accentuation after the string is in motion, as in *lancé*, *porté*, and *louré* bowing.
- **Duration of separation.** Tones separated by small amounts of silence include *martelé*, *spiccato*, and *staccato*.
- **Off-string bowing.** Dropped, lifted or ricocheted strokes are distinct from completely on-string tones. During the decay segment, off-string tones ring where their on-string counterparts are damped. *Piqué*, *spiccato*, *jeté*, and *flying staccato* strokes are played off-string and are distinguished by amount of contact at attack and decay.

The 85th sound example compares several articulations whose envelopes are plotted in figure 15.5.

15.6 Summary

The control system has been tested in several different musical situations, both with hand-entered scores and scores composed by algorithmic means. In experimenting with different instruments, envelope-generating rules

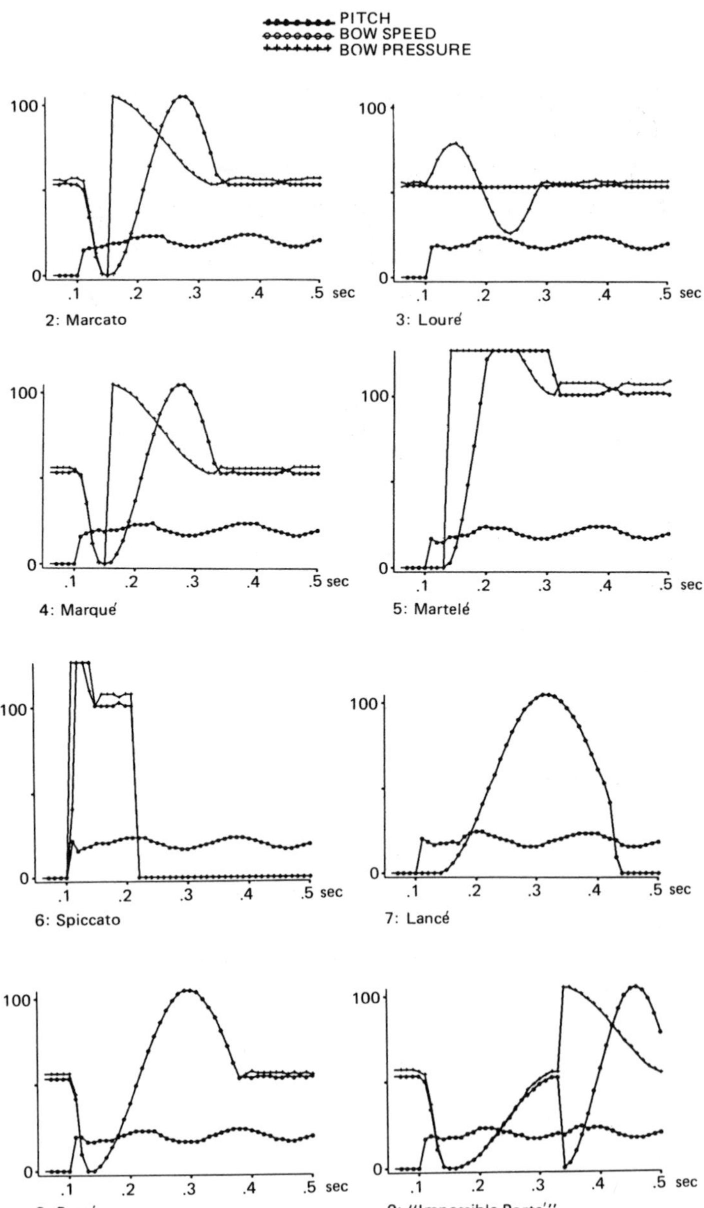

Figure 15.5
Envelopes for various bowed articulations. These envelopes were generated in the process of synthesizing sound example number 85: the comparison of bowed articulations. Graphs show the second stroke of each group of four tones.

have been created that simulate guitar and koto performance. The rule base can be expanded for a selection of musical styles, instruments, or even the personal touch of different performers.

The rules currently in the system have been refined through repeated synthesis trials, in the absence of measurement from actual playing. In the future, such measurement will be possible through instruments that can sense bowing and pitch information. An example is the system of Askenfelt's. Under development at CCRMA are string family MIDI controllers that will allow analysis of live performance, and that will help to determine more precise envelope-generating rules.

Note lists, which are the most common data structure for specifying computer music scores, would be inappropriate for synthesis from physical models of continuous-sounding instruments like the cello. Control of the instrument involves several parallel processes whose synchrony varies depending on the musical texture. Slurs are a simple example of asynchrony between the two hands of a cellist. Subsequent notes continue the sound before the previous note is extinguished. In the note list style of control, only separate and isolated notes can be sounded and slurs are approximated by keyboard style note overlap. Moreover, the state of the synthesizer is reinitialized each note, eliminating the advantages of physical modeling for synthesis of natural-sounding transients.

Recapping the issues that have been considered in the design of the cello control system: Left-hand and right-hand gestures are merged in a way that permits their effects to interact in the synthesis. Gesture segments can coordinate changes in several parameters at once and track evolving phrase conditions. The synthesizer's state is preserved allowing the physical model to be put to full advantage.

Acknowledgment

The author wishes to thank Julius Smith, Xavier Rodet, and Gabriel Weinreich for advice and contributions of software. The system was first implemented in 1984 at IRCAM Paris, France, and again in 1987 at CCRMA.

References

[1] A. Askenfelt, "A Simple Device for the Simultaneous Registration of Bow Motion and Bow Force," Proceedings of the Stockholm Music Acoustics Conference, 1983.

[2] A. Askenfelt "Measurement of Bow Motion and Bow Force in Violin Playing," *J. Acoust. Soc. Amer.*, vol. 80, no. 4, pp. 1007–1015, October 1986.

[3] L. Cremer, *The Physics of the Violin*, MIT Press, 1984.

[4] D. Campbell et al., "The Role of Computation in Nonlinear Science," *Communications of the ACM*, vol. 28, no. 4, pp. 374–384, 1985.

[5] M. E. McIntyre, R. T. Schumacher, and J. Woodhouse, "On the Oscillations of Musical Instruments," *J. Acoust. Soc. Amer.*, vol. 74, no. 5, pp. 1325–1345, November 1983.

[6] M. E. McIntyre and J. Woodhouse, "The Acoustics of Stringed Musical Instruments," *Interdisciplinary Sci. Rev.*, vol. 3, no. 2, pp. 157–173, June 1978.

[7] X. Rodet, "FORMES: Composition and the Scheduling of Processes.," *Computer Music Journal*, vol. 8, no. 3, pp. 32–50, June 1984.

[8] J. C. Schelleng, "The Bowed String and the Player," *J. Acoust. Soc. Amer.*, vol. 53, no. 1, pp. 26–41, January 1973.

[9] J. O. Smith, "Techniques for Digital Filter Design and System Identification with Application to the Violin," Department of Music Technical Report STAN-M-14., Ph.D. Thesis, Department of Electrical Engineering, Stanford University, Stanford, California, June 1983.

[10] G. Weinreich, "Violin Sound Synthesis From First Principles," abstract of paper presented to the Acoustical Society of America Conference, *J. Acoust. Soc. Amer.*, vol. 74, pp. 1S52ff., 1983.

[11] G. Weinreich, "Sound Hole Sum Rule and the Dipole Moment of the Violin," *J. Acoust. Soc. Amer.*, vol. 77, no. 2, pp. 710–718, 1985.

16 Automatic Counterpoint

William Schottstaedt

16.1 Introduction

For several hundred years composers have praised species counterpoint as one of the best ways to learn to write music. In this discipline the student learns to shape and combine simple melodies through a carefully organized sequence of baby steps. One well known exposition is "Gradus ad Parnassum" by J. J. Fux (1725) [1].

A program was written following as closely as possible the exposition of species counterpoint given by Fux. Fux's guidelines and rules were used to solve counterpoint exercises automatically. The rules were then extended and modified until the results of the program were an acceptable match with Fux's examples. All five species in Fux's five modes were implemented, accommodating up to six voices. The program itself with a detailed commentary is available [2].

16.2 Why Write a Counterpoint Solver?

There are several reasons to undertake this task. From a programmer's point of view, it is fun and not particularly difficult to write such a program. The world of species counterpoint is simple enough that the criteria for judging solutions are reasonably clear, and the results look deceptively like music. From a music theorist's point of view, the program can imitate an unusually inept but earnest student whose unexpected mistakes and misunderstandings can make it clear where the rules are inadequate. Finally, from a composer's point of view, species counterpoint seems like a plausible place to start in the development of a smarter working environment for composers of computer music.

16.3 The Rules

Although Fux's definitions and rules are exceptionally clear and carefully presented, they are incomplete. For example, in his list of the ways voices can move, Fux ignores the case in which neither voice moves. Also, in the edition I used, Fux does not explicitly define the difference between a skip and a step. Omissions such as these are easy to handle. It is more difficult to make explicit the proper way to handle trade-offs between rules and guidelines. For example, Fux mentions that it is desirable to maintain "variety" in the melodies. This variety seems to entail a mix of melodic intervals coupled with the avoidance of repetitions of any one pitch. The overall melodic contour should be smooth, but not without some independent character. A program cannot satisfy these constraints unless it can recognize good and bad situations, and make choices among them. The first requires an explicit statement of what "smooth" means; the second requires some explicit weighting and searching method to decide when an acceptable solution has been found. In all but the simplest cases, each solution runs up against at least a few of the guidelines, so the program must be able to choose the "best" from many imperfect solutions.

The basic rules of species counterpoint describe how melodies are formed and combined. Fux repeatedly stresses that most of the rules are guidelines, not absolutes. In our implementation we define the relative importance of the rules by assigning each rule a penalty. The higher the penalty, the worse it is to break the associated rule. The relations among these penalties largely determine what solutions the program finds.

Prohibitions (infinite penalty):

1. Parallel fifths are not allowed.
2. Parallel unisons are not allowed.
3. In two-part counterpoint the final chord must be a unison or an octave; it can include the third or fifth when there are more than two parts.
4. The next to last chord must have a leading tone.
5. Dissonances must be handled correctly (this covers a host of rules).
6. Voices must stay within the mode of the cantus firmus.
7. Some melodic intervals are not allowed.
8. A melody must stay within the range of a twelfth.
9. Cadences must be correct (this covers a host of rules).
10. Direct motion to an octave or fifth over three chords where the intervening interval is not at least a fourth is not allowed.

12. A dissonance as a passing tone must fill in a third.
13. A nota combiata must be resolved correctly.
14. A ligature must be resolved correctly.
15. There are certain situations where a ligature is not allowed.
16. Augmented intervals are not allowed.
17. Doubled leading tones are not allowed.
18. The leading tone must be resolved correctly.

Very bad infractions (penalty is 200):

1. Avoid direct motion to a perfect fifth.
2. Avoid direct motion to an octave.
3. Voices should not move outside certain ranges.
4. Avoid a unison on the down beat.

Bad infractions (penalty is 100):

1. Avoid unisons in two-part counterpoint.
2. Try not to repeat a note on the upbeat.
3. A melody should stay within the range of an octave.
4. Eighth notes should not skip.
5. There are various rules concerning the rhythmic values of tied notes.
6. A six-five chord must be prepared correctly.
7. A six-five chord must be resolved correctly.
8. Avoid direct motion to a tritone.

Other rules (penalty is given in square brackets):

1. Avoid a sixth followed by motion in the same direction [34].
2. Strive for triads [34].
3. In fourth species, avoid passages without ligatures [21].
4. Avoid direct motion to a perfect consonance in the inner voices [21].
5. Avoid tritones near the cadence in lydian mode [13].
6. Avoid a leap to the cadence [13].
7. Avoid moving from a tenth to an octave [8].
8. Avoid a skip to an octave [8].
9. Avoid a sixth preceded by motion in the same direction [8].
10. Avoid a tritone outlined by a melody [8].
11. Avoid skips in all voices at once [8].

12. Avoid a fifth or octave followed by motion in the same direction [8].
13. Avoid a repeated pattern of four notes [7].
14. Avoid notes on the outer edges of the ranges [5].
15. Avoid leaps of an octave [5].
16. Avoid doubling the third [5].
17. Avoid doubling the sixth [5].
18. Try not to skip from a unison [4].
19. Avoid a repeated pattern of three notes [4].
20. Avoid a fifth or octave preceded by motion in the same direction [3].
21. Avoid any skip followed by motion in the same direction [3].
22. Avoid two skips that do not fill in a triad [3]
23. Do not repeat a note on the down beat [3].
24. Avoid a repeated note on the fourth beat [3].
25. Avoid a skip followed by a skip in the opposite direction [3].
26. Avoid direct motion to a tritone in the inner voices [13].
27. Avoid doubling the fifth [3].
28. Avoid doubling the bass twice [3].
29. Avoid a repeated pattern of two notes [2].
30. Avoid perfect consonances [2].
31. Avoid leaps of a sixth [2].
32. Avoid a tritone between voices [2].
33. Avoid a skip followed by a skip [1].
34. Avoid direct motion [1].
35. Avoid compound intervals [1].
36. Avoid any skip preceded by motion in the same direction [1].
37. Avoid upper neighbor notes [1].
38. Avoid lower neighbor notes [1].
39. Strive for variety in a melody (this covers several rules that try to avoid a melody made up entirely of skips, constant repetition of one pitch, constant use of the same interval, and so on) [1].
40. Avoid skips to a down beat [1].
41. Strive for contrary motion [1].
42. Try to keep the upper voices from wandering far apart [1].
43. Avoid repeated voice crossing [penalty dependent on the number of crossings].

These penalty values arise partly from Fux's comments about which rules are more important than others (these get a higher penalty), and partly from experience running the program. Obviously some of the penalties do not apply to every species of counterpoint. The penalties are positive (that is, there are no rewards), because we want to abandon a line as soon as its penalty gets too high. This implies that the penalty function should not be able to decrease. Even the smaller penalties have a noticeable effect on the outcome of the counterpoint search. The solver is consistently "bent" in the direction determined by the penalties.

16.4 Searching for Solutions

There are many ways to search for acceptable solutions to a counterpoint problem. The main constraint is compute time. If we make an exhaustive search of every possible branch of a short (10-note) first-species problem, we have 16 raised to the 10th power possible solutions (there are 16 ways to move from the current note to the next note). Even if we could check each branch in a nanosecond, an exhaustive search in this extremely simple case would take 1,000 sec (about 20 minutes). Because we hope to handle problems far more complex than this simple one and hope to do it reasonably quickly, we must find a smarter search method.

After we made several false starts, Bernard Mont-Reynaud suggested that we use a best-first search. We compute the penalty associated with each melodic interval from the current pitch, then continue recursively using the best result first. If forced to abandon a branch, we back up and try the next best interval until a complete solution is found. Unfortunately, the first such solution may not be very good. By accepting the smallest local penalty we risk falling into a bad overall pathway. If the program is told to search every branch, we once again get bogged down in long computations. To get around this, as soon as we get a solution from one branch, we drop back to the beginning of the exercise, and try a different beginning interval. By trying a new starting interval, we maximize the chance of finding a truly different solution. As before, we abandon any branch when its accumulated penalty is above that of the best complete solution found so far.

Even with these optimizations, fifth species remains a problem. The number of choices increases in this species because it generally has more notes in the counterpoint melody, and because we have several possible rhythmic values to assign each note. Several optimizations can be added to reduce this problem: we search only for those solutions that are much better than the current one, and once a solution has been found we do not spend too much time on any other interval. Compute times for multivoice fifth species remain high despite all this machinery.

In early versions of the program we solved one voice at a time and built up the entire ensemble by layering. This is satisfactory for three voices because the first voice is usually a good melody, and the second voice still has enough degrees of freedom to find an acceptable solution. As more voices are added the later layers become less and less acceptable. To get a solution in which all voices are reasonably good, the entire ensemble must be calculated together.

To illustrate how the rules help the program decide whether one melody is better than another, we shown in figure 16.1 three acceptable counterpoints to the bottom line (the cantus firmus). The number under each note is the penalty associated with that note. Notice that the first (top) solution starts out with the higher penalty but ends with the lower overall penalty. In figure 16.2 we point out in detail how each note in these lines gets its penalty.

16.5 Remaining Problems

Currently the program has no provision for starting a melody with a rest, nor does it reward invertible counterpoint and imitation. It tends to let voices get entangled in each other, and makes inadequate judgments about overall melodic shapes. Certain implied vertical clashes, tritones in particular, are not noticed. Given these caveats the program does well in a reasonably short time.

In figures 16.3–16.8 we give examples of the program's output. It should be kept in mind that species counterpoint exercises are not expected to be great music. The five species are (1) note against note, (2) note against two notes, (3) note against four notes, (4) note against note with ligatures, and (5) note against a "free" counterpoint, that is, a melody in different rhythmic values using any of the possibilities of the preceding species. The numbers running beneath the counterpoint melodies show the penalty associated with that note. The cantus firmus is the voice without any running penalties. Each cantus firmus is taken from Fux.

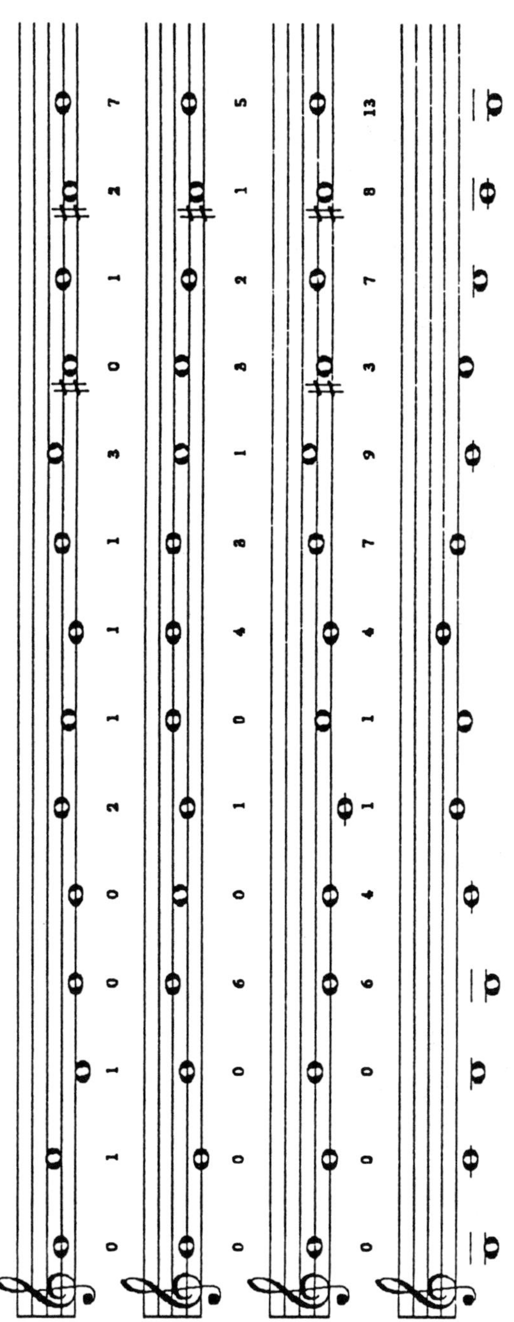

Figure 16.1
Three acceptable counterpoints to a cantus firmus.

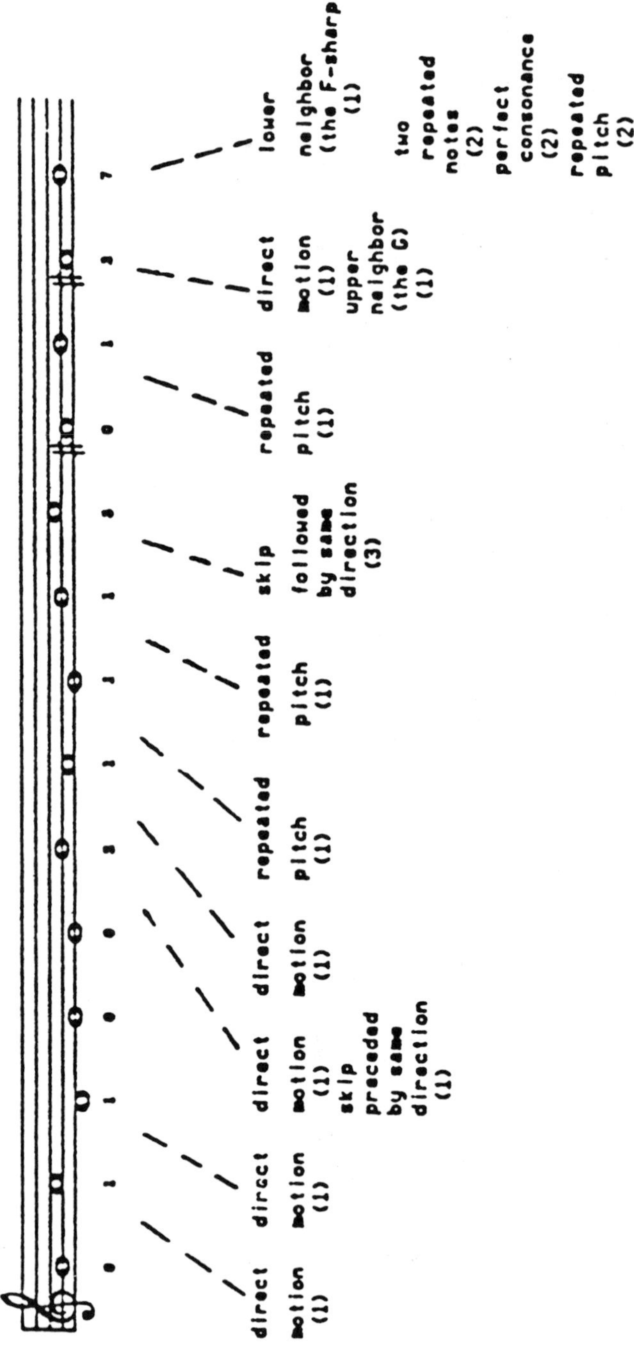
direct motion (1)
direct motion (1)
direct motion (1) skip preceded by same direction (1)
direct motion (1)
repeated pitch (1)
repeated pitch (1)
skip followed by same direction (3)
repeated pitch (1)
direct motion (1) upper neighbor (the G) (1)
lower neighbor (the F-sharp) (1)
two repeated notes (2)
perfect consonance (2)
repeated pitch (2)

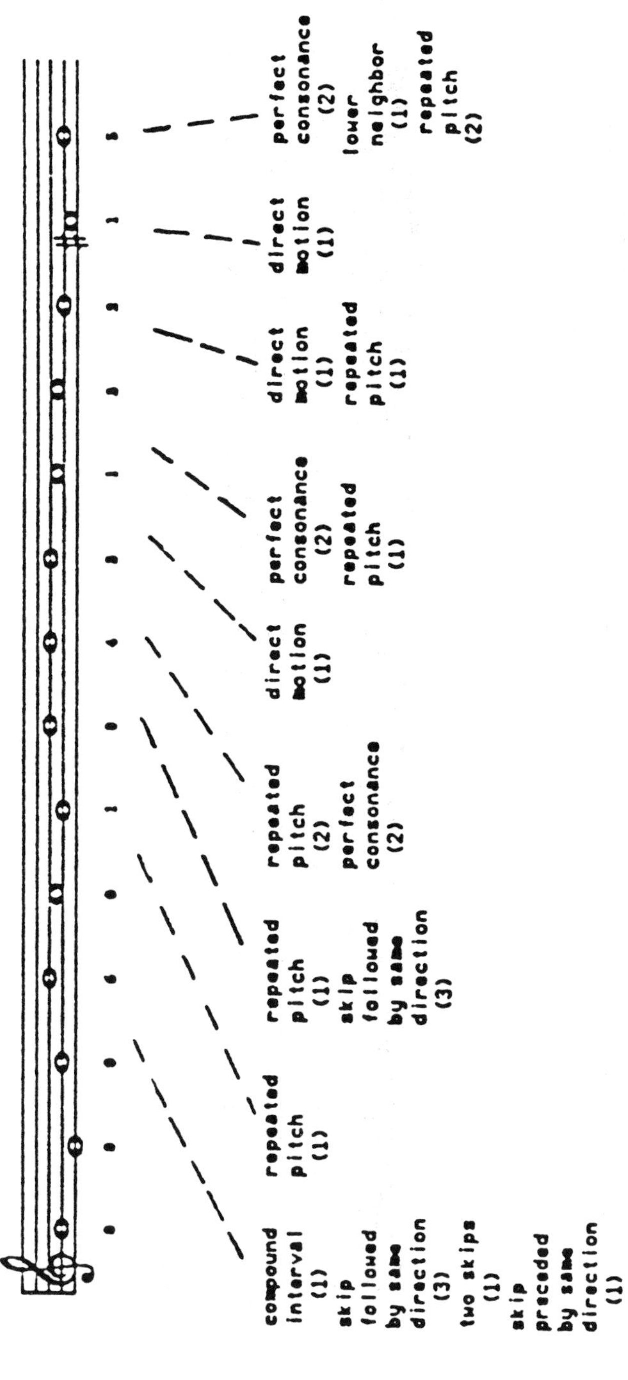

Figure 16.2
Origin of penalties.

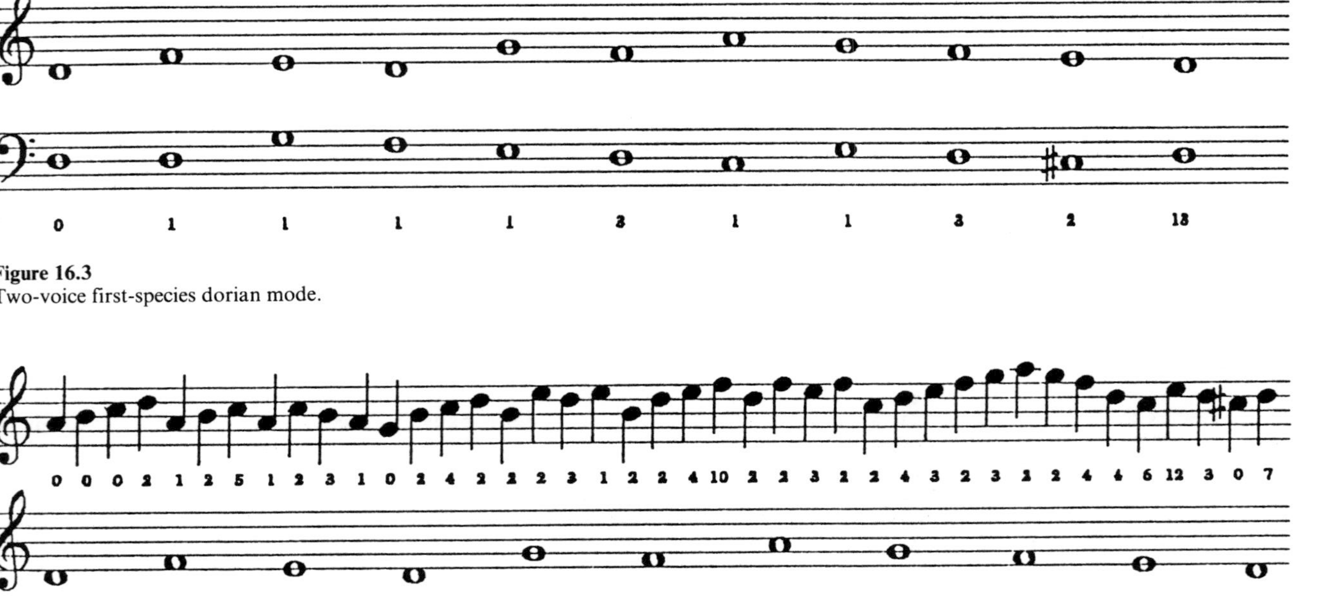

Figure 16.3
Two-voice first-species dorian mode.

Figure 16.4
Two-voice third-species dorian mode.

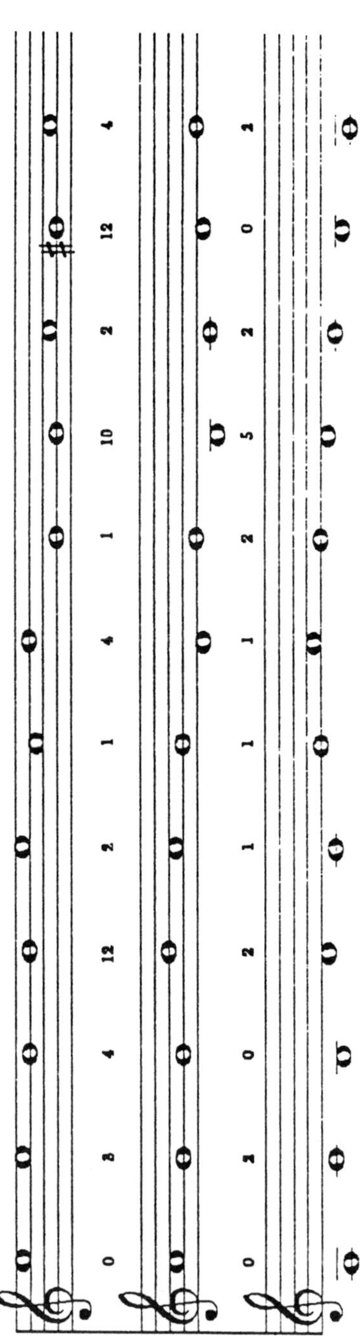

Figure 16.5
Three-voice first-species aeolian mode.

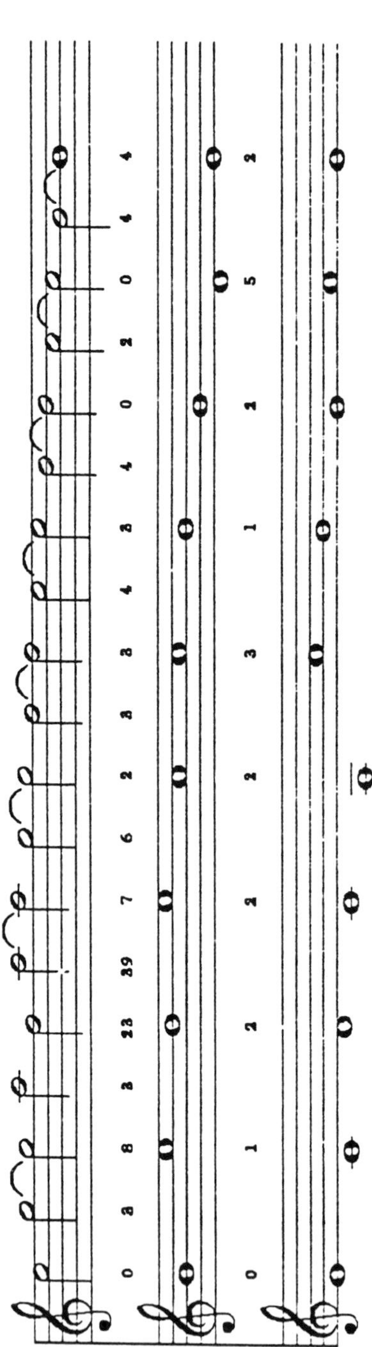

Figure 16.6
Three-voice fourth-species phrygian mode.

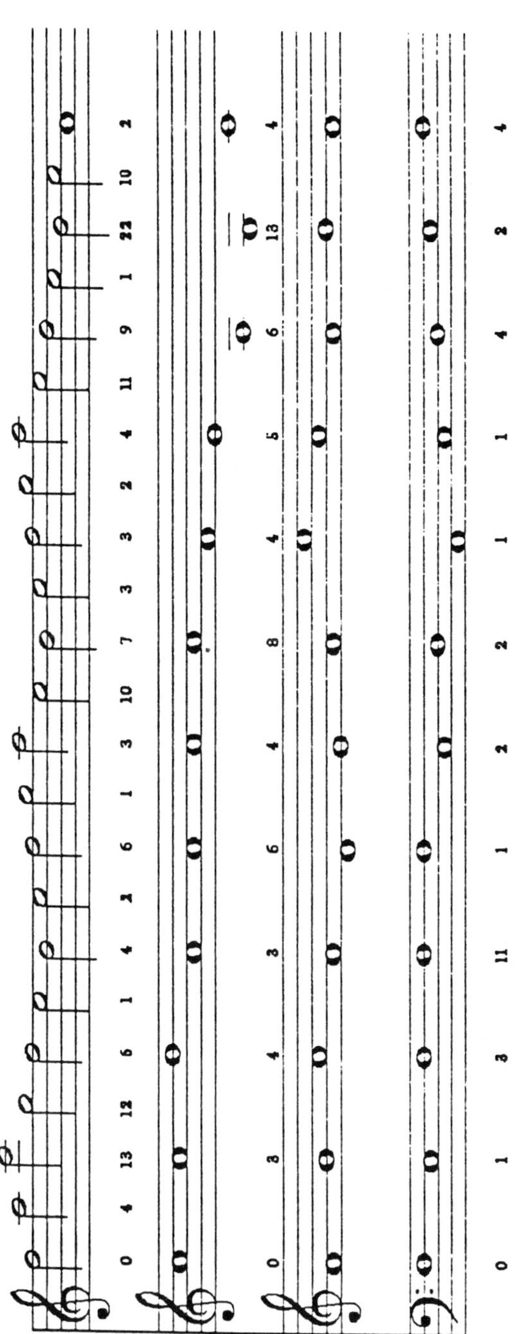

Figure 16.7
Four-voice second-species lydian mode.

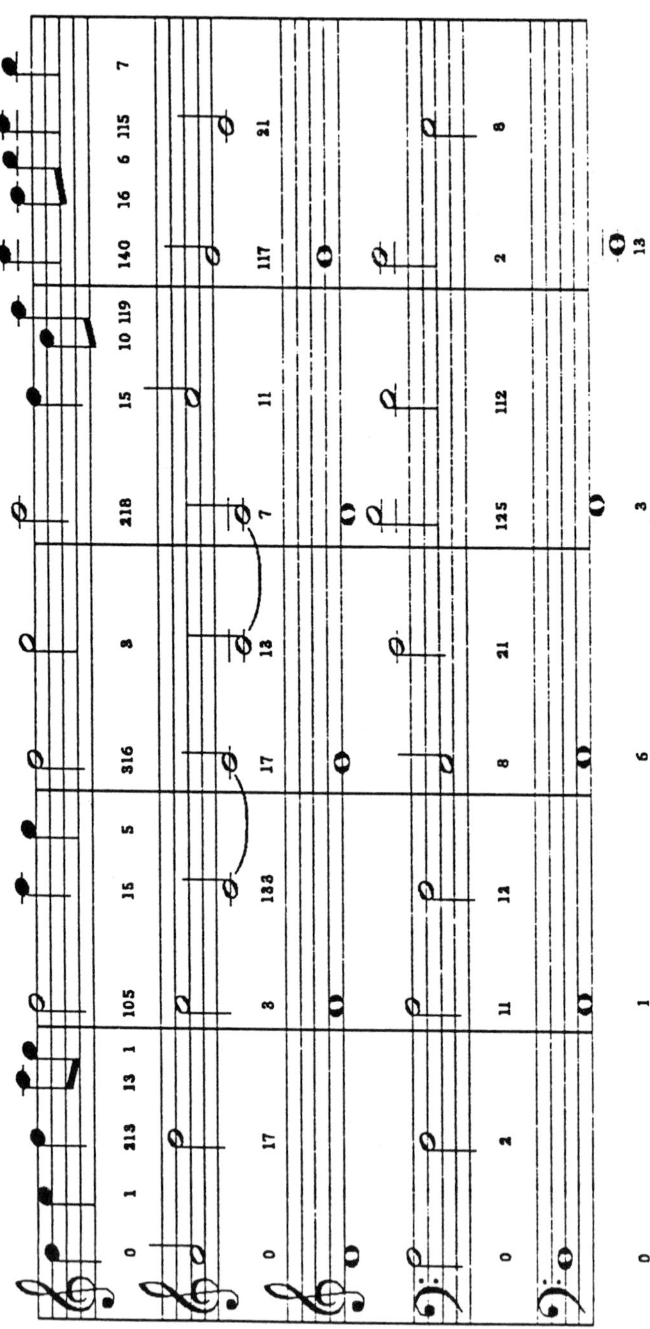
0 1 213 13 1 105 15 5 316 8 218 15 10 119 140 16 6 115 7
0 17 3 133 17 13 7 11 117 21
0 2 11 12 8 21 125 112 2 8
0 1 6 3 13

Figure 16.8
Five-voice fifth-species dorian mode.

References

[1] J. J. Fux (1725). *The Study of Counterpoint from Johann Joseph Fux's Gradus ad Parnassum*, translated and edited by Alfred Mann. W. W. Norton and Co., New York, 1971.

[2] W. G. Schottstaedt (1984). Automatic Species Counterpoint. Stan-M-19, CCRMA, May.

17 A Computer Music Language

William Schottstaedt

The computer has gained widespread acceptance as a sound synthesis engine, an analysis tool, and a graphical score printer. In addition to these uses, many composers are intrigued by the possibility that computer languages can provide new, perhaps valuable, ways to express and explore musical thoughts. Most of the software development effort to date, however, has gone into reinventing computer analogs to existing musical notations. Early compositional tools (Score for example) made it relatively easy to type in twelve-tone piano music. Other systems depend on elaborate menus and icons for access to simple facilities such as "draw a note" and "transpose." There have even been attempts to build translators so that composers can put their thoughts in "natural language."

I believe that these efforts are misguided. Throughout this century composers have griped and moaned about the inadequacy of existing music notations. With the arrival of the computer, notation has become a nightmare. Common music notation, for example, is intended for music based on simple rhythms and twelve divisions of the octave. But many composers want to experiment with other ways to organize pitch and with rhythmic values that are not based on divisions of an obvious beat. In "Water Music," for example, I use two tuning systems based on 13 and 48 tones in the octave. In "You're So Far Away," I divided the octave into 144 tones, then warped the entire fabric of an ostensibly normal twelve-tone piece into a complex overall pitch trajectory. Accurate pitch and rhythm notation is only one aspect of the problem; consider trying to notate the timbre manipulations or the spatial movements that are taken for granted in computer synthesis. But other existing notations do no better. "Natural language" is diffuse and ambiguous; can anyone imagine writing a complete "natural language" specification of an actual piece of music? Graphics-oriented approaches on the other hand can handle only the simplest compositional needs. Even the good ones eventually degenerate into a blizzard of lines and cute hieroglyphs.

This problem cannot be ignored, however; a composer needs an adequate record of his thoughts so that he can remember and reuse them later and communicate them to other composers. It may be satisfying to "click on" an icon and see the screen go through violent spasms, but this action by itself leaves no record that can be easily edited and incorporated into other such sequences. In addition, every detail of the music must be decided somewhere, either by the composer, the performers, or the software controlling the sound synthesis. In hand-holding systems, these decisions are made by the original programmer, who may have only the vaguest notion what things are actually useful. Most serious composers want to get at every detail while exploring arbitrarily speculative ideas. Nothing short of a real computer language can give that access in any reasonable form. Why are we so often told that it is necessary to protect composers from the terrifying arcana of computer languages? Why do composers assume that computer languages are beyond their grasp? My experience has been that computer languages are extremely easy to learn, and that once a composer dispenses with all the well-intentioned but suffocating layers of protection, he finds the freedom and power at his disposal exciting and stimulating.

Let us pretend that Sesame Street's Don Music has decided to tackle the computer. Although our contract says "keep Mr. Music happy," we do not intend to do any more programming than necessary. "But I don't need much," he assures us, "I just want to make a racket"! Once we set about building the Don's music system, we notice that at some point we have to decide what to do next. If we are not satisfied with pure improvisation and performance, we must remember what we did; a list of musical events has to be generated so that a synthesizer or a performer can be told what to do. With this list in hand we can go back later and edit the data to fix musical problems.

In some systems the list of events is only implicit in the scheduling decisions. At CCRMA the list is saved as a text file called, not surprisingly, the note list. It contains a time-ordered sequence of notes. Each "note" is a procedure call that passes to the procedure (normally a synthesizer patch called an "instrument") all the data it needs to produce the right musical event at that moment. Say we have a synthesizer patch that our friends can be convinced to call a "violin." On each note, this violin needs to know its onset time, duration, frequency, and amplitude. To remember this data, we write a text file full of violin notes of the form

```
Violin, 10, 2, 440, .1;
Violin, 11, 1, 660, .1;
```

These two lines produce two violin notes. The first starts at time 10 sec and lasts 2 sec. Its frequency is 440 Hz, and its amplitude is .1 (rather loud). The second violin note starts 1 sec later, lasts 1 sec, and its frequency is 660 Hz.

A list of such calls has several good points. First text editors are very sophisticated these days, so even extensive editing of such lists is easy. Second, there is no necessary limit on the number of parameters, so there is no a priori limit on the extent to which each note can be polished and refined. Third, note list syntax is simple, so programs can easily handle the data in various ways. We can display the note list as a normal score, for example, or mix it with other note lists. Fourth, the note list can contain all the data needed to remake the music. It is often far more straightforward to edit the note list to fix small errors than to change the procedures that generated that note list.

Unfortunately, the note list is often hard to read as music. Computer instruments have become extremely complex, sometimes needing more than 100 parameters on each call. Because synthesizers have become more powerful, it is not uncommon for composers to have more than 50 instruments running at once. Compositions now routinely last more than 20 minutes (a trend that is not universally regarded with approbation), and may call for dozens of notes per second. The instruments are interleaved according to note onset times, and the musical effect of each parameter depends on the instrument (and may therefore be hidden from the reader of the note list). It is not surprising that the note list can become a bewildering morass of undecipherable data. A more limited system may not be able to approach this level of complexity, but that is not something it should brag about.

There are two straightforward ways to make the note list easier to read. First, we can use variables instead of arithmetic expressions. For example, let us transpose our earlier notes:

Variable Transposition, Loud;

Transposition ← 9/8;

Loud ← .1;

Violin, 10, 2, 440*Transposition, Loud;

Violin, 11, 1, 660*Transposition, Loud;

In large note lists, the use of variables can make a major improvement in readability and editability. The second improvement is to use named parameters with defaults for unstated parameters. The note list then contains only the data that are different from the default expectations for that note. Because the parameter names are included in the note list, much of the data has built in explanations as to what it means. Some forms of editing (reorchestration in particular) become easier if all our instruments share a common set of parameter names. For example, if both our bell instrument and our violin have the parameters "Amplitude" and "Frequency," we have a good chance of getting a reasonable result when we interchange which instrument plays which note. The named parameters can occur in any order, so we no longer have to try to remember where each parameter belongs in the parameter list. A simple example is the following, slightly edited excerpt from the fifth movement of "Colony":

```
Violin, 195.0, 9, 51.914*9/8, Amplitude: .020, FmIndex: 2, Reverb: .4;
Violin, 195.0, 9, 103.828*9/8, Amplitude: .020, FmIndex: 2, Reverb: .4;
Violin, 195.0, 9, 207.655*9/64, Amplitude: .020, FmIndex: 2, Reverb: .4;
```

It should be clear that "FmIndex: 2" causes the note to be brighter than usual. If all the violin parameters were present, the number "2" would be hidden somewhere in about sixty other numbers and envelope names. Here nearly all these parameters have taken their default values so the index setting jumps out at the reader. Of course, we had to repeat the message for each note. In common music notation, a mark such as "brighter" or "louder" can apply to hundreds of notes, but to do the same in the note list requires some fooling around.

Even with these improvements Don Music complains that he cannot read his note lists. After a lot of grumbling, we agree to provide arbitrary graphical and pictorial representations of the data. A sophisticated example of such a system is the Sced editor of the SSSP project. At CCRMA graphical representations are provided by a subprogram called NED, which runs under the text editor (E). One of its more useful displays shows the note list data in the current editor window as a normal musical score. Another provides a proportional display (frequency versus time). We have not been able to go as far in this direction as Buxton's group because graphics are not fully supported at CCRMA. We do not have a pointing device, for example, so it is not easy to move around in a graph.

Don Music is still not satisfied. It is very tedious to type out and edit by hand every parameter of every note. Even with fancier graphical facilities, Don Music needs a way to write note lists and specify complex transformations of the data. Unfortunately for our repose, he has noticed that many of his ideas can be expressed as computer algorithms. A crescendo, for example, can be expressed as a simple ramp function applied to the amplitude data. A repeating pattern can be handled with a circular list. Many melodic transformations can be treated as vector operations. In fact most instrument parameters follow algorithms that are extremely tiresome to work out by hand but that are easily expressed in a computer language. Let us develop a language for the Don and call it PLA.

Our first version of PLA is based on Sail, an Algol language that happens to be in heavy use at CCRMA. The Sail part of PLA provides macros, various data types, arithmetic and string operators, conditionals, loops, subroutines, recursion, contexts (for backtracking), and so on. The Lisp part of PLA provides an object oriented facility based on the flavor paradigm of Symbolics Lisp. A few constructs are borrowed from Score [7] (pitch names, rhythm names, motives, and a tempo statement). Besides these, we add a few somewhat unusual features. The first is the notion of a "voice." Composers rarely think of an entire piece in terms that are strictly ordered in time from the start. Since the musical events must be in the right order when they emerge from the loudspeaker, notions such as "melody," "chord," and "phrase" must be sorted in time. In PLA, this is done with voices, sections, and files (note lists).

A voice can be thought of as a musical line, encapsulating the knowledge necessary to produce that melody without making any assumptions about the context in which the melody is expressed. A PLA voice need not have any relation to a voice that appears on a stave of an orchestral score. The voice body is simply a block of code that can, if it wants, instruct that a note or musical event be placed in the note list. The scheduler handles the mixing of voices to ensure that everything is ordered properly for the synthesizer. Because a voice is a process (with local state and a notion of local time), fancy event decisions can be deferred until "run time," thereby enabling the composer to express, at least in a rudimentary manner, the kinds of interactions that happen between performers in chamber concerts. The same capability makes it possible to write authomatic counterpoint solvers and automatic serial music generators.

Another somewhat unusual feature of PLA is the envelope. An envelope is a list of coordinate pairs giving a set of "breakpoints" connected by line segments. Given an x-axis value, PLA then interpolates, if necessary, to find the corresponding y-axis value. Envelopes have been used to control everything from the amplitude of a particular note to the tempo of an entire piece. In fact, several composers have developed huge composing programs based almost exclusively on envelopes as filters of otherwise random selections.

Some examples might make this disucssion less nebulous. We present first a very simple piece of PLA code that calls for a voice and an envelope. The comments in the code may help the computer-naive reader figure out what is going on.

```
Pars Name, Onset, Dur, Freq, Amp;
                          ! these are the instrument parameters;
                          ! "Name" is the instrument name;
                          ! "Onset" is note's starting time in seconds;
                          ! "Dur" is the note's duration;
                          ! "Freq" is its frequency in Hertz;
                          ! "Amp" is its amplitude;
Seg AmpRamp .1 0 .2 10;
                          ! make an envelope named "AmpRamp";
                          ! the odd order (y, x) is a holdover from the
                          distant past;
Voice Simp;
                          ! set up a voice named "Simp";
Begin
                          ! "Begin" marks the start of the voice block;
MyEnd ← 10.0;
                          ! "MyEnd" is when the voice stops;
                          ! there are many ways to decide a voice is done;
                          ! we could have said "Simp(0 : 10)" for
                          example;
Onset ← Onset + Dur*.9;
                          ! each note overlaps the last one slightly;
                          ! the first Onset time will be 0 because Dur
                          starts out 0 (it hasn't been set yet);
Dur ← Rhythm: q, h, q, q;
                          ! q = quarter note, h = half note;
                          ! there are many ways to express an arbitrary
                          list;
                          ! this one is borrowed from Score;
Freq ← [c, d, e, f, g, a, b, c*2];
                          ! another form of a list – c = 261.62 Hz;
                          ! this statement produces a rising c-major
                          scale;
```

```
                          ! the list of expressions in "[ ]" has an internal;
                          ! pointer to the current element which returns;
                          ! to the beginning after the last element;
                          ! An Alberti bass becomes [c, e, g, e]/2 for
                          example;
Amp ← AmpRamp[Onset];
                          ! "Amp" depends on the value of the envelope;
                          !   at the time the note starts;
If Dur > = 2 Then Amp ← Amp*2;
                          ! we want long notes to be louder;
End;
                          ! "End" closes the voice block;
```

The voice "Simp" creates notes until it decides it is done. On each note the voice block is evaluated and the resulting values for the voice parameters are sent to the note list. I think this code presents the actual musical intentions more clearly than the equivalent paragraph of "natural language," and with more specificity than graphical systems can attain. In this particular case, common music notation is better than PLA code, but in more complex cases common music notation suffers the same problems that afflict other pictorial representations. I think that the PLA code is easy to read, write, and edit. The syntax of the PLA code is not very important; the Lisp-based PLA has basically the same good and bad features that the Algol-based PLA has. The important factor is the access to a real language, not its appearance on the screen.

The note list produced by the example given above is

```
! instrument, onset, dur, freq, amp;
  SIMP, .000, 1.000, 261.620, .100;
  SIMP, .900, 2.000, 293.660, .218;
  SIMP, 2.700, 1.000, 329.630, .127;
  SIMP, 3.600, 1.000, 349.230, .136;
  SIMP, 4.500, 1.000, 391.990, .145;
  SIMP, 5.400, 2.000, 440.000, .308;
  SIMP, 7.200, 1.000, 493.890, .172;
  SIMP, 8.100, 1.000, 523.240, .181;
  SIMP, 9.000, 1.000, 261.620, .190;
  SIMP, 9.900, 2.000, 293.660, .398;
```

Assume we are happy with this note list. Next we want to take eight copies of it, staggered by 4 sec, each a ninth of an octave (4/3 semitones) higher than the last, with the individual notes slightly staggered in onset time, and with a little fleck of sound added to each note that happens to be higher than 600 Hz. In PLA a note list (called a "file" here) is just a kind of voice:

```
Pars Name, Onset, Dur, Freq, Amp;
Integer I;
For I ← 1 Step 1 Until 8 Do
  File Scale.Pla;                    ! use our scale 8 times;
    Begin
    Real Transposition, NewStartTime;
    I_Only:                          ! this block is evaluated only upon
                                       voice initialization;
        Begin                        ! "I_Only" is a borrowing from
                                       Mus10;
        Transposition ← 2↑(i/9);     ! each repetition is 2/3 of a tone
                                       higher;
        NewStartTime ← (i − 1) * 4; ! repetitions start at 4 second
                                       intervals;
        End;
    Onset ← Onset + Ran/10 + NewStartTime; ! stagger onsets a little;
    Freq ← Freq * Transposition;
    If Freq > 600                    ! add a little note to each high note;
      Then
        Voice Fleck;
          Begin
          Real Start Time;
          I_Only:
            Begin
            MyNoteNum ← 1;           ! Each Fleck voice produces only
                                       one note;
            StartTime ← Onset;       ! Fleck starts at the same time as
                                       the high note;
            End;
          Onset ← StartTime;
          Dur ← .10;
```

```
        Freq ← 500 + Ran * 500;
        Amp ← .01;
        End;
End;
```

This example is still extremely simple compared to the sorts of things composers actually want to do. I hope it helps demonstrate that there is really no way to determine in advance every compositional procedure that every composer is going to want. Only a system that is completely open-ended is even a satisfactory beginning.

But Don Music is still unhappy. "Oh, I'll never get it," he cries. "Why can't I just play my piano?" To please him, we build the necessary sensors and write the necessary software to capture whatever notes Don Music plays. From this data, we can provide an editable note list approximating his performance. The Don soon discovers, however, that he, like most composers, does not particularly want his fingers thinking for him. Devices like piano keyboards make very definite assumptions about the kind of music we want to produce. But, Mr. Music points out, there is another way to use "real-time" interactions. We can write compositional algorithms, then poke at them while they are running. Our basic input device is the typewriter keyboard. Although the keyboard is noisy, it is superior to a piano keyboard because it is more compact, has more states, and can be used to input arbitrary commands. It is also superior to a device like the electronic violin because the composer does not have to deal with a virtuoso performer, and does not have to learn yet another difficult set of muscular motions just to talk to his instrument. It is not superior in some respects to a rack of knobs and dials, except that the latter are hard to reprogram quickly.

The composer now writes PLA code to specify the actions of his instruments, and to tell the synthesizer how to react to keyboard input. PLA then drives the synthesizer directly, treating all real time input as PLA code. The composer's actions consist of programmatic instructions such as

```
StartViolin       "start up aother violin"
Amp ← .1          "set the global amplitude to .1"
Simp: Att ← .01   "set Simp's attack time to .01"
```

We have had as many as thirty PLA voices running moderately complex compositional algorithms with interactive controls on many aspects of the improvisation (reverberation, FM index, pitch mode, tempo, and so on).

To my surprise, neither the real-time input of data nor the real-time interaction with composing algorithms has generated much interest among other composers. Don Music ends up editing note lists and writing PLA code; our fancy sensors lie forgotten in some corner gathering dust. Perhaps the importance of real-time interaction has been overrated. Certainly composition is not normally a real-time process; I doubt that Don Music even thinks in real time. Composers need reasonably rapid turnaround, but very few of them are interested in a new way to make a one-man band.

At CCRMA, composers normally use the note list as their principal music representation. PLA code produces the first approximation to a phrase or section, and gives the composer numerous ways to try out fancy changes to existing data. Many composers have worked with PLA without unacceptable suffering. I hope that the compositional tools of the future do not restrict composers to anything less than the full power of a real language.

References

[1] Buxton, W., et al. 1979. "The Evolution of the SSSP Score Editing Tools." *Computer Music Journal* 3(4).

[2] Reiser, J, ed. 1976. "SAIL." Report STAN-CS-574. Stanford University Artificial Intelligence Laboratory.

[3] Samuel, A., and M. Frost. 1986. "E." Stanford; SAIL, Stanford University.

[4] Schottstaedt, William. 1982. "Pla—a Composer's Idea of a Language." *Computer Music Journal* 7(1).

[5] Schottstaedt, William. 1985. "Ned." Stanford: CCRMA. Stanford University.

[6] Schottstaedt, William, 1984. "Pla Reference Manual." Report STAN-M-19. Stanford University Department of Music.

[7] Smith, Leland, 1972. "SCORE—a Musician's Approach to Computer Music." *Journal of the Audio Engineering Society* 20(1):7–14.

[8] Tovar. 1977. "Music Manual." Stanford: CCRMA, Stanford University.

[9] Weinreb, D., and D. Moon. 1981. "Lisp Machine Manual." Cambridge Massachusetts: MIT Artificial Intelligence Laboratory.

18 Real-Time Scheduling and Computer Accompaniment

Roger Dannenberg

18.1 Introduction

Some of the most interesting applications of computers in music involve real-time computer music systems. The term "real time" refers to systems in which behavior is dependent upon time. As a simple example, a program that controls a music synthesizer to perform a piece of music is a real-time program. This sort of program is perhaps the least interesting form of real-time computer music system because it ignores the possibility of live real-time interaction between human performers and computer music systems. More sophisticated approaches can be classified into at least three categories: computer music instruments, computer accompaniment systems, and interactive composition systems. Although all of these categories are inspired by traditional terminology, it should be emphasized that the special properties of the computer force a rethinking of the meaning of terms like "instrument" and "composition." This reorganization of meaning is one of the attractions of computer music.

A computer music instrument is, by analogy to acoustic instruments, a device that produces sound in response to human gesture and control. Most electronic keyboard instruments are now computer controlled; thus they provide examples of traditionally oriented real-time computer music systems. A more innovative instrument can be seen in the sequential drum of Max Mathews [11]. This instrument can play stored sequences of notes when triggered by striking a specially instrumented drum. The position and force on the drum can control different aspects of each note.

A computer accompaniment system is based on the model of traditional accompaniment in which a score is initially provided for both the solo and the accompaniment. The job of the accompanist is to synchronize with the soloist. One of the sound examples is a recording of a trumpet solo accompanied by computer [4].

While accompaniment systems are given musical materials in the form of a precomposed score, interactive composition systems use the computer actually to generate musical materials in response to input from live musicians. Other appropriate terms for this type of system include improvisation and composed improvisation [6]. A short version of *Jimmy Durante Boulevard* [5], a work of composed improvisation, is included as

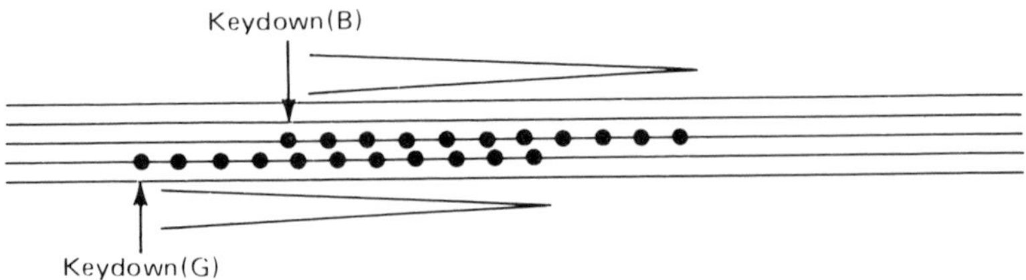

Figure 18.1
A musical timing diagram of a potential execution of the *echo* program. Keydown events are indicated by arrows.

another sound example (given on the accompanying compact disk). In this piece, a keyboard, flute, and trumpet are interfaced to a computer, which also controls several music synthesizers. A number of tasks run simultaneously, analyzing input from the flute and keyboard, recording material from the trumpet, computing musical material to be performed, and controlling the synthesizers.

All of these real-time systems depend upon schedulers as a means of coordinating and ordering the execution of many small tasks over the course of time. To illustrate the role of the scheduler more specifically, the following example presents a moderately difficult real-time programming task and solves it in an elegant manner.

18.1.1 An Example

The problem is to play a sequence of notes with diminishing loudness to simulate an echo. An echo sequence must be triggered whenever a key is pressed on a keyboard, and sequences may overlap in time. Suppose, for example, that a G and a B are pressed at times indicated by arrows in figure 18.1. The resulting sequences of events are seen to interleave in time. A scheduler is essential for the realization of programs with several independent but simultaneous real-time tasks such as this.

A program that realizes this behavior is given below. It is written in a stylized version of C that should be understandable to anyone familiar with a modern programming language like C, Pascal, or Ada. To avoid clutter, the nesting of program statements will be indicated by indentation rather than by explicit symbols. Algol (and Pascal) assignment (: =) and equality (=) symbols will be used in place of the symbols used in C (= for assignment, == for equality). The meaning should always be clear from context. **Keywords** will be printed in **boldface**, *program identifiers* will be printed in *italics*, and CONSTANT VALUES will be printed in SMALL CAPITALS.

```
echo(ptich, loudness)
  loudness := loudness–5
  if loudness > 0
    note(pitch, loudness)
    cause(DELAY, echo, pitch, loudness)

keydown(pitch)
  note(pitch, INITIALLOUDNESS)
  cause(DELAY, echo, pitch, INITIALLOUDNESS)
```

This program is executed in an environment that continuously looks for input from a keyboard. When a key is pushed, *keydown* is called with the pitch of the key. The *keydown* routine schedules the *echo* routine to run after a short delay by calling *cause*.

The *cause* routine is critical to the behavior of the program. Its first argument is a delay and its second argument is the name of a routine. The *cause* routine schedules a call to the specified routine after the given delay. Any other parameters to *cause* are saved and passed to the specified routine when it is called. Thus, the *echo* routine will be called DELAY time units after *keydown*. The *echo* routine begins by decrementing its *loudness* parameter. If the parameter is still greater than zero, *echo* plays the given note (by calling *note*) and uses *cause* to schedule another call to *echo*. This will decrease the loudness further, play another note and schedule yet another call. This process repeats until the loudness goes to zero or below, at which time *echo* does nothing. Since *echo* does not schedule anything else at this point, the sequence of notes comes to an end.

Since each call to *echo* runs for a very short time (typically less than 1 ms), there is plenty of processing time to deal with other actions that are scheduled to occur in between the notes of an echo sequence. In particular, many overlapping echo sequences can be active at once. Each sequence uses the same *echo* routine but is characterized by a distinct *pitch* parameter. (With this version of *echo*, pressing a key a second time during a sequence will start a second sequence with the same pitch, which may be undesirable.)

This example illustrates a few important concepts. Virtually all timing in conventional real-time programs is achieved by explicit calls to service routines like *cause*. It is usually assumed that programs execute very fast except for these calls, which usually have the effect of delaying execution. During the time execution is delayed, there is normally enough time to perform many other actions. By taking advantage of this idle time, other tasks can be processed. The scheduler (in this case *cause*) plays an important role in the management of time-dependent tasks because it is responsible for running tasks in the right sequence and at the right time.

The *cause* routine used in the *echo* program has two nice properties. It not only serves to schedule events, but it also saves parameters and passes them to the events when they are performed. Since saving and passing parameters is largely a straightforward matter of bookkeeping, only the scheduling aspects of *cause* will be considered further.

The *cause* construct is due to Douglas Collinge, who designed the language Moxie [7]. Upon learning about Moxie, this author promptly stole the central idea and the name to create Moxc, a version of Moxie based on the C programming language.[1] Moxc was used to implement *Jimmy Durante Boulevard* and runs on several personal computers.

In the remainder of this chapter, various implementations of real-time schedulers are presented. Then implementations that perform scheduling with respect to a variable-speed time reference are examined. This provides a natural way to implement musical effects such as tempo change and rubato. Finally, a more sophisticated scheduler is presented that incorporates musical knowledge to enhance its ability to adjust tempo dynamically to obtain musical results.

18.2 Real-Time Schedulers

The *echo* program illustrates the need to schedule events for performance at a specific time in the future. This section considers a sequence of scheduler implementations, each one containing an improvement over the previous one. The final implementation will exhibit excellent real-time behavior.

It is convenient to define some primitive operations that will be used by each scheduler. The *gettime*( ) operation reads the current real time; for example,

$t := gettime()$

assigns the current time to t. The *setalarm*(t) operation causes the operation *alarm*( ) to be invoked at time *t*. If *t* is less than the current time, then *alarm*( ) is invoked immediately. If an alarm is pending due to a previous *setalarm*, then invoking *setalarm* again will cancel the effect of the previous *setalarm*. In other words, at most one alarm can be pending. This corresponds to typical real-time systems that have a hardware counter (the reading of which is modeled by *gettime*) and a hardware timer (the setting of which is modeled by *setalarm*). When the timer times out, a hardware interrupt is generated (modeled by invoking *alarm*).

Using these primitives, the goal is to implement a scheduler with the operation *schedule*(*id, time*), where *id* is an event identifier and *time* is the time of the event. The *schedule* operation causes the operation *event*(*id*) to occur at *time* if *time* is in the future. Otherwise, the operation takes place immediately.

The *schedule* and *setalarm* operations are similar in that they each cause another operation (*event* and *alarm*, respectively) to take place in the future. However, *schedule* is more powerful because it "remembers" multiple requests. Since multiple requests can be outstanding, *schedule* associates an identifier with each request. One use of *schedule* is to implement the *cause* routine used in the *echo* program. In this case, *id* would be the address of a block of memory containing a routine entry point and parameters. The *event* operation would run the indicated routine with the saved parameters. Another typical use of *schedule* is to reactivate sleeping processes. In this case, *id* would be the address of the process descriptor that is to be reactivated. Thus, *schedule* is a general building block that can be used in a number of ways.

Two important observations to keep in mind are that (1) the scheduler must keep track of an arbitrary number of pending *schedule* requests, and that (2) the requests do not necessarily arrive in the same order in which they must be satisfied. Thus, a scheduler must have some way to remember a set of pending requests and a method for sorting requests into time order.

In the implementations that follow, the same notational conventions seen in the *echo* program example will be used. Because the C language notation for structures is rather cumbersome, the following conventions will be followed. A structure with elements A, B, . . . , C is created by calling *new*(A, B, . . . , C). The fields FIELD1, FIELD2, . . . , FIELDN of a structure *s* are denoted by *s*.FIELD1, *s*.FIELD2, . . . , *s*.FIELDN.

18.2.1 Implementation 1

A straightforward implementation of the scheduler wakes up and runs at every increment of time and looks at the pending requests to see if one should be satisfied. The data structure consists of *requests*, a list of pairs of *id*s and *time*s, which is initially empty. The variable *t* is used to compute the next time at which *alarm* should be invoked. The scheduler is initialized by setting *t* and invoking *setalarm* (*setalarm* will immediately generate an interrupt that calls *alarm*):

```
initialize( )
   set requests to EMPTY
   t := gettime( )
   setalarm(t)
```

The *schedule* operation adds an *id* and *time* to the *requests* list:

```
schedule(id, time)
   insert new(id, time) into requests
```

The *alarm* operation searches through the list of requests looking for any whose time has come. It then increments *t* and calls *setalarm* so that *alarm* will be invoked every unit of time.

```
alarm( )
   for each r in requests
      if r.TIME <= gettime( )
         remove r from requests
         event(r.ID)
   t := t + 1
   setalarm(t)
```

Note: Since *schedule* and *alarm* operate on the same variables, it is *essential* that *alarm* not be invoked by an interrupt during the execution of *schedule*. In order to simplify this presentation, it is assumed throughout that the executions of *schedule* and *alarm* are always mutually exclusive.

The *schedule* operation has the nice property that it takes a fixed amount of time, assuming *requests* is implemented as a linked list [1]. However, this scheduler suffers from two problems. First, the *alarm* operation must look at every pending request every time it is invoked. As the number of requests goes up, so does the computational cost of *alarm*. Second, *alarm* is invoked

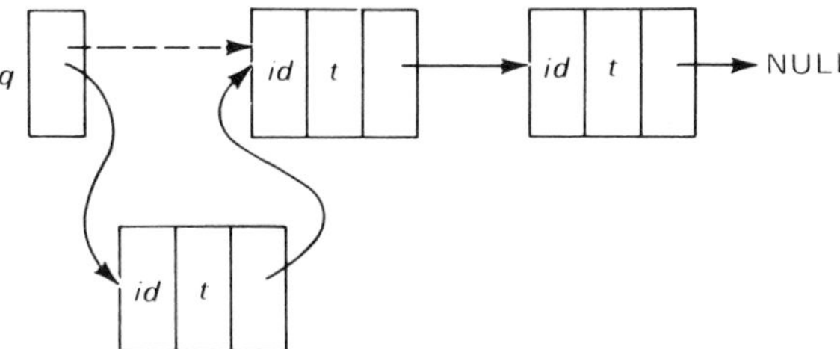

Figure 18.2
Inserting a new element into a linked list.

even when there are no requests to be satisfied. This might be tolerable if the time needed to execute *alarm* were small, but that is not the case here. The next implementation uses a *priority queue* to reduce the cost of *alarm* operations.

18.2.2 Implementation 2

A *priority queue* is a data structure that contains a set of items, each of which has a *priority*. In this case, items will be requests ([id, time] structures), and the priority of an item will be determined by its time component. Priority queues have an *insert* operation, which adds an item to the queue, an *inspect* operation, which returns the [id, time] structure with the highest priority (earliest time), and a *remove* operation that removes the item with the highest priority. Since priorities are static (that is, the priority cannot change after the insert operation), an efficient implementation is to represent the queue as a linked list, sorted by increasing time values. Each list element is a structure with three fields: ID, TIME, and NEXT, where the NEXT field is a link to the next list element. As explained above, *new*(*id*, *time*, *next*) will allocate and initialize a new linked list node. To insert a new *id* and *time* in the list, the *new* function is called to allocate a structure to hold the *id* and *time* and remember (in the NEXT field) a reference to the remainder of the list. Figure 18.2 illustrates the operation of inserting a new item into a list, an operation that will be used throughout this chapter. The operation shown is

$q := new(id, t, q)$

and the value of q before the assignment is indicated by a dotted line. NULL represents a pointer to the empty list.

For the scheduler, the queue is initially a list with one node whose time component is infinity (this simplifies other parts of the implementation).

```
newqueue()
   return new(0, infinity, NULL)
```

An implementation of *insert* is

```
insert(queue, id, time)
   if time < queue.TIME
      return new(id, time, queue)
   pointer := queue
   while t >= pointer.NEXT.TIME
      pointer := pointer.NEXT
   pointer.NEXT := new(id, time, pointer.NEXT)
   return queue
```

To complete the priority queue implementation, *inspect* and *remove* operations must be provided. In the implementation below, *inspect* returns data from the front of the queue, and *remove* returns a reference to the rest of the queue. Notice also that the problems of storage reclamation are ignored to simplify this presentation:

```
inspect(queue)
   return new(queue.ID, queue.TIME)

remove(queue)
   return queue.NEXT
```

A new scheduler can be implemented using a priority queue. This time, *requests* is initialized as a priority queue:

```
initialize()
   requests := newqueue()
   t := gettime()
   setalarm(t)
```

The *schedule* routine is as follows:

```
schedule(id, time)
   requests := insert(requests, id, time)
```

Now, since the request with the earliest time is at the front of the queue, *alarm* only needs to look at the front of the list of requests.

```
alarm( )
   r := inspect(requests)
   while gettime( ) >= r.TIME
      event(r.ID)
      requests := remove(requests)
      r := inspect(requests)
   t := t + 1
   setalarm(t)
```

This implementation solves the first problem of Implementation 1, namely, the *alarm* operation now takes time proportional to the number of requests ready to be satisfied plus a small fixed overhead. This is quite good, since satisfying the requests by calling *event* is likely to dominate the total computation cost. This implementation still suffers from the fact that a small fixed cost is incurred every time unit because *alarm* is invoked whether or not there are pending requests.

Even though this scheduler is a great improvement over Implementation 1, a new problem has been introduced. Recall that in Implementation 1, the *schedule* operation took a fixed amount of time. In the new implementation, the *schedule* operation takes time proportional to the number of pending requests in the worst case. This is because the *insert* operation may have to scan the entire queue in order to find the right place to insert a new item. Thus, *alarm* is now efficient at the cost of making *schedule* rather inefficient. Nevertheless, most real schedulers are essentially identical to Implementation 2.

18.2.3 Implementation 3

One way to improve the previous scheduler is to use a faster implementation of priority queues. Since faster implementations are not common knowledge, at least not as common as they should be, a short digression on fast priority queues is in order to present one algorithm for priority queues.

A data structure called a *heap* provides a fast way to implement a priority queue [3]. The time required to insert and remove elements is proportional to the logarithm of the number of elements in the queue. A heap is a complete (or full) binary tree in which each node stores a value that is less than or equal to the values of its children. Heaps are typically stored in an array where the first element (at index 1) is the root. The children of a node at index i are at array locations $2i$ and $2i + 1$. Figure 18.3 illustrates a heap and its array representation.

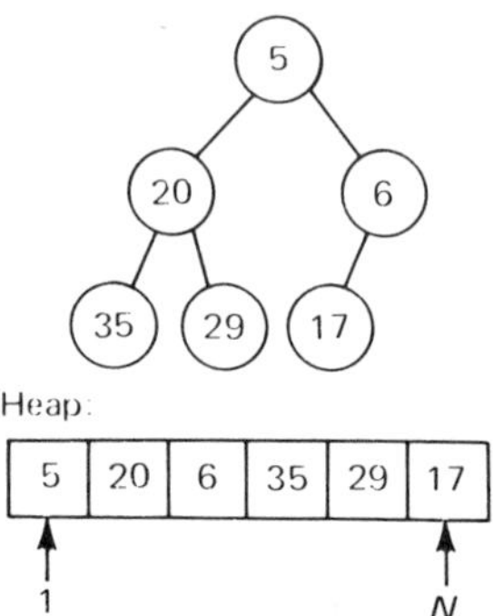

Figure 18.3
A heap data structure uses an array to represent a binary tree.

To treat the heap as a priority queue, *insert* and *remove* operations are needed. Let $H[1]$ through $H[N]$ be a heap. Initially, $N = 0$ and the heap is empty. To insert an element into the heap, the element is added to the end of the heap and is "bubbled up" by iteratively exchanging the element with its parent until the heap property is satisfied. To remove an element from the heap, the first element of the array is taken. To restore the heap property, the last element of the heap is moved to the beginning of the array (the top of the tree) and "bubbled down" as follows: the element is swapped with the smallest of its children until all of the element's children are greater than or equal to the element. The routines follow:

```
initialize()
   N := 0

insert(time)
   N := N + 1
   H[N] := time
   i := N
   while i > 1
      parent := floor(i/2)
      if H[parent] <= time
         return
      swap(H[i], H[parent])
      i := parent

remove()
   H[1] := H[N]
```

```
    N := N − 1
    i := 1
    child := 2 * i
    while child <= N
        if child + 1 <= N
            if H[child + 1] < H[child]
                child := child + 1
        child is now the index of the least child
        if H[i] <= H[child]
            return
        swap(H[i], H[child])
        i := child
        child := 2 * i

inspect( )
    return H[1]
```

In these routines, only the times are stored in the heap. For use in a scheduler, an event must be associated with each time. This is a straightforward extension to make once the algorithms are understood.

Notice that the size of array H sets an upper limit to the number of events that can be stored on the heap. A priority queue based on $2 \cdot 3$ trees [1] offers similar high performance without an intrinsic upper bound on the queue size.

Be redefining *newqueue*, *insert*, *inspect*, and *remove*, the scheduler can be improved without changing either *schedule* or *alarm*! Since this is a straightforward substitution, no further implementation details are presented here.

Using a heap for the priority queue changes the cost of both the *schedule* and the *alarm* operations. The *schedule* operation costs are reduced from something proportional to n to something proportional to $\log n$. This improvement is quite significant when n is large. The *alarm* operation, which formerly cost a fixed amount per satisfied request, now costs something proportional to $\log n$ per satisfied request. This is a small price to pay considering the savings made in the *schedule* operation.

18.2.4 Implementation 4

More improvements are possible. Implementation 4 incorporates an optimization that avoids the *alarm* operation unless necessary. The trick is to use *setalarm* to invoke *alarm* only at the proper time. Both *schedule* and *alarm* must be changed, and *setalarm* is not called when the system is initialized:

```
initialize( )
   requests := newqueue( )

schedule(id, time)
   requests := insert(requests, id, time)
   r := inspect(requests)
   setalarm(r.TIME)

alarm( )
   r := inspect(requests)
   while gettime( ) >= r.TIME
      event(r.ID)
      requests := remove(requests)
      r := inspect(requests)
   setalarm(r.TIME)
```

Notice that both *schedule* and *alarm* end by calling *setalarm*(*r*.TIME), where *r*.TIME is the time of the earliest pending request, as determined by *inspect*.[2] Thus, *alarm* will always be invoked when the next pending request is ready, but never earlier.

Implementation 4 saves a fixed cost at every time increment for which no request is ready. If the unit of time is very short, this can be a significant savings. Many real implementations use this technique to optimize Implementation 2. In most computer music applications, however, a time resolution of several milliseconds is adequate.[3] Therefore, the overhead of invoking the *alarm* operation at every unit of time could amount to less than 1% of the computing resources in a carefully written scheduler.

In a real-time computer music system, frequent operations that consume only a small amount of processing time are not as problematic as less frequent operations that involve significant computation. Following this line of reasoning, Implementation 4 has not led to a substantial improvement: an unimportant aspect of the scheduler has been optimized while significant overheads remain in the form of the priority queue operations invoked by *schedule* and *alarm*. Implementations 5 and 6 will incorporate a strategy that largely removes this problem.

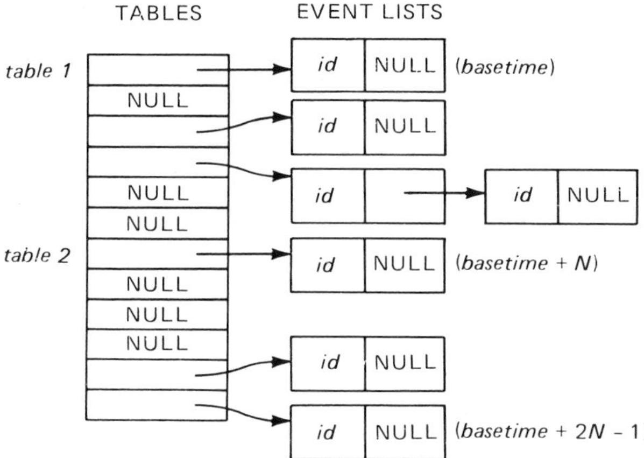

Figure 18.4
table 1 and *table 2*, with lists of events scheduled for times between *basetime* and *basetime* $+2N-1$.

18.2.5 Implementation 5

Implementation 5 is quite similar to Implementation 3, but a different method is used to avoid the overhead of the priority queue. The idea is to use the fact that at a time resolution of several milliseconds, a separate list of requests can be maintained for each unit of time for several seconds into the future. Since there is a separate list for each unit of time (see figure 18.4), scheduling an event amounts to inserting the event *id* in the proper list. This always takes a small constant amount of time. Furthermore, performing events is very fast. At each unit of time it is only necessary to advance to the next list and perform all of the events in the list. Thus, there is a small constant amount of time necessary per event and per time unit to perform events. This is much better than the performance of the previous scheduler when there are many events waiting in the queue.

The scheduler presented in this section will provide constant time scheduling and constant time event dispatching, but it will only allow scheduling a finite amount into the future. This limitation will be removed in the next section.

For reasons that will become clear later, two tables (arrays) of lists called *table1* and *table2* are used, and each will store N lists, named *table1*[*0*] ... *table1*[$N-1$] and *table2*[*0*] ... *table2*[$N-1$]. The operation *swap*(*table1*, *table2*) exchanges the contents of *table1* and *table2*.[4] When the scheduler is started, each table is filled with empty lists, *basetime* is initialized to the current time, and *settime* is used to invoke *alarm*:

```
initialize( )
   for i := 0 to N − 1
      table1[i] := NULL
      table2[i] := NULL
   basetime := gettime( )
   t := basetime
   setalarm(basetime)
```

Now, *table1*[*i*] (for any *i* between 0 and $N - 1$) will be a list of requests scheduled for time *basetime* + *i*, and *table2*[*i*] will hold requests scheduled for time *basetime* + *N* + *i*. In figure 18.4, *table1* and *table2* are shown. The scheduled time for several events is indicated in parentheses to the right of the events. Each table entry stores a possibly empty list of structures with two fields, *id* and *next*. Note that the time of an event is implied by the choice of table entry, so there is no need to store the time in the lists.

At time *basetime* + *N*, all requests in *table1* will have been satisfied, so *table1* can be reused for future events. This is accomplished by swapping *table1* and *table2* and adding *N* to *basetime*. Figure 18.5 illustrates the correspondence between table entries and time before and after a swap operation. Notice how *table1* is renamed and relocated in time to become the new *table2*.

The implementation of *alarm* is simple. First, if the end of *table1* is reached, swap tables. Then get the list of pending requests corresponding to the current time and call *event* for each *id* in the list. Finally, clear the current table entry to allow it to be reused when the tables are swapped.

```
alarm( )
   if t = basetime + N
      swap(table1, table2)
      basetime := t
   requests := table1[t − basetime]
   while requests <> NULL
      event(requests.ID)
      requests := requests.NEXT
```

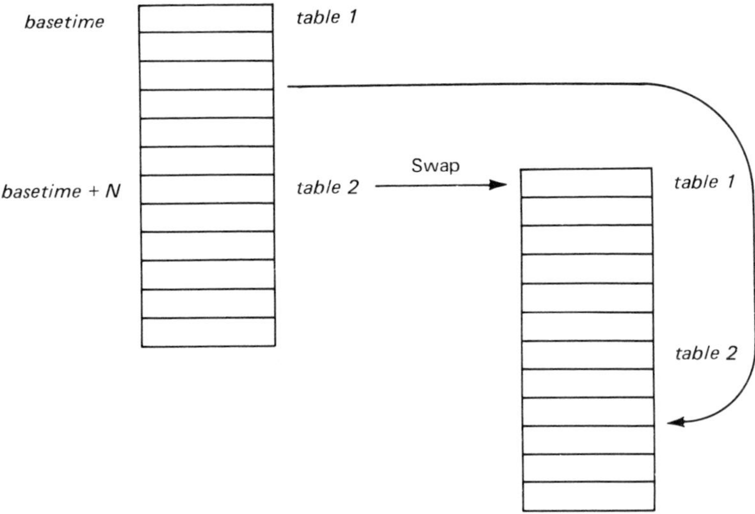

Figure 18.5
Data structures for Scheduler Implementation 5.

```
    table1[t – basetime] := NULL
    t := t + 1
    setalarm(t)
```

The *schedule* operation locates the right list and inserts the *id*:

```
schedule(id, time)
    if time < basetime + N
        table1[time – basetime] :=
            new(id, table1[time – basetime])
    else if time < basetime + (2 * N)
        table2[time – (basetime + N)] :=
            new(id, table2[time – (basetime + N)])
    else error( )
```

Note that just before the swap operation, all lists in *table1* are empty as a consequence of *alarm*. This makes *table1* ready to be reused as the new *table2*.

Both *alarm* and *schedule* now take a *constant* amount of time per request. The only problem with this scheduler is that it does not allow us to schedule

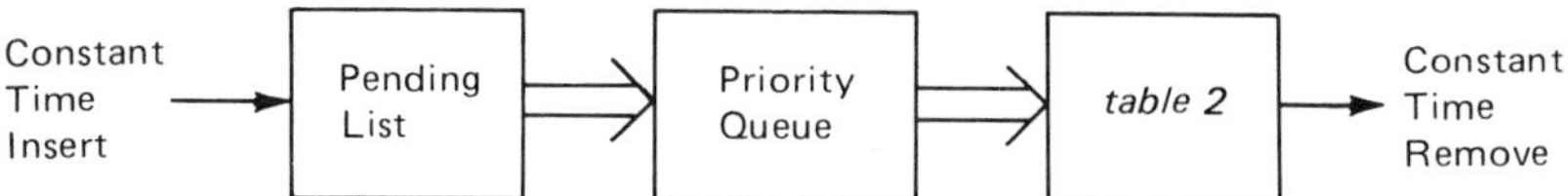

Figure 18.6
Flow of event request data from scheduling time to performance time.

events for further than N time units into the future. (The maximum time at which an event can be scheduled is *basetime* $+ 2N - 1$, and the current time can be as great as *basetime* $+ N - 1$; the difference is N.) Notice that if a request is scheduled further ahead of time than this, there will be no table entry to receive it. However, if requests are always made with times less than N time units into the future, *schedule* will always work, and its real-time characteristics are almost ideal (the only possible reservation being the overhead incurred by invoking *alarm* when there are no requests to be met). The last implementation will extend this one to allow requests to be made at arbitrary times in the future.

18.2.6 Implementation 6

The key idea of this implementation is to use the previous implementation to handle all near-term requests and to add a fallback strategy for long-term requests. Notice that the scheduler has at least N units of time to deal with any far-term request, so it is possible to delegate most of the work to a background process that runs when there is no other work to do. Since practical real-time systems have a large amount of idle time, this strategy is quite reasonable: time-critical (near-term) scheduling operations will execute in constant time, and non-time-critical (long-term) scheduling operations will take more processing time, but will take advantage of otherwise idle processing time.

The algorithm works as follows: any request that cannot be immediately entered into a table is put on a simple linked list called *pending*. Note that this takes only a fixed amount of time. In the background, a process uses idle processor time to remove items from the *pending* list and insert them into a priority queue. It also takes items from the queue and inserts them into tables as this becomes possible. The flow of data for events scheduled after *basetime* $+ 2N$ is illustrated in figure 18.6. The double arrows represent transfers that take place in the background.

The timing constraints on the background process are simplest to understand if the requirements are made a little stronger than absolutely necessary. At the moment just after *basetime* is incremented, *table2* is empty and represents lists of events that are to take place in the interval from *basetime* + *N* to *basetime* + 2*N* − 1. The *pending* list may contain requests for this interval, but no more requests for the interval will be added to *pending* because any new request for that interval will be inserted directly into the table. Thus, when *basetime* is incremented, there are *N* time units in which to insert the *pending* list into the priority queue and then to transfer to *table2* everything in the queue with a time earlier than *basetime* + 2*N*. Since new requests with times of *basetime* + 2*N* or greater might be scheduled while this background task is running, it is convenient to use two lists, *pending1* and *pending2*. Requests will be added to *pending1* and removed from *pending2*. A *swap* operation will exchange them when *basetime* is incremented.

Figure 18.7 illustrates timing relationships. During the time interval labeled 1, events are moved from *pending2* to the priority queue and then to *table2*. Meanwhile, any event scheduled for time interval 2 is placed on *pending1*. At *basetime* + *N*, a swap occurs, exchanging *pending1* and *pending2*, *table1* and *table2*, and adding *N* to *basetime* so that the whole sequence repeats. The resulting scheduler is given below:

```
alarm( )
  if t = basetime + N
    swap(table1, table2)
    swap(pending1, pending2)
    basetime := t
  requests := table1[t − basetime]
  while requests <> NULL
    event(requests.ID)
    requests := requests.NEXT
  table1[t − basetime] := NULL
  t := t + 1
  setalarm(t)

schedule(id, time)
  if time < basetime + N
    table1[time − basetime] :=
      new(id, table1[time − basetime])
  else if time < basetime + (2 * N)
    table2[time − (basetime + N)] :=
      new(id, table2[time − (basetime + N)])
```

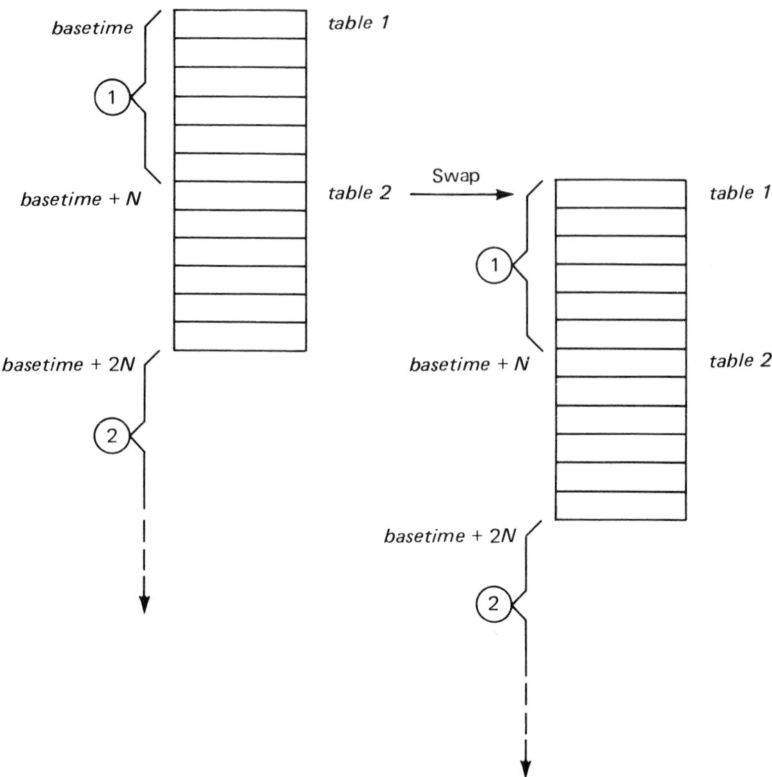

Figure 18.7
Data structures for Scheduler Implementation 6.

```
   else
      pending1 := new(id, time, pending1)

background(starttime)
   mybase := starttime
   while TRUE
      mybase := mybase + N
      while mybase > basetime
         do nothing
      while pending2 <> NULL
         insert(queue, pending2.ID, pending2.TIME)
```

```
    pending2 := pending2.NEXT
  q := inspect(queue)
  while q.TIME < mybase + (2 * N)
    schedule(q.ID, q.TIME)
    queue := remove(queue)
    q := inspect(queue)
  if mybase <> basetime
    error( )
```

The important variables are

table1	events scheduled for *basetime* <= t < *basetime* + N
table2	events scheduled for *basetime* + N <= t < *basetime* + 2N
pending2	temporarily holds events scheduled during *basetime* − N <= t < *basetime* for times greater than *basetime* + N
pending1	temporarily holds events scheduled during *basetime* <= t < *basetime* + N for times greater than *basetime* + 2N

Initialization is as for the previous scheduler, with a few additions:

```
initialize( )
  for i := 0 to N − 1
    table1[i] := NULL
    table2[i] := NULL
  basetime := gettime( )
  t := basetime
  setalarm(basetime)

  pending1 := NULL
  pending2 := NULL
  queue := newqueue( )
  start background(basetime)
```

The background process is started and is passed the initial value of *basetime* as a parameter. The background process uses this value to determine when to perform a cycle of its outer loop that moves requests from *pending2* to *queue*, and then from *queue* to *table2*. After these operations, *background* checks to make sure it has completed its task within N time units. If it has, *mybase* will still equal *basetime*.

For computer music applications, this scheduler is superior to those considered earlier. The *schedule* and *alarm* operations take a constant amount of time to execute in all cases. When events are scheduled far in the future, there is an additional computational expense proportional to $\log n$ per event, but this expense is delegated to a background process. During each regular interval of N time units (where N is an arbitrary number), the background process must enqueue all requests pending from the previous interval and dequeue all requests pending for the next interval. This interval can be made large if desired in order to minimize the effect of "bursts" of scheduling requests.

Notice that if all events are scheduled for times greater than *basetime* + $2N$, then this scheduler will do slightly more work than Scheduler Implementation 4. The extra work arises from moving each event on and off of both a pending list and a table. In addition, the *alarm* routine must be called every unit of time. However, even in the worst case this scheduler still has a significant advantage because events can be scheduled and dispatched in constant time. This is very important in music where events often come in bursts—for example, at the beginning of a chord with many notes. The high performance during bursts of scheduling or dispatching activity more than makes up for the extra work performed by the background process.

The memory space required by the scheduler is proportional to $N + M$, where N is the time interval size and M is the number of pending requests. There is no way to get around M in any scheduler, and the memory space due to tables of size $N = 1{,}000$ might typically be 8,000 bytes, one-sixteenth of a single 1M-bit memory chip. At a time resolution of 1 ms, this would give an interval time of one second.

Experienced programmers may recognize that a circular buffer could be used in place of the double-buffering scheme of two tables used here. The double-buffering scheme is used here because it makes it easier to understand the requirements that must be met by the background process.

(After this chapter was completed, a paper was independently published by Varghese and Lauck [12] that develops algorithms similar to those in this section. Rather than use a background process to schedule future events, all events are immediately entered into a table at the event time mod N. The alarm routine must examine entries in the table and invoke only event requests whose time matches the current time. This is simpler than Implementation 6 but slightly more expensive.)

Scheduler Implementation 6 was designed because other existing scheduler algorithms did not deliver the performance desired for real-time computer music systems. The present design overcomes significant problems associated with other schedulers.

18.3 Scheduling with Virtual Time

In each of the schedulers discussed in the previous section, times are referenced to a single clock that is presumed to correspond to real (physical) time. In computer music programs, it is often convenient to have a time reference or references that do not correspond to real time. Consider the conductor's baton, which (among many other functions) measures time in beats.

Because tempo may vary, time as measured in beats may not have a fixed linear relation to real time. By analogy, one can imagine a software scheduler that uses a nonlinear or variable speed time reference.

This concept can be extended to incorporate several simultaneous but independent time references, analogous to having several conductors conducting at different tempi. A further extension is the composition (in the mathematical sense) or nesting of time references [9]. As an intuitive introduction to this concept, imagine taking a recording of a rubato passage of music and varying the playback speed. The resulting tempo will be a composite of two functions, or *time maps*, that map from one time reference to another: the playback speed and the original tempo. In this section, various ways to implement virtual-time schedulers will be considered, starting with a simple extension to the last scheduler in the previous section.

18.3.1 A Single-Reference, Virtual-Time Scheduler

The simplest virtual-time scheduler contains a single time reference that can be made to advance at any positive speed with respect to real time. For now, it is assumed that the speed of virtual time relative to real time can be changed within the program by calling *setspeed*(s), where s is the new speed of the virtual time. The speed variation can be implemented in either hardware or software.

Usually, real-time computer systems have a programmable real-time clock that generates an interrupt every N cycles of a very fast (often 1–10

MHz) system clock. In terms of the schedulers of section 18.2, an interrupt corresponds to calling *alarm*( ). For example, if the system clock period is 1 μs and the nominal time unit used by the scheduler is 1 ms, then N would be 1 ms/1 $\mu s = 1{,}000$. If N is changed to 900, the interrupt period will be 0.9 ms. Thus, virtual time (the time reference used by the scheduler) would go faster.

In cases where a hardware solution is not possible, software can be used. The software solution described here will not produce truly periodic intervals like the ones generated in hardware. Instead, the approach will produce the correct average period in the long run. The actual advances of virtual time (or calls to *alarm*) will occur on transitions of the real-time clock, which limits the time resolution of the system. This is typically not a problem since the real-time clock interval is small. A schematic of the software solution follows:

```
Initially:
  d:= 0.0

On hardware interrupt:
  d:= d + s
  while d >= 1.0
    d:= d - 1.0
    alarm( )
```

Both d and s are floating point numbers. Note that if s, the speed of virtual time, is exactly 1, then *alarm* is called on every interrupt. The speed can be arbitrary; for example, if $s = 0.71$, then *alarm* will be called 71 times out of every 100 interrupts, and the calls will be spaced fairly uniformly. In general, during an interval of t units of real time, *alarm* is called approximately st times. Thus, the ratio of virtual to real time approaches exactly $st/t = s$, as desired. Also notice that if s is greater than 1.0, *alarm* will at least sometimes be called more than once in response to a single interrupt. This is necessary to get an average *alarm* rate greater than the interrupt rate.

Rather than use floating point numbers as indicated above, fixed point numbers or integers are often used for greater efficiency. The same program can be written with only integer operations. In the version below, the speed s is set to an integer scaled to 1,000 times the desired speed of virtual time. For example, if the desired speed is one-half, s would be 500, and *alarm*( ) would be called on every other hardware interrupt. (The choice of one thousand is arbitrary. Larger numbers allow greater accuracy in the representation of fractions but require larger integers.) Here is the code:

```
Initially:
  d := 0
  ONE := 1000

On hardware interrupt:
  d := d + s
  while d > ONE
    d := d − ONE
    alarm( )
```

18.3.2 Multiple Reference Schedulers

Problems arise if it is necessary to schedule according to several time references. A simple, but potentially expensive, approach is to operate a separate scheduler for each time reference. The interrupt routine presented above is rewritten as follows:

```
Initially:
  d_i := 0.0 for each i

On hardware interrupt:
  for each i
    d_i := d_i + s_i
    while d_i >= 1.0
      d_i := d_i − 1.0
      alarm_i( )
```

In this approach, there is a separate speed (s_i) for each scheduler. Time for scheduler i advances when $alarm_i$ is called. This approach is practical only when the number of schedulers is small because the cost is proportional to the number of schedulers.

18.3.3 An Efficient Compromise

It seems wasteful to compute the advance of each virtual clock at every unit of real time, but this is necessary because the speed of a virtual clock can change at any moment. If changes to s are restricted, this problem can largely be eliminated. One possible restriction is to require complete knowledge of how s will change in the future. It is then possible to compute the real time to which any virtual time will correspond. If the desired real time can be computed when an event is scheduled, there is no need for special virtual-time schedulers.

Unfortunately, for most interactive real-time programs it is too restrictive to require future knowledge of the behavior of s. For example, s might be controlled by a slider in real time. Another possible restriction is to allow s to change only with some small advance notice. This would allow a conversion of each virtual time to a real time shortly before the real time occurs.

This idea can be applied to Scheduler Implementation 6 from the previous section. Recall that in scheduler 6, a background process pulls events from a queue and enters them into *table2* while events in *table1* are activated in sequence. For this new scheduler, there will be a separate queue for each virtual-time reference, and the background process will pull events from each queue, translating virtual times into real times and inserting events into *table2*. Once an event is entered into a table, its real time cannot be changed, which is another way of saying s must be known in advance. The worst-case advance notice (or latency, depending on one's point of view) is twice the table size.

The implementation of this scheduler begins with routines for converting virtual time to real time. The calculation assumes that virtual time moves forward at a rate s from the last time at which s was changed:

virttoreal(*vtime*, *i*)
  return $realref_i + (vtime - virtref_i) * s_i$

The parameter i indicates which virtual-time reference is to be used. For each reference, s_i is the speed, $realref_i$ is the time at which s_i was last changed, and $virtref_i$ is the virtual time at which s_i was changed. Figure 18.8 illustrates this graphically. To change s, the following routine is called:

setspeed(*speed*, *i*)
  $time := gettime()$
  $virtref_i := virtref_i + (time - realref_i)/s_i$
  $realref_i := time$
  $s_i := speed$

The *setspeed* routine computes the current virtual time based on previous values of $virtref_i$, $realref_i$, s_i, and the current real time. Then, $virtref_i$, $realref_i$, and s_i are updated.

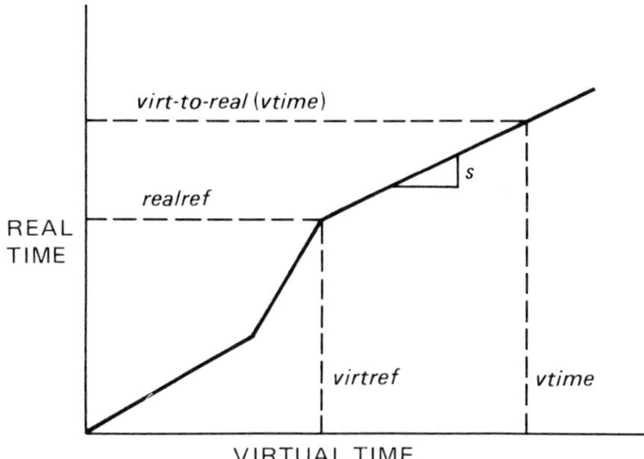

Figure 18.8
The virtual- to real-time calculation.

A new routine, *vschedule*, can now be written.

```
vschedule(id, vtime, i)
  time := virttoreal(vtime, i)
  if time <= gettime( )
    event(id)
  else if time < basetime + N
    table1[time - basetime] :=
      new(id, table1[time - basetime])
  else if time < basetime + (2 * N)
    table2[tme - (basetime + N)] :=
      new(id, table2[time - (basetime + N)])
  else pending1 := new(id, vtime, i, pending1)
```

This routine is similar to *schedule* except it takes an extra parameter (i) that specifies which virtual-time reference to use. If the event is expected to happen during the times represented by *table1* or *table2*, then the event is scheduled for a particular real time. Otherwise, the event is put on the pending queue to be handled by the background process, which is now presented:

```
background(starttime)
  mybase := starttime
  while TRUE
```

```
mybase := mybase + N
while mybase > basetime
   do nothing
while pending2 <> NULL
   i := pending2.I;
   insert(queue_i, pending2.ID, pending2.VTIME)
   pending2 := pending2.NEXT
for each i
   q := inspect(queue_i)
   time := virttoreal(q.VTIME, i)
   while time < mybase + 2 * N
      schedule(q.ID, time)
      queue_i := remove(queue_i)
      q := inspect(queue_i)
      time := virttoreal(q.VTIME, q.I)
if mybase <> basetime
   error()
```

This code is based on that of Scheduler Implementation 6. Notice that the pending queue now specifies which time reference, and therefore which priority queue in which to insert the event. Notice also that now there can be more than one priority queue, so the background process must examine each one.

What has been accomplished with this new algorithm? In the beginning of this section, it was found that computation costs were proportional to the number of virtual-time references. This was true because each virtual time was updated at every unit of real time in order to schedule events properly. The new scheduler saves work by converting all virtual times to real times. There is still a computation cost proportional to the number of virtual-time references, but now this happens on each iteration of the background process rather than every unit of real time. Thus the new scheduler is much more efficient.

The disadvantage of this approach is that there is some latency between the time s changes and the time at which this affects the real time of an event. Barry Vercoe has described programs with this property, presenting them as a model of human physiology [13]. The latency due to fixing performance times slightly in advance of real time is analogous to human reaction time.

To get an idea of the magnitude of the latency, a reasonable implementation might use real time units of 5 ms and tables of length 16. This would give a worst case latency of $5 \times 16 \times 2 = 160$ ms or 0.16 s. Note that this number reflects the worst-case delay before a new s takes effect; if s changes by some percentage p, then the maximum timing error will be roughly $(p/100) \times 0.16$ s. Also note that these numbers are arbitrary and there seems to be a wide range of reasonable choices. The main trade-off is that as the table gets smaller, latency goes down, but so does the amount of time available in the background process to handle a burst of events. Overall, this approach is interesting, but not very satisfying. It is fairly complex, yet an implementation is likely to suffer from too much latency or situations where the background process fails to make its deadline.

18.3.4 Yet Another Scheduler

Another implementation is worth considering. In this scheduler, there will be no latency except that due to the processor falling behind when there are many events to schedule or activate. This scheduler will not be as efficient as the previous one.

The idea is based on Implementation 4 in the previous section. Recall that Implementation 4 uses a priority queue for events and that it uses *setalarm* so that the scheduler does not work until it is time to activate the next event. Now imagine having one priority queue for each virtual-time reference and allowing each one to set an individual alarm. The alarm will be set with the anticipated real time of the next event. (Speed changes will be dealt with later.)

In practice, there may not be an individual hardware timer for each virtual time reference, but this is exactly the problem that schedulers solve! The virtual-time schedulers will use a single real-time scheduler to schedule themselves, and the real-time scheduler will use the hardware timer as always.

Assume that there is an Implementation 6 scheduler that implements the operation *schedule*$(i, time)$ that results in a call to *valarm*(i) at the indicated time. The only change necessary to Implementation 6 is to replace the call to *event* with a call to *valarm*.

The virtual-time scheduler is presented below:

vschedule$(id, vtime, i)$
  $r := inspect(requests_i)$

```
requests_i := insert(requests_i, id, vtime)
if vtime < r.VTIME
    schedule(i, virttoreal(vtime, i))
```

The object is to make sure that *valarm* will be called at the real time corresponding to the next item in the *requests* queue. If the virtual time of the new request (*vtime*) is less than the earliest time of any other event in *requests* (*r.vtime*), then *schedule* is called with the real time corresponding to *vtime*, the new earliest virtual time. The implementation of *valarm* detects and ignores any extra requests:

```
valarm(i)
  r := inspect(requests_i)
  vtime := r.VTIME
  while virttoreal(r.VTIME, i) <= gettime( )
      event(r.ID)
      requests := remove(requests_i)
      r := inspect(requests_i)
  if vtime <> r.VTIME
      schedule(i, virttoreal(r.VTIME, i))
```

Extra requests are detected by the while loop. If it is not yet time to perform the next event in the queue, nothing happens. If one or more events in the queue are performed, then *vtime* will no longer equal *r.vtime* and *valarm* finishes by scheduling the anticipated real time of the next event in the queue. To complete the implementation, here is *setspeed*:

```
setspeed(speed, i)
  s_i := speed
  r := inspect(requests_i)
  schedule(i, virttoreal(r.VTIME, i))
```

This scheduler is interesting because it always schedules *valarm* for the next known event time for each virtual-time reference. Since the real-time scheduler is so efficient, there is little overhead in scheduling extra *valarm* events. Notice that it is never a problem to schedule an extra *valarm* because *valarm* checks to see that it is time for an event before performing it. On the other hand it is important always to have at least one *valarm* scheduled for the real time of the next event, so each call to *setspeed* also schedules *valarm* for the new predicted time of the next event.

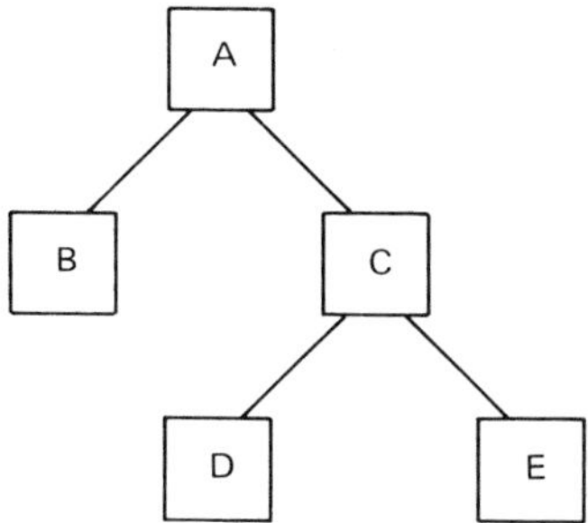

Figure 18.9
A hierarchy of virtual-time schedulers.

In this scheduler, a call to *vschedule* and a subsequent *valarm* has a cost proportional to the log of the number of events in the *request* queue. There is also an added cost of calling *schedule*, but this cost is essentially fixed except for potential background processing. Finally, each call to *setspeed* adds the cost of calling *schedule*.

18.3.5 Composition of Time Maps

After exploring real-time schedulers and virtual-time schedulers, there *is* still one area left to consider. A logical extension to the scheduler is one in which a virtual-time scheduler uses another virtual time as a reference. This allows arbitrary nesting of virtual-time references.

The implementation of such a system uses a tree of schedulers where the root is a real-time scheduler and other nodes are virtual-time schedulers. Figure 18.9 illustrates a tree of virtual-time references. References E and D use C as a time reference, and B and C use A (real time) as a reference. Each scheduler uses its parent to schedule an alarm when it is time for the next event to be activated. Thus, the parent scheduler determines the reference time for its children. It can be seen that the previous scheduler is a two-level tree with this structure.

In a multilevel tree, the cost of performing an event is the sum of the cost at each level. For example, in figure 18.9, the performance of an event scheduled with scheduler E begins with an event scheduled with A, the real-time scheduler. This first event invokes the *valarm* routine of scheduler C, which in turn runs the *valarm* routine of scheduler E. The *valarm* routine of E finally performs the scheduled event. The idea of scheduling alarms that turn out to be useless because of a subsequent speed change is still applicable in a multilevel tree of schedulers.

To reduce the overhead of dispatching events that are many levels deep, it is possible to collapse any tree to two levels. For example, in figure 18.9, D and E would be moved to the level of B and C. To do this, it is necessary to modify *setspeed* to update all affected time references. For example, changing the speed of C must indirectly affect D and E. Finally, the *virttoreal* function must be modified to compute the correct composition of time maps. This approach makes dispatching faster at the expense of a more expensive *setspeed* operation.

Another extension of virtual-time schedulers is to consider using a continuously varying speed. For example, a smooth acceleration might be effected by changing the speed linearly instead of in steps. To incorporate this capability, the only change necessary is in the function *virttoreal*. The real time of a future event at virtual time V_f will be the integral of the speed function $s(v)$ from the current virtual time V_c to V_f. If $s(v)$ can be restricted to a polynomial, then the *virttoreal* function will consist of evaluating the integral of s, also a polynomial [9].

18.3.6 Related Work

The idea of nested virtual-time schedulers is not new, and implementations have been described by Jaffe and by Anderson and Kuivila. Jaffe's article [9] considers a non-real-time system oriented toward computer-aided composition. The system by Anderson and Kuivila [2] is a real-time implementation in which the delay of the next event must be specified as each event is scheduled. Executable processes can be used to specify speed changes, resulting in a very flexible means for specifying time maps.

The work described here makes two contributions to existing methods. First the real-time scheduling algorithm is a significant improvement over the use of heaps or other "fast" methods. Second, all of the virtual-time scheduling algorithms described in this chapter allow events to be scheduled in arbitrary order, and it is unnecessary to know the time of the next event, or whether the next scheduled event will be before or after the present one.

In fairness to the previous work, it is often the case that one knows when the next event will be scheduled, or at least one can often know the order of events. This leads to greater efficiency in the referenced works, insuring that there are no extra calls to *vtime*.

18.4 Computer Accompaniment

All of the schedulers presented so far deal only with time and events and could be used for, say, controlling machinery as well as music. In this section, a scheduler that assumes a musical context is examined. This assumption enables the scheduler to incorporate musical knowledge, resulting in a very sophisticated (but not very general) scheduler.

Computer Accompaniment[5] is a task similar to that of a human accompanist, who listens to another performer, reads music, and performs another part of the music in a synchronized fashion. Computer accompaniment does not involve any improvisation or composition. Instead, the computer is given a score containing a description of the music to be played by each performer. In this model, the *soloist* considers only his or her (or its!) part of the score and determines the tempo of the performance. The (computer) *accompanist* dynamically adjusts its timing to match that of the soloist.

Computer accompaniment has been accomplished by a computer system that can be divided roughly into two parts: the "analytical" part that uses a fast algorithm to perform pattern matching on a symbolic representation of the score and the solo, and the "musical" part that attempts to produce a sensible performance in the face of continual adjustments in tempo. Figure 18.10 separates these parts further into a number of separate tasks that are described below.

18.4.1 Analytical Tasks

The "analytical" part has the job of following the soloist in the score. This part consists of two concurrent tasks. The first task, called the *listener*, is a preprocessor of input from the soloist. Listening in this context means converting sound into a symbolic form to be used by the next task. A single melodic line from, say, a trumpet or flute is processed in real time to obtain time-varying pitch information, which is then quantized to obtain the discrete pitches of a musical scale. Alternatively, a music keyboard whose pitch output is inherently symbolic can be used. In either case, the listener task sends a schematic representation of the soloist's performance to the next task. The delay between the onset of a note and its detection by the listener must be small to achieve responsive accompaniment.

This second task, called the *matcher*, compares the actual performance to the expected performance as indicated in the score. The objective of the

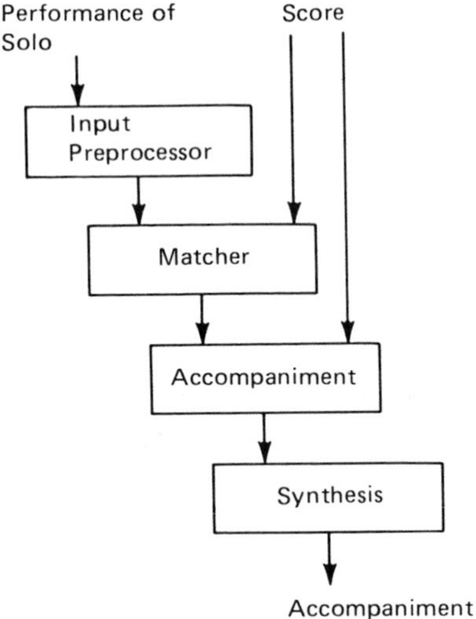

Figure 18.10
Block diagram of a computer accompaniment system.

comparison is to find a correspondence between the performance and the score, thereby relating real time to the timing indications in the score. In accompaniment, the goal is to construct a time map in real time in order to make the virtual times of score events take place at the real times of the performance events. Since either the soloist or the listener task may make mistakes (the listener task makes mistakes because pitch and attack detection, especially in a noisy acoustic environment, is inherently error prone), the matcher must be tolerant of missing notes, extra notes, or notes whose pitches are wrong. Furthermore, the timing of notes will vary from one performance to the next. To deal with this kind of "fuzzy" match, a real-time adaptation of dynamic programming is used. The output of the matcher is a sequence of reports that occur whenever the matcher is fairly certain that a note performed by the soloist corresponds to a particular note in the score. A matcher for monophonic inputs is described in [8] and two matchers for polyphonic inputs are described in [4].

18.4.2 Musical Tasks

The "musical" part contains a third task, called the *accompanist*, which controls the timing of the accompaniment. Note that most of the accompaniment is determined by the score, and timing is the only dimension that varies from one performance to the next. (Other parameters, such as loudness, could be varied as well.) Typically the accompanist will output commands that mean something like "the violin should now begin playing C-sharp," and a synthesizer handles the actual sound generation. The main problem in the accompaniment task is to adjust the timing of the accompanist in a musical fashion.

One approach to providing timing would be to use a virtual-time reference to schedule accompaniment events. Calls to *setspeed* could be used to keep the accompaniment in synchronization with the performance. Although this scheme would work reasonably well, it would be unable to handle jumps to new positions in the score in a musical way. A better approach is to write a scheduler that incorporates musical knowledge. The scheduler gets the clock speed and offset relative to real time from the matcher task. Adjustments must be made carefully if they are to sound musical, and a rule-based approach is used to program the accompanist. For example, one rule says that if the virtual clock is behind the soloist by a moderate amount, it is better to catch up by playing very fast than by skipping part of the accompaniment. Note that this is not as simple as the virtual-time schedulers seen in the previous section. In order to enhance the quality of the accompaniment, the accompanist can repeat parts of the score if virtual time jumps backward, skip parts of the score if virtual time jumps forward by large amounts, and generally alter timing according to the context of the score. The accompanist can be called a *knowledge-based* scheduler because it schedules events based on knowledge of musical interpretation as well as the passage of time.

18.4.3 Implementation

The implementation of the accompanist relies on an underlying real-time scheduler of the sort described in the first section. The overall structure of the accompanist is fairly simple: the accompanist calculates the real time at which the next accompaniment will occur, and an event is scheduled to reactivate the accompanist at that time. Normally, the accompanist will then suspend itself and when the proper time is reached, the accompanist will be reactivated. It then performs the next accompaniment event, and the cycle is repeated.

The accompanist is also reactivated when input arrives from the matcher. Recall that the matcher reports when the soloist plays a note in the score;

therefore, the current real time is known to correspond to the virtual time of the matched note in the score. The accompanist can now recalculate the speed of virtual time, the current virtual time, and the real time of the next accompaniment event. An event is scheduled to reactivate the accompanist at that time.

If the performance time of the matched note is not close to the expected time for that note, the accompanist must take a corrective action. A rule that matches the current situation will determine the action; for example, if the virtual time skips far ahead, the accompanist will stop any notes currently sounding and skip to a new location in the score.

Left to its own, the accompanist always has a single reactivation event scheduled while it is asleep. However, the matcher may intervene with some information that changes that accompanist's notion of when it must next do something. Rather than changing the time of the previously scheduled wakeup event, it schedules a new one. This is analogous to setting another alarm clock after deciding to wake up at a different time. Since the accompanist knows when it should wake up, it can ignore alarms that go off at other times.

18.4.4 Thinking Ahead

One consequence of the accompanist implementation is that the analytical score following tasks are only weakly coupled to the musical accompaniment tasks. This is as it should be, since an accompaniment performance should make a certain musical sense even without the solo it is meant to support. The partial independence allows the accompanist to continue its performance even in the absence of input from the soloist. This is essential for situations where the accompaniment has many notes against a sustained note or rest in the solo part.

Because of this partial independence, it is not true that the accompaniment system must lag behind the soloist. To avoid this potential problem, the latency of the system is determined experimentally and subtracted from the scheduled real time of every accompaniment event. Therefore, the accompaniment anticipates every event by an amount equal and opposite to the latency in the system, just as a tuba player must anticipate in order to compensate for the latency of his instrument. If the soloist and accompanist are to play two notes simultaneously, it is only after the soloist's note is processed that the accompanist can know whether its timing was correct. If not, the discrepancy is used to update the virtual-time reference so that the next note will be timed more correctly. The resemblance to human performance is striking.

18.4.5 Related Work

Computer accompaniment systems have been developed independently by Dannenberg [4, 8], Vercoe [13, 14], and by Lifton [10]. The paper by Bloch and Dannenberg [4] discusses matchers for monophonic and polyphonic performances in detail. The paper by Vercoe and Puckette [14] describes the idea of learning performance timing through rehearsal, and Lifton's paper [10] describes a system for the accompaniment of vocal music.

18.5 Conclusions

Computer music instruments, accompaniment systems, and interactive composition systems are opening new doors for performers and composers. Schedulers are critical components in these systems, and this chapter has presented a collection of schedulers for computer music applications. Scheduler Implementation 6 is a particularly efficient real-time scheduler with a constant cost per scheduled event plus some background processing for events scheduled far into the future. Several virtual-time schedulers were also described. Finally the concept of a knowledge-based scheduler was explored in the context of computer accompaniment systems.

As real-time music systems increase in complexity, the idea of knowledge-based schedulers may very well evolve into the notion of expert performance systems, that is, computer programs that model the behavior of human performers. Composers who use these systems will enjoy the flexibility of computer-generated sounds, without giving up all of the advantages of having human performers play their works. Composers who write their own expert performance systems will be able to explore and develop new standards of performance practice tuned to their own personal musical goals.

Acknowledgments

Most of this chapter grew out of conversations with Ron Kuivila in between concerts and lectures at the 1985 International Computer Music Conference and the Second STEIM Symposium on Interactive Composition in Live Electronic Music. It was during these conversations that the idea for a fast scheduler was born. Barly Truax, Simon Fraser University, Michel Waisvicz, and STEIM deserve special thanks for organizing these conferences, which generated such a sharing of ideas. John Maloney furnished many helpful comments and spotted some errors in an earlier draft. The author would also like to thank the Computer Science Department and the Center for Art and Technology at Carnegie-Mellon University for their support of this work.

Notes

1. Moxc is available as part of the CMU MIDI Toolkit from the Center for Art and Technology, Carnegie-Mellon University, Pittsburgh, PA 15213.

2. The *requests* queue is initialized with a request whose time is infinity, so *inspect* will always return a value. It is assumed that *setalarm*(*infinity*) is defined to disable the alarm indefinitely.

3. Sound travels on the order of a foot per millisecond.

4. In an actual implementation, *table1* and *table2* would be blocks of memory accessed through pointer variables. The *swap* operation merely exchanges the contents of the pointer variables. Thus *swap* is very fast.

5. Computer Accompaniment is the subject of a pending patent.

References

[1] Aho, Hopcroft, and Ullman. *The Design and Analysis of Computer Algorithms*. Addison-Wesley, 1974.

[2] David P. Anderson and Ron Kuivila. A Model of Real-Time Computation for Computer Music. In *Proceedings of the 1986 International Computer Music Conference*, pp. 35–41. Computer Music Association, 1986.

[3] Jon Bentley. Programming Pearls. *Communications of the ACM* 28(3):245–250, 1985.

[4] Joshua J. Bloch and Roger B. Dannenberg. Real-Time Computer Accompaniment of Keyboard Performances. In *Proceedings of the 1985 International Computer Music Conference*, pp. 279–290. Computer Music Association, 1985.

[5] Xavier Chabot, Roger Dannenberg, and Georges Bloch. A Workstation In Live Performance: Composed Improvisation. In *Proceedings of the 1986 International Computer Music Conference*, pp. 57–60. Computer Music Association, 1986.

[6] Joel Chadabe. Interactive Composing: An Overview. *Computer Music Journal* 8(1):22–27, 1984.

[7] D. J. Collinge. MOXIE: A Language for Computer Music Performance. In *Proceedings of the 1984 ICMC*, pp. 217–220. Computer Music Association, 1984.

[8] Roger B. Dannenberg. An on-Line Algorithm for Real-Time Accompaniment. In *Proceedings of the 1984 International Computer Music Conference*, pp. 193–198. Computer Music Association, 1984.

[9] David Jaffe. Ensemble Timing in Computer Music. *Computer Music Journal* 9(4):38–48, 1985.

[10] John Lifton. Some Technical and Aesthetic Considerations in Software for Live Interactive Performance. In *Proceedings of the 1985 International Computer Music Conference*, pp. 303–306. Computer Music Association, 1985.

[11] Max V. Mathews and Curtis Abbott. The Sequential Drum. *Computer Music Journal* 4(4): 45–59, 1980.

[12] G. Varghese and T. Lauck. Hashed and Hierarchical Timing Wheels: Data Structures for the Efficient Implementation of a Timer Facility. In *Proceedings of the Eleventh ACM Symposium on Operating Systems Principles*, published as *Operating Systems Review* 21(5): 25–38, ACM Order No. 534870, 1987.

[13] Barry Vercoe. The Synthetic Performer in the Context of Live Performance. In *Proceedings of the 1984 International Computer Music Conference*, pp. 199–200. Computer Music Association, 1984.

[14] Barry Vercoe and Miller Puckette. Synthetic Rehearsal: Training the Synthetic Performer. In *Proceedings of the 1985 International Computer Music Conference*, pp. 275–278. Computer Music Association, 1985.

19 The Conductor Program and Mechanical Baton

Max V. Mathews

19.1 Principles of Operation of the Conductor Program

The conductor program is intended to be used for the performance of music on a digital synthesizer attached to a small computer. Normally synthesizers are played with keyboards. With the conductor program, a keyboard is not used. Instead, the performer conducts with a mechanical baton called a Daton. The score of the music is in the memory of the computer. The program can be viewed either as a sophisticated sequencer or as an intelligent musical instrument.

The program simulates a number of the functions of an orchestra following the baton of a conductor. The performer sets the tempo by beating time on the Daton. He can change the tempo from beat to beat and the computer will follow his tempi closely. The performer can also control other interpretable qualities of the music such as the loudness and the balance of the various voices. Control is exercised by where he hits the Daton or how he moves a joystick that is also available to him.

The score in the computer memory contains the pitches and durations of the notes to be played. Consequently the performer does not have to select the pitch of any note by a physical gesture. Elimination of pitch selection eliminates one of the traditional tasks of the performer, thus making part of his job easier. In much music, the performer has no interpretive choice about pitch in the sense that if he changes a pitch from that written by the composer, it is considered to be a performer error. Since the performer has no real choice about pitch and since pitch selection can be a very demanding task, it seemed ideal to give this task to the computer. By contrast, duration and loudness are subject to much more performer interpretation, and these tasks are left under his direct control in the conductor program.

19.2 Hardware

A diagram of the equipment on which the conductor program operates is shown on figure 19.1. The central device is a small computer of the IBM PC type, specifically an AT & T 6300 that uses an Intel 8086 processor. However, the program can easily be adapted to most IBM clones. The not completely standard feature required by the program is a millisecond clock,

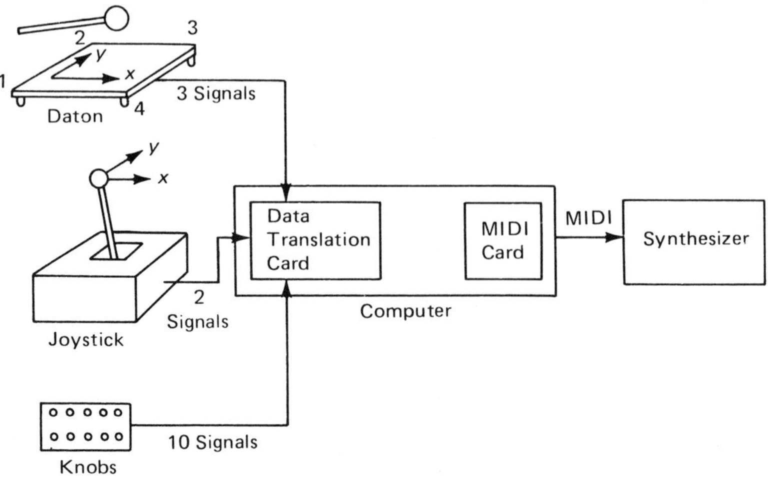

Figure 19.1
Diagram of conductor program hardware.

which we have obtained by changing the speed of one of the existing computer clocks. The program can probably be converted to other popular personal computers such as are made by the Apple Company. However, the IBM clones are particularly convenient since they have a backplane with slots into which special cards can be inserted.

Two such special cards are used by the conductor program. Signals from the various sensors, the Daton, the joystick, and the knobs are A/D (analog to digital) converted and put into the computer memory space by a data translation card. Signals to the synthesizer are sent via a MIDI cable, and a MIDI card, the Roland 401, generates these signals. Although the MIDI card can be used either to send or receive signals from the synthesizer, in this program it is only used to transmit to the synthesizer.

The synthesizer currently used is a Yamaha 816, but as almost all current synthesizers can be controlled with MIDI, almost any can be used without change in the program.

The data translation card is a 2801B (Data Translation Company). It can be used in a number of modes, but the program connects it to one of the DMA (direct memory access) input channels of the computer. The 16 analog inputs going to the card are sampled sequentially at a 16-kHz rate and each sample is stored in a location in the computer memory space.

Thus each analog input is sampled once per millisecond. The A/D converter has an accuracy of 12 bits. Once started, the data input process proceeds without further action by the computer central processor. The conductor program can use the current value of any input simply by reading an appropriate memory location.

The Daton, a current version of the Sequential Drum [11], consists of a light rigid plate about 14 inches square and an inch thick. In order to be both light and rigid, it is made as a laminate with fiberglass-reinforced plastic on upper and lower surfaces and a core of honeycomb paper material. This type of construction is often used in airplanes.

The plate is supported at its four corners by four strain gauges. Each time the plate is struck, four electric pulses are generated by the gauges. Circuitry to analyze the peak value of these pulses computes both where and how hard the plate was hit. For example, the strength of a hit is the sum of the four pulses. The y position of the stroke is the sum of the pulses at corners 2 and 3 (see figure 19.1) divided by the sum of all four.

The accuracy of the Daton is about 5% of the full range in any dimension. This accuracy is sufficient for most conducting purposes. The time constants of the plate are such that it takes about 5 msec to make a reading and perhaps 15 msec more to stabilize before a subsequent stroke occurs. The plate should be hit with a relatively soft drumstick in order to work properly.

The Daton only sends information to the computer at the instant that it is struck. Such "percussive" information is appropriate for controlling time and for controlling the parameters of percussive timbres—for example, for the loudness of a pianolike timbre. However, it is not sufficient to control continuous factors such as the variation of the loudness or vibrato in a violinlike tone within a single note. For this purpose, a joystick, which can send continuous information to the computer, has been built. The joystick is a simple mechanical linkage that connects two potentiometers to the joystick so that the voltages from the potentiometers are proportional to the x and y positions of the stick. The human engineering of the stick has been given some consideration. It is about 10 inches long so as to move an amount that is appropriate for human arm motion. The friction of the motion is carefully controlled by adjustable Teflon bearings so that it is easy to move the stick, but in addition so that the stick will stay in position if it is released.

Finally, a set of knobs sends 10 signals to the computer. These are used to set parameters in the computer program and to control individually the loudness in the synthesizer channels.

19.3 Software Design

The software is developed from a control philosophy proposed by Miller Puckette [6] and was partly written by D. L. Barr [12]. The program called RTLET (for real-time letters) is based on passing messages, or letters, between processes. RTLET consists of two logically distinct sections: the letter delivery section and the control processes. The letter delivery system passes the letters to the control processes, which perform some service. The routine that controls passing of letters is the post office. The actual delivery of the letters is performed by the postman. Control processes are logically distinct from the post office because letter delivery is a simple message-passing system and is application independent. The post office could work well with a variety of real-time control applications.

The operation of the post office may be seen in figure 19.2. A letter is delivered to the post office by some control process. An initial letter, delivered by the initialization routine, starts the process. The posted letter is placed in the letter bin and sorted in order by the delivery time stamped on the letter. The postman reads the destination and delivery time of the top letter in the bin. When real-time equals delivery time it sends the letter to the control process, and transfers control to the control process. The control process runs to completion and returns control to the postman. The postman reads the delivery time of next letter in the bin and waits for that delivery time. Delivery times are specified in beats, an arbitrary unit whose time may be adjusted to vary the tempo of the musical piece. One of the timers in the computer is used as a real-time clock. An interrupt handler keeps a variable, t_time, equal to the current time value in milliseconds. Various tempo algorithms are used to relate t_time and beats. Control processes may send letters to other control processes or to themselves to cycle the delivery process continuously.

Control processes are written specifically to play music. A control process reads the notes from an intermediate score. The intermediate score is compiled from an alphanumeric score that can be prepared on any word processor. The score gives the pitches and durations in beats of each

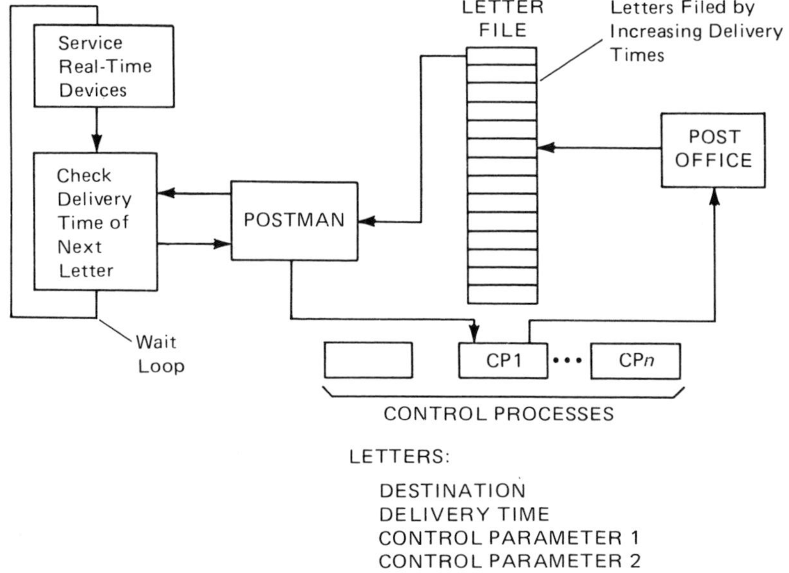

Figure 19.2
Diagram of RTLET program.

note to be played and, in addition, the times in beats between all Daton strokes.

The intermediate score consists of a list of operation codes, each followed by information appropriate to that particular code. The main operation codes are listed in table 19.1. The compiler for the intermediate score was written by D. L. Barr [12].

Before starting to play, the intermediate score is loaded into an array, score [ ], that is read and parsed by the control process. Playing a note is accomplished as shown in figure 19.3. A pointer into score [ ] is maintained by control process CP1. CP1 reads the operation code, and, based on the type of operation, the control process performs the operation. In the case that the operation code is PLAYN, five pieces of information are then read from the score array. The first is the MIDI channel to play on. The MIDI standard allows up to 16 devices to be addressed on the bus at any given time. The second item needed is whether or not the note is part of a chord. This is used to bypass the timing aspects of RTLET when certain notes should happen simultaneously. The control process keeps reading from the score array and playing the notes until all notes of a chord are played. The

Table 19.1
RTLET operation codes

Mnemonic		Meaning
PLAY	OPERATIONS	
	PLAYN:	Play a note with beat timing
WAIT	OPERATIONS:	
	WAITR:	Wait for x beats
MIDI	DEVICE CONTROL:	
	TIMBRE:	Change timbre immediate
REAL	TIME CONTROL:	
	BAT:	Baton stroke
TEST	OPERATIONS:	
	COMPA:	Compare register and value
	COMPR:	Compare two registers
BRANCHING INSTRUCTIONS:		
	JMP:	Unconditional branch
	START:	Start parsing at location (fork)
	SUB:	Jump to sequence at location
REGISTER CONTROL:		
	SETR:	Set register to a value
	INCR:	Increment a register
	DECR:	Decrement a register
TERMINATION CONTROL:		
	TERM:	Sequence termination
	TERMA:	Master termination

third item is the duration of the note, specified in terms of a legato factor. This factor allows a certain amount of control over whether a note is played staccato or legato. This variable can have three values: one corresponds to staccato, in which the note is played for 50 msec; another coresponds to normal, in which the note is on until the start of the next note, and the final is for legato, in which the note is on 50 msec past the start of the next note. The manner of note playing can also be written out in the score by separating the note into a shorter note followed by a rest. The fourth piece of information is the key number of the note to be played, which determines the frequency. The MIDI standard allows for 128 possible pitch values with middle C as value 60. The final item is the delay, in beats, before the next note starts.

The final thing that CP1 does before returning to the postman is to send a letter to itself with a delivery time equal to the current beat plus the delay. This assures that the process will continue. When a termina-

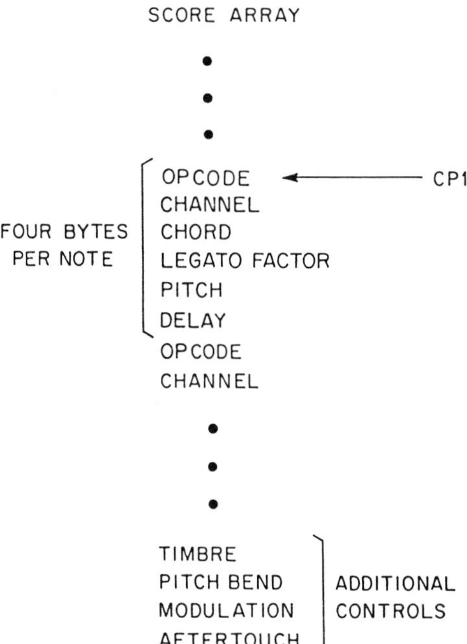

Figure 19.3
Example of score array.

tion opcode is encountered, the final letter is not sent, and post office terminates.

Other opcodes are used to control the execution and flow of the interpreter. For instance, multitrack sequencing may be done in RTLET using the START opcode. The START opcode forces two letters to be sent from CP1. The first letter is the letter that is required to make CP1 continue to interpret the score array for the track containing the START opcode. The second letter starts CP1 again, but at a different location in the score file, thus starting a second track.

Multitrack sequencing is essential in RTLET. Consider the excerpt of the Kreutzer Sonata in figure 19.5. The beginning of the sixth measure contains 2 quarter notes, 2 dotted quarter notes, and a half note, all starting simultaneously. RTLET cannot play these as a chord in one track, since all notes in a chord must both begin and end together. The solution, as given in figure 19.6, is to split the piano part into three tracks, V3, V4, and V5. There is no limit to the number of tracks in RTLET.

19.4 Control Processes as Concurrent, Reentrant, Pure Procedures

Although control processes can be written in a variety of ways, it is often useful to write them as pure procedures. The opcode interpreter procedure CP1 that we have described is such a procedure. The score [ ] array that is read by CP1, and that contains a description of the music to be played, can be looked upon as a program that is interpreted by CP1. Each time CP1 is activated by the postman, another opcode in score [ ] is interpreted and executed.

Only one copy of CP1 exists, even though from the user's standpoint as many "copies" of CP1 as desired may be "simultaneously" playing notes. At any given moment in real time, the pseudo copies of CP1 can be executing opcodes at the same or different places in score [ ]. Commands exist for starting new copies and for terminating copies. Opcodes also exist for both absolute and conditional jumps of the CP1 execution to other locations in score [ ].

In order to be useful, pure procedures must be able to store local variables somewhere while they are not being used. In languages such as C, local variables are pushed onto a single stack. Such storage requires that the procedures be called and return in a hierarchical order and does not work with the RTLET control processes, which can be called in very arbitrary orders by the postman according to the delivery times on letters.

The solution to the storage problem used in RTLET is to pass local variables to a procedure via the letter that activates the procedure. The principal use of a local variable in CP1 is to store the location in score [ ] of the next opcode to be interpreted. Obviously, other local variables can be handled in the same way. For example, if one wanted to set up a loop in score [ ] and to execute a block of opcodes *n* times, the counter for the loop could be set up as a local variable.

Another application of local variables is in passing channel-dependent information along. For instance, if a user wants to play 2 tracks simultaneously at different intensities, the simplest way to handle this is to set the intensities of each track and pass this information as part of the letter. Each channel is set differently, so each is propagated at a different value.

Although we have not attempted to do so, we believe the letter principal would be a good way to handle local variables in a general purpose real-time compiler.

19.5 Servicing of Real-Time Devices

In addition to sending letters to control processes, the postman services any real-time devices that are being used. At present these consist of the Daton, the joystick, the knobs, the computer keyboard, and the synthesizer. Servicing is done by a wait loop in postm ( ). The wait loop also looks at the millisecond clock (t_time) and updates the current beat as appropriate.

All waiting in RTLET is done in the postm ( ) wait loop, and all other procedures return to this loop as rapidly as possible. New real-time devices may be added to the program by rewriting the loop and thus can be guaranteed equal priority in service.

The input devices all put signals into a 16-variable array via the DMA input; each millisecond new samples are read into the array. The wait loop examines this array and acts accordingly. For example, for the Daton, when the total force signal exceeds a threshold, the program watches the other Daton signals, waits until they have reached their peak values, computes x and y, and sets a flag indicating that the Daton has been hit. Signals from the joystick are usually transmitted to the mod wheel and footpedal controls of the synthesizer. The wait loop watches the joystick signals and sends appropriate MIDI signals to the synthesizer only when the joystick has been moved.

Postm ( ) also reads t_time when a drum stroke occurs and computes the implied tempo, btim, as the time difference between the current stroke and the previous stroke divided by the number of beats written into the score between the strokes. Actually btim is the inverse tempo and is the number of milliseconds per beat.

In addition to tempo, some special cases in time control must be treated. The expected beat for the next Daton stroke is written in score [ ] (for example, as V6 in figure 19.6), and the notes played depend on whether the computer arrives at the next expected Daton beat before or after the Daton has been hit. If the computer arrives at the beat first, the program halts execution and waits until the Daton has been hit before playing the next note. If the Daton stroke occurs before the computer halts, the computer jumps immediately to the note in the score that immediately follows the Daton stroke; intervening notes are not played.

This algorithm, which involves stopping and skipping notes in the score, is not the only way that tempo can be regulated. It causes the computer to follow the conductor very closely, and is preferred by most conductors who

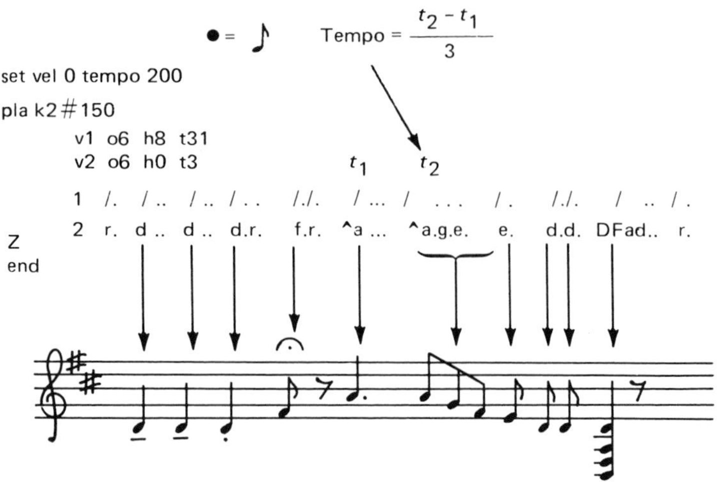

Figure 19.4
Comparison of RTLET score and normal musical notation score.

tried the program. However, it also demands that the conductor beat very evenly in sections in which he wishes to maintain a constant tempo. One can design other algorithms that smooth the tempo variations produced by the Daton.

19.6 A Simple Example of a Conductor Program Score

The use of the conductor program is best understood by discussing a simple example. Figure 19.4 shows a short score written in the appropriate form to be put into the conductor program. The score is entirely alphanumeric and can be written with any word processor. The equivalent score in normal musical notation is also shown.

The first two lines of the score set the key signature to two sharps and set some other initial parameters in the program that we shall not discuss.

The next two lines of the score tell the computer that there will be two voices in the score, the first being the Daton and the second being an instrumental voice. For example, the line "v2 o6 h0 t3" says that the second voice will be played in the 6th octave on synthesizer channel 0 with timbre number 3.

The fifth and sixth lines of the score specify the Daton strokes and the notes to be played. The Daton has a line in the score like any other voice in which a slash, "/," indicates where Daton strokes are to be made. In line 6, the pitches of the notes are written simply as the letter names of the notes AB . . . Gab . . . g over a two-octave range, where capital letters are used for the lower octave. The actual octave in which the notes are played is also determined by the octave constant o6, which can be changed at any time. The letter r indicates a rest.

Durations in the score are written as dots. In this case, the value of a dot is arbitrarily chosen to be an eight note. Thus the first note is written d . . and is a quarter note. The notes DFad cause a chord to be played because there are no dots between the letters.

Daton strokes, indicated in the fifth line, are also separated with dots to locate their position in the score. A stroke can serve several musical purposes. It can start a note or start a group of notes or start a chord or start a rest that is equivalent to stopping a note. Computationally, each Daton stroke after the first stroke sets the tempo that will be used until the next stroke. The tempo computation is shown in figure 19.4 and has already been discussed. The tempo can be changed at each stroke; thus the conductor can accelerate or retard the music. The times of the strokes are measured to an accuracy of 1 msec by a clock in the computer. This accuracy is more than sufficient for human gestures.

We shall now discuss playing the score stroke by stroke. The first stroke is an upbeat, which produces no sound (it plays a rest), and, together with the second stroke, sets the initial tempo. The second and third strokes play the first two d's in the score; these are legato and each note lasts until the next note starts. The next stroke starts a staccato d, which lasts only half of its quarter-note duration. The next stroke starts an f with a fermata, which will sustain till it is cut off by the following stroke. The next two strokes begin and end an "a" which is moved up an octave by the accidental mark, " ^ "; the second of these strokes starts the playing of three eighth notes ^ a.g.e. whose tempo is determined by the time between the two strokes. The next three strokes play three more eighth notes e.d.d. whose times are individually determined by the times of these strokes. The next-to-last stroke starts a chord, DFad, which continues till it is cut off by the final stroke.

This score illustrates most of the basic functions of the Daton. The function of a particular stroke is determined by where it appears in the score in relation to the notes in the playing voices. Depending on its position, the stroke can start a note or stop a note or start a group of notes. As far as the computer program is concerned, all strokes are treated in the same way. Each stroke specifies a tempo and starts the computer playing the group of notes at the specified tempo. It may be musically useful in many cases to have only one note in the group so that the stroke is a trigger for this individual note. But this is only a special case of the general Daton function of tempo setting and triggering a group of notes.

19.7 The Kreutzer Sonata—a More Realistic Example

Figures 19.5 and 19.6, respectively, show the traditional and the alphanumeric score for a short section from the beginning of Bethoven's Kreutzer Sonata. Six tracks V1–V6 are defined by lines 3–8 in this score. All of these tracks will be interpreted by CP1 "simultaneously" and in parallel. Tracks 1 and 2 are the violin part, tracks 3–5 the piano part, and track 6 the Daton.

Track 6 is of particular significance because it is the Daton track. Only Daton strokes are present here. In the first block of tracks 1–6, only the Daton stroke is executed. The other tracks all have rests. This is equivalent to the conductor's upbeat. The time between the first and second Daton strokes is used by RTLET to set the initial tempo of the piece. The first group of four dots (up to the next Daton stroke) is played at this tempo. At the next Daton stroke, the program recalculates the tempo.

The first played notes are in the second block of tracks 1–6. The first track is the only one playing here. It starts with a chord, "AEc^a," which has a quarter-note duration (four dots). The chord is legato and will continue until the next Daton stroke starts the next chord.

At the end of the first measure, we have an example of a slightly staccato chord. The score is

```
1    . . . bd . . . r .
2  r . . .
3  r . . .
4  r . . .
5  r . . .
6    . . ./ . . .   ./
```

The chord "bd" terminates to a rest before the Daton stroke is written. A more staccato chord could be written by moving the rest to the left.

Another function of the Daton can be to cut off a fermata with a separate stroke. This is used in measure 4, where the final "c" plus the chord "AE" are allowed to continue as long as desired by the performer according to the score:

```
1     d....  c..  r..  ....
2   AE....   ..   r..  ....
3     r....  ..   ..   ....
4     r....  ..   ..   ....
5     r....  ..   ..   ....
6     /....  /..  /..  ....
```

19.8 Methods of Putting Scores into the Conductor Program

If the conductor program becomes popular, then there will be a need to put much music into a form that can be conducted. The alphanumeric score shown in figure 19.6 can be prepared with any word processor. Although this is an entirely practical way of working, faster and more accurate procedures can probably be developed.

As a masters thesis at MIT Ruth Shyu [10] developed a simple program for preparing scores in which the notes are displayed in a simplified common practice music notation drawn by the computer on its terminal. The display provides a fast accurate way to proofread the music. The program was designed to minimize the number of keystrokes required to put in the music.

Leland Smith [9] has developed an excellent program for high-quality music printing in which the music is written into the computer on a standard ASCI keyboard using a special language that he has invented. Parts of his program could be adapted to prepare scores for the conductor program. Smith's program also displays a good-quality common practice music notation on the computer terminal, and these displays are helpful for proofreading.

Another possibility is to "play in" the score on a MIDI keyboard. The MIDI interface on the computer can be used either for input or output so that no additional hardware would be needed to implement this option. The procedure would be to play in either some or all the voices of a score and then to edit the computer record to add conducting marks, to correct mistakes, and to quantize the note durations properly. With MIDI, the pitches are automatically quantized by the keyboard, but durations are continuous variables. Hence, they would have to be fitted into some

SONATE
(komponiert 1803)
Op. 47
(Kreutzer-Sonate)
Adagio sostenuto.
Adagio sostenuto.
9.
cresc.
fp
p cresc.

Figure 19.5
Kreutzer Sonata in normal musical notation.

```
set vel 50 tempo 200
pla k3# l50
        v1 o7 h0 t9
        v2 o7 h1 t9
        v3 o6 h2 t0
        v4 o4 h3 t0
        v5 o4 h4 t0
        v6 o4 h5 t0

1 r....
2 r....
3 r....
4 r....
5 r....
6 /....

1 AEc^a.... df.... bd...r.          Gb.... Ee.... ..DG.r.
2 .... .... ....                    .... .... ....
3 .... .... ....                    .... .... ....
4 .... .... ....                    .... .... ....
5 .... .... ....                    .... .... ....
6 /.... /.... /....                 /.... /.... ../..

1 Ca...r. BFd...r. BGd...r.                d.... c..r.. ....
2 r.... .... ....                   AE.... ..r.. ....
3 r.... .... ....                   .... .... ....
4 r.... .... ....                   .... .... ....
5 r.... .... ....                   .... .... ....
6 /.... /.... /....                 /.... /../.. ....

1 r.... .... ....                   .... .... ....
2 r.... .... ....                   .... .... ....
3 ace^a.... $Fad$f.... Dad...r.            ab...r. Ge.... ..G.r.
4 o4 Aa.... Dd.... $F$f...r.               o5 d!E.... .r.b.. e..d.r.
5 .... .... ....                    e.... ...r. e...r.
6 /.... /.... /....                 /.... /....../..
```

```
1 r.... .... ....
2 r.... .... ....
3 a...r.Dd...r.Dd...r.
4 $c...b. a.r.a.. b..$c.r.
5 $f.... ...r. f...r.
6 /.... /.... /....

1 .... $f...r. !$GDb$f...r.          $C$G$c.... ..r.. ....
2 r.... .... ....                    $f.... e..r.. ....
3 Fa$C.... B$G..r.. ....             .... $Ge...r. ae...r.
4 o6 Dd$G.... ..r.. ....             o5 .... $ce...r. $ce...r.
5 r.... .... ....                    .... .... ....
6 /.... /.... /....                  /.... /.... /....

1 .... ^a...r. BF# d^a...r.                Eb^a.... g.... ....
2 r.... .... ....                    .... .... ....
3 e.... # d..r.. ....                      .... BDG...r. B$CG....
4 o5 bf^a.... ..r.. ....             .... o3 e...r. e....
5 r.... .... ....                    .... .... ....
6 /.... /.... /....                  /.... /.... /....

Z
end
```

Figure 19.6
Alphanumeric notation for Kreutzer Sonata.

appropriate set of standard note lengths. Although making a useful and practical system to "play in" a score is undoubtedly more difficult than it appears to be, it can probably be done. It is an interesting question for research in programming and human engineering.

A final possibility would be a music scanner that would read normal printed music and automatically convert it to machine readable form. We believe this is a very difficult task and may be the last of the methods we have discussed to be usefully achieved.

19.9 Uses of the Conductor Program

Just as for any other new musical medium, the conductor program can be used by contemporary composers to perform new compositions [1, 2, 7, 8] especially written for this program. However, in addition to its use in new music, the program may have important uses in playing traditional music. Two possibilities that seem promising and that may be economically important are accompaniment and active listening.

Accompaniment of soloists, which is often done with a piano, is both difficult and uninspiring for the accompanist. Very good reading and ensemble abilities are required from the pianist. He seldom gets a big share of the glory for a good performance. Consequently, it is both difficult and expensive to obtain accompanists. An alternative is to put the accompaniment into the conductor program and to conduct the accompaniment with the Daton. Much less reading skill is required by the accompanist, and he can focus his attention on ensemble. Also, certain soloists, such as singers who have their hands free, can accompany themselves. We have done demonstrations with a soprano [4] showing that this is indeed a promising method.

Active listening is a way of experiencing music that is made possible by the conducting program. Instead of listening to recorded music, the music appreciator would purchase a computer score and conduct his own interpretation of the piece. In addition to allowing an individual style of interpretation, the listener could take the piece apart to focus on individual voices or sections of the music in ways that are not possible with normal recordings and thus quickly gain a deeper understanding of the music. We believe this may become a very popular way of appreciating music.

Active listening could also lead to an entire new music industry—that of preparing scores for the conductor program.

19.10 Demonstration

A video tape of performances using the conductor program is available as an adjunct to this book.

References

[1] Boulanger, Richard, 1986, Shadows, a piece for the conductor program and electronic violin, premiered MIT November 1986.

[2] Chafe, Chris, 1987, Virga, a piece for the conductor program and harp, premiered Stanford April 1987.

[3] Chowning, John, 1988. (The name "active listening" was suggested by John Chowning.)

[4] Chowning, Maureen, 1987, soprano, Mozart recitative and aria, Deh, vieni, non tardar, from *The Marriage of Figaro*, accompanied by the conductor program.

[5] Data Translation Co., 100 Locke Dr. Marlboro, Massachusetts.

[6] Puckette, Miller, 1985, informal discussions during the summer.

[7] Radunskaya, Ami, 1986, Fruit Salad on Pi, a piece for the conductor program, three cellos, and a bass mandolin, premiered at Stanford, October 1986.

[8] Rocco, Robert, 1985, AT&T Bell Labs, Murray Hill, New Jersey, many short pieces and demonstrations composed for the conductor program.

[9] Smith, Leland, 1977–1987, Score (tm), Computer Music Typography System, Passport Designs, Inc.

[10] Shyu, Ruth, 1988, MIT masters thesis in computer science, The Maestro Program.

[11] Mathews, Max, and Abbott, Curtis, "The Sequential Drum," *Computer Music J.*, vol. 4, no. 4, pp. 45–59, 1980.

[12] Barr, D. L., Kohut, J., and Mathews, M. V., "A Music Synthesis System Using a Personal Computer, Drum Sensor, and Midi-Controlled Synthesizer (A)," *J. Acoust. Soc. Amer.*, vol. 79, p. 575, 1986.

20 Zivatar: A Performance System

János Négyesy and Lee Ray

Zivatar is a piece for real-time performance by two musicians, one of whom plays on an electronic violin controller and the other of whom manipulates various electronic sound sources and processors, including a multichannel mixing board. A computer plays a crucial role in mediating the interaction of the violinist and the electronic sound sources. Zivatar is a collaborative and interactive work that varies from performance to performance but that nonetheless remains recognizably the same. A video tape of a performance of Zivatar is available as an adjunct to this book.

The violinist uses two different modes to produce sounds from the performance system. In the first, the acoustic mode, the sounds produced by the excitation of the strings and other parts of the violin by such means as bowing, plucking, and scraping are picked up by piezoelectric elements inset into the bridge of the violin. The signals from each pickup are then conveyed independently to the preamplifier where they are highpass filtered to remove low-frequency noise. From this point the signals follow two parallel paths. On one, the violin signals go to the mixing board for further processing by the synthesist. Since the signals are independent, they can be treated individually. For example, the four strings can be panned across output channels, creating a spatialization of the violin sound. Each string can also be sent in varying amounts to different outboard processors, such as delays, reverberators, and filters. The outputs of these units can in turn be brought back to the mixing board and treated as independent signals that may be further processed.

In the second mode, the controller mode, the individual signals from each of the four strings are sent independently to a note detector. This special-purpose hardware analyzes the variations in voltage over time in each signal and produces estimates of the time-varying loudness and pitch of the sounds from the violin [3]. These estimates are then sent to a 68000-based computer system. The computer is running a program in firmware that performs a statistical analysis of the loudness and pitch estimates and attempts to eliminate noisiness and error from these data. The results are coded into a stream of MIDI key commands. (Each string generates a MIDI stream on a different MIDI channel so that the independence of the strings can be maintained just as it is in the acoustic mode.) These command streams carry the time-varying amplitude of the sounds as a succession of begin times and end times for notes with an associated single intensity or "velocity" level. Similarly, the time-varying pitch of the string signal is carried as a single equal-tempered "key number." The MIDI stream describing the violin performance is then combined with other MIDI data from a MIDI control unit that has various programmable sliders, pedals, and switches. This composite MIDI stream is then directed to various synthesizers and a sampler to give the violinist timing and pitch control of events programmed on those devices.

Zivatar uses the identity function for note translation—a single note played on the violin produces a single MIDI keystroke. (See [1] for a discussion of other possibilities.) However, the aural significance and musical usefulness of the various MIDI keystroke commands depends on the configuration of the synthesizers and sampler. For example, when playing the violin and holding the MIDI "sustain pedal" down, sounds coming from the synthesizers will have their pitch and loudness specified by the notes played on the violin but will last as long as pedal is held down. In this case the violin and pedal function together to produce a situation similar to the use of a sustain pedal on a piano—notes are begun by the action of the hammer striking the string but do not cease ringing until damped by the release of the pedal. (More will be said about the various roles of the synthesizers and sampler in the program notes below.) The outputs from the MIDI-controlled units are then sent to the mixing board for further processing by the synthesist as discussed above.

20.1 Zivatar: Performance System Equipment

The equipment used in the Zivatar performance system on the accompanying video tape is shown in figure 20.1 and described here. The electronic violin was designed and fabricated by San Diego sculptor Michael Monfort based on an instrument by Max Mathews [2]. The preamplifier, hardware pitch detector, and computer were designed, fabricated, and programmed at the Computer Audio Research Laboratory (CARL) of the Center for Music Experiment (CME) at the University of California at San Diego (UCSD) by Gareth Loy, Andy Voelkel, Rusty Wright, and Tom Erbe. The mixer is a Soundcraft Series 200B. Four channels of compression are provided by 2 stereo Symetrix 522s. The synthesizers are the 8-module Yamaha TX816 FM rack. The sampler is the Sequential Circuits Prophet 2002. The delay and echo units are the Yamaha SPX90. The reverb is the Roland SRV-2000.

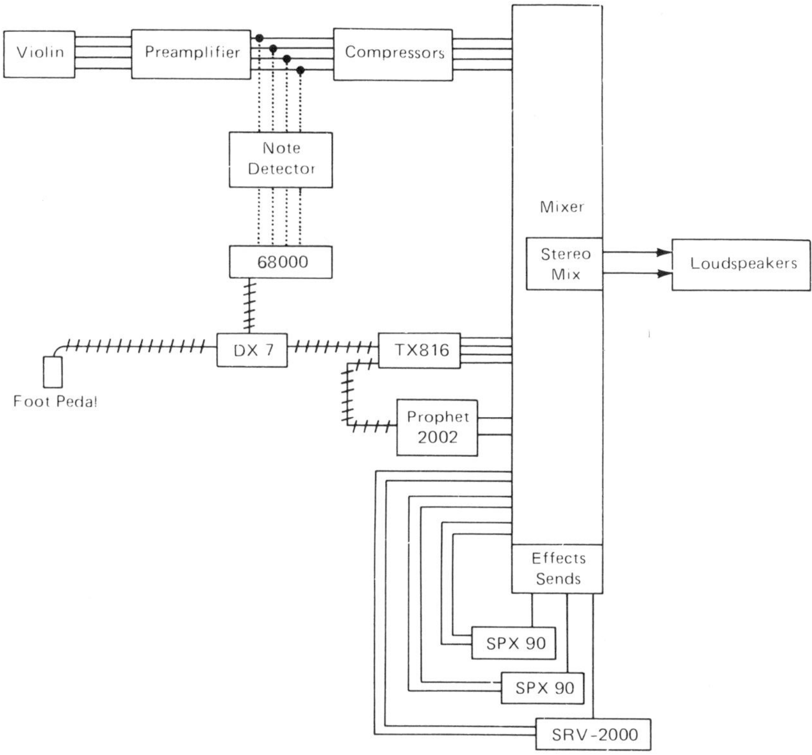

Figure 20.1
Zivatar performance system: solid line, audio; hatched line, MIDI; dotted line, pitch or loudness estimate.

20.2 Zivatar: A Brief Discussion

Musicians—composers and performers alike—can have a musical intention best realized with electronic resources. Their training typically prepares them for dealing with either very specific details of execution or rather abstract and schematic overall views. A host of engineering details, whether they have to do with the fabrication of violins and pianos or integrated circuits, are the speciality of others. Yet just as violins and pianos can be designed for playability, so electronic circuitry can be shaped to the purpose of the musician. General-purpose computers can transform information about the behavior of the musician into commands for synthesizers, samplers, and other powerful machinery. Computer-assisted performance allows musicians to use their musical training and intelligence to control the unique sonic resources that can be created only with electronics.

In Zivatar, the performance system allows for musical control of a diverse array of materials, including arbitrarily tuned sine waves, noise bursts, a violin, bells, footsteps, groans, and whispers. Sounds can be filtered, echoed, delayed, reverberated, and have altered dynamic shapes. The preparation of samples, the programming of synthesizer elements, and the setup of processing units must all be accomplished prior to the time of performance in order to allow an expressive interpretation of the music in real time.

Appendix: A Program Note on Zivatar

A video tape of a performance of the piece "Zivatar" is available as an adjunct to this book.

Zivatar consists of several different sections, each of which features a particular mode of sound production and phrase shaping. The piece is arrayed in a modified sonata form with some compression of sections. Approximate timings for the beginnings of some of the events mentioned below are given in minutes and seconds in parentheses.

Zivatar begins with a barrage of complex synthesizer sounds that produce no definite single sensation of pitch or rhythm (0′00″). The violinist triggers these sounds rather as a conductor might cue instrumentalists who have rehearsed to produce certain phrases. Here the character and pulsatile rhythms of the synthesizer noise are determined by the randomly varying low-frequency oscillator that is controlling the frequencies of modulators of carriers with fixed frequencies. The synthesizer used is the Yamaha TX816. The durations of individual instances of the sounds are controlled by the violinist either by the length of a given bowing or by using the MIDI sustain pedal. The Yamaha DX-7 is used to add "sustain pedal on/off" commands. The loudness and speed of echoes as well as the ratio of direct to reverberated sound are controlled by the synthesist to give the impression of a constantly changing aural perspective throughout the piece.

The second section features the acoustic output of the violin. The novel bowing technique produces low-amplitude noise bursts that are then arrayed in speechlike patterns (1′20″). The noises are filtered using Yamaha SPX90 processors performing "chorusing" or time-varying delays and amplitude modulations. Delays on the order of 2–50 msec are used to introduce formants into the violin sounds, reinforcing their speechlike character. This section overlaps with the following section, which uses sounds generated by the synthesizers. The MIDI note detectors used to trigger the synthesizers perform most satisfactorily when presented with a note of definite pitch, loudness, and duration. In an effort to satisfy these conflicting musical and technological demands the acoustic signals from the violin are processed by Symetrix 522 compressor/limiters. These units, a combination of envelope detectors and voltage-controlled amplifiers, superimpose a paradoxical dynamic on the violin signals by allowing quiet sounds to be greatly amplified while loud sounds are considerably attenuated. The violinist's actual dynamic is thus decoupled from the listener's impression of loudness, and the contribution of vigorously bowed notes to the acoustic sections is reduced while nevertheless giving the MIDI note detector reliable information.

The next section uses the synthesizer "operators" of the TX816 configured as summed sine waves (3′10″). Their envelopes have different slow onsets and decays. In addition, the sensitivity of each sine wave to MIDI key velocity varies from a value of "2" to "7." The greater the value, the more vigorously the string must be bowed in order to give an operator a substantial output. In this way the violinist can use the intensity of attack to control the number of the synthesized tones. Only one of the six sine waves has the same pitch as the MIDI key command. The other five are all transposed by intervals that do not fall in the equal-tempered scale. The duration of the tones is given either by the duration of the string excitation or by the use of the sustain pedal. Quasi-vocal and instrumental sounds fuse and emerge from the massed sine waves only to disappear again. The relative balances and filtering similar to that done in the acoustic section before are adjusted by the synthesist. As in the previous synthesizer section, the violinist's role becomes more like a conductor's than an instrumentalist's since notes, once begun, may take several seconds to be loud enough to be heard. His concern is for the accumulation of elements of a continuous texture rather than the statement of elements with certain pitch/time values.

A sampled sound is then introduced over the continuing sine wave clusters (5′10″). In preparation for the piece, the violinist whispered a brief sentence, which was then recorded via analog-to-digital converters into the CARL software synthesis system at the Center for Music Experiment of the

University of California at San Diego. The recorded sentence was then combined with many delayed and pitch-shifted copies of itself in order to create the sound of a crowd of whispering voices, a sound, once again, with little definite pitch or rhythmic profile. The prepared sound was transferred to the sampling unit used in performance, the Sequential Circuits Prophet 2002. The sample, once triggered by a violin note, persists until its end and then stops. The "key number" gives a transposition level for the sample that, for this sound, shifts the noises up or down in spectrum. No looping or other processing of the sound is done with the sampler. However, the duration of the sample can be shortened by depressing the sustain pedal while bowing. In this case the sample would begin at its beginning and only sound for as long as the string excitation continued.

While the violinist uses the sampled sound the sine wave clusters are faded out and replaced by a new group of synthesized sounds (6′20″) that have two elements—an initial noise burst followed by a cluster of near-unison sine waves, which undergo a small programmed change in frequency over the course of their sounding. As before, the operators are set to be sensitive to the MIDI key velocity, and so the relative contribution of the various operators to the overall sound is controlled by the violinist.

In addition, the spectrum of the noise burst varies from broad band for high velocities to a narrower bandpass region around the frequency of the fingered violin note for low velocities.

A restatement of the speechlike acoustic section follows. Once again the sine wave clusters are introduced underneath the violin sounds and then combined with a vocal sample. This sample is a new one, a pitch-shifted version of voiced speech to which a backward copy of the first sentence has been added. The same procedure as outlined above was used to prepare this sample.

The clusters are replaced by another group of synthesizer sounds, bursts of short, bliplike sine waves (11′30″). Again, only one of the six sinusoids has the same pitch as the fingered note on the violin. However, the other five are this time transposed to pitches that fall in the equal-tempered scale. The onsets of the sinusoids are delayed with respect to the string excitation and to each other by setting the first segment of their envelopes to a level of "0" and then to some rate between "99" and "0" with the higher values introducing less delay. Once again operator velocity sensitivity varies so that a greater or lesser number of sine wave elements can be included by the violinist. Rather than a single "note" being sounded for every fingered note, a phraselike melodic element results. The violinist's performance gives the begin time and transposition level for the phrase, the approximate number of notes in the phrase, and the phrase duration.

A blast of white noise covers the violinist's efforts for a few seconds and signals the coda (11′55″). Here a variety of samples—bells, voiced speech, and footsteps—are interwoven with the echoing bursts. A single note from the acoustic violin is caught in an indefinitely regenerating reverb program running on a Roland SRV-2000 signal processor (16′27″). A final flurry of synthesized, sampled, and processed acoustic sounds ends the performance.

References

[1] D. G. Loy, "Designing an Operating Environment for a Realtime Performance Processing System," Proceedings of the International Computer Music Conference 1985, Computer Music Association, San Francisco, 1985.

[2] M. V. Mathews, "Electronic Violin; A Research Tool," *J. of the Violin Society of America*, Vol. VIII, No. 1, pp.71–88, 1984.

[3] A. Voelkel, "A Cost Effective Input Processor-Pitch Detector for Electronic Violin," Proceedings of the International Computer Music Conference 1985, Computer Music Association, San Francisco, 1985.

21 Composing with Computers—a Survey of Some Compositional Formalisms and Music Programming Languages

Gareth Loy

Before God and as an honest man I tell you that your son is the greatest composer known to me either in person or by name. He has taste and, what is more, the most profound knowledge of composition.
—Joseph Haydn to Leopold Mozart

Is this just a clockworks of fabulous design, or does it actually tell time?
—Virgil Thompson (*The Art of Judging Music*)

There is currently a wave of revolutionary dimensions in the realm of music composition stemming from the confluence of two forces: on the one hand, the widespread availability of digital computers for musicians and composers, and on the other, their availability at this time, when serious composers no longer rely so heavily on convention, but create their own artistic justifications from first principles.

Though composers have always used formal devices in composition, recent musical trends and the availability of computers have made it a practical concern for composers and musicians to develop formal techniques and descriptive and procedural notations in order to express musical ideas in ways mutually understandable to computers and musicians. The application of formal techniques to music is a good place to begin to understand the often conflicting requirements music and computers place upon each other.

The problem of representing music with computers is deep and multifaceted. As an art form, music has high-level expressive requirements that are extremely difficult to formalize. But computers require formal expression for all problems they address. Besides this, the sheer volume of computation required to realize music of any subtlety with computers puts musical computing in league with such problems as vision research and particle physics.

The article begins with an overview of some of the formal methods used historically in composition, and a quasi-historical discussion of how composers and music theorists have thought about and used formal methods such as algorithms to write—and help write—music. This leads to a discussion of music composition programs and programming languages for music, with many examples.

21.1 Introduction

Music, like all other products of human culture, owes its existence to number and process, both of which are free creations of the human mind. Of all the arts, music is considered to be open to the purest expression of order and proportion, unencumbered as it is by material media. The oft-noted affinity between music and mathematics is therefore no mystery. Indeed, in earlier times, music was considered to be a branch of mathematics. Cassiodorus (ca. 485–ca. 575) labeled these as the divisions of mathematics: arithmetic, music, geometry, and astronomy [Cassiodorus 1950a]. What brought these four disciplines together for him as mathematics was that they all dealt in what he termed "abstract quantity": "By abstract quantity we mean that quantity which we treat in a purely speculative way, separating it intellectually from its material and from its other accidents, such as evenness, oddness, and the like.... Arithmetic is the discipline of absolute numerable quantity. Music is the discipline which treats of numbers in their relation to those things which are found in sound" [Cassiodorus 1950a].

Music was used as a vehicle for ritual and magic in prehistoric times, was considered to be a branch of science by the ancient world, and was a vehicle of emotional expression in the Romantic era of the nineteenth century. Berlioz and others regarded music as the direct communication of internal states of being [Barzun 1969a]. There have also been those who view music primarily as a mystical enterprise, and point to its magical properties in shamanistic chant, and its spiritual properties in mantram [Hamel 1976a]. Carl Orff speaks of an "elemental music," which is prerational; the primordial soup out of which all music comes. It is the raw expression of human energies and states of being [Orff 1967a]. Balance between these seemingly conflicting perspectives is difficult: "Unlike a close, non-referential mathematical system, music is said to communicate emotional and aesthetic meanings as well as purely intellectual ones. This puzzling combination of abstractness with concrete emotional experience can, if understood correctly, perhaps yield useful insights into more general problems of meaning and communication, especially those involving aesthetic experience" [Meyer 1956a].

Philosopher Susanne Langer maintains that music is a symbolic system, where the denotata constitute a "morphology of feeling." She has said, "music conveys *general forms* of feelings, related to specific ones as algebraic expressions are related to arithmetic [expressions]" [Langer 1948a]. Music, she is saying, is a kind of algebra for the expression of emotional archetypes. Music thus seems to share the goals of mathematics in the pursuit of a coherent expression of ordering principles.

Clearly a discussion limited to the formal aspects of music can never do justice to the whole of music. However, the charge here is to discuss those aspects that are tractable with computers. And because computers require formal expression for all subjects they are to understand, formalization of music is our first topic. However, we should not lose sight of the content so formalized.

21.2 Compositional Formalisms

The term *compositional formalism* here is taken to mean any systematic ordering, or way of organizing, creating, or analyzing compositional systems (or processes or designs). Other terms, such as *procedure*, *method*, *game*, and *algorithm*, are all formalisms in this way of thinking. Of these, *algorithm* is the most carefully defined because of its place in mathematics. Examples of algorithmic methods include travel directions and the rules of algebra. Just as an algebraic equation specifies *relationsips* between symbolic objects, an algorithm specifies *actions* on symbolic objects.

Most things one does repeatedly with a purpose can be considered algorithmic, though there are some important qualifications, as we shall see. The creation—and sometimes even the appreciation—of formalisms generally takes an exertion of mental effort because one must be holding the goal of the method and the requisite actions in mind, while simultaneously observing and recording what one is doing to achieve the goal. Because of the mental effort required, formalisms are generally only created where the expenditure of effort seems warranted. The analysis of formalisms can therefore reveal important values of an individual or culture. We shall see that the formal methods of a musical style are often deeply salient and revealing.

Because of its precise definition, we shall begin with a short exposition about algorithms, though we shall subsequently see that most formal procedures used in music are not strictly algorithmic. Still, algorithm has received the most careful definition, and other formal techniques can be described with related concepts. Later we shall examine some novel computer programs and languages developed to solve problems in the expression of music and musical formalisms. The purpose of the survey of compositional formalisms is to motivate the discussion that follows on programs and languages.

21.2.1 Algorithm Defined

For a short history of algorithms, I refer the reader to [Knuth 1973a]. The earlier term *algorism* was used to describe the rules of calculating with Arabic numerals. The term *algorithm* is derivative, but more general. An algorithm may describe a set of rules or give a sequence of operations for accomplishing some task, or solving some problem. The following are the criteria for determining an algorithm.

Finiteness—An algorithm must terminate after a finite (and reasonable) number of steps.

Definiteness—There must be agreement as to the precise meaning of each of the steps to be taken.

Input—An algorithm may receive information upon which it is to operate.

Ouput—An algorithm must have at least one result, which is produced by applying the algorithm to its inputs.

Effectiveness—Even if a step passes the criterion of definiteness, it still may or may not be effective. Each step must yield a result in a finite (and reasonable!) period of time. The inputs must be tractable; the action of each step must not depend upon unknowns.

Is a cookbook recipe an algorithm? We can see that while it meets most criteria, it may lack definiteness by allowing such language as "salt to taste." On the other hand, travel directions ought to pass all the tests, or else they are not useful, and so qualify as truly algorithmic.

Knuth gives additional criteria that we use to measure algorithms. Among these are the "aesthetic qualities" of simplicity, elegance, parsimony, and tractability (ease of adaptation to, e.g., a computer). We should also care how efficently an algorithm accomplishes our task, and how well it represents our understanding of the problem. Whereas the first five criteria define what an algorithm is, Knuth says, these aesthetic criteria determine its "goodness."

Before considering musical techniques for their algorithmic qualities, it would be good to consider a clear-cut example from mathematics. We shall start with Euclid's algorithm for finding the greatest common divisor of two integers, that is, the largest number that divides both integers evenly, without remainder [Vinogradov 1954a, Knuth 1973a]. This comes in handy, for instance, in reducing fractions to their lowest form. For example, the greatest common divisor of 9 and 12 is 3. We just "know" that, but *how* do we know it, and how could we represent this knowledge so someone else could know it too? Also, what if we were faced with finding the greatest common divisor of 91 and 416, which we most probably do not know? Euclid developed the following algorithm for positive integers to solve this problem.

1. Given two numbers, m and n, find their remainder, r, after division.[1]
2. If the remainder is 0, then we are done, and n is the answer.
3. Otherwise, set m to n, and n to r, and start over.

In the case of 9 and 12, we have the following steps:

step 1: $m = 9$, $n = 12$, $r = 9$,

step 2: $m = 12$, $n = 9$, $r = 3$,

step 3: $m = 9$, $\underline{n = 3}$, $r = 0$.

That is, we set $m = 9$, and $n = 12$, and take the remainder of m and n, which is $r = 9$. As it is not 0, we set $m = 12$ (i.e., we set it to the value of n) and we set $n = 9$ (i.e., the value of r), and go back to step 1. We continue this process until $r = 0$, whereupon n is the answer: 3. In the case of 91 and 416, we have the following:

$m = 91$, $n = 416$, $r = 91$

$m = 416$, $n = 91$, $r = 52$

$m = 91$, $n = 52$, $r = 39$

$m = 52$, $n = 39$, $r = 13$

$m = 39$, $\underline{n = 13}$, $r = 0$

So the greatest common divisor is 13.

This method qualifies as an algorithm on all counts. It is *finite* because it will always eventually yield a remainder of 0. This is because successive values of r move monotonically toward 0. It is *definite* (for positive integers) because the meaning of division and remaindering for positive integers is unambiguous. (But we must be careful; if we extend the range by only one number to include 0, it no longer passes the effectiveness test because division by 0 is not permitted.) It has *inputs*, m and n, and an *output* (the answer). It is *effective* because the quantities it works on—positive integers—present no ambiguities in calculations.

It meets Knuth's "aesthetic" criteria as well. It is simple (three steps), elegant (goes straight to the point), and parsimonious (does not require extraneous operations). It is also easily adaptable to a computer. Here is a subroutine, written in the C programming language, that implements Euclid's algorithm [Kernighan 1978a]. Symbols in **bold** are C-language reserved words, while *italic* is used for user-defined variable and subroutine names.

```
Euclid(m, n) {
    int r = m % n;
    while (r != 0) {
        m = n;
        n = r;
        r = m % n;
    }
    return n;
}
```

Subroutine *Euclid* receives two arguments, m and n. It declares r to be an **int**, C's keyword for "integer," and assigns it the value of $m \% n$. The "%" operator computes the remainder of m and n. The subroutine then enters a **while** loop, which will terminate only when $r = 0$. In this programming language, the "=" operator assigns the value of the expression on the right to the variable on the left, while the "!=" operator tests whether the values on the right and left are different. When r finally equals 0, the loop is terminated, and the result is in n, the value of which is **return**ed as the answer.

As we have seen, the creation—and even the appreciation—of algorithms generally takes an exertion of mental effort because one must be holding the goal of the method and the requisite actions in mind, while simultaneously observing and recording what one is doing to achieve the goal. One is, so to speak, recursively thinking about what one is thinking about. The analysis of algorithms can be shown to demonstrate not merely clever means to ends, but, more important, it can reveal the value systems —the true aims—of individuals and cultures: because what is formalized into algorithms is always the essence of what is felt to be so central to an enterprise as to warrant such expenditure of effort. For instance, we shall see that the formal elements of a musical style are often its most salient and revealing aspects.

21.2.2 Guido's Method

We take the ancestor of the compositional algorithm for our first musical example. This method was first presented in 1026—nearly one thousand years ago—by the learned Benedictine and famous musical theoretician Guido D'Arezzo. Though so old, we shall find much to ponder in its implications. One of the chapters of his treatise for singers, entitled *Micrologus*, laid out a practical scheme for the production of a musical line from any text whatsoever [D'Arezzo 1955a]. The essence of the method consists in constructing a table of correspondences between the vowels of the text and the notes of the scale.

First he lays out the pitches of the double-octave, which was the standard compass of vocal music of his time,

Γ A B C D E F G a b c d e f g a,

which correspond to the modern pitch letters C-D-E-F-G-A-B... covering the range G below middle-C to A above the treble cleff. Against this he places three iterations of the canonical vowel sequence, a-e-i-o-u, as follows:

Γ	A	B	C	D	E	F	G	a	b	c	d	e	f	g	a
a	e	i	o	u	a	e	i	o	u	a	e	i	o	u	a.

Guido now selects a Latin text and, extracting the vowels from each word, sets about looking up corresponding pitch values from his table. We note that this method supplies three choices for each vowel (four choices for the letter a). This keeps the method from having but one unique solution for each text. Following this procedure, he composes a song for the entire text.[2] Even though given a schematic for the melody by the tables, composers still must exercise their creative and intuitive faculties to yield a suitably musical line by applying other standard musical rules relating to the aesthetics of melodic formation. Guido suggests that by selecting only the best excerpts from several attempts, this method can yield a composition perfectly adapted to the text, and also one that meets the requirements of good compositional practice.

Is Guido's method an algorithm? Certainly the heart of the method—the construction of the table and the lookup operation—is clearly algorithmic. But Guido's admonition that we must make final selections according to other rules not explicitly stated (the aesthetic rules of melody formation) makes that part of the method seem more like the injunction in a recipe: "... and salt to taste." So it runs afoul of the definiteness criterion.

This serves to point out a truism about composers and compositions of all eras and styles: given a method or a rule, what is usually deemed compositionally interesting is to follow it as far as to establish a sense of inertia, or expectancy, and then to veer off in some way that is unexpected, but still somehow related to what has gone before. Like a melody subjected to variations, all formal ordering methods are usually held by composers to be as plastic as the material they order. The criterion of definiteness in the definition of *algorithm* leaves little room for arbitrary aesthetic tempering; therefore, few compositional ordering practices are strictly algorithmic. Such terms as *procedure* and *method* share all but the definiteness rule. It seems preferable, then, to refer to Guido's *method* rather than Guido's *algorithm.*

So we have examined Guido's method in its relation to algorithm. But is it art? (Or more properly, does it produce art?) In a nineteenth-century edition of Guido's *Micrologus*, the editor, Michael Hermesdorff, criticised Guido's method as artistically suspect—a mere form of dalliance—not suitable for such a major figure as Guido. To protect Guido, the editor explained it away as a practical help provided for the incompetent beginner as a way to get results quickly. However, musicological opinion now has it that Guido's method must be taken more seriously [Kirchmeyer 1963a].

This is a common complaint about formal structure of all kinds in music that has not been directed only at Guido. Viewed from this perspective, such techniques take all the work out of composing. Once a system has been established, the argument goes, the only decisive thing has already been done and "composing" reduces to merely making adjustments—much as a cook will season a dish to taste. Kirchmeyer points out, however, that this is not so much a criticism as a statement of truth about all formal methods, "You can never get more out of an automaton than has already been put into it" [Kirchmeyer 1963a].

What has become of composing where formal practices are used is simply the relocation of the compositional decision-making process to a higher position. It means the incorporation of higher-level musical elements, such as algorithms, into the fabric of the compositional process. Some low-level elements of the compositional decision-making process may be taken over by an automatic process, but the composer must still both choose the process and accept the results.

Formal techniques are used as tools in composing in two ways: to achieve an underlying unity and direction in a work, and to determine an independent agent of choice for certain details. In the most abstract sense, algorithmic techniques are merely tools of conceptual explanation that composers use to express their methods of operation. It is the framing in a conscious, explicit way of a generative relationship between elements of a composition. For instance, Guido's method consciously expressed his underlying belief that the purpose of music was to exalt and clarify the biblical text that it set. His method constrained the music to the words, thereby expressing his philosophy of music in a conscious manner. Here we see an example of the analysis of algorithmic techniques revealing the aesthetic agenda of a composer.

21.2.3 Other Antique Formal Practices

There are many other compositional formalisms that have the flavor—if perhaps not always the rigor—of algorithm.

The technique of *isorhythm* is a case in point. It emerged as a characteristic rhythmic organizing technique in the motets of the thirteenth-century composer Philipp de Vitry. His motet tenors were often laid out with a serially repeating rhythmic pattern. The pattern could vary according to certain rules after the lapse of a certain number of repetitions. The tenor's rhythmic line moved very slowly against the faster notes of the upper lines. The slow-moving tenor thus provided a structural template that determined the metrical foundation of a composition.

Another method for establishing a formal anchor for a composition is the canon, wherein a composer generates one or more additional voices by delayed imitation of a melodic line. The technique seemingly first appeared in the music of the Netherlands composers ca. 1450, though there has been little work, until recently, on the automatic generation of canons. Canons are difficult to compose because one must simultaneously obey the canonic imitation rule while satisfying the rules of how voices may combine harmonically (voice leading). Composers do this intuitively, and fairly quickly, but algorithmic solutions for canons of any length require fast computers and lots of time [Dewdney 1987a]. For instance, the Netherlands composer Johannes Ockeghem wrote a famous mass, the *Missa prolationum*, every movement of which is constructed as a double mensuration canon making use of various intervals and various combinations of key signatures [Grout 1980a].

The English *round* is a method for the harmonization of a melody by performers. Here we must differentiate between compositional and performance methods. There is no simple method for composing a round, but the method of performing a round is simple and nearly algorithmic. It is typically a short, unaccompanied vocal canon at the unison or octave. It has definiteness (the rules are simplicity itself: delay so many entries by so many measures and start singing), input (the song), output (the singing), and effectiveness (when suitable choice of melodies is made). It lacks only a termination rule to qualify as algorithmic, though of course one is always provided by the performers, ultimately.

In the fifteenth and early sixteenth centuries, one often encounters so-called canonic riddles embedded within compositions that require the working out of a puzzle in order to perform the work. Again, a distinction must be made: the creation of the puzzle was undoubtedly not methodical, but—once one sees the answer—the solution is. The movement *Agnus Dei III* of Guillaume Dufay's *Missa L'Homme armé* contains the inscription *Cancer et plenus et redeat medius* ("Let the crab proceed full and return half"). Davison and Apel deduce that this "indicates that the cantus firmus is to be sung twice, first in full note values, then in halved values and in retrograde motion (this being indicated by the word 'return'). Since, however, the crab's normal motion is backwards, the 'proceeding' section actually is retrograde, and the 'returning' section, therefore, in normal motion" [Davison 1964a].

21.2.4 Musical Acrostics

The term *soggetto cavato* (literally, "carved out subject") refers to a Renaissance method, related to Guido's, of deriving a musical phrase by taking a significant word or words, extracting the vowels, and obtaining a melody formed by the Guidonian solmization syllables [Kirchmeyer 1963a, Apel 1961a]. A related example is the theme built by J. S. Bach from his own name. In German, in the times of J. S. Bach, the *B* signified our pitch *Bb*, while *H* signified our *B-natural*. The resulting theme, *Bb–A–C–B*, was used by Bach in the last work of his life, the *Art of the Fugue*, in the last, unfinished, fugue. (Planned as a quadruple fugue, it is curious to note that his health gave out just as he introduced the B–A–C–H theme, and he died shortly after.) Many other composers have used this theme as well—for instance, the slow movement of Beethoven's string quartet, opus 59 #2 (in the bass) [Scholes 1964a]. Later users include R. Schumann (*Sechs Fugen über Bach*), F. Liszt (*Fantasy and Fugue on B.A.C.H.*), Reger, Piston, Honegger, Berg, and many others [Apel 1961a, Mies 1925a].

Robert Schumann's delight in musical acrostics is evidenced in his piano compositions, such as his *Abegg Variations* (which spells *A–Bb–E–G–G*). His *Carnival* is based on permutations of the letters in the name of the town of Asch (*A–S–C–H*) near which his fiancée lived. This can be permuted to S–C–H–u–m–A–n, which yields *Eb–C–B–A* in modern notation [Longyear 1969a]. These techniques are mostly just embellishments to compositions that did not depend upon the technique in any substantial way. Things of this kind lend themselves more readily to explanation and memory than many more important—but less verbalizable—things about these works. It is very unlikely that anyone listening to these works would deduce these as ordering principles, but, being so informed, we must admire the works all the more for the artfulness of the compositions despite the formal technical problems being solved at the same time.

21.2.5 Combinatorics

A pervasive compositional method employed by the Viennese composers Arnold Schoenberg, Alban Berg, and Anton Webern was the use of consistent note patterns that contain all twelve pitches. In the methodology initially set out by Schoenberg, an instance of such a pattern of 12 notes is called a *row*, or *set*, or *series*. No note appears more than once within the set. It may be subjected to four linear geometrical transformations: inversion, retrograde, retrograde-inversion, and rectus (also called prime, or the identity function). The four resulting transformations can also be transposed to any degree of the chromatic scale. The result is a structure of 48 rows derived from the original, called a *set-complex*, which formed the source material for pitch organization in a work. The purpose of these transformations is to generate variants that are related to the original intervallic structure of the prime row, to be used as material that can act as variants in developing compositions.

When applying these rows in the process of composing, an unambiguous ordering of the set-forms (the individual rows of the set-complex) is assumed; but the actual compositional procedures employed will vary from composer to composer and work to work quite freely, depending on the stylistic goals of the composer, and the nature of the set-complex.[3] Once begun, all the pitch classes in a particular set-form usually must be used before another set-form is chosen from the set-complex. Also, it was generally the case that a pitch class from a set-form would not be repeated out of turn. But an exception was made by Schoenberg and Berg to allow for pitch repetition—for instance, to allow for ostinati. But once a note was left, it was generally not revisited until its turn came again. Webern, it seems, utterly eschewed such redundancy.

The purpose of this method becomes clear if we realize that Schoenberg and his school were setting up an engine for the logical extension of trends in tonal organization that were culminating in the final and total obliteration of tonal expectation and key-centeredness in European art music. The rows chosen—and their compositional treatment—were such as to defeat our tendency to hear tonal centeredness of any kind. What was substituted for tonality was the inner organization of the row sequence and the selection of set-forms. We see here again the philosophical-aesthetic posture of a composer (or school) revealed in an underlying formal method. "Perhaps the most important influence of Schoenberg's method is not the 12-note idea in itself, but along with it the individual concepts of permutation, inversional symmetry and complementation, invariance under transformation, aggregate construction, closed systems, properties of adjacency as compositional determinants, transformations of musical surfaces through predefined operations, and so on" [Perle 1981a].

21.2.6 Würfelspiel [Dice Music]

It is revealing that composers of such durable stature as W. A. Mozart, J. Haydn, and C. P. E. Bach, living as they were in the Age of Enlightenment, would be found dabbling in compositional techniques based on chance [Potter 1971a].

Because musical aesthetics of the classical era were so strict, it was possible to construct a simple music-making game for composing minuets and other incidental works. The method consisted of iteratively applying the outcome of throwing dice, or spinning a spinner, to choosing which of several possible musical motives would be selected from tables of musical figures. A well-formed piece of music in the classical style would result. "This sort of musical game was in the air in the second part of the 18th century, though clearly regarded as entertainment only. This is, e.g., expressed by Kirnberger—whom we should also regard as the father of musical literature of this sort—in the preface to his composition of this kind (1757). Every game is after all a mirror of the ideas of the times: the rationalistic epoch considers the possibility of mechanical composition" [Gerigk 1936a].

Both Guido's lookup method and Kirnberger's chance method can be broken down usefully into two phases: the first where the options are enumerated, the second where the choices are made. I will refer to these as the *generator* phase and the *selector* phase. In Guido's case, the generator phase is the process of transformation from a vowel to a set of possible pitches. In Kirnberger's case, it is the determination of the set of possible next measures. The selector phase for Guido is the heuristic evaluation of the most suitable choice—based on rules of melody formation—during which one of the possibilities is selected. Kirnberger's selector phase, however, is accomplished by assigning choice to the outcome of an unregardable (i.e., chance) operation.

It was common in that day even for composers of considerable stature to turn to compilations of musical progressions and cadences for solutions to musical problems. The technique, called *ars inveniendi*, was quite widespread from the late Baroque through Classical times. Musicologists and composers alike would make compilations of motives to serve either as a stimulus for the composer's imagination, or as the actual music for the unimaginative. Though a composer might work by stringing these motives together like a chain of beads, there was still the act of choice that kept it authentic. But the introduction of "mere" chance to determine the choice seems to relieve the composer of the last vestage of responsibility. One may reasonably ask whether one is not utterly giving up the compositional process to a blind automation? As if purposefully to raise hackles, a work entitled *A Tabular System Whereby Any Person without the Least Knowledge of Musick May Compose Ten Thousand Different Minuets in the Most Pleasing and Correct Manner* was published by Peter Welcker in London in 1775, and seems to follow Kirnberger's lead [Köechel 1935a].

Some scholars are reluctant to admit that Mozart's *Musikalische Würfelspiel* is authentic. (It was found written on an autograph manuscript of another of his works.) It is difficult to define what *authentic* means in such a case. One can argue that the piece is in his hand, which clearly establishes authorship. But it is difficult to see the hand of the master behind a façade that includes chance, just as it is difficult to make out a face behind frosted glass.

Würfelspiel emerged from the era which saw the advent of the probability calculus of Pascal. In this era, ways were being found to penetrate the enigma of chance, to rationalize it, without, however, being able to reduce it to its essence. Perhaps we must guard against reading too much into such a trifle as *Würfelspiel*; nonetheless, it is true that in chance can be found the Universe's most elemental decision-maker. If one wants to automate a decision-making process, it must be based on chance, *Würfelspiel* being a case in point.

Another observation on chance will perhaps stretch credibility even further, but we can find from this game a bridge to the work of John Cage. Pure chance is ultimately irrational, by which I mean there can be no closed system of explanation that includes it, save for the Universe itself. Because of this, observing pure chance has been looked upon by some as a way of perceiving the direct influence of the Cosmos upon us, so unpredictable outcomes have sometimes been thought of as having prophetic value. This perhaps explains why chance is the root of oracular methods such as the Tarot and the Chinese *I Ching*. The tap root of these oracles is the belief that the chance methods on which they are based are synchronous with the same universal decision-processes that control all things, and hence also fate. Of course, to interpret an oracle in a predictive way requires a successful theory of decoding the supposed message derived from the underlying chance operation. As the histories of the Greek supplicants at Delphi can attest, this is generally very difficult to do and usually requires a leap of faith somewhere! However, if one does not use an oracle in an interpretive way, one can consider that the chance operations one incorporates—for instance, in the act of composition—amount to an echo of the Voice of the Universe speaking through the music. This mystical notion, I maintain, is at the root of Cage's approach [Cage 1961a]. As evidence for the reasonableness of this, Giorgio de Santillana, in his landmark work, *Hamlet's Mill*, discusses several games from very ancient times, in which the choice of piece to be moved in chess, for instance, was determined by a throw of the dice [Santillana 1969a]. Variously called "The Game of the Gods" and "Celestial War," they are documented in texts dating from the fourteenth and fifteenth centuries in India and China. The origins of such games are hard to trace, but probably very ancient. A simple substitution of musical tables for a gaming table produces Kirnberger's musical equivalent, and simultaneously reveals an important antecedent to Cage's philosophy of music.

21.2.7 Principled Composition

Joseph Schillinger was a mathematician of the first half of the twentieth century. His work introduced many of the major themes taken up by the field of computer music in the years after his death. In his magnum opus, *The Mathematical Basis of the Arts*, he lobbied hard for a more practical theory of aesthetic creation than had hitherto been available [Schillinger 1948a]. Much as Langer might, Shillinger states that "a scientific theory of the arts must deal with the relationship that develops between works of art as they exist in their physical forms and emotional responses as they exist in their psycho-physiological forms." So far so good, but then he goes on to say, "As long as an art-form manifests itself through a physical medium, and is perceived through an organ of sensation, memory and associative orientation, it is a *measureable quantity*." Alas for the progress of the cognitive sciences, this is not tenable. The quantification of human experience does not come so easily as he wishes. He then concludes, "Analysis of esthetic form requires mathematical techniques, and the synthesis of forms ... requires the *technique of engineering*" (his italics throughout). We are to understand by this that his goal is the development of a general theory of the compositional process that would be generative as well as analytical; that would aid the composer as much as the musicologist.

He chastises all previous art theory as useless: "It is time to admit that esthetic theories have failed in the analysis as well as the synthesis of art. These have been unsuccessful both in interpreting the nature of art and in evolving a reliable method of composition." Previous theory, he maintains, had for its generative component mere "imitation of appearances (mimicry)," whereas he proposes a method of "creation from principles": "Theories a posteriori are very characteristic forms of art theories in general. Offering nothing in the analysis of the creative processes of art, such theories expose their futility in the contention that a genius is above theories, and that his creativity is free and does not conform to any laws or principles. This is the mythological period of esthetics. There is less and less room for mystery and divinity so far as the manipulation of material elements is concerned." So Schillinger is not just interested in rationalizing and codifying the techniques of artistry, but would like to incorporate creativity itself in his theory. The idea of a theory of musical creativity was also developed later in the work of Lejaren Hiller, Leonard Issacson, Robert Baker, and others, as discussed below. Just as Pascal was able to penetrate chaos with probability theory, but was still unable to rationalize pure chance, Schillinger was bound to fail, as the human creative process seems to have a similarly inscrutable kernel.

But behind this Promethean goal, what obviously motivates his work is the desire to put practical methods into the hands of artists that will give them a mathematician's vision of the nature and extent of their artistic domain. This is his positive contribution. It is this energy that led to the production of his two-volume tome (no other word describes it so well), *The Schillinger System of Musical Composition* [Schillinger 1978a]. Some of his ideas seem banal (some incomprehensible), but others do indeed—as I can attest—give the nonmathematician new vistas of the compositional process.

Schillinger's desire to apply his theories in practice is one of the most compelling aspects of his work. The idea of composing automata was not new, but Schillinger was more than a maker of musical clockworks. One of his composing machines was called the *Rhythmicon.* Built by Leon Theremin, it "is confined to the composition and automatic performance of rhythmic patterns in the acoustical scale of intonation" [Schillinger 1948a]. He planned for the development of "instruments for the automatic composition of music" including rhythm, melody, harmony, harmonization, and counterpoint; combinations of the above for the realization of pieces "with variable tone qualities"; instruments for the automatic variation of existing music; the above coupled with sound production for the purpose of performance during the process of composition or variation; and semiautomatic instruments for composing music. His name for such instruments was "Musamaton." He looked toward their use by anyone, not requiring special training, "suitable for schools, clubs, public amusement places, and homes."

Schillinger expressed his musical formalisms in an abstract mathematics-like notation, accompanied by often cryptic "explanations" that usually further served to mystify the reader. Deducing operations from his numerous examples proved the best means of understanding his methods. This reader has nevertheless felt compelled by the breadth and scope of his vision, if a little disappointed at the direct usefulness of his ideas. One still finds his theories, especially about rhythm, discussed occasionally, as for instance in [Jaxitron 1985a].

21.2.8 Stochos

As is well-known, the categorical break in European music from functional harmonic practice (so-called "common practice" music) came with the advent of the Viennese school of the twentieth century. Given that part of the desiderata of twelve-tone music was the avoidance of tonal effect, Schoenberg and his school used simple deterministic methods that resulted in a uniform distribution of pitches, at least in the basic material—the set-forms—from which compositions were realized.

In the early 1950s, Iannis Xenakis (among others) noted that another way to achieve such pitch distributions—indeed, any shape distribution—would be to use probabilistic, instead of serial, methods. In fact, it was the ultimate extension of the serial method to a completely causal determinism that led him to make the connection [Xenakis 1971a].

Xenakis notes that Olivier Messiaen sought to generalize and systematize the serial pitch-ordering technique of Schoenberg to all parameters of music (though he was working with modal pitch structures, not twelve-tone rows). Composers of the post-World War II era adapted his ideas to serial practices, and postwar serialism was born. However, when the complexity of this totally controlled, deterministic technique was realized in compositions, a curious thing was observed: there was little to distinguish these compositions from utter randomness. In 1954 Xenakis criticised serialism thus: "Linear polyphony destroys itself by its very complexity; what one hears is in reality nothing but a mass of notes in various registers. The enormous complexity prevents the audience from following the intertwining of the lines and has as its macroscopic effect an irrational and fortuitous dispersion of sounds over the whole extent of the sonic spectrum. There is consequently a contradiction between the polyphonic linear system and the heard result, which is surface or mass." So much for the diagnosis, now for the cure. He continues: "This contradiction inherent in [serial] polyphony will disappear [and] what will count will be the statistical mean of isolated states and of transformations of sonic components at a given moment. The macroscopic effect can then be controlled by the mean of the movements of elements which we select. The result is the introduction of the notion of probability, which implies, in this particular case, combinatory calculus. Here in a few words, is the possible escape route from the 'linear category' in musical thought" [Xenakis 1955a].

He thought this in keeping with the emergent world-view in physics of the quantum mechanics. "It is a matter here of a philosophic and aesthetic concept ruled by the laws of probability and by the mathematical functions that formulate that theory, of a coherent concept in a new region of coherence" [Xenakis 1971a]. (Xenakis' attempt to align musical aesthetics with a natural theory is not a new enterprise, of course, but dates back at least to the early Rennaissance music theorist Zarlino, who championed the view that music was an imitation of nature.)

Some of Xenakis' examples in *Formalized Music* seem to be limited to ordering methods of music for traditional musical instruments. Elsewhere in this work he addresses a deeper level of sound organization where he asserts, "All sound is an integration of grains, of elementary sonic particles, of sonic quanta." This compositional metaphor is derived from seminal work done by D. Gabor in 1947 regarding an isomorphism between the Fourier analysis model of hearing and a quantum analysis of his own design [Gabor 1947a].[4] Gabor's original mathematical analysis has been extended and confirmed [Bastiaans 1980a, Roads 1985a].

For Xenakis, "All sound is conceived as an assemblage of a large number of elementary grains adequately disposed in time." He proceeds from this to define a *screen* as a two-dimensional instant of time, having frequency on one axis and amplitude on the other. One composes by filling different regions of successive screens with varying densities of grains of sound.

This choice of compositional metaphor led Xenakis directly from probability theory as the basis of describing the granular nature of his sound objects to lexical and Markovian techniques for describing their behavior in time. This led in turn to the use of symbolic logic for the description and manipulation of compositional objects. Like Schillinger, Xenakis developed a notation derived from mathematics to describe these operations. While there are numerous examples in his book, they seem fragmentary, designed to be hints rather than guides.

What is most interesting, from the perspective of this chapter, is that we find in Xenakis' *Formalized Music* a desire to develop a language for manipulation of musical elements derived from the disciplines of mathematics, logic, and particle physics. Given this burden of theory, it is not surprising that he turned to computers to help him realize some of his works. He enthused, "With the aid of electronic computers the composer becomes a sort of pilot: he presses the buttons, introduces coordinates, and supervises the controls of a cosmic vessel sailing in the space of sound, across sonic constellations and galaxies that he could formerly glimpse only as a distant dream" [Xenakis 1971a]. Xenakis speaks for many of us—as someone who sees in computer-assisted music the possibility of being lifted from the mundane level of the note-by-note compositional process.

21.2.9 Experimental Music

Lejaren Hiller is generally regarded as the first to compose music successfully with computers. He, with the help of Leonard Isaacson and Robert Baker, used the Illiac computer at the University of Illinois to compose a composition entitled *Illiac Suite* in 1957 [Hiller 1959a]. Like Xenakis, chance techniques play a large role in his work, though for quite different purposes. He and Isaacson wrote, "The process of musical composition can be characterized as involving a series of choices of musical elements from an essentially limitless variety of musical raw materials. Therefore, because the act of composing can be thought of as the extraction of order out of a chaotic multitude of available possibilities, it can be studied at least semi-quantitatively by applying certain mathematical operations deriving from probability theory and certain general principles of analysis incorporated in a new theory of communication called *information theory*. It becomes possible, as a consequence, to apply computers to the study of those aspects of the process of composition which can be formalized in these terms" [Hiller 1959a].

It is clear from this that, unlike Xenakis, Hiller and Isaacson desired to simulate the composing process itself with computers, rather than use computers as an aid to composition.[5] They noted, however, that "the composer is traditionally thought of as guided in his choices not only by certain technical rules but also by his 'aural sensibility,' while the computer would be dependent entirely upon a rationalization and codification of this 'aural sensibility.'"

To test this hypothesis, they conducted four experiments, which were incorporated into Hiller's composition, *Illiac Suite*. They used the so-called Monte Carlo method, which requires the generation of large quantities of random numbers that are then subjected to statistical controls. From this process, samples—in the form of machine-coded musical examples—are extracted that conform to the supplied selection rules. The outline of the method resembles *Würfelspiel*. It has a generation phase (a random number generator) followed by a selection phase. But rather than merely requiring a simple table lookup, Hiller's selection phase must test the validity of candidate random numbers against the supplied rule set.

The range of possible solutions is not limited to some precomposed examples.

Hiller and Isaacson transformed rules of various compositional styles—ranging from rudimentary species counterpoint to free atonality—into a set of numeric determinants that could be incorporated in programs running on the Illiac computer at the University of Illinois. The process of composition consisted in sequentially applying each random number generated to the appropriate sets of rules. If the number chosen violated a rule, another number was selected from the random series until all rules were satisfied, and the successful number was appended to the end of the sample being generated. For instance, Experiments One and Two were based on the rules of species counterpoint that were formalized by J. J. Fux in 1725 in his work *Gradus ad Parnassum*, and are used in derivative forms in music pedagogy even to this day [Fux 1943a]. This required the codification of the rules specified by Fux, including melody formation, harmonic rules, and combined rules (such as detecting parallel and direct harmonic motion).

What is noticed by the careful observer of this work is not so much the music produced by the program but rather the hand of the human behind it, like the Wizard of Oz behind the emerald screen. The actual music produced in the *Illiac Suite* "sounds pleasant, but it wanders, and so does the listener's attention" [Pierce 1983a].

At bottom, the implementation of Hiller's model of composition is the process of rule-satisfaction driven by a random sequence generator. Note the difference between this model of composition and that characterized by Kirchmeyer: the human composer's task has only begun with the satisfaction of the rules of composition; what remains is to satisfy one's artistic aims. What distinguishes Hiller's work as *experimental* is that the goal of the work was to observe composing automata, not to try editorially to improve upon the output of the programs he created. We could say that what artistic aims he had were embedded in the design of the experiments. In subsequent compositions, Hiller did not characterize the work as experimental in this narrow sense.

21.2.10 Deterministic Compositional Automata

A criticism that can be laid against the use of random selection as it appears both in Xenakis' and Hiller's music is that "both these approaches are highly limiting to a composer with clear stylistic objectives" [Ames 1982a].

In the case of Xenakis, one controls means and variances in probability distributions to shape a work; for Hiller, one controls rule sets that are applied to random sequences. In both cases, the composer has little control over the fine detail.

In the 1960s, Max Mathews and his colleagues made some simple experiments with deterministic compositional algorithms in ways that provide an antidote to the methods of Hiller and Xenakis. Also, he wished to investigate the usefulness of algorithms not traditionally associated with musical practice.

Mathews and J. E. Miller investigated pitch quantization as a compositional strategy [Mathews 1965a]. In one experiment, they generated a counterpoint between two voices by the following method: choose a pitch for Voice 1, then choose a pitch for Voice 2 such that the interval formed is quantized to the nearest 3rd, 4th, 5th, or 6th from Voice 1. Then choose the next pitch for Voice 1 such that it satisfies the same criteria, and continue. This can of course be generalized to any number of voices, and rules of pitch selection can be modified arbitrarily. Note that this is still a rules-driven-by-noise procedure that can be characterized as a first-order Markov process.

This abstract pitch-generation method was then subjected to further constraints as to allowable pitches. Different examples were generated, ranging from nontonal to diatonic, using absolute frequency (no quantization), quantization into an equal tempered scale, and quantization into a standard diatonic major scale.

Mathews and L. Rosler experimented with a functional representation of musical parameters as part of research which eventually led to the development of the GROOVE system [Mathews 1968a, Hiller 1970a, Mathews 1970a]. This is essentially the same graphical representation of music used by Schillinger in his *System of Musical Composition*. Mathews and Rolser first represented the pitch and rhythmic lines of two folk melodies as functions of time. Then they computed a running interpolation between the two sets of control functions in such a way as to produce hybrid melodies. In one example, based on the tunes *The British Grenadiers* and *Johnny Comes Marching Home*, the hybrid began with *Grenadiers*, and ended with *Johnny*, and in between consisted of a gradual transition from the control functions of the one to the other.

Mathews and Rosler felt "algorithmic composition is the beginning of a revolution in the musical use of computers." They anticipated the day "when computers become fast enough, and cheap enough, for improvisation." They concluded, "Finally, the compositional algorithms can be used to supplement technical knowledge, thus allowing music to be composed by people without formal training. If the day comes when each house has its own computer terminal, these techniques may make music as a means of self-expression accessible to everyone" [Mathews 1968a].

Even though the techniques of Mathews and Rosler are completely deterministic, the result is sequences that are unplanned in fine detail by the composer. This is true of all deterministic techniques, including the precompositional methods typified by the serialists. (One does not know—when developing materials and parameters in the precompositional phase—what will be the artifacts of their combinations, even where the rules of such combinations are to be strictly deterministic, until one actually combines them.) This lack of control over fine detail is essentially the same complaint laid against stochastic processes at the beginning of this section. Both these techniques tend to reduce a composer's control. Of course, this can be good or bad, depending upon the goals of the composer. Where a composer has a strong stylistic objective, these techniques can lead away from—rather than toward—good solutions. On the other hand, a major feature of these techniques is that they provide stimulation to the composer's imagination, suggesting avenues not previously considered.

21.2.11 Travesty

Travesty is another example of a deterministic compositional algorithm [Lansky 1986a]. The composer takes an existing work of music, extracts arbitrary phrases from it, and relinks them together according to some set of rules.

One example of this is reported by Peter Langston. He supplies a table of riffs, each chosen simply to sound "good" against a chordal background (and in no particular order). The next riff is chosen by randomly selecting three possibilities and then using the one whose first note is closest to one scale step away from the last note of the prior riff. The riffs are modified when played, based on position within the solo; they are more likely to elide a note or omit it altogether in the middle of the solo, and to be more "energetic" at the beginning and end. "The idea here is to simulate (somewhat cynically) the process that a high school guitar player goes through when improvising. The search for the next riff is only allowed to consider a small number of possibilities; the one that is easiest to play is used" [Langston 1986a].

Roger Reynolds has studied the restructuring of performed musical excerpts as a compositional device. While this is properly an editing operation, he finds it useful to redefine editing in this context: instead of the usual editorial function of compression and refinement, his aim is the "proliferation and recasting of materials" such that "the result is longer than the original, and will take on a structure that is, in itself, purposeful" [Reynolds 1986a]. He describes one of his methods, called SPIRLZ, this way.

> Begin with a sound file,[6] preferably one that is rather heterogeneous and has a distinctive formal profile. Clarity and diversity in the subject matter of the original file improves the clarity with which the effects of the SPIRLZ procedure can be experienced. Assuming that the beginning and ending of the input file are taken as temporal boundary conditions (alternatively, internal limits can be chosen), select a midpoint from which to begin a process of segment extraction. Set an initial duration for these extracted segments, the "window" through which a sonic snapshot is taken. Subsequently, move forward and backward in the file according to a standard offset which functions alternatively as an increment or decrement. In alternation, then, the output will receive segments of the subject file taken from successively later and earlier positions. The duration of individual segments is constant and a pass terminates when the current window overreaches either the begin or end point. [Reynolds 1986a]

While the method continues through another phase, this is sufficient to give the idea. The effects of this procedure can be heard, for instance, in Reynold's composition *Vertigo*, a 4-channel computer music piece.

21.2.12 Merging the Roles of Composer and Computer

The work of Hiller and Issacson is remembered as an early use of a computer for composition of music, but it is more important for having inaugurated the study of the compositional process with computers. They felt that, whatever musical appeal the *Illiac Suite* had, their experimental technique was of greater importance: they applied no retroactive valuation or editing of the results obtained from running their computer model save the choice of one complete output of the program over another. While this served their scientific purposes, it was no surprise that generating music by driving simple rule sets with noise proved musically weak.

Two avenues opened up at this point. One could attempt to develop more musically convincing formalisms and continue to produce music entirely from automata. On the other hand, one could incorporate an element of human discretion by developing—rather than avoiding—the interaction between program and composer. Either of these avenues could help improve the musicality of automata, or extend the formalizing power of the composer, or both.

Most subsequent development has focused on the latter approach. For instance, in *Stochastic Quartet* (1963) James Tenney assumed control over tempo, tessitura, and dynamics and their ranges; the computer chose the pitches by chance (with but one rule concerning intervals—the avoidance of octaves) [Tenney 1969a].

Further work on human interaction with music-composing automata has been taken up by Gotfried M. Koenig, among others. His programs, Project I and Project II, are in some ways experiments in how to share the compositional process between man and machine [Koenig 1970a, Koenig 1970b, Koenig 1979a]. Project I takes very skeletal input from the composer and, using a combination of serial and stochastic procedures, produces a musical score in alphanumeric format that is *connotative* in the sense that it is purposefully incomplete. While it specifies event order, pitch, dynamics, and attack points, it omits such things as note durations, orchestration, and assignment of attack points to instruments. This gives considerable latitude to the composer to superimpose additional selection criteria on top of the program output to yield a particular aesthetic goal. Project II, on the other hand, requires detailed specifications of the operations the program is to perform. The program produces alphanumeric output that is *denotative* to the extent that a musical score can be directly transcribed from it.

21.2.13 Composing by Programming

There remains unaddressed in Koenig's work (except, of course, for himself) the desire of composers to experiment directly by writing their own composing programs. The central value of computers to composers is that they facilitate the experimental application and dynamic evaluation of compositional rules. Prior to their advent, it was more difficult for composers to experiment with composition from arbitrary principles.

It is only a question of facilitation, however, and it is not the case that even this is universally desired. Consider Conlon Nancarrow's work with temporal dissonance as the central organizing principle for his set of *Studies* for player piano. They were composed and realized literally by hand, a monument to Nancarrow's tenacity. His work clearly would have been facilitated by computers, and many who have been drawn to his work have wondered what the impact of a computer attached to his pianos would have been.

Besides those composers already mentioned, Charles Ames, David Cope, Joel Chadabe, Clarence Barlow, Larry Polansky, and David Rosenboom, to mention a few, take considerable advantage of the experimental approach to composition opened up by computers [Ames 1982a, Ames 1982b, Cope 1987a, Chadabe 1978a, Chadabe 1984a, Clarlow 1980a, Rosenboom 1985a]. The most common goal here is to establish domains of musical parameters over which can be superimposed automatic control structures, the execution of which results in the generation of the structure of a composition. There is a tremendous amount of work taking place now in this area, which must be drastically reduced here to the following examples.

Charles Ames reports on the technique of comparative search to realize *Protocol*, his composition for solo piano [Ames 1982a]. He felt confronted with the dilemma mentioned at the end of the section on deterministic techniques, namely, the limiting effect of deterministic and random techniques alike on a composer who wishes to retain control over fine stylistic detail. His solution is "a *protocol* of algorithmic tests, that is, [a] collection of tests where each test has been ranked according to one's preferences." The protocol is then consulted to direct a search that looks for optimal solutions, backtracking where necessary to remain within constraints imposed by the tests. This approach, developed originally for automatic chess-playing programs, was used by Ames throughout the production phase of this composition.

If a comparative search is enumerated over all possible choices of a musical parameter, the results will be a ranked set of *optimal* solutions. Such enumeration and testing can be expensive because the search must be exhaustive. Hiller and Isaacson noted that as rules were added, the computation time of a piece typically went up, and the probability of finding a solution went down. Faced with the same problem with comparative search, Ames then turned to constrained search for the realization of his composition *Gradient* [Ames 1983a]. A constrained search accepts the first complete solution encountered while rejecting any flawed solution immediately upon discovering a fault. One will get an acceptable, though not necessarily optimal, solution this way. Ames has published a considerable amount of material on automatic composition, including a valuable survey [Ames 1987a].

In the issue of *Die Feedback Papers* devoted to his composition *Çoğluotobüsişletmesi,* Clarence Barlow reveals a penetrating research into computer-assisted composition [Clarlow 1980a]. He says of the work, "The most important general concept underlying this composition is the organisation of texture, defined in this context as being a result of the conformity between various parallel musical streams (in each of which no two events—notes or chords—ever overlap in time) of differing and varying consistency. Conformity here implies the degree of material similarity (of keys and/or metre) between streams, consistency the interaction of eight parameters: harmonic and metric cohesion (ranging down to atonality and ametricism), melodic and rhythmic smoothness (ranging down to pointillism and syncopation), chordal and tactile density (the quantity of pitches per chord, of chords per unit time), as well as dynamics (loudness) and articulation (connectedness)." He sets himself the task of establishing uniform, computable continua for the above-mentioned musical parameters, for which this piece is but one traversal.

His approach to the element of tonality, for instance, is singular. He goes from an intuitive rationale for a scheme that characterizes harmonic tension (i.e., how strongly an interval requires resolution) to a mathematical expression of what he calls tonal "intensity" in such a way that it also predicts harmonic tension of an interval and its polarity in any scale that can be stated or approximated with rational numbers.

The usual explanation is that the consonant intervals are all ratios of small integers, such as the octave (1 : 2) and fifth (2 : 3), because they align with the base of the overtone series. Intervals of larger-numbered ratios supposedly become progressively more dissonant. But this would predict a smooth curve from consonance to dissonance that does not occur; nor does it explain the tonal ambivalence of certain intervals such as the fourth. In practice the fourth appears both as a consonance and a dissonance. And there are intervals with higher-order ratios that are considered more consonant. The fourth has been considered as a consonance when it appears as the inversion of the fifth between upper voices, but as a dissonance when it is exposed between the bottom two voices of a contrapuntal line [Fux 1943a]. The interval of a fourth is also peculiar in that, unlike most other intervals, the upper tone seems weighted more heavily than the lower one. Barlow demonstrates the limitations of previous attempts to account for these phenomena, and then proposes a solution based on the observation of what he calls the "indigestibility" of the numbers that go into an interval. The intuitive framework is that the less numerically "digestible" numbers are, the more inharmonic will an interval be perceived which is made from them. The equation Barlow developed is reminiscent of Euler's function $\phi(n)$, which gives the *relative primeness* of a number—that is, the measure of how indivisible a number is by numbers smaller than itself. Barlow's numerical indigestion function has the further advantage of predicting which note in the interval will be weighted heavier. The reader is referred to [Barlow 1987a] for details.

Barlow utilized this formula compositionally by setting up tonal fields governed by a succession of tonics. He could use it to guide his note selection process to choose pitches that would either reinforce a particular tonic or migrate away from it. Note, however, that the underlying method is still the rules-driven-by-noise approach of Hiller. The result ends up sounding similar to the Stravinskian practice of *tonicization by insistence*, rather than the usual functional harmonic tonicization.

Though out of print, the issue of *Die Feedback Papers* where these ideas are developed is recommended as a glimpse of the extent to which some composers go with computational practices. Many other novelties are put forth, such as an interesting formula for rhythmic "indispensability," which predicts the desirability for an attack point on a particular beat in order to sustain a chosen meter.

21.2.14 Summary

We have seen that musical formalisms as well as algorithmic and methodic practices have long been part of the creation of music. Such practices have been used in two principal ways, as providing an underlying framework for a composition (such as isorhythm) and as an alternative source of compositional decisions (such as *Würfelspiel*).

The rigorous application of musical formalisms based on a priori theories of composition seem only to have developed in this century through the work of such composers as Schoenberg and Hindemith, and such theorists as Schillinger. Efforts at formalization of music theory by Schenker, Schoenberg, Schillinger, Tenney [Tenney 1986a], and Lerdahl and Jackendoff [Lerdahl 1983a], among others, also should be noted. Music typographers [Smith 1973a, Byrd 1984a] and music instructors [Gross 1981a] have also found formal systems to be a natural ally.

Interest in formal methods is growing as computer systems become increasingly available to composers, because of the power of such systems to model formal operations. To realize this capacity, however, requires the development of programming languages with which to express musical ideas. The second half of this survey takes up this subject.

21.3 Introduction to the Survey

[The Engine's] operating mechanism might act upon other things besides number, were objects found whose mutual fundamental relations could be expressed by those of the abstract science of operations. . . . Supposing, for instance, that the fundamental relations of pitched sound in the signs of harmony and of musical composition were susceptible of such expression and adaptations, the engine might compose elaborate and scientific pieces of music of any degree of complexity or extent.
—Ada Lovelace

The communication of instructions to a computer often is modeled as making utterances to the computer out of a limited vocabulary of tokens (machine instructions) that are understood both by the computer and the programmer. The words in the vocabulary only make sense in certain grammatical patterns. Because of these, and other, similarities to properties of natural languages, the term *programming language* has arisen to describe this communication. The problem of using computers musically is first of all to define appropriate musical programming languages. The building blocks for all such languages are the vocabularies and grammars that computers can recognize.

The sources of input to computers are broader on the surface than the previous paragraph suggests. Computer-music interfaces have been analyzed into five categories: composition and synthesis languages, graphics score editing tools, real-time performance systems, digital audio processing tools, and computer-aided instruction systems [Pennycook 1985a]. There are other models for communicating with computers that are beginning to appear that provide alternatives to the linguistic metaphor. However, the root of all of these sources of input eventually translates into a stream of atomic instructions, so that the model of this process as *linguistic* still seems to be fundamental.

Because one is so strictly constrained by the linguistic limitations of computers, programming languages are a very cramped medium for the representation of any rich symbolic system, be it in an artistic or scientific idiom. Music obviously contains a considerable wealth of knowledge that is not expressible in any language. On the other hand, there is a *meta*level of music representation that people use to talk *about* music. This aspect of musical communication consists of the more-or-less formalized rules of music, i.e., those aspects of music available to our consciousness, as opposed to those aspects we can only experience subjectively.

Computers can certainly be given the task of organizing these formal aspects of musical representation. Computers can also be used as a research tool to explore alternative formalizations of music. This has the beneficial effect of opening our eyes to new musical possibilities. However, there is a danger in becoming habituated to the restriction of one's musical vision to what can easily be represented this way. John Rahn speaks of a "Metaphorical Fallacy," which is "the fallacy of carrying over to whatever is being modeled inappropriate features of the structure being used as a model" [Rahn 1980a]. Model building is *characterization*; it necessarily avoids completeness in order to work at all.

21.3.1 Differentiating Languages, Programs, and Systems

Strictly differentiating among computer languages, computer programs, and computer systems is hard, but an intuitive understanding is sufficient anyway. A *program* is a self-contained schedule of computer instructions that accomplishes some goal of the user, and that usually depends on the services of a computer system for utility functions (such as information entry and display). A system (sometimes called *operating system*) is generally regarded as a program or collection of programs that, taken together, provide some (it is hoped) coherent rationale to the user for associating instructions to the computer with desired results.

Take, for instance, so-called *turn-key* systems, those that run a fixed program when switched on (like video games or elevators). Though they have computers in them, the users of these machines do not program them; they *operate* them. Using a word processor or music editor is still considered operating a computer, not programming it. Instead, some programmer somewhere has created a preexisting program that the operator uses as a translator of his or her input.

But there is a hitch in this explanation: programming languages also are implemented as preexisting programs (called compilers) that act as translators of user's input. So what distinguishes the operator from the programmer here? One way to differentiate the problem is to notice that while an operator provides input and control information, a programmer provides the map between input and output that defines the meaning of the inputs and controls in terms of the problem being addressed. An analytic way of saying this is, "The meaning of each program in the resulting program space could be deduced and related systematically to the structure of the language" [Loy 1985a].

A programming language is usually implemented by a compiler (that is, a computer program) that takes statements from the user written in the language the compiler implements. The compiler translates them into machine instructions that have an equivalent semantic meaning when executed by the computer. If the resulting machine instructions are executed on the spot, we say the language is *interpreted.* If they are saved in a form that can be executed later, we say the language is *compiled.* So programming languages provide ways to extend the repertoire of a computer's behaviors by creating yet more programs—including, perhaps, more programming languages, and even operating systems. For instance, the UNIX operating system is written (almost) entirely in the C programming language (save for a few lines of assembly language), and one of the programs available under the UNIX operating system is the C compiler. Using the compiler, one can write other programs (for instance, musical applications), or one can rewrite UNIX or create a new computer language, or even new operating systems.

21.3.2 Common Practice Notation

Is so-called common practice music notation (CPN) a programming language? No—it is not because one can not relate the "program" encoded in a piece of music to the structure of any language. Music theory treats the task of analyzing CPN output back into some archetypal form, but this is not the same as "decompiling" CPN back into some prototypical language, because the "language" does not exist. There is no concrete meaning or signification carried by music itself—apart from any external knowledge we may have of a composer's intent (as in so-called program music), lyrics, etc.

CPN is designed to serve the needs and processing abilities of performing musicians. Musicians are under considerable realtime constraints in performance with regard to what they can visually digest about the music they are to play. What CPN does to allow this is to telescope many levels of description together, resulting in a system that packs a tremendous quantity of information into a relatively small number of symbols. But as a result, CPN is formally incoherent.

Music, taken as a straight pressure waveform, has a very large acoustical information content—or data rate—per unit of time. In order to cover effectively the entire range of human hearing, current systems sample a waveform on the order of 50,000 times per second to a precision of one part in 65,536, or 2^{16}, for each channel. The data in any extended musical work are thus on the scale of that needed to encode a multivolume encyclopedia. Reducing the level of data down to what humans can manage requires considerable abstraction. This is most evident in CPN, where pitch and rhythm are quantized out of the continuous musical stream into discrete notes. Few of the observable dimensions of music are encoded by CPN, and they are by no means always the most important ones. Pitch, time, dynamics, and articulation are coded directly. Of these, only pitch and time are given anything resembling a formal expression. Timbre is not notated systematically but is a by-product of specifying which instruments play, as well as what, when, and how they play. The rest of the musical dimensions are transmitted by coded icons that have evolved over hundreds of years of performance practice. When these fail to convey the necessary instructions for proper interpretation, CPN resorts to exhortations in a natural language, traditionally Italian.

The trick that CPN accomplishes is to allow the information not carried in the score to be recovered through the application of the CPN score to a set of interpretive rules. Musicians are trained to apply the rules in order to reconstitute the music from the CPN score. Some of the rules are manifest, but the majority of them can be verbalized only with great difficulty. The extent of this unwritten body of lore is made painfully evident by attempts to formalize it.

21.3.3 Iconic versus Symbolic Representation in Music

There are two classes of representation that seemingly must coexist in any robust music programming language: symbolic and iconic. By *symbolic*, I mean that the tokens of the language that stand for particular sonic events bear no overt resemblance to the sonic event. Rather, a table of correspondences—a symbol table—must be maintained that relates musical symbols to sonic events. This is in contrast to *iconic*, by which I mean that the tokens do resemble the sound being represented. The closer the resemblance, the greater the fidelity.[7] CPN is a mixture of symbolic and iconic elements. Pitch coding is iconic because height on the musical staff line corresponds to height of pitch. Other iconic elements are the indications for dynamics, crescendo, and diminuendo. Such elements as time signature, cleffs, accidentals, bar lines, etc., are symbolic. Besides CPN, there are a tremendous number of alternative notations, traditional and modern, that have arisen [Cage 1969a].

Both symbolic and iconic elements seem necessary in music notational systems and languages. Most music programming languages attempt to accommodate both, though the two representations are in some ways incompatible. Languages that are predominately symbolic lend themselves to an asynchronous event-oriented structure, whereas iconic languages tend toward synchronous, function-oriented structures. Function-oriented representation is ultimately necessary in order to represent sound as air pressure-wave functions. So iconic representation tends to predominate in these languages. Event-oriented representation is usually most useful when dealing with the abstract form of sounds, such as are represented by CPN. So symbolic representation usually predominates in these languages.

To summarize, synthesis languages deal with the translation of symbolic and/or iconic representations of musical sound into one of three things: (1) a symbolic score such as CPN, (2) an iconic score such as a pressure-wave function, or (3) a stream of machine instructions that, when processed, yields either (1) or (2). Languages usually mix symbolic and iconic representations of music.

21.3.4 Types of Music Languages, Programs, and Systems

Three strategies have been commonly employed in developing compositional uses of computers. A composer experienced at programming might experiment by writing a composition program in an existing general-purpose programming language [Koenig 1970a, Koenig 1970b, Xenakis 1971a, Clarlow 1980a]. The languages chosen vary widely, and include also generative grammars [Holtzman 1981a, Green 1980a, Roads 1985b]. Another strategy is to develop libraries of utility subroutines that implement common operations on musical data structures. Then composition programs can be written in some standard programming language that makes calls on the library subroutines [Hiller 1966a]. If the language can be interpreted, a fairly responsive interactive compositional system can result [Nelson 1977a].

While neither of these approaches can be said to involve the practitioner in the development of programming languages, these methods have been used quite frequently by composers to embody particular compositional systems [Hiller 1966a, Koenig 1970a, Koenig 1970b].

A third approach is to write a programming language as the embodiment of a musical paradigm through which a wide range of compositional strategies can be realized. Programming languages for music typically go beyond standard general-purpose languages in implementing special musical data types and operations, methods for representing the flow of time, and methods to represent the forms of recursion and parallelism commonly found in music.

We must discriminate between four categories within this latter approach. There are

- languages used for music data input,
- languages for editing music—using textual, graphic, and/or sonic representations,
- languages for specification of compositional algorithms, and
- generative languages—used to compute musical scores from a program input.

Most actual languages are a mixture of more than one category; however, they usually emphasize one or the other aspect. Examples of pure descriptive languages used to capture existing music in manuscript form for music printing or musicological analysis include DARMS [Erickson 1975a], MUSTRAN [Wenker 1972a], and EUTERPE [Smoliar 1971a]. Some music data input languages provide simple compositional processing facilities, such as SCORE [Smith 1976a], SCOT [Gold 1980a], and YAMIL [Fry 1980a]. Examples of editing systems are Bill Buxton's SCED score editor [Buxton 1980a] and Shawn Decker's ELED score editor [Decker 1985a]. Languages for specifying compositional algorithms, such as PLA, usually also come with descriptive musical data structures, but emphasize compositional processing [Schottstaedt 1983a].

Generative languages, such as Hiller's MUSICOMP, Koenig's Project I and Project II, and Daniel Scheidt's MC language [Scheidt 1985a], generally include music data structures and sometimes also ways of specifying compositional algorithms, though to write such algorithms one must be able to program in the base language.

The range of available models to represent music data is quite broad, and includes mathematical models such as stochastic and combinatorial techniques (Hiller, Xenakis, Koenig), linguistic models such as grammars (Holtzman and Roads), algorithmic models such as are found in typical high-level structured programming languages, process models such as those found in object-oriented programming and parallel processing, and other models derived from artificial intelligence (AI) [Roads 1985c].

21.3.5 Caveat on the Scope of the Survey

In the survey that follows, the sequence of the examples is not strictly cataloged by the categories at the end of the previous section, but is laid out in a way that will hopefully foster the appreciation of the different strategies and goals addressed. This survey is mostly limited to languages and systems that

- generate waveforms (section 21.4.1),
- control synthesizers (sections 21.4.2 and 21.4.3),
- facilitate writing compositional formalisms (sections 21.4.2 and 21.4.3), and
- automatically generate musical compositions (sections 21.4.3 and 21.4.4).

Even in these areas, the goal is to suggest lines of inquiry rather than to be grimly thorough. Only secondarily do I address music data entry languages such as DARMS, MUSTRAN, SCOT, and YAMIL [Fry 1980a]. Music editing languages are left out almost entirely, and I have given short shrift to some important developments in musicology and computer-aided music instruction. Some otherwise appropriate systems and languages have been left out, such as the MIDIM/VOSIM system at the Institute for Sonology, Utrecht [Kaegi 1986a, Kuipers 1986a], and the work on representing structure in music with Petri Nets done by Goffredo Haus at the Laboratorio Informatica Musicale in Milan. Some very interesting, and relevant, work on grammars as representations of music is not included here [Holtzman 1981a, Roads 1978a]. Also ignored are the numerous commercial MIDI-based systems,[8] some of which have impressive attributes for music notation, editing, and even compositional algorithms. Some of this work has been discussed in [Yavelow 1986a, Yavelow 1985a].

Another area I have mostly ignored is the use of existing general-purpose languages—without major extensions for special musical operations—to musical problems. Notable among this work is that of David Wessel to produce a MIDI system using LeLisp [Boynton 1986a], Jan Vandenheede's experiments with Prolog [Vandenheede 1986a], and Hyperscore, Stephen Pope's current research with Smalltalk. A very interesting series of guest articles, collectively entitled "Machine Tongues," has appeared over the years in *Computer Music Journal* that explore developments in general-purpose computer languages and language theory as they apply to music. References for this set of articles is in the bibliography. Other work is being done on graphic programming languages for music [Desain 1986a].

While I have covered certain composer's work with computers in the section on compositional algorithms, there is much more, as evidenced by its section in the bibliography.

Finally, there are a number of interesting systems that have become known to me too late or about which I have little information. These include FORMULA [Anderson 1986a], MUSICIAN [Ban 1986a], and Miller Puckette's MAX system [Puckette 1986a]. Much of the work in this area is reported in *Computer Music Journal*, *Interface*, *Perspectives of New Music*, and the *Proceedings* of the International Computer Music Conference. Interested readers are directed to these publications.

21.4 Waveform Compilers

The term *waveform compiler* or *acoustical compiler* is applied to a program that produces air pressure-wave functions as their direct output. Most also have data types and operations that support iconic representation of sampled functions of time [Mathews 1961a].

While the rationale for this representation strategy was given above, there are also historical factors that show the importance of this approach. The basic ordering principles of digital music synthesis can be seen as extensions into the digital domain of ideas derived from analog electronic music. The early analog devices were in turn derived from the modular test equipment found in early radio stations and recording studios such as amplifiers, modulators, filters, and oscillators. When first developed, the most important feature of electronic musical instruments was felt to be their ability to allow musicians to dig into the acoustical microstructure of sound. This allowed the musical dimension of timbre, which was previously constrained by the physical limitations of traditional musical instruments, to grow into a major dimension of musical interest and concern. This was largely a result of the interest of composers of the time in the novel musical perspective revealed by this technology [Bussoni 1962a, Cage 1961a, Risset 1969a, Xenakis 1971a]. In some cases, timbre overtook all other musical parameters, as in Schaeffer's *musique concrète* [Schaeffer 1952a]. The switch to digital techniques was a natural result of the limitations of analog techniques: lack of precision and repeatability, and limited macro- and microlevel control. However, some of the most successful waveform compilers maintain the analog modular paradigm. Given the importance of timbre, most waveform compilers define a musical note as the *specification of an acoustical event*. That is, a note consists of a collection of acoustic parameters that are applied to a synthesis procedure of some sort such that an acoustical waveform is generated that is determined by the combination of parameters and synthesis technique.

By going directly from the level of note-as-acoustic-specification to the acoustical waveform, a very precise means of controlling the exact properties of the waveform is provided. This is both an advantage and a liability. It is an advantage insofar as it allows composers freedom of expression at the timbral level far in excess of what was available before. With waveform compilers it is possible to define and realize sounds that are physically impossible for any vibrating object but a loudspeaker to produce.

It is a liability insofar as the composer who wishes to work this way now must take on the additional burden of specifying the microstructure of sound, which was formerly the domain of the performing musician. This turns out to be a very serious problem, as it seems that the information added to the music by instrumental performers is crucial for the quality of aliveness of musical sounds. We shall take up this problem again below.

21.4.1 Music N

The first programming languages for musical sound synthesis and signal processing were the suite of programs written by Max Mathews at AT&T Bell Laboratories in the late 1950s and 1960s named Music I through Music V [Mathews 1961a, Mathews 1963a]. This early work spawned numerous descendants, and recent designs still emulate important features of two of these languages, Music IV and Music V. We shall use the term Music N to refer to this extended family of programs [Mathews 1969a]. These programs were derived to a certain extent from earlier work in analog circuit modeling in which continuous electrical signals are represented as discrete functions of time, and are passed using a data flow metaphor between stream operators that emulate the effects of electrical components, such as capacitors and resistors [David 1958a].

To adapt this strategy to music meant simply to consider the signals as audio waveforms. Thus, the audio signals are represented as a sequence of audio samples. Signal generators such as oscillators and random number generators create these streams of audio data while signal modifiers such as filters, amplifiers, and modulators process these streams, in Music N systems. The universal term for all signal generators and modifiers is *unit-generator*. Networks of these unit-generators can be dynamically patched together; each resulting network is called an *instrument*, by analogy to regular musical instruments. The action of the instrument is defined by the connectivity graph of the unit-generators as well as by acoustical parameters that control the actions of the unit-generators (parameters such as frequency and amplitude for oscillators, for instance). The acoustical parameters are supplied in a score to be described below.

In operation, Music N is a program running in a computing environment that includes, besides a central processing unit (CPU), a fast-access mass-storage medium such as a large magnetic disk, and a set of DACs—digital to analog converters (and possibly ADCs—analog to digital converters). When run, Music N expects two things. First come instructions about how to configure networks of unit-generators into instruments. Each instrument is given a name and a time at which it is to come into existence. Next comes the musical score, consisting of a set of *note statements*. A note statement conveys three essential elements: (1) the begin time and duration of the note, (2) the name of the instrument that is to play the note, and (3) the acoustical parameters that will control the operations of the unit-generators.

Music N creates instrument templates, instantiates them at the right times, and binds the acoustical parameters to the unit-generators. It also merges the outputs of the various instruments into an arbitrary number of final outputs (usually mono, stereo, or quad). This output is stored on the mass-storage device rather than sent directly to the DACs. This is because most general-purpose CPUs are not fast enough to compute the final waveform in real time. However, it is usually possible for most such computers to send the precomputed audio data from a disk to the DACs in real time. In practice, music of any subtlety usually requires many times real time to compute the final waveforms. Thousands of calculations usually go into each output sample, and anywhere from 20k to 50k samples are required per second for reasonable-quality audio.[9] If the compute-time to real-time ratio is less than 1, the program is running at or faster than real time, and the output could theoretically go directly to the DACs. But in practice, compute ratios on the order of 200 to 1 are not uncommon.

At a ratio of 60 to 1, it takes an hour to compute a minute of sound. So efficiency was a major concern in the design of Music N sound synthesis programs. At the same time, it was necessary to find a design whose expressive capabilities could combine simplicity, uniformity, and power. The solution to these problems consisted of a three-fold approach:

1. Synthesis algorithms are specified as combinations of unit-generators, with flexible means of configuring them into data-flow subprograms called instruments.

2. The activation of instruments is controlled by *note statements* that bind the instrument, the action times, and the acoustical parameters together. A *score* is a collection of note statements and instrument definitions.

3. Efficiency concerns are addressed by localizing the computational load into the unit-generators, and by emphasizing the use of lookup tables and simple transforms, especially for such things as generating waveforms and applying amplitude or frequency envelopes to them.

Operation of Music N consisted of three passes. In pass 1, acoustical parameters are converted from mnemonic codes into appropriate machine representations. For instance, a composer might have given "A4" as a pitch; the actual machine value to use depends on the sampling rate and other details of the implementation. Pass 2 sorts all statements into strictly increasing time order, if it was not already so. Pass 3 does the actual synthesis.

21.4.2 Variants of Music N

Music I through Music III were experimental versions written in assembly language. Music IV and Music V were written in the then-novel high-level programming language FORTRAN. (Unit-generators were still hand-coded for efficiency.) Because of the portability of FORTRAN, Music IV and Music V became the models of subsequent development. I shall compare and contrast them in preparation for discussing how their differences affected subsequent designs.

Music IV lacked reentrant instruments, a feature added in Music V. A code module is said to be *reentrant* if multiple instances of it can be active at the same time. This can be achieved if the module is a *pure procedure*, that is, if the module consists only of program instructions and constants, using separate areas of memory for storage of (possibly multiple copies of) variable data that are to be unique to each instance of the module. The chief benefit of reentrancy comes when generating sounds to be heard simultaneously, such as chords. In Music IV, one would need as many separately defined instruments as there were notes in the densest chord in a piece, even if they all were to produce the same sound. Music V allowed a score to refer simply to an instrument as a template, which was then automatically instantiated as many times as necessary to produce the chord.

Music IV computed samples by parsing the instruments into an execution tree that was traversed once for each sample. Music V instruments were parsed into a block-at-a-time execution tree. Music IV's method was more flexible in terms of program flow, in that the execution tree could be modified for each pass through the tree, allowing synthesis operations to change for each sample, if necessary. But it was less efficient, since operands for unit-generators were usually used only once per pass, resulting in much wasted access to main memory to fetch and store them. Music V corrected this inefficiency by computing a block of samples for each unit-generator on each pass. This allowed the computer repeatedly to use the operands already loaded into high-speed accumulators, or cache memory, before having to fetch the operands for the next unit-generator.

Among the Music IV variants developed in the late 1960s and early 1970s were Music IVB and Music IVBF, written by Hubert Howe and Godfrey Winham [Howe 1975a]. Music V variants included Music 360 and Music 11 for the IBM 360 and the PDP 11 computers, respectively, written by Barry Vercoe, Roger Hale, and Carl Howe of the Electronic Music Studio at MIT [Vercoe 1979a]. There have been two recent implementations of the Music V model: *cmusic*, written by F. R. Moore at UCSD (University of California at San Diego), so named because it is written entirely in the C programming language, and Csound,[10] written by Barry Vercoe at MIT, likewise written in C [Moore 1982a, Vercoe 1986a]. While each of these implementations added numerous useful features, they all adhere to the original model in the three ways described at the end of the previous section. Vercoe's Music 11, for instance, introduced control flow statements in instruments similar to FORTRAN **if** and **goto** statements. This allowed instruments to make decisions about their behavior apart from the instructions given by the score, as performers do. Also as a computational efficiency, he introduced a separate, slower sampling rate for control signals, since such signals typically do not have the bandwidth requirements of audio waveforms.

The most radical version of Music IV is MUS10, developed originally at Stanford by David Poole, to run on a DEC PDP-10 computer [Tovar 1976a, McNabb 1981a]. MUS10 implemented a substantial ALGOL-style programming language and also provided unit-generators. Instruments could be written from a combination of high-level programming language statements as well as unit-generator calls. This facility allowed composers to create very complex instruments in a high-level language, and also increased the intelligence an instrument could display toward information it received from note statements and from its environment, including other executing instruments. MUS10 was implemented with the same concern for efficiency: it compiled an instrument definition into PDP-10 machine instructions, which were then run to generate the samples. The most compute-bound algorithms were put into the unit generators in hand-coded assembly language.

Another feature of MUS10 was its introduction of **I_only** code, which is part of an instrument definition, but is run only before the first sample of each note. **I_only** code can perform functions such as those in Pass 1 of Music V, or more interestingly, it can be used to "interpret" its note statement to allow for slurs and glissandi across note statements, or coupling broader structural elements in the score.

It is worth pointing out that the starting point of MUS10 was an existing Algol parser, modified for music synthesis. We shall see several examples of this later where the language designer simply took an existing language compiler and modified it to suit musical requirements. This is a very simple but effective way to start a language design.

21.4.3 Critique of Music N

The principal advantage of the Music N paradigm is the flexible and yet efficient method of synthesis specification via stored functions and unit-generators. Another advantage is the homogeneous, nonhierarchical event specification via note statements. Where no hierarchy superimposes itself, the musician is free to superimpose structure on the stream of sound as desired, within the constraints of the note concept itself. This lack of structure is very attractive to composers attempting to forge new approaches to composition. We shall also see that it can be a liability. Music N synthesis languages still impose the constraint of the *note as acoustical specification* model, even though event specifications are unconstrained. We shall consider languages where this paradigm is unwanted.

The most killing limitation of Music N languages is that they do not run in real time.[11] It is stifling to compose without being able to hear near-term results. Some counter this complaint by arguing that composers of symphonies, for example, are often forced to wait weeks or months to hear their works played, but this is naive. The difference is that orchestration of traditional instruments is so well-known as to offer few surprises to the experienced arranger; it is quite a different matter to be in charge of the sample-by-sample calculation of an acoustical waveform. In this case, all issues of how the music sounds—its musical interpretation—must be resolved by the composer in addition to all strictly compositional issues. The effect of not having real-time feedback is like trying to play an instrument by touch only, and having to complete the performance before being able to hear a single note. In addition, it often means waiting overnight before the playback can begin! If the lag time becomes too severe, keeping a compositional train of thought going becomes impossible, unless the composing process is largely automatic. This means there is a theoretical size and complexity limit for music made with waveform compilers for compositions where the burden of decisions is on the composer. This in and of itself suggests one reason why compositional algorithms are of such interest to composers in this medium: to provide some momentum against the sluggishness of such systems.

But that is not the only liability of waveform synthesis. Having no real-time feedback is tantamount to eliminating musical performance practice. This can be an advantage where one is seeking to avoid the characteristic touch that human gestures inevitably produce. If this is not the goal, however, it is a difficult problem to reinject a human touch into non-real-time synthesis. Unless this is done, music created with non-real-time waveform compilers can suffer from a wooden disjointedness remeniscent of mechanical musical automata such as player pianos and nickelodeons. Those who have gotten around this have done so either by careful choice of material, by brute force, or by treating the problem as a research project. Roger Reynolds' use of his SPIRALZ algorithm is an instance of careful choice of material.[12]

The brute-force technique is to extract elements of recorded performance such as attack time and velocity and use them directly as the time and amplitude controls of a synthesized composition. A part of the SCORE system allowed a composer to tap out a rhythm on a key; the resulting timing information could then become the basis of timing of a phrase of a score [Smith 1976a]. A more formal approach is to try to deduce the rules of some appropriate style of performance practice, and code these rules into a program that can make automatic adjustments in a score prior to its realization [Sundberg 1986a, Sundberg 1983a, Clynes 1984a]. While this latter field is blossoming into a research domain all its own, as far as practicing musicians and composers are concerned, it is more relevant simply to incorporate some level of real-time synthesis in a system, at least enough to allow the capture and analysis of gestural information.

Another liability of waveform compilers, discussed previously as an advantage, is the homogeneous, nonhierarchical specification of note statements. Music N is most successful where

- all the relevant control information about a note is available when it is started (since score parameters are passed only when the note is instantiated), and
- distinct notes can be treated as independent entities.

More frequently however, musical notes tend to have a life of their own, especially with instruments like the violin where bowing and vibrato often change subtly throughout a phrase. The relationships between notes are many, and are of great musical significance. It is possible to model these relationships with Music N by using global variables to share information between instruments. But this technique burdens the composer with unnecessary bookkeeping detail, and becomes conceptually untractable for scores of any complexity. We shall return to this problem.

21.4.4 Music Data Entry System for Waveform Synthesis

The information content of a Music N note list is mostly acoustical parameters given as arithmetic expressions or constants, which can be a frustration to composers who are more used to thinking in musical terms. In Music IV and Music V a composer could add subroutines to accomplish particular tasks of parameter conversion in Passes 1 and 2, but this required a knowledge of programming, and the necessity to run a FORTRAN compiler and link-editor each time the routines must be changed. SCORE was originally developed as an improvement of Pass 1 and Pass 2 [Smith 1976a].

The basic idea of SCORE is to make character-based mnemonics out of standard common practice notation (CPN) terminology so that a musician can deal with familiar rhythmic and pitch structures, rather than seconds and Hertz. Pitches are specified in the usual textual way, where A4 is taken as 440 Hz, the A in the 4th piano octave. Rhythms are specified as the denominator of a fraction where the numerator is a whole note. Thus, 4 is a quarter note, 8 an eighth note, 12 a triplet (because there are 12 triplets in a whole note). Dots after such numbers have the usual CPN sense that they augment by 1/2 the duration of the rhythm, so "4." equals three 8th-notes. Rhythms for distinct notes are grouped between slashes, so for instance, the sequence

4 16 / −8. / 2 8. / 16 / 1.. /

is equivalent to the musical sequence of a quarter tied to a 16th; a dotted eighth rest (the '–' indicates a silent duration); a half tied to a dotted eighth; a sixteenth; and a doubly-dotted whole note. Dynamics are notated in their CPN nomenclature also, ... *pp*, *p*, *mp*, *mf*, *f*, *ff*, ..., which are assigned a doubling of amplitude for each symbol. Simple numeric and literal data can also be represented.

In SCORE, music is specified by making sequences of these symbols. (Here we see again the carryover of metaphors from analog to digital synthesis: the sequencer was a primitive event ordering device of analog synthesizers.) In the simple case, a tight correspondence exists between a particular sequence and one particular parameter field of the resulting Music N note list. Thus, elements from a sequence of pitches might end up as the sequential numeric values in parameter field 5 (notated **p5**) of a set of note statements. This binding of sequence to parameter field is stipulated in the syntax of SCORE. For instance,

eghn /p2 rhy/8/12 rep 3/4./8/2;

specifies that field **p2** of the note statements generated by SCORE for the instrument **eghn** will have the sequence of rhythms given. (The notation **12 rep 3** specifies three triplet eighths.)

A way to identify motives is given that resembles a macro facility. Motives are the sequence elements between parentheses, and are identified by a letter preceding the left parenthesis. The named motive is expanded where the identifier is preceded with the "@" character. Thus,

p2 rhy/ a(8/16/8/8) / @a;

produces

p2 rhy/ 8/16/8/8 / 8/16/8/8;

Facilities for retrograde, inversion, and transposition of motives were provided.

Collections of such sequences are grouped together to form *instruments*. These are analogous to Music N instruments, in that the named collection of sequences is collated into a sequence of note statements (a score) that are destined for a Music N instrument of the same name. So, the first sequence might be pitches, which might together constitute the melody; the next sequence might be the rhythms, one for each pitch; then dynamics; and last sequences for parameters dealing with the details of the synthesis technique used by the instrument that will receive the score. Where any sequence is shorter than the others in an instrument, the interpreter simply wraps around to the beginning of the shorter sequence, continuously.

SCORE handles polyphony by collating multiple sequences from simultaneously evaluated instruments in correct time order. Tempo can be specified for all instruments together, and/or for each instrument independently. Accelerando, ritardando, and rubato effects can be given for all instruments and/or each instrument separately.

Additional features of SCORE include ways to specify that linear interpolation through time is to be used to fill in values between given end points, rather than having to specify each point in a sequence. One can also have random selection within a range for a sequence element. The ranges of random selection can also be linearly interpolated through time. And of course the escape hatch of providing a way of linking in user-provided FORTRAN subroutines was theoretically available, though with the same caveats as given above for Music N.

Along with DARMS and MUSTRAN, SCORE was an early attempt at computer representation of CPN for music synthesis, music printing, and musicological research [Erickson 1975a, Wenker 1972a, Smoliar 1971a, Smith 1973a]. Smith attempted to make a SCORE-like notation for his music printing program, MS, which dates from the same time, but it became evident quickly that the useful information for synthesis was sufficiently different from that required to typeset a score that the notations had to diverge in nontrivial ways.

SCORE is not so much an exercise in programming language design so much as an attempt to develop a shorthand for entering CPN scores from a computer terminal. Another view is to call it a specialized macro processor for Music N. This is especially evident in its motivic identification feature. Even though it has some operators that can be applied to motives, and can do such things as random selection and linear interpolation, its scope is painfully limited in comparison to more recent systems. PLA and Player (described below), both borrow considerably from SCORE's character-based music data notation.

A different approach to a similar problem was taken by Alan Ashton in his 1970 PhD thesis, which describes a "linear music code" used by Ashton to control an electronic organ [Ashton 1970a]. Ashton's original idea was taken up by Charles Ames, who developed from it a score-transcription utility called ASHTON written between 1977 and 1985 [Ames 1985a]. Ames criticizes SCORE for requiring that musical parameters be unnaturally broken out into parallel sequences. This scatters the information for a single event across all the sequences for an instrument. To delete (or insert) one note from the middle of a score, for instance, requires that one delete (insert) an element from (into) the correct place in all parallel sequences of parameters for this instrument—an error-prone task. If it is done incorrectly, the sequences get out of phase in ways that are often difficult to identify. With ASHTON the information for related compositional structures is localized where it can be more easily manipulated as a unit by the composer.

Ames implemented many extensions to Ashton's original work, leaving behind the model of an organ control language. Extensions include nested instrument descriptions—called *choires*—where instruments defined within common blocks share common attributes. A score is broken into static and time-bound sections. In the static section one defines instruments, establishes scales, and groups instruments into choires. In the time-bound section one can (among many other things) define sections, bars, and note events and supply durations, pitches, and group events with slurs or ties.

From published examples, ASHTON scores seem like they are probably more compact and readable than would be the SCORE equivalents, and also seem more manipulable. The liability of both ASHTON and SCORE is that they are not extensible: they limit the user to built-in operations on quasi-CPN music representations. One can quickly imagine desired musical representations and operations that one cannot perform with such nonextensible systems. Indeed, the user may not define compositional algorithms with either system. On the other hand, they both facilitate the transcription of CPN-type musical information that a general-purpose programming language will not do. An alternative approach considered in the next sections is to provide a set of musical primitives within the context of a general programming language.

21.4.5 EUTERPE

Stephen Smoliar's 1971 PhD thesis concerned a parallel processing model of musical structures [Smoliar 1971a]. He made a direct association between formal representations for music and computer programs by noting the apparent similarity between musical phrase structure and the flow of control in a computer program. He built a music programming language on the model of a generalized assembly language. Scores look for all the world like assembly language programs for a computer that would produce music from its native machine instructions. In fact, EUTERPE was simply an extension of the PDP-6 assembly language compiler at the MIT Artificial Intelligence Laboratory, and most of the machine instructions of the PDP-6 were available in EUTERPE. One could write programs that could thread through six coroutines simultaneously, thereby implementing a basic form of parallelism. Full EUTERPE programs could execute in real time, and drive a resident DAC system for sound conversion of up to six voices.

21.4.6 PILE and SSP

When musicians began the exploration of timbre space with digital technology, the major new area of exploration was the control of the microstructure of sound. Two major lines of investigation were initiated, the differentiation of which depended upon the concept of the musical note. The branch initiated by Mathews with Music N preserved the concept of musical note as acoustical specification. The task of composition was split between developing sonic microstructure and developing scores. Specifying sample-level microstructure depended upon knowledge of scientific disciplines such as signal processing, acoustics, and psychoacoustics. As a result, signal processing techniques came to influence the macrostructural compositional process as well. Because they preserved the note concept, Music N languages were conducive to realizing notated music, and studying performance practice.

Another major direction—which inherited the ideas of European serialism—abandoned the musical note and treated the sound-stream as an utterly homogenous, undifferentiated medium, which was subject to a single, uniform compositional discipline on both the sample level and the macrostructural level. One consequence of this was that conventional scores—and related ideas such as polyphony—became difficult to represent. This also had the effect of discarding most of the artifacts of human performance. Both of these can be seen as liabilities or advantages, depending upon one's persuasion.

PILE is an example of a music programming language driven by the latter concerns [Berg 1979a]. In PILE, no acoustical model is supposed. The usual parameters of synthesis are not implicit, but are constructed by writing programs in PILE. In a sense, PILE is equivalent to a programming language for implementing unit-generators, although it is generally not used for this. PILE is usually used for direct application of algorithmic operations on the waveform not based on any acoustical model. This allows for the imposition of compositional procedures—which were formerly restricted to the note level and higher—to be applied to the microstructure of sound: composing directly for the audio stream. PILE programs can run in realtime. They look very much like a macro assembly language with symbolic variables, assignment statements, arithmetic operations, flow control, and I/O statements. This very simple program in PILE,

```
TOP  RANDOM;
     CONVERT
          SEND:-
          CHANNEL: 1;
     BRANCH
          TO: TOP;
```

generates uniform random numbers and sends them to DAC channel 1.

SSP is another approach to the direct computation of the sound-stream [Berg 1980a]. PILE has no acoustical presumptions whatsoever. SSP allows only two: instantaneous amplitude and time. Again, the regimen consists of a generation/evaluation process (which we have seen in many previous contexts) whereby amplitude and time parameters are generated and then subjected to selection rules. The process is analogous to using Koenig's Project Two to control the microstructure of sound. This leads one "to describe the composition as one single sound, the perception of which is represented as a function of amplitude distribution in time" [Berg 1980a].

21.4.7 CHANT

When Xavier Rodet and his associates desired to develop a model of vocal synthesis, they faced the dilemmas of identifying an appropriate synthesis technique and an appropriate production model. Their solution was unique on both accounts. With respect to the production model, they observed the limitations pointed out above about the Music N model that "patch languages that exist are weak in their ability to specify the elaborate control levels that resemble interpretation by an instrumentalist, for example, expressiveness, context-dependent decisions, timbre quality, intonation, stress and nuances," all of which were elements that would be central to the implementation of the naturalistic vocal model they sought [Rodet 1984a]. To overcome this they adopted a hierarchical synthesis-by-rule methodology.

The synthesis technique itself posed problems. The mode of vocal production in humans and animals is indeed the process of filtering glottal impulse functions or aspirative noise. Linear predictive coding (LPC), phase vocoder, and related analysis/synthesis techniques based on filtering are computationally expensive, difficult to control, difficult for composers to understand, and require large data-bases for storage of analysis data. Their solution was a synthesis technique termed FOF (French: *Forme d'Onde Formantique*), which simulates the behavior of two-pole filters (resonators) being fed an impulse train.[13]

By using FOF generators in parallel one can easily describe arbitrary time-varying spectra in ways that are at once simpler and more stable than the equivalent resonator sections, especially for time-varying spectra. In addition, the model can easily be generalized beyond the original vocal model to a wide range of other sounds.

The method of controlling the collection of FOF generators is through a large set of global parameters that can be changed by the concurrent execution of cooperating subroutines that implement the synthesis rules corresponding to the vocal model under development. Besides the parameters mentioned above, CHANT allows the control of fundamental frequency, random variations of the fundamental, vibrato, random variations of vibrato, formant spectrum, general spectral shape, sound intensity, spectral evolution, and miscellaneous other controls.

All the parameters begin with default values, which, when executed, produce a normalized vocal synthesis. Libraries of previously developed routines that implement various rule sets are available for composers; as well, there are facilities to create new rule sets and to modify and extend existing ones. By this means, Rodet speaks of the accumulation of *knowledge models* of different productions. Knowledge models for such things as a *bel canto* voice and Tibetan chant have been developed. Extremely convincing examples of *bel canto* have been demonstrated.

It became clear to the CHANT group at IRCAM that, as the cooperating rule sets grew and became more complicated, that it was turning more and more into an AI problem to represent the control flow. The FORMES language, based on LISP, was developed for this purpose, and will be described later.

This synthesis technique ordinarily produces direct waveform output, but the CHANT program has been modified to produce synthesizer control instructions in order to run on various realtime synthesizers, such as the Systems Concepts Synthesizer at CCRMA, Stanford, the 4X synthesizer at IRCAM, Paris, and recently an implementation on the TMS-32010 has been demonstrated [Rodet 1987a].

21.5 Programming Languages for Specifying Compositional Algorithms

There really is no appropriate single title that accurately characterizes the languages in this section. Perhaps "Programming Languages for Synthesis Control" would have been better, but the ability to specify compositional algorithms seemed more pertinent. The confusion serves to bring up a point, that when dealing with sample-level and control-level signals, one turns naturally to algorithmic techniques as a way of insulating oneself from the tedium of specifying detail at this level. This is to be expected from the standpoint of pure practicality, as well as tradition, since these aspects are usually autonomous from the composer, and some are involuntary aspects even from the performing musician.

21.5.1 GROOVE

Max Mathews and F. Richard Moore developed a system for real-time control of analog synthesizers called GROOVE at AT&T Bell Telephone Laboratories in the late 1960s and early 1970s [Mathews 1970a]. GROOVE used a digital computer to control analog synthesizer modules, which is called "hybrid" synthesis. GROOVE ran on a Honeywell DDP-224 computer with a bank of twelve 8-bit and two 12-bit DACs, controlling a set of synthesizer modules. In addition, it contained a variety of graphical and tactile control systems. Music was described as a set of time-ordered control functions that could be generated either from performance gesture-capture devices, such as keyboards and knobs, or by algorithm. Several modes of operation were possible.

The standard method was to read functions of time from a disk and from various user inputs such as knobs, switches, and keyboards, in real-time at some relatively slow sampling rate (slow, that is, by audio requirements), and to have the DDP-224 perform calculations on these input functions in interactive realtime according to some user-supplied program. Some 100 functions could be read in at a rate of up to about 200 Hz. The resulting values were then written out to the DACs. The DACs would in turn control the analog synthesizer.

A variable-frequency oscillator was hooked up to the interrupt line of the DDP-224, so that on each interrupt, one sample from each input source (one sample from each of a maximum of 100 functions from the disk, plus user inputs) was read. Then a set of transforms was applied to scale the samples, an iteration of the user-supplied program was passed over the samples, and the function values were applied to the outputs. The modified functions could be simultaneously written back to disk as a record of the changes. Also, a real-time display was available that showed three contiguous groups of functions: those currently being referenced were in the center of the display (with a cursor over the current sample set); the right of the display showed the function values that would become the current functions, and the left showed those that had just been finished.

The user program was in two parts; a set of expressions could be specified that would apply arithmetic and assignment statements to the input samples. This would result in values of functions being scaled and offset, combined into expressions, and possibly mapped to other functions that would become the final output. If this was not enough, a user could supply a program that would be run next that could further modify the input or output samples. In the extreme case, the user program could ignore all inputs and synthesize all outputs if necessary.

As with many Music N languages, GROOVE skirted the problems of music representation by viewing music from the perspective of the system's implementation. Music was described as a set of time-ordered control functions that represented everything from acoustic parameters to the performer's gestures to high-level compositional control. There was no attempt within the GROOVE paradigm to abstract the functions into higher musical terms such as notes, though an enterprising user could accomplish this by analyzing the control functions. This in fact was often done, and provided a credible approach to translating from iconic to symbolic representation. This functional model provided the advantage of an unflavored environment in which to experiment, which was surely its primary goal. It could be used in real-time contexts, thereby allowing inquiry into performance practice. Its main limitation was the comparatively poor sound quality from the analog synthesizer, and the limited control over it, due to restrictions of the analog synthesis components.

21.5.2 PLAY

PLAY, like GROOVE, was another early real-time control language developed for hybrid synthesis. It was later reimplemented for the digital synthesizer built by New England Digital Co. (NEDCO). [Chadabe 1978a]. Since the architecture of the NEDCO synthesizer is fixed, the main focus of the language is not in expressing synthesis models, but in building patches and assigning parameters to synthesizer registers. The control model of PLAY, like GROOVE, is very reminiscent of the sequencer of an analog synthesizer. Like Music N, it implements a data-flow language where operators read, manipulate, and output streams of data. Also like Music N, the data-flow metaphor is extended to allow the generation of data with respect to time. Again like Music N and GROOVE, the language is interpreted, not compiled, and facilities exist so that a program can be changed even while it is running.

Music N and GROOVE view functions as uniformly sampled. That is, the sample period is fixed at some rate, and each action of the Music N or GROOVE program is conditionally executed on each clock tick. PLAY generalizes this by introducing triggers, by which modules (i.e., the "unit-generators" of PLAY) can start each other, possibly at submultiples of the sampling frequency. Modules may be triggered directly from the system clock or from each other in ways that can produce regularly or irregularly spaced events.

The language has three principal data types: functions, triggers, and ordinary integers. Algebraic expressions of triggers and integers can be formed. Functions are defined as either step functions or piecewise linear functions by supplying values to a function interpreter. The interpreter can be invoked during program execution to alter the values of any function on-the-fly. Once defined, the functions can be applied to modules that act to bind the successive values of the functions to moments of time defined by the interaction of modules with triggers. There are several varieties of module: one produces only triggers; another produces both triggers and values from its associated function; another produces triggers and values from an ADC (or other input device) or random values; still others are designed as sources of system triggers and DAC output.

The language was designed to operate on small machines, which means it does not have many extra features. For instance, for the version of PLAY documented in [Chadabe 1978a], function data must be entered from a terminal; alternate function representations are not available; no means of recording program I/O is available, nor is there any means of mixing previous performances with live ones. Nothing in the language itself would preclude these things, and in fact easy solutions spring readily to mind. The main difficulty with PLAY is that it lacks any ready means of encapsulation of code modules into subprograms, making the generation of larger programs difficult and subject to error. This too could be solved, for instance, with the addition of a macro preprocessor.

21.5.3 MUSBOX

The Systems Concepts Digital Synthesizer (SCDS), built by Peter Samson for CCRMA in 1977, implemented a large complement of signal generating and processing elements all executing in parallel, and capable of running in real time. There are 256 digital oscillators, 128 signal modifiers (filters, reverb, amplitude scalers, etc.), a scratch-pad memory for communicating values between processing elements, and a large memory for reverberation and table storage.

One of the challenges in developing a compiler for this machine was how best to provide a convenient transform from the parallelism in the hardware architecture to the serial ordering of von Neumann style computers (ordinary computers) typically used to control them. Another challenge was to develop a language that would provide backward compatibility with existing software synthesis (MUS10), so a compiler was written by this author that simulated MUS10 but generated SCDS commands instead of waveforms [Loy 1981a]. The compiler, called MUSBOX, was written in the SAIL language, and utilized SAIL's parallel processing simulation facilities not just to model the parallelism in the synthesizer, but also the parallelism in musical and compositional structures [Reiser 1976a]. The structure of MUSBOX consisted of a command interpreter, a collection of user-supplied subroutines that acted in a role reminiscent of the Music N instrument, and a library of routines that could generate commands to patch synthesizer modules and bind values to synthesizer registers.

The MUSBOX command interpreter read the score, processed note statements, and evaluated any arithmetic, assignment, or boolean expressions. When note statements were encountered, an instance of a correspondingly named user-supplied instrument was created, and passed the values of the parameter fields of the note statement. Like Music N, each instrument could be instantiated any number of times. Unlike Music N, an instrument was not made up of data-flow operators, but instead consisted of regular SAIL language statements and subroutine calls. The instrument's main task was to call synthesizer command generating routines that emit time-tagged synthesizer instructions.

The command interpreter and the user-supplied "instrument" subroutines operated in a *process scheduling discipline*. In ordinary programming languages, when a subroutine is called, the rest of the program is inactive until the subroutine returns or calls another subroutine in turn. However, when subroutines execute a process discipline, each subroutine —whether it be the command interpreter or any instance of an instrument created by the command interpreter—is best thought of as an autonomous program executing "simultaneously" with all others. These autonomous, concurrently executing subroutines are called processes. The process discipline is really a fiction: only one thread of code can execute at a time on a single CPU; but, when the CPU goes to run a different subroutine, it saves the contents of its registers and program counter in such a way that at any time it can resume the subroutine *where it left off* instead of having to enter it at the beginning again.

In the process paradigm, subroutines are taken as code templates, and any number of processes can be instantiated from any subroutine. To clarify this, note that a subroutine is just the combination of all of its data variables and the machine instructions to be applied to them. If multiple copies of the data variables can be kept separately from the instructions, we call them instances. If, further, each data variable set has room to store a copy of the machine's program counter and registers, then we have a way of stopping the execution of an instance with the possibility of resuming it later at the exact point where it left off. In this case, we call the instances *processes*.

This process paradigm allows—among other things—the simulation of the flow of time. A special routine called **Wait_Until**(*time*), when called by any process, causes it to suspend execution until the value given in *time* is reached, whereupon the execution of the process would pick up where it left off.

In operation, the command interpreter process reads note statements and instantiates one such instrument process for each note statement read. The instantiated instrument processes are not started up immediately, however, but merely caused to come into existence, and put on a list of processes waiting to be executed (or resumed if they were previously suspended). The processes on the queue are always sorted in the order of their begin times, so newly instantiated instrument processes always go at the head of the queue.

The command interpreter continues reading note statements and instantiating instruments as long as the begin time of each note statement equals the current time. When finally a note statement is scanned that indicates a later begin time, the command processor executes a **Wait_Until**(*time*), where the value of *time* is the begin time of the note statement just scanned. This causes the command process itself to be suspended, and placed on the queue of processes waiting to run, just like all the other processes it has just instantiated. Since the command processor has requested to run at some time in the future, its request is placed after all of the processes it just instantiated.

Now it is time to run the next process. The first process waiting on the queue is removed (it would be the first instantiated instrument process created by the command interpreter before it suspended itself), the value of a global variable that stores the current time is updated to the begin time of this new process, and the process is then executed.

The action of each instrument process is first to deduce from the parameters of its note statement what it is to do. It would then accomplish its action by calling library subroutines to issue the appropriate synthesizer commands, for instance, to turn on an oscillator. Having done so, it must wait until it is time to turn the oscillator off, which is given by the sum of the begin and duration parameters. It does this by executing **Wait_Until** (*begin_time* + *duration*). In doing so, it is suspended, and put in the queue after all other processes that want to run sooner than it. Eventually, when that time arrives, our instrument is resumed, and issues more synthesizer instructions to turn off the oscillator. Having no further purpose, it then exits.

Eventually, the time at which the command process requested to be resumed will arrive. When reawakened, the command process will instantiate the note statement that caused it to be suspended, and continue to read note statements until it again encounters a begin time greater than the current time, and the process just described repeats. When the score is exhausted, the command process executes **Wait_Until**(∞), which guarantees that the command process will not be run again until all other processes currently waiting to be executed have run their full course. So when the command process is next resumed, it knows it can go about cleaning up and quitting with impunity.

This process discipline also proved useful compositionally. For instance, suppose we wish to specify the placement of sounds in loudspeaker space along a certain trajectory. With the process discipline, one process is assigned the task of computing the current direction on the path and broadcasting this information to interested processes. The trajectory process simply computes the first vector, then suspends itself until the direction changes. When resumed it computes the next vector, then suspends itself again, and so on. All interested processes can read the broadcasted information and follow (or deviate from) the trajectory. This localizes the information about the path to be followed in a single expert process by creating a simple hierarchy of cooperating processes.

Another obvious application of the same sort of approach would be to designate one process as a conductor, the rest as instrumentalists, and have the conductor broadcast tempo and dynamics. One could also imagine simulating the cross currents of an orchestra section's response to a conductor, as happens in real orchestras. So the notion of processes as autonomous entities, communicating and synchronizing with other entities toward a common goal, works well as a model of the musical task. Musical knowledge can be represented both within and among instruments. Knowledge within instruments consists of the rules that implement their own characteristic behavior. Knowledge among instruments is characterized by the shape of the network, and what is communicated across it. The **cause** and **interrogate** features of SAIL were used to implement this method of interprocess communication, known as message passing.

21.5.4 FMX and Cleo

FMX is a patch language developed by Curtis Abbott for Andy Moorer's Audio Signal Processor (ASP) at Lucasfilm Limited [Abbott 1982a, Loy 1985a]. Developed for film sound, this machine emphasizes general signal processing more than synthesis, though it can do quite a lot of both.

Like the Systems Concepts Digital Synthesizer, the central problem of writing software for the ASP is modeling its hardware organization so that it is both intellectually and computationally efficient. The ASP implements a highly parallel architecture that is controlled through horizontal microcoding. That is, the various parallel computing resources are controlled through bit fields in very wide machine instruction words. One creates machine instructions for the ASP in much the same spirit—but on very different terms—as one creates unit generators in Music N. Microcode word sequences are stored in a writable control store—a special memory that the hardware reads from which serves to define the vocabulary of instructions the machine can perform. Code to be loaded can be time tagged in hardware, facilitating dynamic, real-time changes of both parameters and programs.

The machine is claimed to be easy to microcode, but in practical circumstances excessive detailed knowledge is required. FMX provides several essential services, all characterized as facilitating instrument design. The main thing to accomplish is to avail the user of the comprehensive computing resources of the ASP, which FMX does in its facilities for unit-generator definition. The main task comes when one wishes to combine unit-generators in an instrument. FMX handles the allocation and optimization of ASP computational resources by a method of stratifying the required operations across the available processing resources so as to maximize the utilization of the machine. The third major thing FMX accomplishes is the patching—or plugging together—of unit-generators to other data sources and sinks. The effect of plugging two data streams together is to make them into equivalent functions. GROOVE and PLAY do essentially the same thing, but in FMX, all signal sources and sinks are uniformly described, which obliterates the distinction between control functions, triggers, and sound samples. One is left merely with functions of time that are handled at different sampling rates.

Curtis Abbott also provided a high-level score language for the ASP, called Cleo. At first glance, Cleo resembles a version of the C language with some attention paid to cleaning up the syntax of variable declarations. In fact it is considerably more, incorporating features of FMX and a scheduling model based on Abbott's 4CED language, to be described next.

21.5.5 4CED

4CED is an earlier language of Curtis Abbott, developed for the 4C, an experimental synthesizer developed by Pepino di Giunio at IRCAM in Paris in the mid-1970s [Abbott 1981a]. The 4C implements a mixed collection of unit-generators ranging from oscillators and envelope generators down to discrete arithmetic-logic units and fast multipliers, all of which are connected via a scratch-pad memory. The 4C appears to its host computer much as an ordinary computer peripheral. A range of the address space of the host is mapped to the settable registers of the 4C. The host sets variables in the 4C in response to interrupts from the 4C. Envelopes, for instance, are implemented in the 4C as a starting value, an increment, and a final value. When the final value is reached, the 4C triggers an interrupt to the host, which responds by reinitializing these registers with the next slope from the function. The result is the generation in hardware of piecewise linear functions of time.

Given this architecture, the task of the controlling computer can be viewed as the host *intervening* in the actions of the synthesizer. This suggested a process discipline called *intervention scheduling* as the model for both synthesizer control and music representation. In this model, separate processes are called *schedule instances*, and are thought of by the programmer as running only at instantaneous, uninterruptible moments, called *interventions*. Each intervention is triggered by an event, which can be the arrival of a hardware interrupt from the 4C (such as an envelope timeout or other programmed delay), or real-time performance inputs (such as a button being pushed), or triggers simulated in software by other schedules.

Scores are implemented as schedules, which either run as sequences or trigger each other directly by generating software events, in a way reminiscent of PLAY. Envelopes are likewise implemented simply as schedules.

Intervention scheduling is contrasted with priority scheduling. In the latter, events are graded by the importance of having an instantaneous response, with lower-priority events being deferred until the CPU is not occupied by higher-priority events. Response latency is a probablistic function of interrupt level. For the highest-priority interrupts the latency is the (constant) hardware interrupt response time of the host computer—effectively instantaneous.[14] For lower priorities, latency ranges from a minimum of near-instantaneous (no other higher-level events are pending) to a typical worst-case value equal to the sum of service response intervals of higher events to a maximum of never, if the system is flooded with higher-priority events. Priority scheduling is not a very good model for real-time because of the ambiguity of these delays. Another problem with priority-coded schemes is that they require relatively complicated methods of sharing mutual resources between the various prioritized contexts that must be handled with interlock mechanisms such as semaphores, monitors, and message passing.

Intervention scheduling deals with both of these concerns by flattening the priority scheme to only two levels: background (no intervention) and foreground. Within the foreground, the service time associated with each intervention is considered to be infinitesimal, so that there is never more than one event being serviced at a time. This eliminates the need for interlocks and "guarantees" a flat response function for all events. Of course, the service time of interventions is not really zero, so small delays creep into program flow that is supposed to be controlled by time. A program has to be referenced to an external clock or it will eventually start running slow.

In 4CED, a small expression language is available to define interventions, allowing evaluation of arithmetic expressions, assignment to local and global variables, and assignment to scratch-pad registers in the 4C. Data are available in the form of constants, references to array elements, and an operator that reads a potentiometer or other user performance device. Two kinds of arrays are available, one that functions as a normal (one-dimensional) lookup table and one implicitly referenced by the program counter, providing data for the "current event." This latter feature is again reminiscent of GROOVE and PLAY. Other operators include control flow (a form of **if-then-else**, and a **goto**), as well as a mechanism to trigger other schedule instances.

Besides the score sublanguage just described, there is also a patch sublanguage. Even though the 4C implements fixed unit-generators, one can combine collections of low-level unit-generators into higher ones hierarchically. This is handled by an extended macro system that handles memory and unit-generator resource allocation and interconnection through scratch-pad memory. Parallelism in the hardware is likewise represented in the patch sublanguage, and translates into concurrent operations in the synthesizer. The outermost layer of variables in an instrument definition is globally exported, and can be addressed symbolically in the code that handles interventions.

21.5.6 Event-Driven versus Periodic Abstractions

4CED is the first example of a real-time language we have encountered where program execution is not strictly periodic and chronological. GROOVE and PLAY and all languages with a strict functional model of music implement real-time by polling at fixed intervals. They assign the function of controlling the passage of time to a clock. When the clock interrupts the processor, input devices are polled, and outputs are calculated. I/O devices "speak only when spoken to" by the polling program. No event other than the clock can cause an asynchronous response by the processor. If a button is pushed halfway between two clock ticks, response will be deferred to the next clock tick, and the time tag it receives will be rounded up to the higher tick.

4CED, on the other hand, allows multiple asynchronous events. Time is handled as the transition from one state to the next. The semantics of some of these states, such as envelope generation, cause the flow of time.

Of course, a sampled function of time can be viewed as just a set of synchronously chained events, and an event can be seen as a sample, so these data abstractions can be resolved into each other, though usually with some loss of efficiency, depending on the type of information being recorded.

In practice, event-oriented models usually incorporate a level of abstraction of the modeled phenomenon that is missing in functional models. Remember that a musical note is an event representation of the continuous pressure-wave of the note as performed. The gestures of the musician to realize the note are best represented as unabstracted functions of time: bow or lip pressure, fingering, etc. Such performance information must then be abstracted to yield musical notes as isolated events.

21.5.7 Handling Musical Information Density Fluctuations

The information density curve of most musical scores has large temporal fluctuations that take the form of sharp spikes associated with the onset of musical simultaneities, such as at downbeats. The ratio of the maxima to the mean of these functions is quite large. For instance, compare the information frequency in the downbeat of an orchestral *tutti* to that played *senza ripieni*. This control problem is handled by massive parallelism in a symphony orchestra, but must usually be dealt with by a small number of serial processors in a computer system, raising the problem of how best to record and represent this information.

Functional and event-oriented systems solve the problem of efficiently representing these functions in complementary ways. In the functional model, an arbitrary limit on bandwidth is applied, and the resulting capture ability is controlled by the Nyquist theorem. Thus, the functional strategy is to stipulate a fixed order and fixed rate of observation of all inputs. The rate is determined by trading off the input signal bandwidths against the sustainable computation rate of the hardware. The sustainable computation rate is then divided up between examining inputs and computing and storing outputs. The positive side of functional systems like GROOVE and PLAY is that input from all sources is guaranteed for each sample; the negative side is that information above the Nyquist rate is aliased down, or, if properly lowpass filtered, it is thrown out. Also, all signals—even those that do not change—must be continuously recorded at each sample interval, which introduces a lot of redundancy in the record of the performance.

In the event model of input capture, there is no notion of sample rate: the rate at which sampling occurs is a function of the frequency of events. It is as though the event model implements a variable-sample-rate functional model where the rate is controlled by the density of information in the input signals. There is a de facto upper limit on bandwidth, however, which coincides with the minimum period of interrupt service time.

Sampling is induced asynchronously by the recognition of events, the rate of which fluctuates. This is good because, instead of the rate being defined a priori as in the functional approach, the rate "floats" as a function of the actual density of information we want to record. Thus, the event strategy implements no fixed order or rate of observation of all inputs. This is good, because it means we are only sampling inputs when we need to, which reduces the volume of recorded information, and simultaneously provides a layer of abstraction on the input data. However, if we look for a moment at an event system as a variable-sample-rate functional system, we see its bad side.

There is a knowable time function associated with any deterministic calculation, including, for instance, the process of recording input data. Consideration of this time is made in the functional approach in determining the sampling rate. Event systems cannot take this into account, however. There is no way of limiting the number of significant events during peaks of information density, and consequently no way of limiting the frequency of interrupts the responding system must be able to handle.[15] Thus, where the frequency of events approaches the maximum frequency of interrupt response latency (i.e., the "maximum sampling rate" of our variable-sample-rate perspective), the responding system must spend progressively more time handling interrupts and has less time for other tasks, such as analysis and response to events. When interrupt frequency is equal to the peak interrupt service time, the recording system is flooded, and can only record and cannot respond. When interrupt frequency exceeds this rate, even the recording process breaks down, and we drop out of real time. In particular, events are either lost or they are given an incorrect "too late" time stamp when they are finally processed, depending on how the system handles this case.

So we have this trade-off: functional systems guarantee capture regardless of input bandwidth fluctuations but alias (or discard) information whose frequency is above the Nyquist rate and produce inefficient representations of the recorded performance when the information density is much less than the sample rate. Event systems eliminate the redundancy of functional representations, but are susceptible to flooding in a way that could jeopardize real-time response.

The bottom line is this: no matter what abstraction is chosen, care must be taken that response time does not increase (degrade) under load beyond perceptible psychoacoustic and musical limits. While it is important that the time response of a musical system to any input signal be "quick," it is more important that the response time be consistent than that it be fixed. But the worst case is where response time is a function of how many other events are simultaneous with it. In systems that process this information serially (all current systems), this is a real problem. A recent paper by [Kuivila 1986a] considers this problem in detail.

Of the systems reviewed in the survey section below, the functional model seems to be preferred for such low-level tasks as waveform synthesis, recording of performance gestures, and waveform-level synthesizer control, because this abstraction differentiates information quantitatively, not qualitatively. That is, it does not discriminate on the basis of kinds of information, only on frequencies of information. With event-based systems all you ever capture is what you go looking for; functional systems capture everything that occurs with a frequency less than the Nyquist rate. The second reason—which is really only a corollary of the first—is that functional systems are more resistant to real-time degradation. The event model is generally preferred for high-level music processing, such as representing scores or editing such things as CPN.

21.5.8 SSSP

William Buxton and his Structured Sound Synthesis Project (SSSP) at the University of Toronto has focused considerable attention and thought on the design of a composer's aid for a synthesizer they developed [Buxton 1979a, Buxton 1978a]. For Buxton, this meant first providing a general-purpose computing environment, and enriching it with special-purpose tools for musical composition. SSSP was a computer system, not just a single language. The data structures and methods of invocation were tightly integrated as far as possible with each other and the underlying general-purpose system. Like CHANT, defaults were provided everywhere both to aid the naive and to allow a composer to focus first on what was thought important. Tasks solved by the system bore out a musical taxonomy familiar to musicians. SSSP seemed to strike a happy balance between providing automatic structures to composers and providing a general computational workspace that was not overly biased by strict theoretical underpinnings.

Graphics played an important role in the SSSP system, and Buxton was among the first in this line of research to realize the potential of the mouse-driven bit-mapped graphics user interface first developed at Xerox PARC by Alan Kay and now known to millions through the Apple Macintosh. This interface practically made obsolete the standard teletype terminal for user I/O in the SSSP system and was a major factor in its simplicity, generality, and responsiveness, compared to computer keyboard-driven systems.

The mouse-driven graphics made the system easy to learn; additionally, the system was designed to hand over control gracefully as the user matured. A then-novel hierarchical music data structure was implemented to represent scores internally, and a variety of user interfaces were built on this to represent scores to the user in complimentary ways.

21.5.9 Moxie

Moxie sets out to solve many of the same problems that 4CED and PLAY addressed, but is interesting for the simplicity of its approach, the comparative ease of programming it, and its consequent portability to other systems [Collinge 1984a, Collinge 1980a].

Moxie was developed by Doug Collinge at the University of Victoria, in Victoria, Canada, in the late 1970s and early 1980s. It was targeted first for the NEDCO synthesizer, the same one as PLAY. The native programming language of the NEDCO host computer is XPL. Moxie simply consists of a combination of a macro package and a library of routines that implement the Moxie scheduling apparatus. Moxie programs are written in XPL, moderately extended by the macro package. The NEDCO consists of a synthesizer coupled across a bus to a host computer that communicates with the synthesizer in an event-oriented manner similar to that of the 4C system. There are foreground and background processes that run along the lines of the intervention scheduling model of Abbott. A symbol table relates events from I/O devices and the synthesizer to *action components* of the foreground process. These action components correspond in function to 4CED schedules. One advantage of Moxie over 4CED is that it is embedded within a general-purpose programming language whereas 4CED was written from scratch. This meant Moxie was easier to create and easier to maintain and to port to other computer systems.

Moxie's simplicity derives in part from having only a single means for programs to schedule delayed execution. The **cause** subroutine could be expressed in pseudo-C as follows:

cause(time, routine, $arg_1, arg_2, arg_3, \cdots, arg_N$)

Calling this routine will cause the deferred execution of the routine whose address appears as the second argument at a time specified by the first argument. The remaining arguments to **cause** are saved in an internal table and passed to the routine when it is finally invoked. A routine can thus cause any other routine to execute at any time (including immediately);

equally, it can reschedule itself. **Cause** is essentially a noninterlocked time-tagged message passing discipline.

In some ways, the syntax of **cause** is problematical, because few languages provide dynamic variation of the number of actual arguments to a subroutine; one must usually fix the number of arguments to some amount. The original implementation specified that there could be four arguments that would be passed via **cause** to the routine. Of course one can use the arguments as pointers to datagrams or messages, so long as what is pointed to is guaranteed to be there still when the caused routine is executed.

Two new versions of Moxie have been written in widely portable languages. Moxie has been reimplemented in interpreted form by Doug Collinge in the FORTH programming language. A compiled form in the C programming language, called Moxc, has been implemented by Roger Dannenberg at Carnegie-Mellon University [Dannenberg 1986a; cf. also Dannenberg's chapter in this book].

21.5.10 HMSL

Developed by Larry Polansky and David Rosenboom at the Center for Contemporary Music at Mills College in Oakland, HMSL stands for "Hierarchical Music Specification Language" [Rosenboom 1985a]. It is designated by its authors as a real-time environment for formal perceptual and compositional experimentation. The theoretical and musical underpinnings come from a music theory developed originally by James Tenney [Tenney 1986a], and later extended with Polansky [Tenney 1980a]. Tenney's pioneering theory, developed from some ideas of gestalt psychology, is a listener-centered music theory that attempts to describe and predict the aggregates in which listeners hear music in time. Traditional music theory had mostly focused on analyzing a score without reference to temporal aspects of perception. The heart of the theory is a hierarchical taxonomy of musically salient perceptual units. HMSL "depends on the assumption that many of the perceptual processes that distinguish musical entities on one level . . . are archetypically the same as those which group larger units . . ." [Rosenboom 1985a].

A set of values and their ordering is termed a *morphology*, or shape. One can establish hierarchies of such morphologies such that a shape may be a determinant of a set of underlying shapes. HMSL deals in the design of morphologies, their ordering in hierarchies, and the rules governing their transformation into other morphologies. With the idea of morphological transformation comes the notion of a *morphological metric*, an indication of the perceptual distance between any two morphologies. This in turn gives rise to the idea of compositional manipulation of these metrics such that each morphology can be represented as a point in a metric space of some kind. Then correlations between morphologies can then be viewed as distances in this space. A composer can then work in terms of plotting trajectories across this space. HMSL is implemented in three functional units: CREATE, PERFORM, and EXECUTE. CREATE deals with the establishment of basic compositional elements, primarily through the use of mouse-based graphics. PERFORM is an optional scheduling step that establishes the "stimulus-response" behavior of the system, that is, the connection between events and actions. EXECUTE, as the name implies, makes it all happen. The system is implemented and running, and numerous compositions have been realized with it.

21.5.11 Arctic

Arctic is an experimental language through which Roger Dannenberg is exploring the applicability of John Backus's funtional programming model to real-time control problems, such as music [Dannenberg 1984a, Backus 1978a]. Arctic is a *declarative* rather than a *procedural* language, meaning that the programmer of Arctic writes in a kind of algebra of functions, and Arctic turns this into an executing program.

In Arctic, one declares that functions of time have certain relations, rather than stipulating a procedure that produces such relations.

Flow of time is made explicit in the language of Arctic, as it is in Music N, where adjustments due to sampling rate are buried in the implementation. In event-oriented languages such as 4CED, Moxie, and MUSBOX, time is represented as successive transitions of state; in function-oriented languages such as GROOVE and PLAY, time is represented as a sequential sampling interval. In both event and functional abstractions, the actual flow of time is dependent on a clock that is external to the language.

In Arctic, declarations and procedure calls are replaced by *prototypes* and *instances*. A prototype is a declaration of either a computed function or a stream of input or output data. Instances are created from prototypes by applying them over particular time intervals. The time assignments (or the conditions leading to such assignments) are stated explicitly in expressions of the language. Besides operators to assign and scale instances in time, there are operations such as addition, multiplication, division, and assignment and logical operations that can be applied to functions. However, these operations apply to entire functions, not, as in GROOVE, to the current sample from each function. Variables exist, but they do not store state information; they are merely used as pointers to instances that are external to a particular program module.

The trouble with Arctic is that it is close enough to a regular programming language in its syntax that one becomes lulled into thinking it ought to act like one, but the semantics are quite unusual, as all operations relate to manipulating functions. Dannenberg has been experimenting with a non-real-time interpreted prototype version of this language. This allows the assumption that all inputs and outputs are fixed when a program is begun. A separate facility is provided for graphic construction of prototypes that are modeled as piecewise linear time functions.

He expects that the program can be made to operate in real-time by time-division multiplexing a processor among concurrent instances, or by using small-grained multiprocessing architectures to the same effect. One suspects that the underlying implementation of Arctic may resemble GROOVE and Music IV to some extent, since there will then be the necessity of discretizing the time functions and providing an execution tree for successive moments of time, which is basically what GROOVE and Music IV do.

21.5.12 PLA

PLA is arguably the most thoroughly implemented programming language for music in existence [Schottstaedt 1983a]. PLA is described in another chapter by Schottstaedt, so I shall merely comment upon it here. It started out as a language interpreter written in SAIL, a baroque dialect of Algol [Reiser 1976a]. PLA gradually came to incorporate not only the entire SAIL language, but formidable extensions to SAIL as well, all within an interpreted system. Important language models for PLA included SCORE, MUSBOX, SAIL, LISP, Zetalisp, and Smalltalk. From SCORE came PLA's music data notation; MUSBOX provided a model for note-list parsing and a model of the parallel processing run-time capabilities of SAIL; LISP provided a good model for processing the lists of SCORE-type music data, including *eval* operations; and Smalltalk and Zetalisp provided models for object-oriented message passing programming. Schottstaedt says that the message passing aspect got added not so he could remain *au courant* with language design so much as because he thought it would be a good way to manage complexity.

The management of complexity is an extremely important issue in machine representations of music. CPN derives its conciseness by connoting much, denoting little. It gives some objective information, but mostly provides inferences to musicians that key off of their considerable knowledge of the context of the music being represented. Imagine composers having to write scores such that, in addition to telling the performers what to play, they had to tell them in explicit detail with what feeling they should play. Though so-called *expert systems* research is a hot topic in AI, even the current state of the art does not yet provide a means of automatically discovering and representing this kind of informal, covert knowledge. Every musical rule must be explicitly stated somewhere by a programmer, and it is not enough just to represent the objective dimensions of music (such as pitch, rhythm, and loudness).

But even the objective dimensions of music are very taxing of the representational abilities of even the most robust languages surveyed here. This is nowhere more evident than how synthesis parameters are handled in note statements. For instance, SCORE mostly turns one kind of list (sequential parameter data) into another kind of list (sequential note statements). ASHTON improved on SCORE's representational efficiency, but is still mostly an unprogrammable data-entry system. MUS10 mitigated the amount of parameter data that must be passed from score to instruments by providing so-called **I_only** code blocks that allowed an instrument to interpret the arguments it receives from a note statement, somewhat the way a musician does. MUSBOX extended this by allowing instruments to be written within a multiprocessing discipline, allowing considerable musicianly knowledge to be embedded within the body of the instruments that interpret the score. PLA carried this a step further with the introduction of object-oriented programming techniques.

At the core, the ideas underlying message passing and object-oriented programming are simple: a subroutine not only receives data as arguments, but also gets an indication as to what subset of its code it is to execute. This argument is called the *message*, and the code executed inside the subroutine as a consequence of its receipt is called the *method.* A subroutine responding in this way we call an *object*. Also, instead of using global variables to store information that is needed in various parts of a program, one encapsulates these variables and all actions that manipulate them into an object, the address of which is global. This serves three purposes: (1) it provides an interlock to keep the variables from being inadvertently or incorrectly modified by other routines; (2) it localizes into one place all the operations on the data and hides implementation details within the object; (3) to effect a change, one need only send a concise symbolic message indicating what needs to be done without worrying about how it will actually be accomplished. Hierarchies of objects of increasing sophistication can then be built up to solve complex problems.

It is easy to see how this strategy extends the concept of modular programming an extra step, and tends to break down and hide complexity. Of course, programs of arbitrary complexity can be written in any reasonable language. But for linear growth in program complexity there is usually a nonlinear growth in the difficulty of modifying a program. So as a program grows, it tends to reach a limit determined by the language, not the problem. Programming disciplines, like message passing, help to solve this by factoring complexity into a hierarchical collection of cooperating objects. However, it is only a discipline; undisciplined programmers can still wreak havoc.

The other major contribution of PLA is in the development of alternative representations of scores. Language primitives and libraries of useful subroutines are supplied from which one can create arbitrary representations of scores. Schottstaedt has provided a note-list editor, a program editor, a function-of-time editor, and a pseudo-CPN editor.

21.5.13 Player

Player was written by this author in 1983 as a platform for music language research. Its heritage is MUSBOX, SCORE, PLA, and Music N [Loy 1986a]. There were a number of goals to be accomplished in its design.

• **Portability**: The implementation language of Player is the C programming language, a modern, high-level language [Kernighan 1978a]. A major goal of the C language was to achieve machine independence as a part of the language design. As a result, wherever there is a C compiler for a machine, Player can run on it too. This bypasses the problem faced, e.g., by PLA that it is implemented in a nonportable language, and cannot easily migrate to more modern (less expensive and more powerful) computers as they become available.

• **Familiarity**: Player is a strict superset of the C language, so programmers familiar with C can learn to program quickly in Player.

• **Tight integration with UNIX**: The UNIX operating system is almost entirely written in C, and is widely available. It is an excellent program development environment, and programs written in Player can cooperate with the large base of other programs for musical applications available for UNIX [Moore 1985a].

• **Real-time**: As a timesharing operating system, UNIX is unsuitable for real-time applications. In order to run in real time, Player programs must be able to run stand alone on dedicated microprocessors. Player has libraries of runtime routines that allow it to operate without benefit of UNIX support.

• **Fast execution**: Speed of execution helps guarantee timely response to input events, and allows complex operations to be performed in realtime. C's portability is not at the expense of its speed. It compiles directly into native machine instructions, and so, therefore, do Player programs.

• **Music representation**: Player borrows from several other languages, notably PLA and SCORE, for its music data types, though it regularizes and extends them somewhat. Tools are provided for programmers to define arbitrary music representations, and to provide easy conversion between them.

• Player implements a *pseudo*process discipline similar to MUSBOX. As there is no support in the C language for so-called "lightweight" processes, this had to be added. Doing so without requiring access to the computer's subroutine stack frame has maintained Player's portability, but makes its process discipline somewhat resemble Moxie's.

• **Time flow**: Player implements Curtis Abbott's intervention scheduling method of process synchronization. Processes can synchronize their execution based on external events, actions of other processes, or the lapse of a time interval.

Player has music data types and libraries of supporting routines for graphic and textual representation of common practice notation. The language itself is by no means limited to this, but provides basic CPN data types as a basis from which to develop others. The specification shown below outlines a hierarchical music data structure very close to CPN, which can be cast in terms of either a page of music graphics or a textual representation. This chart is in BNF (Backus-Nauer form), which defines items on the left of a colon as one or more things on the right. This dialect of BNF is from a compiler-cimpiler language called Yacc [Johnson 1975a]. A compiler-compiler is a language for implementing computer languages. The Portable C Compiler was written in Yacc, for instance [Johnson 1978a, Johnson 1975a].

A *piece* is defined as *systems*, which in turn are defined as one or more *system*. A *system* in turn is defined as a collection of *staves*, and *staves* are defined as one or more *stafflines*. The symbol ":" separates the thing being defined from its definition, the "|" symbol means "or," and ";" terminates the definition. The way to define things as "one or more of" something in Yacc is to define the something in terms of some other thing, or itself followed by some other thing. For instance, *staves* : *staffline* | *staves staffline* says that *staves* can be either a *staffline* or *staves* followed by a *staffline*. So *staves* is a way of accumulating sequential stafflines.

For clarity, I have included only the most general parts of the specification. The symbols that are not defined here, i.e., that do not appear at all in the left hand column, are given in CAPITALS.

```
piece           : systems
systems         : system | systems system ;
system          : staves ;
staves          : staffline | staves staffline ;
staffline       : staff | directive ;
staff           : voice_list voice_items ;
voice_list      : SYMBOL | voice_list ;
directive       : statement ;
statement       : ARITHMETIC | assignment | proc_call ;
assignment      : SYMBOL = value_list ;
proc_call       : SYMBOL (ARGS) ;
value_list      : VALUE | value_list, VALUE ;
voice_items     : voice_item | voice_items voice_item ;
voice_item      : note_list | MEASURE | BEGIN_SLUR
                | END_SLUR | BEGIN_MOTIVE | END_MOTIVE ;
note_list       : note | note_list note ;
note            : note_items ;
note_items      : note_item | note_items note_item ;
note_item       : /* empty */ | note_elements ;
note_elements   : note_element | note_elements NOTE_ELEMENT ;
```

This form establishes the connection between an entire piece and the individual *note_elements* of which it is composed. This particular form is biased toward textual representation.

The kinds of *note_elements* built in to Player include **Notes**, **Rhythms**, **Exprs** (arithmetic expressions), and **Strings**. Facilities are provided to create arbitrary *note_elements*, such as microtonal scales. The format of *note_elements* is likewise defined in BNF. For instance, the textual notation for chromatic pitch:

```
pitch            : pitch_class
                   | pitch_class acc_list
                   | pitch_class acc_list octave
                   | pitch_class octave
                   | directive ;
pitch_class      : a | b | c | d | e | f | g | r ;
acc_list         : acc_list accidental | accidental ;
accidental       : n | f | s ;
octave           : NUMBER | rel_octave ;
rel_octave       : plus_list | minus_list ;
plus_list        : + | plus_list + ;
minus_list       : - | minus_list - ;
directive        : key_signature | time_signature | metronome_mark ;
key_signature    : K NUMBER s | K NUMBER f ;
```

Examples of pitches include *a4* (A440), *cs7* (C sharp in the seventh piano octave), *eff* (E double-flat), *fn* (F natural), and *b* - - (B two octaves below last pitch). Key signatures can be given: *K3s* is the key of A-major/F-sharp-minor. Notes affected by signature can be overridden by accidentals, which hold until the end of a bar-line. Rhythmic values are slightly generalized from SCORE. The relationship between a number, N, and a duration in seconds is $4/N$. Thus, the rhythmic value of a quarternote is represented by the number 4, which equals one second duration at MM = 60. Appended dots increase a duration recursively by 1/2 of its previous value for each dot appended. There is a fractional format where one can replace the numerator of $4/N$ with X/N, which allows any compound rhythm. For example, a quarter tied to a sixteenth is five sixteenths tied, expressed as 5/16. Rhythmic values can be formed into expressions: 4. + 15/16 + 12.

The Player language system consists of a Player program recognizer, written in Yacc, and a package of run-time routines that implement the music data structures and the scheduling paradigm. The Player program recognizer reads Player source programs and translates Player constructs into equivalent C language statements. The resulting C program is compiled normally and linked with the run-time library routines. The result is an executable program.

In the following code example, we have a Player (which is Player's equivalent of PLA's Voice declaration and MUSBOX's Instrument declaration) that does a melodic/rhythmic interpolation between two motives. In this case, the two motives being interpolated are a three-note phrase and its retrograde. Over the course of 24 seconds, the rhythmic phrase {16 4. 8} will gradually become {8 4. 16}, and the pitch sequence {c3 ef3 c4} will become {c4 ef3 c3}. This example is given in the spirit of Max Mathews' experiments in melodic transformation discussed in the section on compositional algorithms.

```
# define interp (f, p, q) ((f) * (q) + (1.0 − (f)) * (p))
# define rhy "16 4. 8"
# define mel "c3 ef4 c4"
Player retrophrase (0, 24){
    int now = Norm_time (Self);
    P4 = interp (now, Rhythms (rhy), Rhythms (Retrograde (rhy)));
    P5 = interp (now, Pitches (mel), Pitches (Retrograde (mel)));
    Wait_until (P2 = Abs_time (Self) + P4);
}
```

The macro *interp* implements linear interpolation. This is like a pan-pot where *f* is he "knob" and *p* and *q* are the inputs. The output is their sum weighted from *p* to *q* as *f* traverses the interval [0,1).

Player *retrophrase* is instantiated from time 0 for 24 sec duration. The melodic retrograde will take place once over its lifetime. The statement **Norm_time (Self)** is a Player system routine that returns a value that goes from 0 to 1 as Player *retrophrase* progresses from 0 to 24 sec. (**Norm_time** provides time evaluation equivalent in function to the implicit unit-interval duration parameter of Arctic.) (The argument **Self** means compute the value for the current Player. It is possible to get the value for any other Player by the appropriate substitution for **Self**.) The value from **Norm_time** is assigned to *now*, and is used as the "knob" on the melodic pan-pot. **P4** is assigned successive rhythmic durations while **P5** receives pitches. The macro *interp* receives as arguments the value *now*, an element from the cyclic list of rhythms being evaluated by the **Rhythms** routine, and the retrograde of this same cyclic list. The interpolated rhythm is assigned to **P4**. The same method is applied to the cyclic lists of pitches being evaluated by the **Pitches** routine, and its retrograde. The interpolated pitch is assigned to **P5**.

Finally, the time to rerun this Player is determined. **Abs_time** returns the current value of absolute time (either simulated time or realtime depending on whether this is being run under timesharing or on a dedicated microprocessor.) **P2** is assigned the value of the current absolute time plus the duration of the note just interpolated in **P4**. The result is passed as an argument to the routine **Wait_until**, which will cause the next execution of this Player to "wait until" the computed future time.

Another facility provides for a Player to wait on a condition or event, instead of the lapse of a time interval. **Wait_for** is a routine that takes as its argument the address of a subroutine that will return a nonzero value if the condition of interest has occurred. The address of the subroutine is given to the Player scheduler, which polls it at specifiable intervals. If the subroutine returns true, each Player that invoked it with **Wait_for** is scheduled to run immediately. A Player may call both **Wait_until** and **Wait_for** to make a deadline such that the Player gets called if the event does not occur within a certain period. All of Player's tokens for music representation are lexically different, allowing them to be mixed into the same cyclic list.

Player came out of the same milieu as PLA, and did some explicit borrowing from PLA, MUSBOX, and SCORE. In comparing it to these antecedents, PLA is interpreted, and written in SAIL, a nonportable language, and is primarily useful as a way of generating, editing, and representing scores in a timesharing context. Player is compiled, and written in C, an efficient, portable language. This makes Player useful in realtime microcomputer systems for the control of musical performance and interactive composition. Because it is a strict superset of C, it does not implement a true process discipline. So it has less room to manouver than do PLA and Formes in process modeling. On the other hand, sticking with C means it is easy to port to any processor with a C compiler. Real-time versions exist for various dedicated microprocessors with and without floating point support. Player was taken by R. Rowe and O. Koechlin as the basis of their 4XY language for controlling the 4X synthesizer at IRCAM [Favreau 1986a], and by Rick Bidlack at UCSD for his CIRCE system.

One limitation of both Player and PLA is that—to a certain extent—they are trying to do with SAIL and C what ought to be done with languages more properly capable of handling the complexity of the material with which they must deal. In particular, neither applies a model for organizing and controlling the operation of large sets of communicating parallel processes. While this provides great flexibility, it also requires a composer to take on this nontrivial responsibility. The next language, Formes, provides a more structured approach to this problem.

21.5.14 Formes

As discussed at the end of the section on CHANT, the synthesis-by-rule approach to modeling the singing voice eventually led to the situation where the synthesis technique was well developed, but the task of elaborating the rules for its control was becoming increasingly more difficult. This was for the reasons discussed in the section on PLA, that most general-purpose programming languages asymptotically approach a saturation level of complexity where the difficulty of further changes in a program precludes their continued elaboration. When this situation was faced by the CHANT group, it was realized that they must address the complexity problem at its roots [Rodet 1984b, Cointe 1983a]. Because of these origins, Formes is an example of a system that is *not* a top-down design, a pattern that is familiar in many other applications of artificial intelligence.

Formes has the advantage over PLA of being written in a language that directly implements message passing and inheritance, VLISP [Chailloux 1978a]. The main goal of the language is the isolation and production of models of *musical knowledge*. The emphasis is on models that are relevant to CHANT synthesis, which means the main task is the generation of time functions.

The framework provided by Formes consists of a time-ordered, genealogical hierarchy of program objects. The objects are connected to the tree through parents, siblings, and children. Higher layers of the tree correspond to more abstract rules of synthesis. For instance, at the bottom might be objects that determine synthesis parameters, such as fundamental pitch, and placement and bandwidth of formants, glissando, and voicing. Above them might come objects relating to fine-grained modeling of performance, such as vibrato and articulation. Above this might come objects that control vocal style, etc. Levels above this might relate to compositional rules, etc.

On each tick of a software clock, the tree of objects is evaluated. The Formes scheduler may modify this tree based on criteria of timing, hierarchy, and certain precedence rules relating to the production of ligatures between notes of a score. Each tree traversal results in one set of synthesis parameters being passed to the CHANT program.

The following example of a program written in Formes, derived from [Cointe 1985a], illustrates a compositional technique of Jean-Baptiste Barrière in his composition *Chreode*, written in 1983 at IRCAM in Paris. In this example, Barrière defined a Formes process to realize a damped sinusoidal function, which would control most of the important parameters of the piece. The function would be offset to the nominal value of the parameter being controlled, and would then lend its characteristic fluctuation to that parameter.

The chosen function of time is

$$\sin(2\pi\omega x - \phi)\cdot(1 - x)^{\alpha}, \qquad x\in[0, 1],$$

where ϕ is phase, ω is the number of periods, and α is the damping factor. The result is a damped sinusoid. The equivalent definition in VLISP is

```
(dmd trajectoire (x α φ ω)
              '(mul
                 (power (subtract 1., (eval x)), α)
                 (sin (subtract (multiply (multiply 2π, (eval x)), ω), φ))))
```

Barrière wished to use the four geometrical transformations of this damped sinusoid: prime, retrograde, inverse, and retrograde inverse. The first step is to define a process that will yield the transformations:

```
(dp rouge
    first-time:  ((setq quantum 0.1))
    each-time:   ((setq f1 (trajectoire (if (fmy sens) '(1-tnorm) '(tnorm))
                 (fmy n) (fmy phase) (fmy np))))
    env:         (duration 10 sens t n 4. phase π/2 np 7.))
```

dp stands for "define process." *rouge* has three components. The label **first-time** corresponds to MUS10's **I_only** code; i.e., it is done once the first time the process is called. Its action is to set the time between calls to *rouge* to 0.1 sec. **env** provides a list of local variables and their default values in pairs. The *duration* is 10 sec; *sens* is **t**, which means "true" in LISP: *n* is the damping factor; and *phase* is $\pi/2$, meaning not inverted. The variable *sens* determines whether the damped sinusoid is traversed forward or backward (retrograde). If *sens* is **t** (as it is initialized to be), the function is traversed backward.

Because **quantum** is set to 0.1, **each-time** is called at 0.1-sec intervals. Its action is to set global variable **f1** to the return value of a call to *trajectoire*. Doing so fulfills the purpose of this process. The method of obtaining the value of local environment variables is to apply the operator **fmy**, so the expression (**fmy** *phase*) evaluates in this example to $\pi/2$.

There is an implicit variable in Formes processes called **tnorm** that behaves identically to Player's **Norm_time** routine, in providing a value in the interval [0, 1) that corresponds to the current moment in the life of the process. The first argument to *trajectoire* evaluates to '(**1-tnorm**) if *sens* is **t**, which it is by default. This yields the retrograde form. If *sens* is **nil** (LISP for "not true"), then the first argument to *trajectoire* is '(**tnorm**), yielding the prime form. The rest of the arguments to *trajectoire* are *n*, the damping factor, *phase*, and *np*, the number of periods.

We activate *rouge* with the statement

(*rouge* '**play**),

which produces the retrograde damped sinusoid and deposits it in **f1**. We can now make three new instantiations of *rouge* to yield the remaining transformations with the statements below. Each new instance of *rouge* inherets the state of the previous one. Thus, the first produces the prime form, the second the inverse, and the third the retrograde inverse.

(**send** '*rouge* '**new** '*verte* '**env:** '(*sens* **nil**))
(**send** '*verte* '**new** '*jaune* '**env:** '(*phase* $-\pi/2$))
(**send** '*jaune* '**new** '*orange* '**env:** '(*sens* **t**))

rouge receives a message that instructs it to instantiate a new processes with the name *verte*. In this new process, the *sens* variable is changed to **nil** (all other variables are inherited unchanged in the new process), which produces the function in prime form. A similar message is applied to *verte*, with its environment variable *phase* set to $-\pi/2$, which creates the process *jaune*, which produces the inversion (since it inherits *sense* = **nil**). Last, *jaune* is instructed to create *orange*, which produces the retrograde inversion.

We see that every process in Formes has a generative potential, one from which can be derived other genetically related formes. It is in this sense that models of musical knowledge can be stated and then subjected to structured elaboration to a higher purpose.

Of course, one can characterize any program—in fact, any algorithm—as a model of some kind of knowledge. But if the knowledge is not available outside the context of its program, it cannot be built upon. The goal of Formes is to provide a system that is not just resistant to complexity saturation, but—as we have seen—is capable of absorbing new knowledge and relating it to models developed previously. The CHANT group wants libraries of successful models to be available as starting points for further exploration.

This requires a higher-level discipline than just object-oriented programming can solve. The authors of Formes have expressed this discipline as a number of rules for programmers.

- **Generality**—models must be dependent as little as possible upon such things as programming language and synthesis technique.
- **Universality**—models should be conveyed using universal concepts.
- **Compatibility**—models must be easy to integrate with each other.
- **Hierarchy**—complex rules should be developed from simpler ones.
- **Derivability**—models must be able to inherit attributes from each other.
- **Ease**—the bottom line and consequence of the above criteria is that the resulting system must be easy to use.

At this point, Formes itself seems to fall down on the generality criterion, at least as far as its forms of output, since it is so far totally devoted to CHANT synthesis. It has succeeded quite well on the criterion of hierarchy. Ordinarily, when using systems like Music N with a composition language like PLA, there is a weak link in the expressivity of the rules of musical performance, because the tendency is to push all synthesis-related issues into Music N and all composition-related issues into PLA, leaving performance interpretation as an orphan in the middle. The CHANT-Formes axis makes possible a smooth continuum from the most basic issues of synthesis, through the regions of performance practice, and on to the higher realms of compositional algorithms. This also means that Formes is not a synthesis-independent programming discipline, but assumes that the output is for CHANT. One could use it with some other synthesis technique that can be similarly driven by time functions, but it would be beyond its scope to use it to drive event-oriented systems.

21.6 Automatic Composition Generating Systems

Systems in this section can be divided into three groups. A generative system can be an *automaton*—a program that provides a built-in model of the compositional process that is sufficiently detailed that it can produce compositions with little or no guidance from the user. Or it may be a *toolkit*—a set of operations embedded within a programming language with no supplied generative algorithm, but with the expectation that one is to be provided by the composer/programmer. Or, it may be an *amanuensis*—a programming language that provides a generative algorithm along with means of modifying or replacing the built-in techniques.

Koenig's Project I and Project II obviously belong in this section, but their brief discussion earlier in this chapter will have to suffice.

21.6.1 MUSICOMP

The granddaddy of all programming systems for automatic music generation is MUSICOMP, written in the late 1950s and early 1960s by Robert Baker and Lejaren Hiller [Hiller 1966a, Hiller 1970a]. (Another system by the same name, which appears to have had nothing to do with Baker's work, was developed by the National Research Council of Canada in the early 1970s [Tanner 1972a].) Hiller used this system to produce several compositions which followed along the lines established by his *Illiac Suite* [Hiller 1964a].

MUSICOMP consisted of a collection of Illiac machine-language (and perhaps FORTRAN) subroutines. Again, we see the familiar generator/modifier/selector approach at work that we saw in the discussion of Hiller and Isaacson's work in the section on compositional algorithms.

Generation was provided by a core of stochastic procedures for developing melodic and rhythmic figures, such as uniform random selection, weighted selection, and Markov-chain techniques. Modification techniques included facilities for serial manipulations, such as the four geometric transforms and certain kinds of permutations. Selection rules included some derived from his work of encoding common-practice melodic/harmonic usages. Musical material was stratified into hierarchies of phrases, sections, and works.

This system was a toolkit, in that a composer working with this system was expected to supply a program that would thread the subroutines together in an appropriate way for the composition being programmed.

Any additional capabilities of the resulting program had to be supplied by the composer/programmer. The author's expectations were that as the system was used, additional routines would be accumulated, and if well integrated, would allow the system to grow. Their work has continued along the same lines, though one gathers that the initial framework of MUSICOMP has been left behind [Hiller 1970a].

21.6.2 POD

POD, like SSSP, represents a unique approach to structuring composition that is useful for this discussion. The POD system is a suite of programs developed by Barry Truax at Simon Fraser University in Vancouver, Canada. It is derived from his work at the Institute for Sonology in Utrecht in the early 1970s [Truax 1977a]. Truax uses standard signal processing models for sound material, such as FM synthesis [Chowning 1973a] and granular synthesis. A collection of more-or-less standard synthesis techniques are embedded within a parameterized random selection compositional system. An ostensible aim of the system is to provide a model of the compositional process much like Koenig's. Recalling the continuum I proposed, which placed automatic composition on one side and manual composition on the other, Truax's system covers a broader area of the continuum than either Projects I or II. POD has the ability to shift the burden of compositional selection dynamically from the machine to the user within a certain range, based on the capacity of the composer progressively to assert command through increasing skill and knowledge.

The focus of the compositional process is the specification of functions of time that act as moving random selection ranges and density functions for such parameters as pitch, timbre, vertical density, amplitude, and spatial location. The specific data for each event within these "tendency masks" are determined by a Poisson random distribution function. All parameters come with initial defaults, so that a composer can begin to get aural feedback on questions of compositional structure very quickly. Contrast this to Music N, where the compositional process must be built up from basic operations on signals, a tedious and error-prone procedure. On the plus side, the user is liberated from laborious precompositional strategising, and is free to concentrate on structural design. Truax justifies his method as follows: "The POD system incorporates strong, specialized strategies for both synthesis and composition, hence its limitations and its potential. These strategies are in recognition of the fact that most composer-users do not possess the detailed numerical knowledge required to use a generalized system effectively, and yet they are capable of quickly judging the well-formedness of acoustic results, and learning control strategies to modify results when the feedback time is sufficiently short. The strong, specialized program, then, allows the composer to work within a system already structured at every level in a manner conducive to his activity, instead of requiring such a structure to be imposed by every user on a basic, generalized facility" [Truax 1977a].

Strong, specialized programs do allow users to get started quickly, but usually become stumbling blocks quickly too. Ultimately the aesthetic/philosophical underpinnings of any specialized approach will channel—and therefore limit—one's compositional choices unless the system provides a graceful transition to a more general environment. Granting this, Truax still maintains that "the use of specialized approaches (where needed) does not preclude use of more general purpose models for tasks where they are appropriate, whereas the converse does not seem to me to be true" [Truax 1987a].

More recently, Truax has described a system for the DMX-1000 programmable digital synthesizer [Truax 1985a]. It provides general utilities for score and sound object specification and editing. The facilities of the earlier POD system are available as specialized composition programs whose output can be subsequently manipulated by general utilities [Truax 1985a].

21.6.3 Flavors Band

Christopher Fry has developed two systems for the automatic generation of improvisatory-style music. Written at the MIT Experimental Music Studio, his first system is very reminiscent of Koenig's and Truax's work, but with the difference that the base language is LISP, and the style of the output is cast in terms of jazz [Fry 1980b].

His later work, Flavors Band, was a toolkit that presented the user with the means of constructing networks of interacting compositional structuring elements called *phrase processors*. These are LISP routines that act within a processlike discipline and can be linked together. A piece (or a category of composition) is described by its network and by the data supplied for is operation. The bottoms of such tree-structured networks are usually note generators; above them are phrase modifiers, and phrase processors at higher levels affect the flow of execution of lower elements.

Again, we see the generate/modify/select method. The fundamental generator is the *notes* processor, which, like its Music N counterpart, specifies begin time, duration, and pitch. There is a way to attach various diatonic and chromatic scales and modes to note generators to constrain their output. It generates one event per note produced.

Some of the phrase modifiers are **coerce-into-scale**, **transpose**, **harmonize**, and **context-mapper**. Some of the flow control processors are **concat**, **repeat**, **coerce-time**, **gate**, **invert**, **filter**, and **merge**. One can create arbitrary phrase processors that resemble the modules of an analog synthesizer. One can also program any desired phrase processor in LISP.

Working libraries can be constructed of previously made compositional choices that can be consulted to guide later choices. This is an important feature because it makes it possible to generate compositions with homomorphic identity.

21.6.4 MC

In his 1985 MS thesis, Daniel Scheidt presented prototype elements of a generative system for music composition [Scheidt 1985a]. His abstract describes the work as "The design and implementation of a software package capable of generating original music compositions. The system's compositional model is based on feedback-driven parallel processes which cooperatively interact toward the creation of coherent musical structures. The feedback mechanism is based on an analysis/synthesis paradigm in which domain-specific algorithms are applied to distinct musical components. The system allows the user/composer to supply initial musical information which is used by the generative processes as the basis of a composition. The compositional model provided can be extended through the addition of new analysis/synthesis routines and processes in order to meet the goals of a wide range of compositional approaches." Scheidt states that the long-range goal of this work is the development of a *composer's apprentice* (or amanuensis, in terms of the definition given above), that is, a program that is capable of learning musical skills through observing and analyzing the behavior of musicians and composers. It is not clear that this is a system that learns, because—for one thing—new rules of analysis and synthesis are not abstracted by the process. It does adapt, but only on the basis of precoded rules. But Scheidt has succeeded in implementing an interesting analysis/synthesis paradigm, putting human-produced music into the compositional loop as a model.

21.6.5 Musamaton Revisited

As synthesizers and personal computers become more affordable, and their interconnection with MIDI has become possible, a market has opened up for software to control this new resource. Software developers initially focused on supplying backward-looking tools that were typically built upon such stock metaphors as the multitrack tape recorder into which one could record performances and then play them back. Ideas reminiscent of the old analog sequencer were also in evidence. Shortly, facilities for editing MIDI data became available, and "voice librarians"—programs that facilitate adjusting acoustical parameters controlling synthesis—began to appear.

It was only later that vendors and their public began to realize the algorithmic compositional possibilities inherent in this combination of hardware. Commercial software began to appear that combined the performance capabilities of systems like GROOVE with compositional algorithms like Flavors Band and MC to produce working, affordable versions of performance/composition processing systems reminiscent of Joseph Schillinger's prophetic idea of the Musamaton.

Laurie Spiegel's *Music Mouse* is an early example of this genre. Her program provides a fixed palette of prototypical rhythmic structures, scales, and modes, which the operator can combine and traverse linearly, using a track-ball or mouse pointing device. When played polyphonically, the result is vaguely reminiscent of *fauxbourdon*. The pointing device controls the location of points of intersection of the x and y axis, which are used to control pitch and tempo, respectively. This can be compared to the compositional algorithms described in [Mathews 1965a], where prototypical continuous functions of time are quantized in pitch and discretized in time by a class of other functions controlling scale and rhythm in order to achieve a class of related melodies. Spiegel was an active member of Mathews's GROOVE project in the early 1970s, so this should not be surprising.

Other examples of this genre are *M* by Joel Chadabe and *Jam Factory*, written by David Zicarelli, [Zicarelli 1986a]. *Jam Factory* somewhat resembles MC, as it implements a performance analysis/synthesis loop, but *Jam Factory*'s paradigm is based on Markov-chain techniques. A player's performance is captured and analyzed into first-order through fourth-order Markov transition tables. The Markov order number is a measure of how many preceding notes of the captured performance are considered in deducing the probability of the next note. It is unlike MC in that it does not implement a programming language interface; thus it is mostly a composing automation.

21.7 Availability

It is remarkable how few of the languages and systems documented above are generally available. Some of the early work is obsolete because the computer systems employed no longer exist. This is the fate of MUSICOMP and GROOVE. Competition from other languages has done in some of them: the Music IV and Music V programs have been largely supplanted by their variants, such as cmusic. Because of the availability of the Systems Concepts synthesizer, perhaps MUS10 was not considered worth the effort to port from the SAIL DEC PDP-10, where it was written, to the subsequent Foonly computer now used by CCRMA. Languages such as PLAY have presumably evolved beyond their original specifications and no longer exist in their documented forms. Many languages become dead tongues when their implementors move on to other places or projects and cease supporting them. This has been the fate of MUSBOX. In some cases, special languages or equipment form the basis of a system, which makes them generally unavailable. FMX is useless unless you have an ASP—likewise 4XY, unless you have a 4X. This is also the trouble with PLA, since it is written in SAIL, which is itself a wonderful, though terminally ill, language being kept alive by the Herculean efforts of Bill Schottstaedt. In other cases, the synthesizers the languages were written for have become obsolete, which is the fate of GROOVE, PLAY, 4CED, and Buxton's SSSP software. (But see [Free 1986a] for a discussion of their attempts to revive Buxton's work for more modern architectures.)

Of the languages in existence at the publication time of this article, Moxie and Moxc are generally available, as is Player, HMSL, and FORMULA (written in FORTH). FORMES, with versions written in VLISP and LeLisp, is easily ported, and versions of CHANT exist in FORTRAN, SAIL, C, and also for various array processors, synthesizers, and DSP boards. Other systems that are available in theory include Truax's POD systems, Smith's SCORE (written in FORTRAN F4), ASHTON (likewise in FORTRAN), Moore's cmusic, and Vercoe's Csound.

21.8 The Myth of the Composer's Amanuensis

From the foregoing examples, it is evident that we are on the edge of a historically important new domain of music-making, stimulated by the economics and availability of home computers and synthesizers. This subject warrants careful attention because of its potential significance to music. The projected scope and importance of this new technology on music can be gauged by recalling the impact of the previous technological revolution of comparable magnitude: the introduction of recording.

Recording technology had a profound and sustained impact on the economy of music, and upon musical aesthetics. In almost all areas, recording has come to dominate the music-making process to such an extent that making records (and more recently, music videos) has become the principal creative outlet of most musicians. But once made, a recording is the same forever. If even "perfect" performances wear thin after too many literal repetitions, lesser performances quickly become utterly unbearable. In classical recording, only those capable of rendering flawless performances are commercially successful, regardless of their artistic depth. In popular music, the Top-40 format evolved to mitigate the deadening effect of literal repetition. Because the recording now stands between the artist and the listener, record makers—recording engineers and marketing executives—have become the arbiters of taste, and this responsibility has been lifted from the hands of both the musicians and the listening public, who are now coached on what to produce and what to expect, respectively. Live performance is now often merely a spectacle staged to promote record sales [Atali 1985a].

A tantalizing analysis of the future is to imagine that the computer/synthesizer explosion currently in progress will reverse this, putting potentially sophisticated and easy-to-use compositional tools in the hands of everyone who wants them. My theory is that the lure of reproduction—of hearing Glenn Gould play the *Goldberg Variations* for the five hundredth time—will wain as a cultural magnet when we discover how much *fun* making music can be when an intelligent instrument appears capable of meeting us halfway. I believe it was in a similar spirit that Max Mathews said, "The intelligent instruments that already exist promise a new age of communication in which the attention of musicians can be on their inner messages. Musicians need not worry as to whether the instrument will be powerful enough to represent the message. They need not worry whether they will be virtuosic enough to play the music. These concerns can be left to the instrument itself [Roads 1985a].

It is very easy to have strong positive or negative feelings about such a development. For instance, what becomes of virtuosity in such a case—or even musicianship? As one composer groused, "The next concern that can be left to these instruments is the synthesis of the very 'inner messages' themselves, and then we can all let our computers listen to this music while we go out for a drink" [Anonymous 1986a].

Mathews' words were evidently written in very much the same spirit as those of Kirnberger in elucidating his musical dice game. "Kirnberger's *Ever-Ready Minuet and Polonaise Composer*, is a symptom of 'galant' trivialization and popularization: the trivialization of music's ancient and honorable relation to number, and the popularization of the art of composition for the sake of a rising generation of middle-class amateurs—two developments that unmistakably spelled the beginning of a new age" [Helm 1966a]. As the example of *Würfelspiel* shows, this is not the first time that a radical shift to a broader aesthetic base has taken place. Can it be that *Würfelspiel* was the *Jam Factory* of its day; that all that has changed is that the automatons that implement it are microelectronic, rather than mechanical?

The answer is (with any luck) no. The avenues to music-making have been *broadened* by computer technology, not shortened. In fact, the avenues have been *lengthened* by virtue of the new domains of knowledge that are essential to the effective artistic control of this technology.

"What we really want, so we are told, is a musical data-entry system where composers need know nothing of the machine. But composers are expected to learn the rudiments of other instruments; why should the computer be different?" [Schottstaedt 1983a]. With new knowledge comes new ranges of choice. The thoughtful act of music composition is just as hard as it ever was. but this should not be daunting. Here is the good news: "No matter what your level of musical sophistication, you can write a program to mimic the way you *intend* to treat given material. Effectively then, you can ask the computer what *your* music would be like if you did such and such. There has never been so powerful an instructor or decision-making tool for helping you determine which methods have promise and which do not" [Jaxitron 1985a].

The domain of compositional control has certainly been extended by computer technology down into the microstructure of sound and up into the macrostructure of musical composition. However, I believe this survey demonstrates that no one has yet figured out how to harness this new expressive power effectively. We observe instead that research is preoccupied with identifying and refining suitable computable fomalisms for music. The easy-to-formalize parts of the problem are at least being addressed, but there is no particular standardization emerging on how to do even such basic things as machine representation of common practice music. Even if these problems are solved, the ultimate task, that of defining what we want to hear—Mathews' *inner messages*—will still be up to us, and is decidedly nonformalistic.

There is no doubt that this technology is already facilitating composing and music-making. A personal computer with synthesizer and printer is now quite standard for personal music studios. This means that, in theory, many of the research topics described in this chapter are now within the reach of anyone with moderate resources. However, it seems rare to find either manufacturers with the willingness or musicians with the curiosity to develop systems of a general enough nature actually to pursue the inherent musical promise. Evidence of this is the popular MIDI specification, which implements an extremely normative conception of music [Loy 1985b]. The need for informed practitioners has never been greater.

Just as the fantasy of a thinking automaton has led the field of AI to some striking results—but not the production of a thinking automaton—so the fantasy of the composer's amanuensis has produced some important knowledge about music, but has not—and probably will not—yield a viable simplification of the art of composition. Quite the opposite! The fact that computers can only deal with formal systems is a blessing and a curse. The curse is that formalization of music is very difficult; attempts to do so often yield very normative conceptions of music. The blessing is that this approach to music can be the liberation from intellectual constraints of all kinds, and can serve to awaken the voice of the Muse slumbering in the midst of all this technology.

Acknowledgments

I wish to thank Margaret Mikulska for the translation of [Gerigk 1936a] from the German. I also wish to thank my numerous and sometimes caustic reviewers, some of whom are subjects of discussion in these pages, and who yet were kind enough to correct my numerous failures of understanding and lapses of scholarship. I hope they feel their efforts have been sufficiently rewarded.

Notes

1. Since we are restricted to positive integers for both inputs and outputs we must use integer division, which yields a whole-number remainder. E.g., 12 divided by 9 is 1 with a remainder of 3; 9 divided by 12 is 0 with a remainder of 9.

2. For a 1-vowel text there are 3 possible one-note "melodies," for a two-vowel text there are 3^2 melodies of two notes, and for an N-vowel text there are 3^N melodies. Thus, the number of possible melodies grows explosively for longer texts. He takes pain to suggest to anyone who should feel his system to be too constraining that they expand it by adding another line of vowels under the notes with a different starting point, effectively doubling the number of choices!

3. For instance, there is a general avoidance of major and minor triads, use of leading tones, octave repetition of a pitch, and intervalic repetition; in general, all the trappings of tonal expectation are to be avoided.

4. Gabor's *quantum of information* can be thought of as a sample amplitude of a channel signal of a phase vocoder, whether the channel be broad or narrow [Dolson 1987a]. A high resolution in time implies a low resolution in frequency, and a high resolution in frequency implies a low resolution in time. Ideally, in a properly implemented phase vocoder the sum of the sampling rates necessary for all channels is equal to the sampling rate necessary for the signal before it is divided among frequency channels, or after the channels have been combined to recreate the signal. Ideally, a signal of bandwidth B can be represented by $2B$ samples per second, whether it is taken as a whole (high time resolution) or properly divided into a few or many frequency bands (greater frequency resolution). In his original paper, Gabor cites experimental data of Bürk, Kotowski, and Lichte, published in 1935, and of Shower and Biddulph, published in 1931, which he interprets as indicating that the accuracy of the joint time and frequency resolution of the ear corresponds to about one sample, regardless of channel width [Pierce 1987a].

5. While this is true for the *Illiac Suite*, it is not necessarily true of Hiller's later collaborations.

6. That is to say, a digital recording.

7. Fidelity is only meaningful in iconic representations.

8. MIDI stands for the *Musical Instrument Digital Interface*, which is a standard means of communicating performance parameters among commercial synthesizers.

9. The Nyquist theorem states that one must sample at a minimum of twice the rate of the highest frequency one desires to capture or reproduce. Since human hearing ranges up to 20 kHz, this implies a rate of better than 40 kHz. In practice, rates both less and more than that are sometimes used with the expected consequences of enhanced or reduced frequency response. Lower rates are often used for doing test runs of scores to get the bugs out because fewer samples per second must be computed.

10. Vercoe's Csound program is not to be confused with a soundfile system for UNIX, likewise called *csound*, which this author wrote in 1982 [Loy 1982a].

11. A *real-time* system is one that computes sound samples at—or faster than—the audio sampling rate at which they are played back. That is, the *compute ratio*, the ratio of the time

it takes to compute versus the time it takes to play back, is less than 1. Music N languages generally do not run in real time, but store their waveforms on a disk, for later playback in real time.

12. If anything, one would expect that chopping up musical material without regard to its underlying metrical structure would produce a very disjointed effect. All the more astonishing then is the fact that, in his hands, it produces very convincing and coherent musical lines. Besides his skill, we can note that the material he cuts up is prerecorded, and therefore contains characteristic human musical gestures, which serves to rebind the musical fragments. Thus, he bypasses the problem by imbedding the human touch in the material.

13. The FOF technique is simply the multiplication of a decaying exponential function by a sinusoid as described by

$$s(k) = Ge^{-\alpha k} \sin(\omega_c k + \phi),$$

where ω_c is the center pulsation, and α controls the -6dB bandwidth of the skirts of the formant peak. It produces a power spectrum that is very close to a two-pole resonator.

14. The *interrupt response* time is how long it takes the processor to switch its context to service the interrupt, it is not to be confused with the *service response* time, which is the time it takes to execute the service code and restore the interrupted context. A typical microprocessor will have an interrupt response time in the range of a few microseconds; of course, service response time depends upon the complexity of the response.

15. One can use interrupt prioritizing schemes only as a way to decide the order in which the events must be serviced, but not, e.g., to filter out interrupts.

References

[Abboutt 1981a] Curtis Abbott, "The 4CED program," *CMJ* 5(1) (1981).

[Abbott 1982a] Curtis Abbott, "System level software for the Lucasfilm ASP system," Technical memorandum #58, Lucasfilm Ltd., San Rafael, CA (1982).

[Ames 1982a] Charles Ames, "*Protocol*: motivation, design, and production of a composition for solo piano," *Interface* 2(11) (1982).

[Ames 1982b] Charles Ames, "Crystals: recursive structures in automated composition," *CMJ* 6(3) (Fall 1982).

[Ames 1983a] Charles Ames, "Stylistic automata in *Gradient*," *CMJ* 7(4) (Winter 1983).

[Ames 1985a] Charles Ames, "The ASHTON score-transcription utility," *Interface* 14 (1985).

[Ames 1987a] Charles Ames, "Automated composition in retrospect," *Leonardo* 20(2) (1987).

[Anderson 1986a] David P. Anderson and Ron Kuivila, "A model of real-time computation for computer music," *Proc. ICMC*, San Francisco, CMA (1986).

[Anonymous 1986a] Anonymous, *private communication*, 1986.

[Apel 1961a] Willi Apel and Ralph T. Daniel, *The Harvard brief dictionary of music*, Harvard University Press, Cambridge (1961).

[Ashton 1970a] Alan Conway Ashton, "Electronics, music, and computers," Ph. D. dissertation, University of Utah (1970).

[Atali 1985a] Jaques Atali, *Noise—the political economy of music*, University of Minnesota Press, Minneapolis (1985).

[Backus 1978a] John Backus, "Can programming be liberated from the von Neumann style? a functional style and its algebra of programs," *Communications of the ACM* 21(8) (August 1978).

[Ban 1986a] A. Ban and J. A. Makowsky, "MUSICIAN—a music processing and synthesis system," Department of Computer Science technical report 435, Israel Institute of Technology, Haifa, Israel (1986).

[Barlow 1987a] Clarence Barlow, "Two essays on theory," *CMJ* 11(1) (1987).

[Barzun 1969a] Jaques Barzun, *Berlioz and the romantic century*, 3rd. edition, 2 volumes. New York, 1969.

[Bastiaans 1980a] M. Bastiaans, "Gabor's expansion of a signal into Gaussian elementary signals," *Proceedings of the IEEE* 68 (1980).

[Berg 1979a] Paul Berg, "PILE—a language for sound synthesis," *CMJ* 3(1) (March 1979).

[Berg 1980a] Paul Berg, Robert Rowe, and David Theriault, "SSP and sound description," *CMJ* 4(1) (Spring 1980).

[Boynton 1986a] Lee Boynton, Pierre Lavoie, Yann Orlarey, Camilo Rueda, and David Wessel, "MIDI-LISP, a LISP-based music programming environment for the Macintosh," *Proc. ICMC*, San Francisco, CMA (1986).

[Bussoni 1962a] Ferruccio Bussoni, "Sketch for a new esthetic of music," in *Three classics in the aesthetics of music*, Da Capo Press, New York (1962).

[Buxton 1978a] William Buxton, William Reeves, Ronald Baeker, and Leslie Mezei, "The use of hierarchy and instance in a data structure for computer music," *CMJ* 2(4) (1978).

[Buxton 1979a] W. Buxton, R. Sniderman, W. Reeves, S. Patel, and R. Baecker, "The evolution of the SSSP score-editing tools," *CMJ* 3(4) (1979).

[Buxton 1980a] W. Buxton, "A tutorial introduction to SCED," draft manuscript (1980).

[Byrd 1984a] D. Byrd, "Music notation by computer," Ph. D. dissertátion, Indiana University Department of Computer Science, Bloomington (1984).

[Cage 1961a] John Cage, *Silence*, The MIT Press, Cambridge, Massachusetts (1961).

[Cage 1969a] John Cage, *Notations*, Something Else Press, New York (1969).

[Cassiodorus 1950a] Cassiodorus, "Institutiones II, iii," in *Source readings in music history*, ed. O. Strunk, W. W. Norton & Co, Inc., New York (1950). Footnote 6.

[Chadabe 1978a] Joel Chadabe and Roger Meyers, "An introduction to the Play program," *CMJ* 2(1) (July 1978).

[Chadabe 1984a] Joel Chadabe, "Interactive composing: an overview," *CMJ* 8(1) (Spring 1984).

[Chailloux 1978a] J. Chailloux, "VLISP 10.3, manuel de référence," *Report RT 16-78*, Vincennes, Université de Paris 8 (1978).

[Chowning 1973a] John Chowning, "The synthesis of complex audio spectra by means of frequency modulation," *Journal of the Audio Engineering Society* 21(7) (1973).

[Clarlow 1980a] Clarlow, "Bus journey to Parametron," *Die Feedback Papers*, Köln (1980).

[Clynes 1984a] Manfred Clynes, "Secrets of life in music," *Proc. ICMC*, San Francisco, CMA (1984).

[Cointe 1983a] Pierre Cointe and Xavier Rodet, *Formes: a new object-language for managing a hierarchy of events*, IRCAM, Paris (1983).

[Cointe 1985a] Pierre Cointe, "Formes par l'exemple," draft manuscript, IRCAM, Paris (1985).

[Collinge 1980a] D. Collinge, *The Moxie user's guide*, School of Music, University of Victoria, Victoria, B. C., Canada (1980).

[Collinge 1984a] Doug J. Collinge, "Moxie: a language for computer music performance," *Proc. ICMC*, San Francisco, CMA (1984).

[Cope 1987a] David Cope, "An expert system for computer-assisted composition," *Computer Music Journal* 11(4) (1987).

[Dannenberg 1984a] Roger B. Dannenberg, "Arctic: a functional language for real-time control," *Conference Record of the 1984 ACM Symposium on LISP and Functional Programming* (August 1984).

[Dannenberg 1986a] Roger Dannenberg, "The CMU MIDI toolkit," *Proc. ICMC*, San Francisco, CMA (1986).

[D'Arezzo 1955a] Guido D'Arezzo, "Guidonis Aretini Micrologus," in *Corpus scriptorum de musica IV*, ed. Jos. Smits van Waesberghe, American Institute of Musicology, Rome (1955).

[David 1958a] E. E. David, Jr., M. V. Mathews, and H. S. McDonald, "Description and results of experiments with speech using digital computer simulation," *Proceedings of the 1958 National Electronics Conference* (1958).

[Davison 1964a] Archibald T. Davison and Willi Apel, *Historical anthology of music*, Harvard University Press, Cambridge, Massachusetts (1964).

[Decker 1985a] Shawn L. Decker and Gary S. Kendall, "A unified approach to the editing of time-ordered events," *Proc. ICMC*, San Francisco, CMA (1985).

[Desain 1986a] Peter Desain, "Graphical programming in computer music, a proposal," *Proc. ICMC*, San Francisco, CMA (1986).

[Dewdney 1987a] A. K. Dewdney, "Computer Recreations," *Scientific American* 256(4) (April 1987).

[Dolson 1987a] Mark Dolson, "A tutorial introduction to the phase vocoder," *CMJ* 10(4) (1987).

[Erickson 1975a] R. Erickson, "The DARMS project: a status report," *Computers and the Humanities* 7(2) (1975).

[Favreau 1986a] E. Favreau, M. Fingerhut, O. Koechlin, P. Potacsek, M. Puckette, and R. Rowe, "Software developments for the 4X real-time synthesizer," *Proc. ICMC*, San Francisco, CMA (1986).

[Free 1986a] John Free, Paul Vytas, and William Buxton, "Whatever happened to SSSP?," *Proc. ICMC* (1986).

[Fry 1980a] Christopher Fry, *YAMIL reference manual*, MIT Experimental Music Studio, Cambridge, Massachusetts (1980).

[Fry 1980b] C. Fry, "Computer improvisation," *CMJ* 4(3) (Fall 1980).

[Fux 1943a] J. J. Fux, *Steps to Parnassus (Gradus ad Parnassum)*, W. W. Norton & Co, Inc., New York (1943).

[Gabor 1947a] D. Gabor, "Acoustical quanta and the theory of hearing," *Nature* 159(4044) (1947).

[Gerigk 1936a] H. Gerigk, "Wuerfelmusik," *Neue Zeitschrift für Musik* (1936).

[Gold 1980a] M. Gold, J. Stautner, and S. Haflich, *An introduction to SCOT*, MIT Experimental Music Studio, Cambridge (1980).

[Green 1980a] M. Green, "PROD: A grammar-based computer composition program," *Proc. ICMC*, San Francisco, CMA (1980).

[Gross 1981a] Dorothy Gross, "A computer-assisted music course," *Computing in the humanities*, Lexington, Massachusetts, D. C. Heath & Co. (1981).

[Grout 1980a] Donald Jay Grout, *A history of Western music*, Norton, New York (1980).

[Hamel 1976a] Peter Michael Hamel, *Through music to the self*, Shambhala Publications Inc., Boulder (1976).

[Helm 1966a] E. Eugene Helm, "Six random measures of C.P.E. Bach," *Journal of Music Theory* 10(1) (Spring 1966).

[Hiller 1959a] Lejaren Hiller and Leonard Isaacson, *Experimental music*, McGraw-Hill Book Company, Inc., New York (1959).

[Hiller 1964a] Lejaren Hiller and Robert Baker, "*Computer Contata*: a study of compositional method," *Perspectives of New Music* 3(1) (1964).

[Hiller 1966a] Lejaren Hiller, Antonio Leal, and Robert A. Baker, "Revised MUSICOMP manual," Technical Report 13, University of Illinois, School of Music, Experimental Music Studio (1966).

[Hiller 1970a] Lejaren Hiller, "Music composed with computers," in *The computer and music*, ed. Harry B. Lincoln, Cornell University Press, Ithaca (1970).

[Holtzman 1981a] S. R. Holtzman, "Using generative grammars for music composition," *CMJ* 5(1) (Spring 1981).

[Howe 1975a] Hubert Howe, *Electronic music synthesis*, W. W. Norton, New York (1975).

[Jaxitron 1985a] Jaxitron, *Cybernetic music*, Tab Books Inc., Blue Ridge Summit, PA (1985).

[Johnson 1975a] S. C. Johnson, "Yacc—Yet Another Compiler-Compiler," Comp. Sci. Tech. Rep. No. 32, Bell Laboratories, Murray Hill, New Jersey (July 1975).

[Johnson 1978a] S. C. Johnson, "A portable compiler: theory and practice," *Proc. 5th ACM Symp. on Principles of Programming Languages* (January 1978).

[Kaegi 1986a] Werner Kaegi, "The MIDIM language and its VOSIM Interpretation," *Interface*, Lisse 15(2–4), Swets & Zeitlinger B. B. (1986).

[Kernighan 1978a] B. W. Kernighan and D. M. Ritchie, *The C programming language*, Prentice-Hall, Englewood Cliffs, New Jersey (1978).

[Kirchmeyer 1963a] Helmut Kirchmeyer, "On the historical constitution of a rationalistic music," *Die Reihe* 8 (1963).

[Knuth 1973a] Donald E. Knuth, *The art of computer programming volume 1—fundamental algorithms*, Addison-Wesley, Reading, Massachusetts (1973).

[Köchel 1935a] L. von Köchel, *Works of Mozart*, Sixth edition, 1935.

[Koenig 1970a] G. M. Koenig, "Project One," *Electronic Music Reports 2*, Utrecht, Institute of Sonology (1970).

[Koenig 1970b] G. M. Koenig, "Project Two," *Electronic Music Reports 3*, Utrecht, Institute of Sonology (1970).

[Koenig 1979a] Gotfried M. Koenig, *Protocol*, Institute of Sonology, University of Utrecht (1979).

[Kuipers 1986a] Pieter Kuipers, "CANON: a system for the description of musical patterns," *Interface*, Lisse 15(2–4), Swets & Zeitlinger B. B. (1986).

[Kuivila 1986a] Ron Kuivila and David P. Anderson, "Timing accuracy and response time in interactive systems," *Proc. ICMC*, San Francisco, CMA (1986).

[Langer 1948a] Susan Langer, *Philosophy in a new key*, New American Library, New York (1948).

[Langston 1986a] Peter Langston, "(201) 644-2332—Eedie & Eddie on the Wire, An Experiment in Music Generation," *Proceedings of the Usenix Conference* (1986).

[Lansky 1986a] Paul Lansky, *private communication*, 1986.

[Lerdahl 1983a] Fred Lerdahl and Ray Jackendoff, *A generative theory of tonal music*, The MIT Press, Cambridge (1983).

[Longyear 1969a] Rey M. Longyear, *Nineteenth-century romanticism in music*, Prentice Hall, Englewood Cliffs, New Jersey (1969).

[Loy 1981a] D. Gareth Loy, "Notes on the implementation of MUSBOX: a compiler for the Systems Concepts digital synthesizer," *CMJ* 5(1) (Spring 1981).

[Loy 1982a] Gareth Loy, "A sound file system for UNIX," *Proc. ICMC*, San Francisco, CMA (1982).

[Loy 1985a] Gareth Loy and Curtis Abbott, "Programming languages for computer music synthesis, performance, and composition," *ACM Computing Surveys* 17(2) (1985).

[Loy 1985b] Gareth Loy, "Musicians make a standard: the MIDI phenomenon," *CMJ* 9(4) (1985).

[Loy 1986a] Gareth Loy, "Player," technical memorandum, Center for Music Experiment, UCSD, La Jolla (1986).

[Mathews 1961a] Max V. Mathews, "An acoustical compiler for music and psychological stimuli," *Bell System Technical Journal 40* (1961).

[Mathews 1963a] M. V. Mathews, "The digital computer as a musical instrument," *Science* 142 (1963).

[Mathews 1965a] Max V. Mathews, "Pitch quantizing for computer music," *Journal of the Acoustical Society of America* 38 (1965).

[Mathews 1968a] M. V. Mathews and L. Rosler, "Graphical language for the scores of computer-generated sounds," *Perspectives of New Music* 6(2) (1968).

[Mathews 1969a] Max V. Mathews, Joan E. Miller, F. R. Moore, J. R. Pierce, and J. C. Risset, *The technology of computer music*, The MIT Press, Cambridge, Massachusetts (1969).

[Mathews 1970a] Max V. Mathews and F. R. Moore, "GROOVE—a program to compose, store, and edit functions of time," *Communications of the ACM* 13(12) (1970).

[McNabb 1981a] Michael McNabb, "Dreamsong: the composition," *CMJ* 5(4) (Winter 1981).

[Meyer 1956a] Leonard B. Meyer, *Emotion and meaning in music*, University of Chicago Press, Chicago (1956).

[Mies 1925a] Paul Mies, "B-A-C-H, stillistisches und statistisches," *Zeitschrift für Musik* XCI(3) (1925).

[Moore 1982a] F. Richard Moore, "The Computer Audio Research Laboratory at UCSD," *CMJ* 6(1) (Spring 1982).

[Moore 1985a] F. Richard Moore, Gareth Loy, and Mark Dolson, "The CARL startup kit," Users manual for the CARL software distribution (1985).

[Nelson 1977a] Gary Nelson, "MPL—a program library for musical data processing," *Creative Computing* (March–April, 1977).

[Orff 1967a] Carl Orff, *Gespräche mit Komponisten*, Züric, 1967.

[Pennycook 1985a] Bruce W. Pennycook, "Computer-music interfaces: a survey," *ACM Computing Surveys* 17(2) (1985).

[Perle 1981a] George Perle and Paul Lansky, *Serial composition and atonality*, University of California Press, Los Angeles (1981). Quotation from essay on "Twelve-Note Composition" in *Grove's dictionary*, sixth edition.

[Pierce 1983a] John R. Pierce, *The science of musical sound*, Scientific American Books, New York (1983).

[Pierce 1987a] John Pierce, *Private communication*, 1987.

[Potter 1971a] Gary Morton Potter, "The role of chance in contemporary music," Ph. D. dissertation, Indiana University (1971). Available through University Microfilms.

[Puckette 1986a] Miller Puckette, "Interprocess communication and timing in real-time computer music performance," *Proc. ICMC*, San Francisco, CMA (1986).

[Rahn 1980a] John Rahn, "On some computational models of music theory," *CMJ* 4(2) (Summer 1980).

[Reiser 1976a] John F. Reiser, "SAIL," Report No. STAN-CS-76-574, Stanford Artificial Intelligence Laboratory, Stanford University, Stanford, CA (1976).

[Reynolds 1986a] Roger Reynolds, "Musical production and related issues at CARL," *Proc. ICMC* (1986).

[Risset 1969a] J.-C. Risset, "An introductory catalogue of computer synthesized sounds," Bell Telephone Laboratories unpublished memorandum, Murray Hill, N. J. (1969).

[Roads 1978a] Curtis Roads, "Composing grammars," *CMA Reports*, San Francisco, CMA (1978).

[Roads 1985a] Curtis Roads, "Granular synthesis of sound," in *Foundations of computer music*, ed. Curtis Roads and John Strawn, The MIT Press, Cambridge, Massachusetts (1985).

[Roads 1985b] Curtis Roads, "Grammars as representations for music," in *Foundations of computer music*, ed. J. Strawn, The MIT Press, Boston, Massachusetts (1985).

[Roads 1985c] Curtis Roads, "Research in music and artificial intelligence," *ACM Computing Surveys* 17(2) (1985).

[Rodet 1984a] Xavier Rodet, Yves Potard, and Jean-Baptiste Barrière, "The CHANT project: from the synthesis of the singing voice to synthesis in general," *CMJ* 8(3) (Fall 1984).

[Rodet 1984b] Xavier Rodet and Pierre Cointe, "FORMES: composition and scheduling of processes," *CMJ* 8(3) (Fall 1984).

[Rodet 1987a] Xavier Rodet, *Private communication*, 1987.

[Rosenboom 1985a] David Rosenboom and Larry Polansky, "HMSL (Hierarchical Music Specification Language): a real-time environment for formal, perceptual and compositional experimentation," *Proc. ICMC*, San Francisco, CMA (1985).

[Santillana 1969a] Giorgio de Santillana and Hertha von Dechend, *Hamlet's mill*, David R. Godine, Boston (1969).

[Schaeffer 1952a] Pierre Schaeffer, *A la recherche d' une musique concrète*, Paris, 1952.

[Scheidt 1985a] Daniel J. Scheidt, "A prototype implementation of a generative mechanism for music composition," M.S. Thesis, Queen's University, Kingston, Ontario, Canada (1985).

[Schillinger 1948a] Joseph Schillinger, *The mathematical basis of the arts*, The Philosophical Library, New York (1948).

[Schillinger 1978a] Joseph Schillinger, *The Schillinger system of musical composition*, Da Capo Press, New York (1978).

[Scholes 1964a] Percy A. Scholes, *The concise Oxford dictionary of music*, Oxford University Press, London (1964).

[Schottstaedt 1983a] Bill Schottstaedt, "Pla: a composer's idea of a language," *CMJ* 7(1) (Spring 1983).

[Smith 1973a] Leland Smith, "Editing and printing music by computer," *Journal of Music Theory* 17(2) (1973).

[Smith 1976a] Leland Smith, "SCORE—a musician's approach to computer music," *Journal of the Audio Engineering Society* 20(1) (1976).

[Smoliar 1971a] Stephen W. Smoliar, "A parallel processing model of musical structures," Department of Computing and Information Science Report AI TR-242, Massachusetts Institute of Technology, Cambridge, Massachusetts (1971).

[Sundberg 1983a] Johan Sundberg, Anders Askenfelt, and Lars Fryden, "Musical performance: a synthesis-by-rule approach," *CMJ* 7(1) (Spring 1983).

[Sundberg 1986a] Anders Friberg, Johan Sundberg, "A Lisp environment for creating and applying rules for musical performance," *Proc. ICMC*, San Francisco, CMA (1986).

[Tanner 1972a] P. P. Tanner, "MUSICOMP, an experimental computer aid for the composition and production of music," ERB-869, Radio and Electrical Engineering Division, National Research Council of Canada (August 1972).

[Tenney 1969a] James Tenney, "Computer Music Experiences, 1961–1964," *Electronic Music Reports* 1(1) (1969).

[Tenney 1980a] James Tenney and Larry Polansky, "Hierarchical temporal gestalt perception in music: A metric space model," *Journal of Music Theory* 24(2) (1980).

[Tenney 1986a] James Tenney, *Meta + Hodos and META Meta + Hodos*, Frog Peak Music, Box 9911, Oakland (1986).

[Tovar 1976a] J. Tovar and L. Smith, "MUS10 Manual," unpublished, Center for Computer Research in Music and Acoustics, Stanford University (1976).

[Truax 1977a] Barry Truax, "The POD system of interactive composition programs," *CMJ* 1(3) (June 1977).

[Truax 1985a] Barry Truax, "The PODX system: interactive compositional software for the DMX-1000," *CMJ* 9(1) (Spring 1985).

[Truax 1987a] Barry Truax, *Private communication*, 1987.

[Vandenheede 1986a] Jan Vandenheede, "Musical experiments with Prolog II," *Proc. ICMC*, San Francisco, CMA (1986).

[Vercoe 1979a] B. Vercoe, *Music 11 reference manual*, M. I. T. Experimental Music Studio, Cambridge, Mass. (1979).

[Vercoe 1986a] Barry Vercoe, *Csound*, Experimental Music Studio, MIT (1986). Documentation about Csound is available from its author.

[Vinogradov 1954a] I. M. Vinogradov, *Elements of number theory*, Dover Publications, Inc. (1954). Translated from the Fifth Revised Edition by Saul Kravetz.

[Wenker 1972a] J. Wenker, "MUSTRAN II—an extended music translator," *Computers and the Humanities* 7(2) (1972).

[Xenakis 1955a] Iannis Xenakis, "The crisis of serial music," *Gravesaner Blätter* (1955).

[Xenakis 1971a] Iannis Xenakis, *Formalized music*, Indiana University Press, Bloomington (1971).

[Yavelow 1985a] Christopher Yavelow, "Music software for the Apple Macintosh," *CMJ* 9(3) (Fall 1985).

[Yavelow 1986a] Christopher Yavelow, "The impact of MIDI upon compositional methodology," *Proc. ICMC*, San Francisco, CMA (1986).

[Zicarelli 1986a] David Zicarelli and Joel Chadabe, "Jam Factory—MIDI music software for the Macintosh," user's manual, Intelligent Music, Albany, NY (1986).

Bibliography

This bibliography constitutes a snapshot of my working references at the moment of publication, and is not claimed to be comprehensive in any sense. Were this to be a definitive statement of what is in print, there would be glaring omissions, especially when broken into separate categories as it is. In addition, I am sure I have left out at least one paper or book that is dear to the heart and/or a constant reference guide to each and every reader. However, I trust that the length, if not the scope, of this bibliography speaks to the earnestness with which I pursued the relevant primary research areas. The intention here, as in the rest of this chapter, is not to be dogmatically comprehensive, but to suggest lines of pursuit.

The bibliography is in nine sections as follows: (1) general programming languages that have been discussed within the context of computer music language research; (2) music programming languages, construed loosely; (3) theory of programming and theory of music systems and languages; (4) documentation of works done with computers where the composer actually exposes the formal elements of the compositional process or describes a method; (5) automated composition; (6) realtime/interactive performance/composition theory and practice; (7) music theory; (8) music representation; (9) other, including psychoacoustics, digital signal processing, linguistics, computer aided instruction, artificial intelligence, etc., etc.

Many of the papers in the first three volumes of the *CMJ* are available in [Roads 1985a]. The reader's attention is directed in general to *Computer Music Journal, Interface, Leonardo*, and *Perspectives of New Music*. A special issue of the *ACM Computing Surveys* 17(3), 1985, was devoted to computer music. The *Proceedings* of the International Computer Music Conference are also recommended.

General Programming Languages

Curtis Abbott, "Machine tongues I," *CMJ* 2(1), pp. 4–5 (Jul 1978).

Curtis Abbott, "Machine tongues II," *CMJ* 2(2), pp. 4–6 (Sep 1978).

Curtis Abbott, "Machine tongues III," *CMJ* 2(3), pp. 7–10 (Dec 1978).

Curtis Abbott, "Machine tongues V," *CMJ* 3(2), pp. 6–11 (Jun 1979).

Lee Boynton, Pierre Lavoie, Yann Orlarey, Camilo Rueda, and David Wessel, "MIDI-LISP, a LISP-based music programming environment for the Macintosh," *Proc. ICMC*, San Francisco, CMA (1986).

J. Chailloux, "VLISP 10.3, manuel de référence," *Report RT 16-78*, Vincennes, Université de Paris 8 (1978).

L. Gilman and A. J. Rose, *APL—an interactive approach*, Wiley & Sons, New York (1976).

Ellis Horowitz, *Programming languages, a grand tour*, Computer Science Press, Rockville, MD (1987).

Jaxitron, *Cybernetic music*, Tab Books Inc., Blue Ridge Summit, PA (1985).

William A. Kornfeld, "Machine tongues VII: LISP," *CMJ* 4(2), pp. 6–12 (Sum 1980).

Glenn Krasner, "Machine tongues VIII: The design of a Smalltalk music system," *CMJ* 4(4), pp. 4–14 (Winter 1980).

David Levitt, "Machine tongues X: constraint languages," *CMJ* 8(1), pp. 9–21 (Spr 1984).

Henry Lieberman, "A preview of Act 1," *AI Memo 625*, Cambridge, Massachusetts, MIT Artificial Intelligence Laboratory (1980).

Henry Lieberman, "Machine tongues IX: object-oriented programming," *CMJ* 6(3), pp. 8–21 (Fall 1982).

Yann Orlarey, "MLOGO: un langage de programmation orienté composition musicale," *Proceedings of the International Computer Music Conference*, San Francisco, Computer Music Association (1984).

Yann Orlarey, "MLOGO—a MIDI composing environment for the Apple IIe," *Proc. ICMC*, San Francisco, CMA (1986).

C. Roads, "Machine tongues IV," *CMJ* 3(1), pp. 8–13 (Mar 1979).

C. Roads, "Machine tongues VI," *CMJ* 3(4), pp. 6–8 (Dec 1979).

Jan Vandenheede, "Musical experiments with Prolog II," *Proc. ICMC*, San Francisco, CMA (1986).

D. Weinreb and D. Moon, *Lisp machine manual*, Artificial Intelligence Laboratory, Cambridge, Massachusetts (1981).

Music Programming Languages and Systems

Curtis Abbott, "A software approach to interactive processing of musical sound," *CMJ* 2(1), pp. 19–23 (Jul 1978).

Curtis Abbott, "The 4CED program," *CMJ* 5(1), pp. 13–33 (Spr 1981).

A. Ban and J. A. Makowsky, "MUSICIAN—a music processing and synthesis system," Department of Computer Science technical report 435, Israel Institute of Technology, Haifa, Israel (1986).

Paul Berg, "PILE—a language for sound synthesis," *CMJ* 3(1), pp. 30–41 (Mar 1979).

Paul Berg, Robert Rowe, and David Theriault, "SSP and sound description," *CMJ* 4(1), pp. 25–35 (Spr 1980).

Pierre Boulez, Trevor Wishart, Denis Smalley, Bruce Pennycook, Mike McNabb, Bary Truax, Jonathan Harvey, and Tod Machover, *The language of electroacoustic music*, Macmillan Press (1986).

Lee Boynton, Pierre Lavoie, Yann Orlarey, Camilo Rueda, and David Wessel, "MIDI-LISP, a LISP-based music programming environment for the Macintosh," *Proc. ICMC*, San Francisco, CMA (1986).

Donald Byrd, "An integrated computer music software system," *CMJ* 1(2), pp. 55–60 (Apr 1977).

Joel Chadabe and Roger Meyers, "An Introduction to the Play program," *CMJ* 2(1), pp. 12–18 (Jul 1978).

Pierre Cointe and Xavier Rodet, *Formes: a new object-language for managing a hierarchy of events*, Institut de Recherche et de Coordination Acoustique-Musique, Paris (1983).

D. Collinge, *The Moxie user's guide*, School of Music, University of Victoria, Victoria, B.C., Canada (1980).

Doug J. Collinge, "Moxie: a language for computer music performance," *Proceedings of the International Computer Music Conference*, San Francisco, Computer Music Association (1984).

Roger Dannenberg, "The CMU MIDI toolkit," *Proc. ICMC*, San Francisco, CMA (1986).

Roger B. Dannenberg and Paul McAvinney, "A functional approach to real-time control," *Proceedings of the International Computer Music Conference*, San Francisco, Computer Music Association (1984).

Peter Desain, "Graphical programming in computer music, a proposal," *Proc. ICMC*, San Francisco, CMA (1986).

John Duesenberry, "The Yamaha CX5M music computer: an evaluation," *CMJ* 9(3) (Fall 1985).

J. Stephen Dydo, "Surface control of computer music," *Proceedings of the International Computer Music Conference*, San Francisco, Computer Music Association (1982).

John Free and Paul Vytas, "Whatever happened to SSSP?," *Proc. ICMC*, San Francisco, CMA (1986).

Christopher Fry, *YAMIL reference manual*, MIT Experimental Music studio, Cambridge, Massachusetts (1980).

M. Green, "PROD: A grammar-based computer composition program," *Proceedings of the 1980 International Computer Music Conference*, San Francisco, Computer Music Association (1980).

Patrick Greussay, Jacques Arveiller, Marc Battier, Chris Colere, Gilbert Dalmasso, Giuseppe Englert, and Didier Roncin, "Musical software: descriptions and abstractions of sound generation and mixing," *CMJ* 4(3), pp. 40–47 (Fall 1980).

Lejaren Hiller, Antonio Leal, and Robert A. Baker, "Revised MUSICOMP manual," Technical Report 13, University of Illinois, School of Music, Experimental Musical Studio (1966).

S. Holtzman, "Music as system," *Interface* 7(4) (1978).

S. Holtzman, "A generative grammar defitional language for music," *Interface* 9(1) (1980).

S. R. Holtzman, "Using generative grammars for music composition," *CMJ* 5(1), pp. 51–64 (Spr 1981).

Raymond F. Jurgens, "Algorithmic music language, a music emulator and assembler-compiler for analog synthesizers," *Proceedings of the International Computer Music Conference*, San Francisco, Computer Music Association (1980).

Marc LeBrun, "Notes on microcomputer music," *CMJ* 1(2), pp. 30–35 (Apr 1977).

Dennis Lorrain, "A panoply of stochastic cannons," *CMJ* 4(1) (1980).

D. Gareth Loy, "Notes on the implementation of MUSBOX: a compiler for the Systems Concepts digital synthesizer," *CMJ* 5(1), pp. 34–50 (Spr 1981).

Gareth Loy, "An experimental music composition language with real-time capabilities," *Proceedings of the International Computer Music Conference*, San Francisco, Computer Music Association (1983).

Gareth Loy and Curtis Abbott, "Programming languages for computer music synthesis, performance, and composition," *ACM Computing Surveys* 17(2) (1985).

Frederick L. Malouf, "A System for interactive music composition through computer graphics," *Proceedings of the International Computer Music Conference*, San Francisco, Computer Music Association (1985).

J. Marc, "Computer music language aids interaction between composer and choreographer," *Proceedings of the International Computer Music Conference*, San Francisco, Computer Music Association (1982).

Max V. Mathews, "An acoustical compiler for music and psychological stimuli," *Bell System Technical Journal 40* (1961).

M. V. Mathews, "The digital computer as a musical instrument," *Science* 142 (1963).

Max V. Mathews, Joan E. Miller, F. R. Moore, J. R. Pierce, and J. C. Risset, *The technology of computer music*, The MIT Press, Cambridge, Massachusetts (1969).

Max V. Mathews and F. R. Moore, "GROOVE—a program to compose, store, and edit functions of time," *Communications of the ACM* 13(12) (1970).

F. Richard Moore, "The Computer Audio Research Laboratory at UCSD," *CMJ* 6(1), pp. 18–29 (Spr 1982).

James A. Moorer, "The Lucasfilm audio signal processor," *Computer Music Journal* 6(3) (1982).

John Myhill, "Some simplifications and improvements in the stochastic music program," *Proceedings of the International Computer Music Conference*, Computer Music Association (1978).

John Myhill, "Controlled indeterminacy: a first step towards a semi-stochastic music language," *CMJ* 3(3), pp. 12–14 (Sep 1979).

Gary Nelson, "MPL—a program library for musical data processing," *Creative Computing* (March–April, 1977).

Yann Orlarey, "MLOGO: un langage de programmation orienté composition musicale," *Proceedings of the International Computer Music Conference*, San Francisco, Computer Music Association (1984).

Yann Orlarey, "MLOGO—a MIDI composing environment for the Apple IIe," *Proc. ICMC*, San Francisco, CMA (1986).

Bruce W. Pennycook, "Music languages and preprocessors: a tutorial," *Proceedings of the International Computer Music Conference*, San Francisco, Computer Music Association (1983).

Bruce W. Pennycook, "Computer-music interfaces: a survey," *ACM Computing Surveys* 17(2) (1985).

Miller Puckette, "Interprocess communication and timing in real-time computer music performance," *Proc. ICMC*, San Francisco, CMA (1986).

Curtis Roads, "Automated granular synthesis of sound," *CMJ* 2(2), pp. 61–62 (Sep 1978).

Curtis Roads, "Composing grammars," *Computer Music Association Reports*, San Francisco, Computer Music Association (1978).

C. Roads, "Interview with Max Mathews," *CMJ* 4(4), pp. 15–22 (Winter 1980).

Xavier Rodet, Yves Potard, and Jean-Baptiste Barrière, "The CHANT project: from the synthesis of the singing voice to synthesis in general," *CMJ* 8(3), pp. 15–31 (Fall 1984).

Xavier Rodet and Pierre Cointe, "FORMES: composition and scheduling of processes," *CMJ* 8(3), pp. 32–50 (Fall 1984).

David Rosenboom and Larry Polansky, "HMSL (Hierarchical Music Specification Language): a real-time environment for formal, perceptual and compositional experimentation," *Proceedings of the International Computer Music Conference*, San Francisco, Computer Music Association (1985).

Robert Rowe, "Recur: composition and synthesis," *Proceedings of the International Computer Music Conference*, San Francisco, Computer Music Association (1984).

M. Santojemma, "Formal representation of basic blocks for sound synthesis," *Proceedings of the International Computer Music Conference*, San Francisco, Computer Music Association (1982).

Brian L. Schmidt, "A natural language system for music," *Proc. ICMC*, San Francisco, CMA (1986).

Bill Schottstaedt, "Pla: a composer's idea of a language," *CMJ* 7(1), pp. 11–20 (Spr 1983).

Bill Schottstaedt, "Automatic species counterpoint," STAN-M-19, CCRMA, Stanford University (1984).

Leland Smith, "SCORE—a musician's approach to computer music," *Journal of the Audio Engineering Society* 20(1) (1976).

Stephen W. Smoliar, "A parallel processing model of musical structures," Department of Computing and Information Science Report AI TR-242, Massachusetts Institute of Technology, Cambridge, Massachusetts (1971).

Anders Friberg and Johan Sundberg, "A Lisp environment for creating and applying rules for musical performance," *Proc. ICMC*, San Francisco, CMA (1986).

P. P. Tanner and Richard Teitelbaum, "The digital piano and the patch control language system," *Proceedings of the International Computer Music Conference* (1984).

J. Tovar and L. Smith, *MUS10 manual*, Stanford University, Center for Computer Research in Music and Acoustics (1976). Unpublished user's manual.

B. Vercoe, *Music 11 reference manual*, M. I. T. Experimental Music Studio, Cambridge, Mass. (1979). Unpublished.

J. Wenker, "MUSTRAN II—an extended music translator," *Computers and the Humanities* 7(2) (1972).

Christopher Yavelow, "Music software for the Apple Macintosh," *CMJ* 9(3) (Fall 1985).

Christopher Yavelow, "The impact of MIDI upon compositional methodology," *Proc. ICMC*, San Francisco, CMA (1986).

Theory of Programming

Curtis Abbott, "Intervention schedules for real-time programming," *IEEE Transactions on Software Engineering* SE-10 (May 1984).

David P. Anderson and Ron Kuivila, "A model of real-time computation for computer music," *Proc. ICMC*, San Francisco, CMA (1986).

Joel Chadabe, "Some reflections on the nature of the landscape within which computer music systems are designed," *CMJ* 1(3), pp. 5–11 (Jun 1977).

E. E. David, Jr., M. V. Mathews, and H. S. McDonald, "Description and results of experiments with speech using digital computer simulation," *Proceedings of the 1958 National Electronics Conference* (1958).

Ron Kuivila and David P. Anderson, "Timing accuracy and response time in interactive systems," *Proc. ICMC*, San Francisco, CMA (1986).

D. Gareth Loy, "Designing a computer music workstation from musical imperatives," *Proc. ICMC*, San Francisco, CMA (1986).

F. Richard Moore, "Applications for an integrated computer music workstation," *Proc. ICMC*, San Francisco, CMA (1986).

Lauri Spiegel, "Sonic set theory: a tonal music theory for computers," *Proceedings of the Second Annual Symposium on Small Computers and the Arts* (1982).

Barry Truax, "The inverse relation between generality and strength in computer music programs," *Interface* 9 (Dec 1980).

Documentation of Compositions

Charles Ames, "*Crystals*: recursive structures in automated compositions," *CMJ* 6(3), pp. 46–64 (Fall 1982).

Charles Ames, "Stylistic automata in *Gradient*," *CMJ* 7(4), pp. 45–56 (Winter 1983).

Klarentz Barlow, "Bus journey to Parametron," *Die Feedback Papers*, Köln (1980).

Thomas Blum, "Herbert Brun: Project Sawdust," *Computer Music Journal* 3(1) (1979).

Aad te Bokkel, "The Errant Syncretizer," *Proc. ICMC*, San Francisco, CMA (1986).

Richard Boulanger, "Interview with Roger Reynolds, Joji Yuasa, and Charles Wuorinen," *CMJ* 8(4) (Winter 1984).

William Buxton, "Design issues in the foundation of a computer-based tool for music composition," CSRG-97, Computer Systems Research Group, University of Toronto (1978).

William Buxton, "Music Software User's Manual," Computer Systems Research Group, University of Toronto (1980).

Jonathan Harvey, Denis Lorrain, Jean-Baptiste Barrière, and Stanley Haynes, "Notes on the realization of *Bhakti*," *CMJ* 8(3), pp. 74–78 (Fall 1984).

Lejaren Hiller, "Programming the *I Ching* oracle," *Computer Studies in the Humanities* 3 (1970).

Lejaren Hiller, "Composing with computers: a progress report," *CMJ* 5(4), pp. 7–21 (Winter 1981).

Lejaren Hiller and Charles Ames, "Automated composition: an installation at the 1985 International Exposition in Tsukuba, Japan," *Perspectives of New Music* 23(2) (1985).

Hubert Howe, *Electronic music synthesis*, W. W. Norton, New York (1975).

Stephan Kaske, "A conversation with Clarence Barlow," *CMJ* 9(1) (Spring 1985).

Gary S. Kendall, "Composing from a geometric model: Five-Leaf Rose," *CMJ* 5(4), pp. 66–73 (Winter 1981).

Gareth Loy, "Nekyia," D.M.A. Thesis, Stanford University, Stanford, CA (1980).

Larry Polansky, "Interview with David Rosenboom," *CMJ* 7(4), pp. 40–44 (Winter 1983).

Roger Reynolds, "Musical production and related issues at CARL," *Proc. ICMC*, San Francisco, CMA (1986).

Jean-Claude Risset, "Computer music experiments," *CMJ* 9(1) (Spring 1985).

J.-C. Risset, "An introductory catalogue of computer synthesized sounds," Bell Telephone Laboratories unpublished memorandum, Murray Hill, N.J. (1969).

C. Roads, "An interview with Gottfried Michael Koenig," *CMJ* 2(3), pp. 11–15 (Dec 1978).

Neil B. Rolnick, "A composer's notes on the development and implementation of software for a digital synthesizer," *CMJ* 2(2), pp. 13–22 (Sep 1978).

Barry Truax, "Timbral construction in Arras as a stochastic process," *CMJ* 6(3), pp. 72–77 (Fall 1982).

Horacio Vaggione, "The making of Octuor," *CMJ* 8(2), pp. 48–54 (Sum 1984).

Automated Composition

Charles Ames, "Notes on *Undulant*," *Interface* 12(3) (1983).

Charles Ames, "Applications of linked data structures to automated composition," *Proceedings of the International Computer Music Conference*, San Francisco, Computer Music Association (1985).

Marc Battier, "A composing program for a portable sound synthesis system," *CMJ* 3(3), pp. 50–53 (Sep 1979).

Alfonso Belfiore, "ALGOMUSIC: an algorithm for the genesis of musical structures," *Proceedings of the International Computer Music Conference*, San Francisco, Computer Music Association (1982).

Tommaso Bolognesi, "Automatic composition: experiments with self-similar music," *CMJ* 7(1), pp. 25–36 (Spr 1983).

K. Ebcioglu, "Computer counterpoint," *Proceedings of the International Computer Music Conference* (1980).

K. Ebciogu, "An expert system for Schenkerian synthesis of chorales in the style of J.S. Bach," *Proceedings of the International Computer Music Conference* (1984).

Giuseppe Englert, "Automated composition and composed automation," *CMJ* 5(4), pp. 30–35 (Winter 1981).

Christopher Fry, "Flavors Band: a language for specifying musical style," *CMJ* 8(4) (Winter 1984).

C. Fry, "Computer improvisation," *CMJ* 4(3), pp. 48–58 (Fall 1980).

S. Gill, "A technique for the composition of music in a computer," *The Computer Journal* 6(2) (1963).

C. Hatzis, "Towards an endogenous automated music," *Interface* 9(2) (1980).

Lejaren Hiller and Leonard Isaacson, *Experimental music*, McGraw-Hill Book Company, Inc., New York (1959).

Lejaren Hiller, "Stochastic generation of note parameters for music composition," *Proceedings of the International Computer Music Conference*, San Francisco, Computer Music Association (1982).

G. M. Koenig, "Project One," *Electronic Music Reports 2*, Utrecht, Institute of Sonology (1970).

G. M. Koenig, "Project Two," *Electronic Music Reports 3*, Utrecht, Institute of Sonology (1970).

Marco Ligabue, "A system of rules for computer improvisation," *Proc. ICMC*, San Francisco, CMA, (1986).

Curtis Roads, "Interactive orchestration based on score analysis," *Proceedings of the International Computer Music Conference* (1982).

Bill Schottstaedt, "Automatic species counterpoint," STAN-M-19, CCRMA, Stanford University (1984).

Marilyn Taft Thomas, "VIVACE: a rule based AI system for composition," *Proceedings of the International Computer Music Conference*, San Francisco, Computer Music Association (1985).

Sever Tipei, "MP1—a computer program for music composition," *Proceedings of the Second Music Computation Conference*, Urbana, University of Illinois (1975).

Real-Time/Interactive Composition and Performance

Jon Appleton, "Live and in concert: composer/performer views of real-time performance systems," *CMJ* 8(1), pp. 48–51 (Spr 1984).

Jon H. Appleton, "The computer and live musical performance," *Proc. ICMC*, San Francisco, CMA (1986).

Martin Bartlett, "A microcomputer-controlled synthesis system for live performance," *CMJ* 3(1), pp. 25–29 (Mar 1979).

Martin Bartlett, "The development of a practical live-performance music language," *Proceedings of the International Computer Music Conference*, San Francisco, Computer Music Association (1985).

Douglas L. Bayer, "Real-time software for a digital music synthesizer," *CMJ* 1(4), pp. 22–23 (Nov 1977).

Joel Chadabe, "Interactive composing," *Proceedings of the International Computer Music Conference*, San Francisco, Computer Music Association (1983).

Joel Chadabe, "Interactive composing: an overview," *CMJ* 8(1), pp. 22–27 (Spr 1984).

Roger B. Dannenberg, "Arctic: a functional language for real-time control," *Conference Record of the 1984 ACM Symposium on LISP and Functional Programming* (August 1984).

Emanuel Ghent, "Interactive compositional algorithms," *Proceedings of the International Computer Music Conference*, San Francisco, Computer Music Association (1977).

Emanuel Ghent, "Further studies in compositional algorithms," *Proceedings of the International Computer Music Conference*, Computer Music Association (1978).

James Lawson and Max Mathews, "Computer program to control a digital real-time sound synthesizer," *CMJ* 1(4), pp. 16–21 (Nov 1977).

Curtis Roads, "The Second STEIM symposium on interactive composition in live electronic music," *CMJ* 10(2) (Summer 1986).

Anders Friberg, Johan Sundberg, "A Lisp environment for creating and applying rules for musical performance," *Proc. ICMC*, San Francisco, CMA (1986).

Johan Sundberg, Anders Askenfelt, and Lars Fryden, "Musical performance: a synthesis-by-rule approach," *CMJ* 7(1), pp. 37–43 (Spr 1983).

Barry Truax, "The POD system of interactive composition programs," *CMJ* 1(3), pp. 30–47 (Jun 1977).

Barry Truax, "The PODX system: interactive compositional software for the DMX-1000," *CMJ* 9(1) (Spring 1985).

Music Theory

Giovanni Degli Antoni and Goffredo Haus, "Music and causality," *Proceedings of the International Computer Music Conference*, San Francisco, Computer Music Association (1982).

Claudio Baffioni, Francesco Guerra, and Laura Tedeschini Lalli, "The theory of stochastic processes and dynamical systems as a basis for models of musical structures," in *Musical grammars and computer analysis*, ed. M. Baroni and E L. Callegari, Olschki, Florence (1984).

William Buxton, William Reeves, Ronald Baeker, and Leslie Mezei, "The use of hierarchy and instance in a data structure for computer music," *CMJ* 2(4), pp. 10–20 (Late Dec 1978).

Donald Byrd, "User interfaces in music-notation systems," *Proc. ICMC*, San Francisco, CMA (1986).

D. Byrd, "Music notation by computer," Ph. D. dissertation, Bloomirgton, Indiana University Department of Computer Science (1984).

Lounette M. Dyer, "Toward a device independent representation of music," *Proceedings of the International Computer Music Conference*, San Francisco, Computer Music Association (1984).

R. Erickson, "The DARMS project: a status report," *Computers and the Humanities* 7(2) (1975).

S. Holtzman, "Music as system," *Interface* 7(4) (1978).

Christoph Lischka and Hans-Werner Güsgen, "MvS/C: a constraint-based approach to musical knowledge representation," *Proc. ICMC*, San Francisco, CMA (1986).

Max V. Mathews and L. Rosler, "Graphical language for the scores of computer-generated sounds," *Perspectives of New Music* 6 (1968).

Michael R. Rogers, "The golden section in musical time: speculations on temporal proportion," Ph. D. thesis, University Microfilms, University of Iowa (1977).

Leland Smith, "Editing and printing music by computer," *Journal of Music Theory* 9.

James Tenney, *Meta + Hodos and META Meta + Hodos*, Frog Peak Music, Box 9911, Oakland (1986).

Music Representation

Gérard Assayag and Dan Timis, "A toolbox for music notation," *Proc. ICMC*, San Francisco, CMA (1986).

Ferruccio Bussoni, "Sketch for a new esthetic of music," in *Three classics in the aesthetics of music*, Da Capo Press, New York (1962).

Donald Byrd, "User interfaces in music-notation systems," *Proc. ICMC*, San Francisco, CMA (1986).

John Cage, *Silence*, The MIT Press, Cambridge, Massachusetts (1961).

John Cage, *Notations*, Something Else Press, New York (1969).

Chris Chafe, Bernard Mont-Reynaud, and Loren Rush, "Toward an intelligent editor of digital audio: recognition of musical constructs," *CMJ* 6(1), pp. 30–41 (Spr 1982).

Peter J. Clements, "A system for the complete enharmonic encoding of musical pitches," *Proc. ICMC*, San Francisco, CMA (1986).

Burnett Cross, "Percy Grainger's free-music machine," in *The Percy Grainger Companion*, ed. Lewis Foreman, Thames Publishing, London (1981).

Paul E. Dworak and Philip C. Baczewski, "A vector field model of compositional creativity," *Proceedings of the International Computer Music Conference*, San Francisco, Computer Music Association (1980).

Lounette M. Dyer, "MUSE: an integrated software environment for computer music applications," *Proc. ICMC*, San Francisco, CMA (1986).

Johann Joseph Fux, *Gradus ad Parnassum*, W. W. Norton & Co., Inc., New York (1965). Edited and translated by Alfred Mann with John Edmunds, from the original 18th-century edition.

Kenneth Gaburo, "The deteriorization of an ideal, ideally deteriorized: Reflections on Pietro Grossi's Paganini Al Computer," *CMJ* 9(1) (Spring 1985).

Craig Harris and Alexander Brinkman, "A unified set of software tools for computer-assisted set-theoretic and serial analysis of contemporary music," *Proc. ICMC*, San Francisco, CMA (1986).

Paul Hindemith, *The craft of musical composition*, Associated Music Publishers, New York (1937).

Thomas E. Janzen, "Aesthetic appeal in computer music," *CMJ* 10(3) (Fall 1986).

Gottfried Michael Koenig, "Aesthetic integration of computer-composed scores," *CMJ* 7(4), pp. 27–32 (Winter 1983).

Otto Laske, "Composition theory in Koenig's Project One and Project Two," *CMJ* 5(4), pp. 54–65 (Winter 1981).

O. E. Laske, "Toward an explicit cognitive theory of musical listening," *Computer Music Journal* 4(2) (1980).

Fred Lerdahl and Ray Jackendoff, *A generative theory of tonal music*, The MIT Press, Cambridge (1983).

Barton McLean, "Symbolic extension and its corruption of music," *Perspectives of New Music* 20 (1982).

Harry Partch, *Genesis of a music*, University of Wisconsin Press, Madison (1949). Reprinted by Da Capo Press, New York, 1974.

Walter Piston, *Harmony*, W. W. Norton, New York (1978).

Stephen T. Pope, "The development of an intelligent composer's assistant, interactive graphics tools and knowledge representation for music," *Proc. ICMC*, San Francisco, CMA (1986).

P. Prusinkiewicz, "Score generation with L-systems," *Proc. ICMC*, San Francisco, CMA (1986).

John Rahn, "On some computational models of music theory," *CMJ* 4(2), pp. 66–72 (Sum 1980).

Jean-Philippe Rameau, *Traité de l'harmonie*, Broude Brothers, New York (1965). Facsimile of 1722 Paris edition.

Curtis Roads, "Grammars as representations of music," in *Foundations of computer music*, C. Roads and J. Strawn, eds., The MIT Press, Boston, Massachusetts (1985).

Curtis Roads, "Symposium on computer music composition," *CMJ* 10(1) (Spring 1986).

C. Roads, "Report on the International Conference on Musical Grammars and Computer Analysis," *CMJ* 7(2), pp. 36–42 (Sum 1983).

Pierre Schaeffer, *A la recherche d'une musique concrète*, Paris, 1952.

Joseph Schillinger, *The Schillinger system of musical composition*, Carl Fischer, New York (1941). Reprinted by Da Capo Press, New York, 1978.

Arnold Schoenberg, *Style and idea*, Philosophical Library, New York (1950).

James Tenney and Larry Polansky, "Temporal gestalt perception in music," *Journal of Music Theory* 24(2) (1980).

Edgard Varèse, "The liberation of sound," in *Perspectives on American composers*, ed. B. Boritz and E. Cone, W. W. Norton & Co., New York (1971).

Iannis Xenakis, *Formalized music*, Indiana University Press, Bloomington (1971).

Miscellaneous

Charles Ames, "A. I. in music," in *Encyclopedia of artificial intelligence*, ed. Stuart Shapiro, Wiley & Sons, New York.

Jacques Arveiller, "Comments on university instruction in computer music," *CMJ* 6(2) (Sum 1982).

Gerald J. Balzano, "Changing conceptions of pitch and timbre: a modest proposal," Presented at the 106th meeting of the Acoustical Society of America, San Diego (1983).

W. R. Bennett, "Spectra of quantized signals," *Bell System Technical Journal* 27 (1948).

Nicola Bernardini, "Computer music: the state of the nation," *Proc. ICMC*, San Francisco, CMA (1986).

Noam Chomsky, *Aspects of the theory of syntax*, The MIT Press, Cambridge, Massachusetts (1965).

John Chowning, "The synthesis of complex audio spectra by means of frequency modulation," *Journal of the Audio Engineering Society* 21(7) (1973).

John M. Grey, "An exploration of musical timbre," Department of Music STAN-M-2, Stanford University (1975).

Dorothy Gross, "A computer-assisted music course," *Computing in the humanities*, Lexington, Massachusetts, D. C. Heath & Co..

Harry Lincoln, ed., *The computer and music*, Cornell University Press, Ithaca (1970).

L. Rabiner and A. Schaffer, *Digital processing of speech signals*, Prentice Hall, Englewood Cliffs, N.J. (1978).

J. R. Ragazzini and G. F. Franklin, *Sampled-data control systems*, McGraw-Hill, New York (1958).

Curtis Roads, "Interview with Marvin Minsky," *Computer Music Journal* 4(3) (1980).

Curtis Roads, "Music and Artificial Intelligence: a survey," *ACM Computing Surveys* 1(1) (1985).

Curtis Roads, "Research in music and artificial intelligence," *ACM Computing Surveys* 17(2) (1985).

C. Roads, "Artificial intelligence and music," *CMJ* 4(2), pp. 13–25 (Sum 1980).

Xavier Rodet, "Time-domain formant-wave-function synthesis," *CMJ* 8(3), pp. 9–14 (Fall 1984).

Peter Samson, "A general-purpose digital synthesizer," *Journal of the Audio Engineering Society* 28(3) (1978).

R. N. Shepard, "Circularity in judgements of relative pitch," *Journal of the Acoustical Society of America* 36 (1964).

Appendix: Description of the Sound Examples on the Accompanying Compact Disk

This appendix gives short descriptions of the 88 sound examples that illustrate the topics discussed in the chapters of this book. For most chapters, the first examples are technical demonstrations and the last example is a short excerpt from a piece of music that makes use of the technology being described.

In order to facilitate location and playing of a particular example, each has been put on a separate track on the compact disk. In this appendix, each example is numbered (1 through 88) by its track number on the disk.

Chapter 2 (Lansky)

1. Transformations of speed, pitch, and formant frequencies of a short utterance:

a. An original recording of a female speaker saying "For some time after I went to bed, I could not sleep." This is taken from a piece of mine called *As it Grew Dark*, and is based on a text from Charlotte Bronte's *Jane Eyre*. The reader is Hannah MacKay.

b. A straight resynthesis of the speech with no pitch, time, or timbral alterations. This was done at a 28k sampling rate with 32-pole filters. The frame rate is 112 frames per second. It is not difficult to notice that some critical components of the timbre have been lost, but it is worth noticing that the synthesis does an excellent job of reconstructing the basic human qualities of the speech.

c. The speech is slowed down and the pitch is raised. The frame rate of unvoiced segments is, however, held at 112 frames per second. The formants are unaltered, so the effect is as if the same speaker were speaking with a higher voice.

d. The speech is transposed down in pitch and played at its original speed. The formants are unaltered, but notice the peculiar effect on the resultant timbre from the lower frequency in the excitation function. There is a kind of highpass effect due to the fact that there is so little energy being applied to the fundamental.

e. The speech is transposed down in pitch, played at its original speed, and now the formants are shifted down proportionately. This now sounds like a different speaker, while example (d) sounded like the same speaker with a sore throat. Here there is more energy being applied in the region of the fundamental, and it sounds like a healthier, although probably larger, individual.

f. The speech is transposed up, speeded up, and the formants are also shifted up proportionately. The results are as expected.

g. The synthesis is at the original speed with no timbral alteration, but the pitch contours are turned upside down, effectively changing the inflected meaning of the speech, albeit in mysterious ways.

h. An arbitrary manipulation of the pitch contours. Different segments are transposed and altered in different ways. Equally mysterious.

i. A flat pitch contour, not based on the pitch of the original, is applied. Note the machinelike quality of the result.

j. The timbre and pitch are shifted down linearly over the duration of the segment as if the original speaker were changing size and gender as she/he spoke.

2. Transformations of a short utterance as used in a musical example:

a. A segment of the poem *Wasting*, by Richard Kostelanetz, read by the poet. "On my 25th birthday I was 81 inches high, and weighed 333 pounds."

b. A resynthesis of this segment from a setting of the entire poem that I did with two of my students, Brad Garton and Andrew Milburn. Here formant shifting and time alteration are used to make the voice of the speaker reflect the physical facts of his self-description. A generous dose of reverberation is added to heighten the effect.

c. Another segment of this composition in which an electric guitar is used as the excitation function, rather than a pulselike signal, to personify the musical predilections of the subject's late teen years. The guitarist is Steven Mackey. This is a powerful extension of LPC. The composer Tracy Peterson has made extensive use of this technique.

3. A segment of movement 1 of my *Six Fantasies* on a Poem by Thomas Campion: Here the speech is slowed down somewhat and combined in three transpositions to project an intensified version of the pitch contours of the speech. The idea was to confuse the image of an individual speaking to get the listener to notice the pitch contours of the speech to a greater extent. (The entire composition is available on Composer's Recordings Inc. SD-456.)

4. A segment of movement 4 of the *Fantasies*: The desired effect is the synthesis of a chorallike texture. The pitches are not based on those of the original. In order to overcome the machinelike quality that is often a result

of this method of synthesis because it is not based on a manipulation of the original pitch contours, I made extensive use of flanging and choir-tone synthesis.

5. A segment of movement 5 of the *Fantasies*: Percussive sounds are made by recycling unvoiced segments through banks of comb-filters. Most of the signal heard here is the ‘ch’ sound from the word “cheek’d.”

6. Excerpt from movement 2 of my composition *Folk Images*: The piece in this segment is one of a set of five folk song settings, using violin synthesis. Here the tune is actually created by shifting the formants of an over-specified analysis of a high violin note. Since most of the original signal was much lower in pitch, and I did not decrease the number of poles for this segment, the poles here fell on the harmonics of the note rather than on its formants. The tune in this case is therefore actually created by using a single input pitch and shifting its formants/harmonics according to modifications of amplitude and frequency contours taken from another segment of the analysis.

7. A segment of my composition *Idle Chatter*: Randomlike distributions of small speech fragments overlay a choral sound created by a high-density recycling of similar small segments. The various flavors of percussive sounds are created by placing different kinds of lowpass filters and envelopes on a wide variety of synthesized fragments, while also shifting the formants of many of them. The entire composition is available on a Wergo compact disk, number 2010–50.

Chapter 3 (Dodge)

8. Recording of the poem for the fourth song, “The days are ahead,” as read by the composer and recorded onto analog tape. The text is

The days are ahead.
1,926,346 to 1,926,345.
Later the nights will catch up.

9. Repeated syntheses of the opening of the poem at different speeds.

10. “The days are ahead” synthesized with an edited pitch contour. Here the words, edited from the same analysis of the original recording as that used for Sound Example 2, are set with a melody composed of a new musical pitch for every syllable of the text.

11. Interpolation applied to fundamental frequency of speech. Here, after specifying the beginning and ending frames of the segment to be altered, a program is invoked to interpolate between the frequencies of the initial and final frames. The sound of this alteration heard extensively in the middle of the fourth song where glissandoing voices counting the numbers in the text follow each other up and down. This example displays three different glissandi, each with a different timing and interval span. The first glissando sounds twice and the second and third glissandi three times each.

12. Several syntheses played together to create a chorus of a desired density.

13. The entire speech song "The days are ahead." It consists of a variety of textures from a single synthetic voice to choruses of up to six synthetic voices. (All the vocal sounds are synthetic, even those that sound simply spoken.) The segments for the song were computed separately and recorded onto analog tape. The composition was assembled by splicing together the analog tape. As indicated above, all the mixing was done in digital form on the computer disk.

Chapter 4 (Bennett and Rodet)

14. The concluding phrase of the madrigal "Moro lasso" by Carlo Gesualdo from the *Libro sesto dei madrigali* . . . (1611) sung by five different voices.

15. A short vocalise sung successively by bass, tenor, countertenor, alto, and soprano voices.

16. A short group of examples beginning with the raw synthesis and adding successively attack and decay, vibrato and fluctuation of the fundamental frequency.

17. Three short examples to show the relation between perceived loudness, spectral tilt, and vibrato.

18. Two short examples to show the effect of legato phrasing.

19. An excerpt from the Queen of the Night's aria "Der Hölle Rache kocht in meinem Herzen" from *The Magic Flute* by W. A. Mozart.

20. An excerpt from *Winter (1980)* by G. Bennett illustrating the use of CHANT for nonvocal sounds.

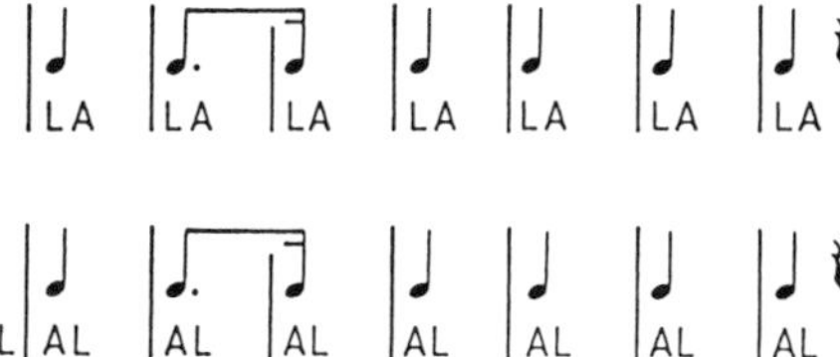

Figure A1
Two ways to locate syllable boundaries: (top) wrong segmentation and (bottom) correct segmentation.

Chapter 5 (Sundberg)

21. LA: *a, la, la, la*, etc., sung in a triad pattern pitches. In (21a) the pitch is changed during the end of the previous vowel. In (21b) the pitch changes after the end of the previous vowel (during /l/), which is better.

22. Vowel qualities and consonant durations: A short melody sung with the sound *la*. In (22a) the vowels are all the long /a:/ and the consonants /l/ have the same durations. In (22b) the stressed notes are sung with the long vowel /a:/ and the unstressed vowels with the short vowel /a/; these vowels have different formant frequencies. In (22c) the vowels are as in (22b); in addition, the consonant /l/ has a greater duration after a short vowel and a lesser duration after a long vowel.

23. Syllable boundaries: In the previous examples the time needed was taken from the note duration of the following vowel, as in (23a) here, illustrated at the top of figure A1. In (23b), illustrated at the bottom of figure A1, which sounds better, the duration of the /l/ is taken from the note duration of the preceding vowel.

24. Crescendos: In (24a) the melody is sung without crescendos or diminuendos. In (24b) the intensity is increased according to chord rules previously enunciated, so that intensity increases as harmonically charged chords are approached and decreases as less harmonically charged chords are approached. This sounds too neutral. In (24c) the crescendos and diminuendos are increased 50%. This sounds better, but not good enough.

As in (24d), the spectrum should change during a crescendo, the higher overtones gaining more than the lower overtones as the sound level is increased. Finally, in (24e), vibrato is used to fuse or concentrate the overtones. The amplitude of the vibrato increases with intensity.

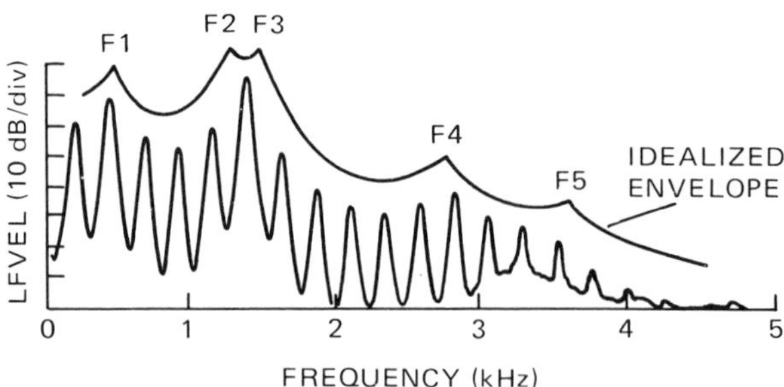

Figure A2
Emphasis of sixth partial by the second and third formants.

25. Coloratura: In the coloratura passage of (25a) an exercise is sung without special coloratura rules. This is inadequate. In (25b) the fundamental frequency is one semitone flat at the beginning of each note and one semitone sharp at the middle of each note, as shown in figure 5.5. This sounds better, but the singer is flat at the peaks of the coloratura sequence. In (25c) the fundamental frequency is made almost two semitones sharp at the middle of the peaks of the coloratura passage. This sounds quite acceptable, although somewhat energetic.

26. Formants as flags: In (26a) the formants of two singers are used; the formants of the different singer is used in one vowel, and this is noticeable. In (26b) all the formants were taken from one singer's voice and the effect is better. In (26c) the vowel /o:/ in *mano* seems "off track" or aggressive. In (26d) the formant frequencies have been changed in order to avoid this.

27. Let the formants sing: In sound example (27a) the second and third formants are very close in frequency, as shown in figure A2 so that they emphasize the sixth partial. As the tone persists we hear this partial as an insistent pitch. In (27b) different formant frequencies are emphasized and play a tune.

Consider the frequencies of the harmonics of a "tonic tone," a second tone a fifth down from the tonic, and a third tone a fifth up from the tonic. Among the harmonics of these three tones are all of the pitch frequencies of the diatonic scale. In (27c) *Jingle Bells* is played by emphasizing harmonics chosen from three such tones.

28. Synthesis example: In (28a) the Lachrymosa theme from Verdi's *Messa da Requiem* has been synthesized using appropriate rules discussed in this paper. In (28b) the same synthesis is accompanied by a piano.

29. Another synthesis example: Six vowels sung by 8 choral singers were analyzed with regard to the formant frequencies. Using these formant frequency values, all these $6 \times 8 = 48$ vowels were synthesized on the MUSSE synthesizer and one period from each was stored in a CASIO digital sampler synthesizer. A small fundamental frequency discrepancy, ranging from 16 cents for the bass part to 4 cents in the soprano part, was introduced between the two voices in each part. In order to generate the particular chorus effect, the fundamental frequency of each individual voice was individually randomized. Thereby, the random function built into the sampler was used, although it is far from being realistic.

In sound example 29 this choral sound has been used for the chorus part in the first movement from Claudio Monteverdi's Maria Vesper from 1610. The first line is sung by MUSSE as tenor soloist, and in the subsequent music the choir is sung by the ensemble of eight MUSSE choral singers performing as a choir on the CASIO sampler synthesizer according to the recipe mentioned. The orchestra was synthesized by two additional synthesizers. All three synthesizers were synchronized and controlled from a Macintosh microcomputer in accordance with our performance rules.

Chapter 6 (Chowning)

30. A short example of synthesized female vocal tones in a musical context.

31. These five examples show the importance of small amounts of pitch fluctuation through the course of a tone:

a. a tone with no pitch change;
b. a tone with random vibrato;
c. a tone with periodic vibrato;
d. a tone with random and periodic vibrato;
e. a tone with random and periodic vibrato and with portamento during the attack.

32. The importance of the exponents for the overall amplitude A in equation (3) is shown in the following examples:

a. five tones having overall amplitudes of 1.0, 0.5, 0.25, 0.125, 0.062, where the exponents are not applied;
b. the same five tones with the exponents showing decreasing vocal effort;
c. repeat of (b);
d. as in (a) above with the addition of a constant amount of reverberation—the changing ratio of the energy of the tone having

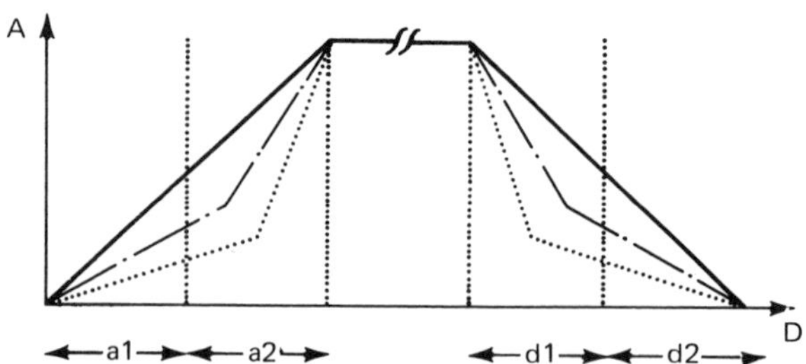

Figure A3
Amplitude envelopes for three formants: solid line, A1; dot-dash line, A2; dotted line, A3.

a constant spectrum relative to the energy of its reverberation strongly suggests an increase in distance.

33. Naturalness of a tone is improved when the attack and decay envelopes applied to the formants are such that the higher the formant, the slower its initial rate of amplitude increase during the attack and the faster the rate of decrease during the decay.

a. All three formants rise and fall according to the single envelope, A1 from figure A3.

b. Each formant has its own envelope A1, A2, and A3, respectively, providing a more natural attack and release.

34. A natural-sounding crescendo depends as well upon independent envelopes for the three formants.

a. A note of 6 sec duration having a crescendo of a2 = 5.67 sec from equation (4), but where the amplitude envelope of all three formants is A1 as shown in figure A3.

b. Applying the three independent envelopes to the three formants produces a more natural feeling of increasing vocal effort.

35. The importance of periodic and random vibrato in the perception of vocal tones is demonstrated by presenting first the fundamental alone, then by adding the harmonics, and finally by adding first a random and then a periodic vibrato. It is striking that the tone only "fuses" and becomes a unitary percept with the addition of the vibrato.

a. a tone at C4;

b. a tone at C4 · 5/4;

c. a tone at C4 · 3/2;

d. the sum of the above three examples (a + b + c) where each has an independent vibrato pattern.

36. A group of sinusoids having belllike envelopes at the attack are continuously transformed into voices where each of the sinusoids gradually becomes a fundamental to a set of harmonics while at the same time vibrato is added.

37. A male vocal tone can be synthesized with a small modification to the algorithm. The modulating signal is itself frequency modulated in order to produce an increase in the number of frequency components in the modulated carriers. An example is presented of a "basso profondissimo" that has extremely low formants.

38. A section of "Phone" (1982) by the author that demonstrates the compositional use of continuous timbral transformations and synthesized voices.

Chapter 7 (Kendall, Martens, and Decker)

These examples were prepared for presentation over loudspeakers in a small room with little reverberant sound, such as an average living room. The loudspeakers ideally should be placed near to ear level with a separation of 90° relative to the listener. The reproduction will provide the best results when there are no sound-reflecting surfaces near the speakers or listener that will return early reflections to the listener from the reproduction environment.

39. Circular saw: The circular saw is heard before and after computer processing with spatial reverberation. The saw was recorded in an anechoic chamber with a single microphone; neither the saw nor the microphone was moved during the recording process. The recording was then transferred to the computer and processed to add spatial motion and room ambience. The first sound presents the original mono recording; the sound image should be centered between the speakers. The second sound demonstrates the saw moving rapidly in a large room toward the listener's head.

40. Footsteps: These footsteps were originally recorded by placing a microphone close to the feet of someone walking in place. Neither the microphone nor the person changed position. This recording was processed to simulate the motion of footsteps climbing up a tall stairwell. The listener is diagonally oriented to the stairs: the footsteps begin away on one side, move up and toward the listener, and then turn the corner up away

toward the top of the stairs. The two versions of this example demonstrate the simulation of different environments. In the first version the walls have been covered with drapes and little reverberant sound is heard. In the second version, the walls are uncovered and made of painted concrete, one of the "worst-sounding" acoustic reflecting surfaces imaginable. The reverberation in the second case sounds like the stairwell of a high-rise apartment.

41. Scene with Sarah swinging: The musical excerpt was composed by Mickey Hart of the Grateful Dead for a segment of the "Twilight Zone" television series. In this particular scene, a young girl named Sarah is observed swinging on a small swingset by the story's main character, a father whose daughter is critically ill. The father suspects that Sarah is not an ordinary child; in fact, she is the spirit of a child who died many years before. As the scene progresses, the father wavers back and forth in his suspicions about Sarah.

While the original version of the music captured much of the underlying mood of the scene, we attempted to add an additional dimension to the music by linking the distance of music from the listener to the father's wavering uncertainty. We also attempted to capture his sense of doubt by having the music move in and out of darkness. The darkness was created by simulating unusually high air absorption, so that distance sounds were unnaturally dark. We also attempted to capture some of the "unearthly" quality of the situation by moving the sound in a path that caused extreme Doppler shifting of wall reflections.

42. Composition in progress by Shawn Decker: This except from the beginning of "Northern Migrations" by Shawn Decker demonstrates one creative use of spatial reverberation. This particular section contrasts sound paths that are clearly circular with paths that undulate.

Chapter 8 (Moore)

All sound examples that accompany this presentation were generated on a VAX-11/780 computer system in the Computer Audio Research Laboratory (CARL) at UCSD's Center for Music Experiment (CME) using the *space* unit generator contained in the author's cmusic sound synthesis and processing program [6, 8]. The cmusic space unit generator is based on the spatialization model described in this article. In this particular implementation of the model only direct and first-order reflections from the four walls of a rectangular room are used to form an early echo response for each loudspeaker channel, along with dense reverberation building up only after about 80 msec.

43. Distance versus loudness: The first set of sound examples briefly demonstrates the inverse square, inverse cube, and inverse fourth power "laws" (relationships). Loudness plays an important role in the subjective interpretation of distance to an auditory event. Each example consists of four sounds at successively smaller intensities. In the first set, the intensity diminishes at each step by a factor of 6 dB, corresponding to successive doublings of distance according to the inverse square law of intensity for direct sounds. In the second set of four sounds, the intensity diminishes by a factor of 9 dB per step, corresponding to successive doublings of distance according to an "inverse cube law." In the third set, a factor of 12 dB per step (corresponding to an "inverse fourth power law") is heard for comparison. At average listening levels and especially for unfamiliar sounds, the "inverse cube law" (based on halvings of subjective loudness) often yields the strongest impression of successive doublings (equal ratios or intervals) of distance. The inverse square law seems to result in successively smaller intervals of distance, while the "inverse fourth power law" seems to take larger and larger steps into the distance. The examples consist of

a. four sounds, −6 dB per step (inverse square law),
b. four sounds, −9 dB per step ("inverse cube law"),
c. four sounds, −12 dB per step ("inverse fourth power law").

44. Azimuth control: The second set of sound examples demonstrates control of azimuth (angle on the horizontal plane). These are four basic cases involving movements among discrete positions versus continuous motions, and movements along straight-line paths versus movements along paths that remain at a constant distance from the listener (arcs). In the first example we hear seven sounds at a sequence of positions moving from left to right along a straight-line path. In the second example we again hear seven sounds at a sequence of position moving from left to right along a curved path that remains a constant distance from the listener (who is assumed to be in the center of the listening space). In the third example the sound moves continuously from its starting point on the left to its final position to the right along a straight-line path. The fourth example demonstrates continuous motion along a curved path that remains a constant distance from a listener in the center of the listening space. Notice that, in accordance with the model, as the sound moves nearer the "hole in the

wall" represented by the loudspeakers, it becomes slightly louder than when it is either to the extreme left or right or in the center (straight-ahead) position. The examples consist of

a. seven discrete positions, constant y (linear path),
b. seven discrete positions, constant distance (arc),
c. continuous path, constant y (linear path),
d. continuous path, constant distance (arc).

45. Distance control: Each of these four sound examples illustrates progression along a straight line that runs from near left to far right. The first example consists of the same sound at seven positions starting near the listener and moving away with amplitudes computed according to the inverse square law. The second example moves from far to near using the inverse square law. The third and fourth examples are the same as the first two except that the inverse cube relation is used to compute amplitudes. The examples consist of

a. seven discrete positions, near-far (inverse square),
b. seven discrete positions, far-near (inverse square),
c. seven discrete positions, near-far (inverse cube),
d. seven discrete positions, far-near (inverse cube).

46. Azimuth and distance control: We may combine controls for azimuth and distance in order to make sounds move along arbitrary paths on the horizontal plane. The first two sound examples illustrate a sound moving along a simple elliptical path in front of the listener, starting to the right and moving with accelerating-then-decelerating speed clockwise around the ellipse, eventually coming to rest in the starting position. The elliptical path is centered 5 meters in front of the listener and is 8 meters wide and 6 meters high (as viewed from above). first the inverse square, then the inverse cube distance relations are heard. Notice the Doppler shift introduced by the **do_delay** procedure when the sound moves quickly. The second pair of examples is similar except that the path surrounds the listener, starting to the right, then moving clockwise behind. The ellipse in these two examples is 8 meters wide and 16 meters high as viewed from above. The examples consist of

a. continuous ellipse front (inverse square),
b. continuous ellipse front (inverse cube),
c. continuous ellipse (inverse square),
d. continuous ellipse (inverse cube).

47. A musical example: Sound paths such as those illustrated in the previous examples provide a powerful tool for musical expression, as illustrated by the final example, which is an excerpt of a composition entitled "The Vanity of Words" by UCSD composer Roger Reynolds. In this composition—which is based entirely on digitally processed spoken and sung text—sounds are made to move along multiple simultaneous paths, the shape of which provides a dramatic element in the music. All sound-path distances in this example were computed according to the inverse cube relationship.

Chapter 9 (Dolson)

48. Time expansion of speech: The first example presents a traditional use of time scaling as it might be encountered in the speech-processing community. A telephone-answering-machine message is heard, first as it was originally recorded, and then time expanded via the phase vocoder by a factor of two. Since speech is by no means a simple harmonic signal, this example provides a good indication of the fidelity of the phase vocoder under the demanding conditions imposed by real sounds.

49. Time expansion of music: Nevertheless, it may be noted that speech is monophonic, and also that we may have higher standards for evaluating the fidelity of purely musical sounds. The second example indicates that the phase vocoder can be equally successful in time expanding a polyphonic musical example—in this case, a brief violin passage. Again, the original recording is heard first, followed by a factor-of-two time expansion.

50. An extreme time expansion: At first, it might seem that a facility such as this would be most useful for adjusting the fine timing of recorded musical excerpts. In a compositional context, however, a more compelling usage turns out to be the generation of new and timbrally rich sonic material from recorded natural sounds. This is vividly presented here. A brief flute sforzando is followed by a time expansion of thirty-two times. The new sound is clearly derived from a flute, yet the connection is unlike any that we are familiar with.

51. Another extreme time expansion: Another application of extreme time expansion is presented. The first part is a digitization of a brief solo flute excerpt from the piece "Transfigured Wind" by UCSD composer Roger Reynolds. In the actual piece, the soloist plays this passage live, after which a radically time-expanded version (derived from a prerecorded perfor-

mance) is echoed on the accompanying tape. The second part of the example is the extreme time expansion (by a factor of thirty) of the beginning of the phrase. The effect here can be likened to that of an "acoustic microscope" in that rapid microvariations in the sound are expanded in time to the point where they are perceived as audible macrovariations in the pitch, loudness, and timbre.

52. An extreme pitch transposition: In this example, a familiar flute passage is presented, first as it was actually recorded, and then transposed down a factor of four (i.e., two full octaves). The transposition results in a timbre that is evocative of a woodwind instrument, yet not of any identifiable one.

53. Transposing speech: An additional consideration in performing transpositions is whether to transpose pitch alone or both pitch and spectral envelope. The method outlined above yields the latter result by default, because all harmonics are transposed directly. Hence, an octave transposition will shift not only the pitch but also any broad peaks or resonances in the spectrum by a factor of two. In the case of speech, these resonances (known as "formants") are particularly prominent and perceptually crucial. This is presented here by an upward pitch transposition by a factor of three, first in the default mode, and then with a built-in correction to preserve the original spectral envelope shape. While both results have the same pitch, the latter is clearly the more intelligible.

54. Time-varying time scaling and pitch transposition: All the examples to this point have been based on the assumption that the time-expansion or pitch-transposition factor is a constant. However, this is by no means the only possibility. Example 54 presents the two steps required for applying a time-varying pitch transposition (i.e., a "glissando") to a speech signal. First, a time-varying time expansion is applied in conjunction with a time-varying spectral warping that shifts the formants to progressively lower and lower frequencies. This warping manifests itself as a changing intelligibility throughout the first part of the example. The second part of the example is the desired glissando, created simply by playing back the first part of the example at a progressively higher and higher sampling rate. (In practice, we do not have access to variable sample rate D/A converters, so a time-varying sample-rate conversion is performed instead.)

55. Radical alternations of individual harmonics: Last, as a final example of the transformational power of the phase vocoder, we consider the

independent alteration of individual harmonics. Example 55 consists of a brief recorded flute passage, followed by a fairly radical restructuring of this passage obtained by time shifting and pitch shifting different individual harmonics by different amounts. This effect is to be contrasted with those in the preceding examples in which all harmonics were modified in the same way. The modification of individual harmonics clearly presents virtually unlimited musical possibilities, but the painstaking effort required in specifying the individual variations is currently more than most composers can reasonably undertake.

56. Sounds as resonators: Whenever we speak into a resonator (e.g., shouting into an open piano), we are essentially shaping the spectrum of our speech according to the spectrum of the resonator. To be more precise, we are filtering our speech according to the characteristic sound that the resonator itself would produce if excited by a single acoustical impulse. In practice, we can simulate this state of affairs by taking any two musical sounds and using a short-time Fourier analysis-synthesis technique to weight dynamically the spectrum of one sound by that of the other. Example 56 presents this effect. A recorded speech excerpt is spectrally shaped by a brief toy-piano sound to produce a result somewhat akin to talking into the piano. (In the example, a few words of the original speech are followed by the toy-piano sound and then by the combination of the two.) This example was created by UCSD composer Lee Ray, working with a recording of a lecture by John Cage. A more complete presentation of the "sounds as resonators" concept is contained in [3].

Chapter 10 (Wawrzynek)

The sounds you hear on the recording were all generated in real-time using VLSI sound-synthesis chips containing UPEs. The hardware comprises a MIDI keyboard, a computer workstation, and a board containing interface electronics and the VLSI sound-synthesis chips. A keyboard is used to control the sounds: When a key is pressed or some other control information is sent from the keyboard, the computer converts the information into coefficients that are then sent to the chips. Outputs from the keyboard may be stored by the computer and modified for later playback.

57. Fanciful marimba: Although duplicating the sounds of acoustic musical instruments is not our ultimate goal, it is our starting point. Simulation of existing musical instruments provides a means to validate the flexibility

and controllability of our sound-synthesis technique. Also, we can generate many new sounds as simple extrapolations of the models of physical instruments. This sound is that of a fanciful marimba. We have developed control parameters for a marimba model that not only cover the range of a standard four octave marimba, but also scale over the entire range of a seven-octave piano keyboard.

58. Primitive sounds: This sample demonstrates the two classes of sounds that we have modeled: struck and blown. We have chosen simple objects that make these sounds—bars, strings, and pipes—and have duplicated their sounds. The first example is a synthesis of a struck aluminum bar. The bar was struck with moderate force, in its center, with a hard rubber mallet. Our analysis of the physical bar indicated many strong normal modes of oscillation. We included only the 10 most prominent modes in the simulation.

Solving the wave equation for an ideal string clamped at its ends yields normal modes, the frequencies of which are integer multiples of the fundamental. The parameters of the resonators for the next sound are based on this idea. The resulting sound is that of a plucked, tightly strung string, without a resonating chamber.

We generated the last sound in this sample using our dynamic model for blown instruments. The object is a brass pipe measuring approximately 0.5 inches in diameter and 6 inches in length. The pipe is sounded by covering one end and blowing across the other.

59. Musical inflection on the marimba: Dynamics, phrasing, articulation, and timbral expression are crucial to interesting musical performances. Our synthesis models include controls for a variety of attacks and timbres. In particular, coefficients in the attack section of our struck-instrument model permit the simulation of the effect of a variety of mallets and striking forces. In real marimbas, and in other struck instruments, a more forceful strike generates not only a louder but also a brighter sound—any realistic simulation must include this effect. In the first example, an excerpt from Gershwin's *Porgy and Bess* is played on our marimba with no accent information. In the second example, the same excerpt is repeated, but this time with the velocity information from the keyboard controlling coefficients in the attack section of the model. This example demonstrates how the control adds musical inflection. The third example repeats the same excerpt with the coefficients in the attack section of the model modified to simulate the effect of a softer mallet, such as a yarn-wrapped mallet.

60. Articulation on the recorder: In wind instruments, as in struck instruments, articulation is important. In wind instruments, the playing force controls not only the volume of the sound but also its brightness. This sample demonstrates the blown-instrument model played with a variety of blowing forces and articulations. In our model, the blowing force is controlled by the velocity of a keypress. A slowly pressed key generates a soft pure tone; a quickly pressed key corresponds to a larger blowing force, and hence to a louder, harsher sound.

61. Excerpt from Bach's Brandenburg Concerto, on flute: This sample further demonstrates the level of musical inflection possible with our blown-instrument model. Also, we have made a variation in the parameters of the mouthpiece section. This variation models the effect of the player changing embouchure, thus achieving a richer tone, that contains a greater proportion of even-numbered harmonics.

62. Overblowing the flute: Overblowing in flutes and other blown instruments (or soda bottles) is the process of exciting stable oscillations of a normal mode other than the fundamental one. This effect may be desired, as in playing the high register on the flute, or may simply be the result of improper technique. Overblowing results from increasing the blowing force or modifying the embouchure. At times, a flute will overblow for a short instant at the beginning of a note, then will jump to the fundamental mode. Our electronic simulation of a flutelike instrument demonstrates overblowing that is a direct consequence of the relation of this model to a physical instrument. In this sample, we generated all notes without changing any control parameters in the instrument except the loop gain, which is, in effect, the blowing force.

63. Multiple bell strikes: In this sample, a simulated large bell is struck repetitively. Several effects not usually heard with other synthesis techniques are evident. After the first strike, each additional strike adds energy to the already sounding bell. In our model, there is no limitation that requires the previous "note" to be stopped when a new one is started; therefore, the effects of many strikes are present at once. The bell responds to the repetitive inputs by sounding at a variety of time scales—from the high frequencies of the striker itself to the low-frequency "drone" tone that develops through the course of the sample.

64. ICD Waltz: Relax and enjoy!

Chapter 11 (Risset)

65. Shepard's original pitch paradox: This example was made by copying a tape loop; hence it can last as long as desired. The loop contains twelve pairs of tones. The perception is that the pitch of each tone is equal to, or greater than, that of its predecessor. Actually every 24th tone is identical.

66. Knowlton's rhythm paradox: This example is also made by coping a tape loop. The speed of a somewhat irregular series of pulses seems always to increase. Actually, the pulses are repeated about every 20 sec.

67. Risset's paradoxical sound: This example, lasting 40 sec, presents a sound with paradoxical features. The pitch glides down the scale, yet it becomes gradually shriller, and it ends much higher than where it started. The sound is scanned by a pulse that constantly slows down, yet that is much faster at the end than at the beginning. Finally this sound, played in stereo, should also give the illusion of rotating in space. These are only instances of the effects that can be obtained by exploiting both the precision of computer synthesis and the specificities of auditory perception. I have used this sound in the third movement of my piece "Moments newtoniens" [5].

Chapter 12 (Risset)

68. Three approximations to a bell sound:

  a. All frequency components decay synchronously.
  b. Different frequency components decay at different rates. The higher the frequency of the component, the faster it decays.
  c. Decay rates are the same as in (b), but the two lowest partials are split into two components to produce a beating effect.

69. Tone derived from a bell timbre by modifying envelopes: The frequencies and the durations are as in the third bell approximation but this time the envelope (i.e., the amplitude as a function of time) is changed to a nonpercussive envelope. The buildup of each component now takes a quarter of the duration instead of 3 msec, as in tones 1–3. Hence the various components reach their peak amplitude at different times; thus, just as white light can be separated into its colored components by a prism, the tone components can be heard building up in succession out of a fluid texture, instead of fusing into a single percussive tone.

70. Inharmonic tones and transformations in a musical context: This example is in two parts. The first part consists of inharmonic tones synthesized according to the process exemplified by the third tone of the simple example above: it evokes music played on gongs and bells.

The second part consists of exactly the same components—the same frequencies and same durations—as the first part, except that the envelope has been changed to a nonpercussive envelope, as in tone 2 in the example above. Hence the belllike tones are changed into fluid textures—while they retain the same underlying harmonic pattern. The passage from the first part to the second part thus involves an intimate transformation that keeps the harmonic content invariant but changes the curve that determines the time behavior of the components. In the first part the listener tends to perceive individual objects—"bells"—whereas in the second part the fusion of partials into individual objects is hindered by the asynchronous envelopes, which helps one hear out the partials in succession. This kind of transformation was used extensively in my piece "Inharmonique."

Chapter 13 (Mathews and Pierce)

71. The scale, the major chord, the minor chord, a harmonized scale.

72. Minuet by Alyson Reeves.

73. Canon 4 by Alyson Reeves.

74. *Eros Ex Machina* by Jon Appleton.

Chapter 14 (Pierce)

75. Two-component scale: A just scale played by two sinusoids separated by 220 Hz. The successive pitches of the lower sinusoid go from 220 Hz, the A below middle C, to 440 Hz, the A above middle C, as shown by the lower pair of dots in figure 14.4. After the end of the scale, the initial note of the scale is played, followed by the final note.

76. Three-component scale: The same as the 1st example, but a third sinusoid 220 Hz above the topmost sinusoid of this example has been added, as shown in figure 14.4.

77. TOP-All tones: In these 4 pairs of tones, all sinusoidal components are successive harmonics of 220 Hz. In ALL, harmonics 1–6 are present with equal intensities. In TOP2, only the top 2 harmonics are present; in TOP3 only the top 3 harmonics are present; and so on. As shown in figure 14.5, the 4 pairs presented are

TOP2, ALL,
TOP3, ALL,
TOP4, ALL,
TOP5, ALL.

78. ALL-TOP scales: A whole-tone scale descending from 880 Hz (an octave above the A above middle C) to 55 Hz, a descent of 4 octaves.

As in the 3rd example above, and as shown in figure 14.6, the tones in the scale alternate between ALL and a TOP. The succession of pairs is the same as the 3rd example above.

79. Differences tune I: The difference frequency of a pair of sinusoids around 2,000 Hz is use to play a tune at a low level. The frequency difference lies in a range from the A below middle C to the A above middle C.

Then the same thing is repeated at a level 20 dB higher. Turning and moving the head enhances the effect of hearing the high-level difference tone "inside the head" or "inside an ear."

80. Harmonics tune I: The same tune as in the 5th example, but played by the tenth and eleventh harmonics of transposed notes of the tune, harmonics that lie around 2,000 Hz. Repeated at high level.

81. Scale difference tune II: Another tune played as the difference frequency of two sinusoidal tones in a range around 2,000 Hz: at a low level, and at a level 20 dB higher. In this case the upper of the two sinusoids goes up and down a scale, and the frequency of the lower tone is lower than that of the upper tone by the frequency of the melody. Repeated high.

Chapter 15 (Chafe)

The first four synthesis examples were completed in 1988 using INTERLISP-D software with array processor support. For simplicity, several limitations were imposed: only a single bow point was computed (as though the bow had one hair), bow changes did not invert waveform phase, and no body transfer function was used (just the raw string vibration was output, slightly reverberated). The last example, completed at IRCAM in 1984, was computed with an FPS-100 array processor under control of the FORMES version of the software.

82. Tuning up: Simulating a cello soloist, this example is a good test for the entire system. Any "off-by-one" programming error and it will not tune up.

83. Fiddle tune: A country fiddle tune is played in the cello register. The score was taken from a transcription of the tune "Wrassled with a Wildcat," in scordatura (with strings tuned A-E-A-E).

84. Repeated tones with dynamic and position changes: A diad is played on two strings with changing dynamic level and contact position of the bow.

85. Articulations: Several synthesized bowed articulations are compared:

1. *"novice"*: a squeaky stroke resulting from an imbalance of bow speed versus pressure;
2. *marcato*: an accented bow change;
3. *louré*: a lightly accented *legato*;
4. *marqué*: a heavily accented *legato*;
5. *martelé*: a separated, accented stroke (*detaché*);
6. *spiccato*: a lifted bow stroke;
7. *lancé*: a softer *spiccato*;
8. *porté*: soft attack, with a delayed accent;
9. "*impossible porté*": *porté* with an abrupt midstroke accent.

86. Automatically improvised hot jazz: The player system was hooked up to the output of a melody improvisation algorithm. Using a set of rules designed by André Hodeir, the algorithm created a violin line to fit a set of chord changes that were given as input. The guitar accompaniment uses the same synthesis model as the violin.

Chapter 18 (Dannenberg)

87. Accompaniment demonstration: The sound example illustrates a computer accompaniment program dealing with a range of problems in real time. The score given to the computer is a literal transcription of "Greensleeves," with no information about how the performance will proceed. Any deviation of the solo (trumpet) part from a strict metronomelike interpretation requires real-time adaptation by the program. The song has a repeated AA′BB′ form and each repetition has a total of 2 measures in 3/4 time.

The first 32 measures are played in fairly strict time (but notice the delayed entrance at measure 17). The second 32 measures illustrate extreme tempo variations. When the tempo slows down, the accompanist repeatedly runs ahead until the next note is played by the trumpet. At this point, the accompanist realizes it is ahead and backs up. The accompanist persists in running ahead, trying to resist the tempo change, but eventually adapts to the slower tempo. The balance between persistence and willing adaptation is an adjustable parameter. When the trumpet speeds up, the accompanist will hear trumpet notes long before they are expected, and responds by jumping ahead in the score. Jumping ahead usually sounds much better than backing up, so the accompanist seems to deal better with speeding up than with slowing down, even though the program does not differentiate between the two.

The last 16 measures illustrate the effectiveness of the matcher. Although the expected solo is exactly the one played in the first 16 measures, the performed solo deviates with many added pitches and altered rhythms. Since the accompanist is not a composer, it does the best it can to follow the underlying melody and pace its accompaniment accordingly. The purpose of this section is to illustrate that the system can cope with performance errors. The accompanist is not intended to deal with ornamentation or improvisation.

On hearing demonstrations like this one, many listeners get the impression that the accompanist cannot deal very well with tempo changes, but this is not true. In a performance (as opposed to demonstration) situation, all planned tempo changes are encoded into the score by notating them or by recording an exemplary performance. Then the accompanist expects the tempo change and makes it instantly. Adaptation is only necessary to correct for discrepancies between the anticipated tempo change and the one actually made by the performer, so the musical result is far superior to the given sound example.

The accompaniment software for this example was written by Roger B. Dannenberg and Joshua Bloch, and the interface was implemented by Ralph E. Bellofatto for Cherry Lane Technologies. The program runs on a Commodore Amiga computer, which is based on a Motorola 68000 processor. The trumpet is interfaced to the Amiga using a mouthpiece-mounted pressure transducer by Barcus-Berry, which is connected through a microphone preamp to an IVL Pitchrider, a pitch follower with MIDI output. A MIDI interface for the Amiga completes the string of input processors and provides a MIDI output as well. The accompaniment sounds were synthesized by a Yamaha DX7. The pressure transducer was used only for the trumpet-to-computer interface, and an ordinary microphone was used for the recording. The sound example was made in real time with no post production editing at Audiomation, with recording engineering by Gregg Vizza and digital recording by Graham Grubb.

88. Composed improvisation: The piece *Jimmy Durante Boulevard* was started in July 1986 in Pittsburgh, and a first version was ready by the end of July. The current version was completed in the three next months through electronic mail between San Diego, Paris, and Pittsburgh. It makes use of CMU and CARL MIDI software, and uses the Moxc scheduler written by Dannenberg and modified by Chabot. The piece was premiered at STEIM, Amsterdam, in October 1986.

The piece aims at a concept called "composed improvisation." Ideally, in composed improvisation, the computer is in charge of the long-term (compositional) decisions, while the live performers are in charge of the local aspects of the performance. But there must be a relationship between the long-term and short-term aspects of a composition. Therefore, the instrumentalists also provide the material with which the computer "composes." The individual sound of each performing group is theoretically taken into account by the processes. The nature of the compositional algorithm, however, participates in the sound of the piece; this algorithm is similar to the traditional participation of the composer.

In *Jimmy Durante Boulevard*, the concept of composed improvisation is implemented in the following manner. The compositional algorithm uses two sorts of musical material, MAT1 and MAT2. MAT1 (in this performance assigned to the trumpet) is melodic in essence. The trumpet melody is recorded and cut and these "cuts" are reshuffled. The reshuffling follows predetermined permutation patterns and the durations of the cuts follow geometric series of variable ratio. MAT2 (in this case assigned to the keyboard) is harmonic in essence. It consists of a series of chords that can be set in advance and/or modified as the performance goes on. As the piece progresses, MAT1 is multiplied (in Boulez's sense) by MAT2. Different levels of structure are created: "parts," "phrases," and finally "cuts." A "structure" is a synthesized sequence that contains N (from 1 to 10) parts separated by silences. Each part is composed of N2 (from 1 to 7) phrases themselves composed of N3 cuts. The time layering of these levels along the geometric series and the harmonic progression of the chords do provide a directionality with or against which the live performers play. This compositional algorithm is applied to two independent voices.

The performers can react, of course. The trumpet can "record" a new material: the length of the recorded material directly affects the length of the computed musical structure; the trumpet has a direct action on the density and the general pitch content. The keyboard can play new harmonic material: a chord analysis method devised by Julio Estrada is applied to the keyboard input and is used to transpose the cuts. Textures that appear often will replace already existing ones. Two simultaneous melodic analyses are performed on the flute data: "contour" and "concavity" analysis. The results of these analyses are used to compute the amount of percussive sounds ("timpanilike" and "kotolike") to be put in the computer part, otherwise using a "pianolike" sound designed for the DX7 by Mark Burnel at the Carnegie-Mellon Computer Music Studio. The triggerlike characteristics of MIDI made us prefer keyboard-type sounds. The piece, as it is, needs a computer keyboard operator in charge of starting new structures with given geometric series characteristics.

Technical realization: Center for Art and Technology (Carnegie-Mellon University) and Center for Music Experiment (University of California, San Diego).

Performers: Roger Dannenberg, trumpet; Xavier Chabot, flute; Georges Bloch, keyboard and operator.

Recording Assistant: Robert Willey.

List of Contributors

Gerald Bennett
Swiss Center for Computer Music
Oetwil am See, Switzerland

Chris Chafe
Music Department
Stanford University
Stanford, CA

John M. Chowning
Music Department
Stanford University
Stanford, CA

Roger Dannenberg
Computer Science Department
Carnegie-Mellon University
Pittsburgh, PA

Shawn L. Decker
Computer Music Studio
Northwestern University
Chicago, IL

Charles Dodge
Music Department
Brooklyn College
Brooklyn, NY

Mark Dolson
Music Department
University of California at San Diego
La Jolla, CA

Gary S. Kendall
Computer Music Studio
Northwestern University
Chicago, IL

Paul Lansky
Music Department
Princeton University
Princeton, NJ

Gareth Loy
Music Department
University of California at San Diego
La Jolla, CA

William L. Martens
Computer Music Studio
Northwestern University
Chicago, IL

Max V. Mathews
Music Department
Stanford University
Stanford, CA

F. Richard Moore
Music Department
University of California at San Diego
La Jolla, CA

János Négyesy
Music Department
University of California at San Diego
La Jolla, CA

John R. Pierce
Music Department
Stanford University
Stanford, CA

Lee Ray
Music Department
University of California at San Diego
La Jolla, CA

Jean-Claude Risset
LMA, CNRS, and Faculté
des Sciences de Marseille-Luminy
Marseille, France

Xavier Rodet
IRCAM
Paris, France

William Schottstaedt
Music Department
Stanford University
Stanford, CA

Johan Sundberg
Speech Communication and Music Acoustics Department
Royal Institute of Technology
Stockholm, Sweden

John Wawrzynek
Department of Electrical Engineering and Computer Sciences
Computer Science Division
University of California at Berkeley
Berkeley, CA

Index

Page numbers in *italics* refer to figures.